The
RISE
of
AMERICAN
DEMOCRACY

VOLUME II

DEMOCRACY ASCENDANT
1815–1840

Books by Sean Wilentz

The Rise of American Democracy: Jefferson to Lincoln (2005)

The Rose & the Briar: Death, Love and Liberty in the American Ballad (ed., with Greil Marcus, 2004)

David Walker's Appeal to the Coloured Citizens of the World (ed., 1995)

The Kingdom of Matthias (with Paul E. Johnson, 1994)

The Key of Liberty: The Life and Democratic Writings of William Manning, "A Labourer," 1747–1814 (with Michael Merrill, 1993)

Major Problems in the History of the Early Republic, 1789–1848 (ed., 1992)

Rites of Power: Symbolism, Ritual, and Politics since the Middle Ages (ed., 1985)

Chants Democratic: New York City & the Rise of the American Working Class, 1788–1850 (1984)

The
RISE
of
AMERICAN
DEMOCRACY

VOLUME II
DEMOCRACY ASCENDANT
1815–1840

Sean Wilentz

W. W. Norton & Company
New York London

ISBN-13: 978-0-393-93007-8(pbk)
ISBN-10: 0-393- 93007-6(pbk)

The Library of Congress has catalogued the one-volume edition as follows:

Wilentz, Sean.
The rise of American democracy : Jefferson to Lincoln / Sean Wilentz.—1st ed.
p. cm.
Includes bibliographical references and index.
ISBN 0-393-05820-4 (hardcover)
1. United States—Politics and government—1783–1865. 2. Presidents—United
States—History—18th century. 3. Presidents—United States—History—19th
century.
4. Politicians—United States—History—19th century. 6. Democracy—United
States—History—18th century. 7. Democracy—United States—History—19th
century. I. Title.

E302.1.W55 2005
973.5—dc21

2004029466

W. W. Norton & Company, Inc.
500 Fifth Avenue, New York, NY 10110
www.wwnorton.com

W. W. Norton & Company Ltd.
Castle House, 75/76 Wells Street, London W1T 3QT

1 2 3 4 5 6 7 8 9 0

A NOTE ON THE COLLEGE EDITION

The three-volume College Edition of *The Rise of American Democracy: Jefferson to Lincoln* has two chief goals. First, many students and teachers, as well as many general readers, are mainly interested in one or two phases of the long history covered in the larger work. Publishing each of the book's three major parts as separate volumes allows those readers to focus on their period or periods of special interest. Second, many readers prefer a version without the elaborate scholarly apparatus of the original, but with pointers on further reading. The College Edition includes a list of select additional titles pertinent to each volume, while it eliminates the endnotes in the full edition. Not a word of text from the larger work has been omitted.

To enhance continuity, brief synopses of events covered earlier in the general work appear in volumes II and III.

—S.W

To P.B. and L.W.
& to all my dearest

CONTENTS

LIST OF ILLUSTRATIONS

(The following illustrations appear between pages 292 and 293.)

1. J. Wood/C.G. Childs, "Genl. Andrew Jackson/Protector of Beauty and Booty/Orleans/1828." A campaign engraving.
2. Timothy Clamright, "Maine Not to Be Coupled With the Missouri Question," Brunswick, Maine, 1820. Clamright, no doubt a pseudonym, opposed the compromise proposal that linked the admission of Missouri as a slave state and Maine as a free state, because of the basic antagonism of freedom and slavery: "They too lazy to work, drive slaves, whom they fear;/We school our own children, and brew our own beer."
3. Gilbert Stuart, *Rufus King*, 1819–20.
4. After Matthew Harris Jouett, *Henry Clay*, ca. 1818.
5. Asher Durand, *Andrew Jackson*, 1835.
6. Henry Inman, *Sequoyah*, ca. 1828. A Cherokee who fought beside Jackson against the Creeks in 1814, Sequoyah here holds up the Cherokee alphabet, for which he is credited with inventing.
7. George Caitlin, *Virginia Constitutional Convention*, 1829–30.
8. "The Doctors Puzzled or The Desperate Condition of Mother U.S. Bank," ca. 1834–35. While President Jackson (with his sidekick, the fictional Major Jack Downing) peer through the window with delight, Henry Clay, Daniel Webster, and John C. Calhoun worry over the condition of the monster bank. On the bed, Nicholas Biddle attends to the BUS, while it

MAPS

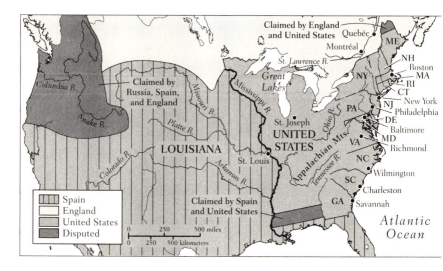

NORTH AMERICA, 1783

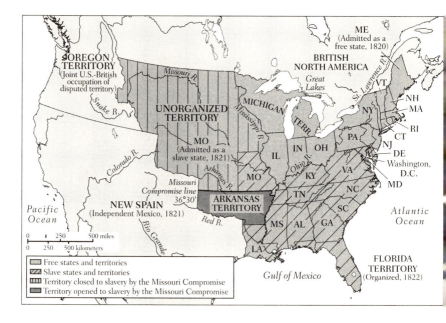

THE MISSOURI COMPROMISE, 1820

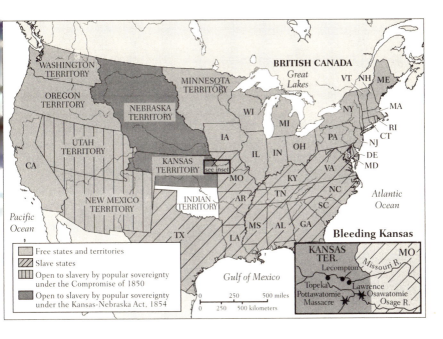

THE KANSAS-NEBRASKA ACT, 1854

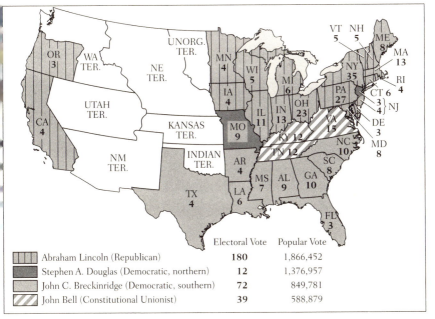

	Electoral Vote	Popular Vote
Abraham Lincoln (Republican)	180	1,866,452
Stephen A. Douglas (Democratic, northern)	12	1,376,957
John C. Breckinridge (Democratic, southern)	72	849,781
John Bell (Constitutional Unionist)	39	588,879

THE ELECTION OF 1860

PREFACE TO VOLUME II

The simple title of the general work from which this volume is drawn, *The Rise of American Democracy*, describes the historical arc of the overall subject. Important elements of democracy existed in the infant American republic of the 1780s, but the republic was not democratic. Nor, in the minds of those who governed it, was it supposed to be. A republic—the *res publica*, or "public thing"—was meant to secure the common good through the ministrations of the most worthy, enlightened men. A democracy—derived from *demos krateo*, "rule of the people"—dangerously handed power to the impassioned, unenlightened masses. Democracy, the eminent political leader George Cabot wrote as late as 1804, was "*the government of the worst.*" Yet by the 1830s, as Alexis de Tocqueville learned, most Americans proclaimed that their country was a democracy as well as a republic. Enduring arguments had begun over the boundaries of democratic politics. In the 1840s and 1850s, the arguments centered increasingly on slavery and slavery's expansion, and led to the Civil War.

The change was astonishing, but it was neither inevitable nor providential. American democracy did not rise like the sun at its natural hour in history. Its often troubled ascent was the outcome of human conflicts, accommodations, and unforeseen events, and the results could well have been very different than they were. The difficulties and the contingencies made the events all the more remarkable. A momentous rupture occurred between Thomas Jefferson's time and Abraham Lincoln's, in which the elitist presumptions and institutions of the infant republic gave way to far broader conceptions of popular sovereignty and to new forms of mass political participation, in and out of elections. The polity that emerged contained the lineaments of modern democratic politics. The rise of American democracy is the story of that rupture and its immediate consequences.

Democracy is a troublesome word, and explaining why is one of *The Rise of American Democracy's* larger purposes. A decade before the American Revolution, the early patriot James Otis defined democracy in its purest and simplest form as "a government of all over all," in which "the votes of the majority shall be taken as the voice of the whole," and where the rulers were the ruled and the ruled were the rulers. As fixed descriptions go, this is as good as any, but its abstractness, of course, begs explication. Since the Revolution, citizens, scholars, and political leaders have latched onto one or another particular aspect of government or politics as democracy's essence. For some, it is a matter of widened political rights, usually measured by the extent of the suffrage and actual voting; for others, democracy means greater opportunity for the individual pursuit of happiness; for still others, it is more of a cultural phenomenon than a political one, "a habit of the heart," as Tocqueville put it, in which deference to rulers and condescension for the ruled give way to the ruder conventions of equality.

All of these facets are important, but I think we go astray in discussing democracy simply as a form of government or society, or as a set of social norms—a category or a thing with particular structures that can be codified and measured. Today, democracy means, at a minimum, full enfranchisement and participation by the entire adult citizenry. By that standard, the American democracy of the mid-nineteenth century was hardly a democracy at all: women of all classes and colors lacked political and civil rights; most blacks were enslaved; free black men found political rights they had once enjoyed either reduced or eliminated; the remnant of a ravaged Indian population in the eastern states had been forced to move west, without citizenship. Even the most expansive of the era's successful democratic political reforms encompassed considerably less than half of the total adult population, and at best a bare majority of the free adult population.* But to impose current categories of democracy on the past is to block any understanding of how our own, more elevated standards originated. It is to distort the lives of Americans who could barely have anticipated political and social changes that we take for granted. It is to substitute our experiences and prejudices for theirs.

By democracy, I mean a historical fact, rooted in a vast array of events and experiences, that comes into being out of changing *historical* human relations between governors and the governed. Stopping *Process* history cold at any particular point and parsing its political makeup negates that historical flow and stifles the voices and activities of actual people attempting to define the operations of government. Only over an extended period of time is it possible to see democracy and democratic government grow out of particular social, intellectual, and political contexts.

Democracy appears when some large number of previously

---

* This is based on the figures gathered in the federal census for 1850, which show that 44.5 percent of the adult population (twenty years and older) and 51.0 percent of the free adult population were white males. Noncitizens and Indians are not included in the calculations. The numbers are crude indicators, but the main point of comparison with the present is obvious.

excluded, ordinary persons—what the eighteenth century called "the many"—secure the power not simply to select their governors but to oversee the institutions of government, as officeholders and as citizens free to assemble and criticize those in office. Democracy is never a gift bestowed by benevolent, far-seeing rulers who seek to reinforce their own legitimacy. It has always to be fought for, by political coalitions that cut across distinctions of wealth, power, and interest. It succeeds and survives only when it is rooted in the lives and expectations of its citizens, and continually reinvigorated in each generation. Democratic successes are never irreversible.

Since Tocqueville, there has been a long tradition of scholarship devoted to understanding the democratic rupture that the general work describes. The rise of American democracy engaged the attention of great historians now forgotten by the general reading public (Dixon Ryan Fox, J. Franklin Jameson), as well as such acknowledged giants as Charles and Mary Beard, Frederick Jackson Turner, Richard Hofstadter, and, most recently, Gordon S. Wood. But modern study of the subject owes the most to Arthur M. Schlesinger Jr.'s *The Age of Jackson*, published in 1945. Before Schlesinger, historians thought of American democracy as the product of an almost mystical frontier or agrarian egalitarianism. *The Age of Jackson* toppled that interpretation by placing democracy's origins firmly in the context of the founding generation's ideas about the few and the many, and by seeing democracy's expansion as an outcome more of struggles between classes than between sections. More than any previous account, Schlesinger's examined the activities and ideas of obscure, ordinary Americans, as well as familiar political leaders. While he identified most of the key political events and changes of the era, Schlesinger also located the origins of modern liberal politics in the tradition of Thomas Jefferson and Andrew Jackson, and in their belief, as he wrote, that future challenges "will best be met by a society in which no single group is able to sacrifice democracy and liberty to its interests." Finally, Schlesinger examined and emphasized the shattering moral and political dilemmas that an expanding southern slavery posed to American democracy, leading to the Civil War.

Since *The Age of Jackson* appeared, a revolution in historical studies has focused scholars' attentions on groups of Americans and aspects of American history that held minor interest at best in the historical profession in 1945. That revolution has altered historians' views of every detail of our past. The tragedy of Indian removal; the democratic activities of ex-slaves and other free blacks; the ease and sometimes the viciousness with which some professed democrats, North and South, championed white racial supremacy; the participation of women in reform efforts (and, in time, in electoral campaigns), along with the ridicule directed at the fledgling woman suffrage movement; the liberal humanitarian impulses that informed important strains of supposedly "conservative," pro-business politics; the importance of ethnicity and religion in shaping Americans' political allegiances—each of these, either ignored or slighted sixty years ago, has generated an enormous scholarly literature.

Yet if the social history revolution has profoundly changed how historians look at the United States, it has not diminished the importance of the questions *The Age of Jackson* asked about early American democracy. On the contrary, it has made those questions—especially about democratic politics, social class, and slavery—all the more pertinent to our understanding of the dramatic events that led from the American Revolution to the American Civil War. Some important recent works have attempted to raise those questions anew, and bridge the so-called new style of history with the older. The most ambitious of them have reinterpreted the connections between society and politics before 1860 as part of a larger market revolution that swept across the country. But these admirable studies have generally submerged the history of politics in the history of social change, reducing politics and democracy to byproducts of various social forces without quite allowing the play of politics its independent existence and importance. *The Rise of American Democracy* offers a different interpretation of these connections, with a greater focus on the vagaries of politics, high and low.

The general work's subtitle, *Jefferson to Lincoln*, reaffirms the importance of political events, ideas, and leaders to democracy's rise—once an all-too-prevalent idea, now in need of some rescue and repair. Thomas Jefferson, more than any other figure in the early Republic, established (and was seen to have established) the terms of American democratic politics. Abraham Lincoln self-consciously advanced an updated version of Jefferson's egalitarian ideals, and his election to the presidency of the United States caused the greatest crisis American democracy has yet known. By singling out Jefferson and Lincoln, I certainly do not mean to say that presidents and other great men were solely responsible for the vicissitudes of American politics. One of the book's recurring themes is how ordinary Americans, including some at the outermost reaches of the country's formal political life, had lasting influence on the exercise of power. But just as political leaders did not create American democracy out of thin air, so the masses of Americans did not simply force their way into the corridors of power. That Jefferson and not John Adams was elected president in 1800–01—a fact that nearly did not come to pass—made a vast difference to subsequent political developments. So did the presence of other public officials, elected and unelected, from the top of American public life to the bottom. Featuring Jefferson and Lincoln in the subtitle of the larger work is a shorthand way of insisting on what ought to be a truism: that some individuals have more influence on history than others. The title, by referring to a broader history, insists that these individuals cannot make history just as they please, constrained as they are by a host of forces and persons beyond their control and anticipations.

The Rise of American Democracy can be read as a chronicle of American politics from the Revolution to the Civil War with the history of democracy at its center, or as an account of how democracy arose in the United States (and with what consequences) in the context of its time. Either way, the general work has a few major themes. One, given special attention in the first volume of the College Edition, is that democracy, at the nation's inception, was highly contested, not a given, and developed piecemeal, by fits and starts, at the state and local as well as the national level. A second theme, taken up in the second volume, is that social changes barely foreseen in 1787, chiefly the rapid commercialization of the free labor North and the renaissance of plantation slavery in the South, deeply affected how democracy advanced, and retreated, after 1815.

Third, Americans perceived these social changes primarily in political terms and increasingly saw them as struggles over contending ideas of democracy. Americans of the early nineteenth century lived in a different mental universe from ours with regard to politics. Above all, they inherited from the Revolutionary era a republican perspective that regarded political institutions as the foundation of social and economic relations, and not the other way around. Certain kinds of societies appeared more conducive than others to a just and harmonious government. Americans sharply disagreed about which societies were superior. But if order and happiness abounded, they believed it was because political institutions and the men running them were sound: disorder and unhappiness stemmed from unsound institutions or from the corruption of sound institutions by ambitious and designing men. Across the chasm of the Civil War, the era of high industrialism, and the conflicts of the twentieth century, we are more likely to see economic power and interests as the matrix for politics and political institutions. For Americans of the early Republic, politics, government, and constitutional order, not economics, were primary to interpreting the world and who ran it—a way of thinking that can wrongly look simplified, paranoid, and conspiracy-driven today.

A fourth theme concerns the constancy of political conflict: democracy in America was the spectacle of Americans arguing over democracy. If the word became a shibboleth for new and emerging political parties and movements, it did not on that account become degraded and bland. Precisely because opposing groups claimed to champion the same ideal, they fought all the harder to ensure their version would prevail. There was no end to the possible qualifying labels Americans could devise to illustrate exactly what sort of democrats they were—not just with separate major- and third-party labels (Democratic, Whig, State Rights, Know-Nothing, and so on) but with the blizzard of names for factions within the parties that always bemuse uninitiated readers: Loco Foco, Barnburner, Hunker, Silver Gray.* In part, these labels connoted patronage connections for political insiders. But in an age when elections came to be conducted more or less year-round, they also reflected beliefs and deep commitments above and beyond party machinations—while for a radical such as William Lloyd Garrison they were craven and sinful, and for a corrosive skeptic such as Herman Melville they inspired ambivalence and dread.

5. Arguing the fate of slavery

Fifth, the many-sided conflicts over American democracy came, in the 1840s and 1850s, to focus on an issue of recognized importance since the Republic's birth: the fate of American slavery. Throughout the decades after the Revolution, but with a hurtling force after 1840, two American democracies emerged, the free-labor democracy of the North and the slaveholders' democracy of the South—distinct political systems as well as bodies of thought. Although they often praised identical values and ideals, and although they were linked through the federal government and the national political parties, the two were fundamentally antagonistic. The nation's political leaders suppressed those antagonisms, sometimes in the face of powerful protests and schismatic movements, from the 1820s through the early 1850s. By 1860, the conflict could no longer be contained, as a

---

* From 1856: "Thus every party and sect has a daily register of the most minute sayings and doings, and proceedings and progress of every other sect; and as truth and error are continually brought before the masses, they have the opportunity to know and compare. There are political parties under the names of Whigs, Democrats, Know-nothings, Freesoilers, Fusionists, Hunkers, Woollyheads, Dough-faces, Hard-shells, Soft-shells, Silver-greys, and I know not what besides; all of them extremely puzzling to the stranger, but of great local significance." Isabella Lucy Bird, *The Englishwoman in America* (London, 1856), 422–23.

democratic election sparked southern secession and the war that would determine American democracy's future.

The work's /final theme/ is implied in the others: the idea of democracy is never sufficient unto itself. Since the Second World War, and even more since the great democratic revolutions of 1989–91, the world has witnessed the continuing resilience and power of democratic ideals. So swiftly have former tyrannies turned into self-declared democratic governments that the danger has arisen of taking democracy for granted, despite its manifest fragility and possible collapse in large parts of the globe. As the early history of the United States shows, the habits and the institutions of modern democracy are relatively new in the larger span of history. Their breakthrough, even in the most egalitarian portions of the New World, required enormous reversals of traditional assumptions about power and legitimacy. As those habits and institutions began taking hold, different American social orders produced clashing versions of democracy, generating enmities so deep that they could only be settled in blood. Thereafter, democratic ideas, both in the United States and elsewhere, have had to be refreshed, fought over, and redefined continually. The rise of American democracy, from Jefferson's era to Lincoln's, created exhilarating new hopes and prospects, but also fierce conflicts and enormous challenges about what democracy can be and should be. Along with democracy's hopes and prospects, its conflicts and challenges persist. So do its vulnerabilities.

This second volume of the College Edition of *The Rise of American Democracy*, entitled *Democracy Ascendant*, takes the story from the conclusion of the War of 1812 to the presidential campaign of 1840, which marked the coming of age of a democratic system driven by mass electoral parties.

The previous forty years had witnessed significant alterations in American politics, including an uneven enlargement of democratic institutions. In 1782, Charles Thompson, an expert in Latin who was helping to design the Great Seal of the United

States, suggested including the motto "Novus Ordo Seclorum." Borrowed from an eclogue by the classical poet Virgil, the phrase translated roughly as "A New Order of the Ages," and signified the belief that a new American era in history had begun in 1776. Yet only five years after Thompson's suggestion, Americans found themselves framing and ratifying a national constitution to replace the Articles of Confederation in force in 1782. Under that new federal framework, fresh conflicts arose over foreign as well as domestic affairs that raised anew a question asked during the War for Independence: how democratic should the new American republic be?

This crisis of the new order led directly to the so-called Revolution of 1800, which elevated Thomas Jefferson to the presidency and handed control of Congress to Jefferson's Republican allies. Yet the crisis continued, fed by protracted struggles over foreign affairs as well as over the proper structure of American politics and government. In 1812, Jefferson's successor, James Madison, led the country into a war with Britain that would prove a watershed in the nation's history and the unsteady, at times contradictory, history of the expansion of American political democracy. By the war's end, certain democratic propositions and institutions initially distrusted by the Revolutionary generation, including a widened suffrage and the rudiments of mass political parties, had come into being. But the resolution of the crisis of the new order did not quell the continued arguments over American democracy, which became entangled more and more with the future of American slavery. These matters became the subject of heated conflict over the decades to come, undertaken by a new generation of Americans, whose leaders included the greatest military hero of the War of 1812, Andrew Jackson.

The

RISE

of

AMERICAN
DEMOCRACY

VOLUME II

DEMOCRACY ASCENDANT

1815–1840

1

THE ERA OF BAD FEELINGS

As 1815 ended, James Madison was jubilant. During the summer and autumn, off the coast of Africa, Commodore Stephen Decatur had subdued the plundering corsairs of Tunis, Tripoli, and Algiers, ending once and for all their sporadic attacks on American shipping. After reporting on this latest military triumph in his seventh annual message to Congress, Madison was free to concentrate on domestic matters for the first time during his presidency. His rhetoric lacked fire, but his postwar plans were lofty.

Madison's speech affirmed that the war had reinforced the evolution of mainstream Republicanism, moving it further away from its original agrarian and localist assumptions. The war's immense strain on the treasury led to new calls from nationalist Republicans for a national bank. The difficulties in moving and supplying troops exposed the wretchedness of the country's transportation links, and the need for extensive new roads and canals. A boom in American manufacturing during the prolonged cessation of trade with Britain created an entirely new class of enterprisers, most of them tied politically to the Republicans, who might not survive without tariff protection. More broadly, the war reinforced feelings of national identity and connection. "The people have now more general objects of attachment with which their pride and political opinions are connected," Albert Gallatin wrote to his old associate, the fiery democrat-turned-manufacturer Matthew Lyon. "They are more Americans."

Madison and the moderate Republican nationalists did not advance unchallenged. The war's conclusion brought a resumption of the tensions between pro-development Republicans and country and city democrats, notably William Duane of Philadelphia. Southern Old Republicans were incensed at what they considered Madison's neo-Federalism. In 1814, the most thoughtful of the Virginia Quids, John Taylor of Caroline, published his *Inquiry into the Principles and Policy of the Government of the United States*—an informed if rambling attack on the Hamiltonian system, more than twenty years in the writing, that registered Taylor's disgust at Madison's apostasy. Over the next five years, Taylor's criticisms turned into a more exacting argument that federal consolidation threatened the private property rights of ordinary citizens, including the rights of southern planters to their peculiar property in black people. In back of that sharpening lay a renascence of plantation slavery.

The South's deepened commitment to slavery accompanied (and was aggravated by) growing antislavery sentiment in the North. By 1804, every state north of the Mason-Dixon Line had taken some step toward the eventual elimination of slavery. Emancipation, in turn, sharpened northern resistance to the spread of slavery into the territories and newly admitted western states. That resistance, and the furious southern reaction to it, threatened, for a time, to dissolve the Republican coalition along sectional lines, and left behind a rupture that would never fully mend. And political leaders in both the North and the South also faced another, very different set of provocations. After 1815, democratic reformers in various states seized upon the wartime services and sacrifices of ordinary soldiers and pressed for an expansion of suffrage rights and an equalization of political representation. At the height of that agitation, in 1819, the American economy, red hot with postwar expansion, melted down, leading to the first national depression in American history. Quickly, outcries for widened democracy became attached to collisions of class caused by the economic disaster—and to fresh attacks by city and country democrats on banks, paper money, and the Republican nationalists.

Except for a few apprehensive souls such as Taylor, it was nearly impossible for Americans to foresee this turbulence amid the celebrations of 1815. For the moment, the nation's sections and classes seemed more tightly knit than at any time since the Revolution. The fading of Federalism left only one party, the Republicans, to run the nation's affairs. "Discord does not belong to our system," Madison's successor James Monroe declared upon entering the restored and freshly whitewashed Executive Mansion—forever after known as the White House—in 1817. A Boston Federalist newspaper surveyed the harmony and proclaimed the commencement of an "ERA OF GOOD FEELINGS."

That era would last less than four years before giving way to a much longer Era of Bad Feelings.

DEMOCRATIC STRUGGLES IN NEW ENGLAND

Aside from the quasi-feudal polity of Rhode Island, no state in the nation was formally more undemocratic in 1815 than Connecticut. The Royal Charter of 1666 remained the basic plan of state government. Political innovations since 1800, including the notorious *viva voce* Stand-Up Law of 1801, had reinforced Connecticut's theocratic establishment, dubbed the Standing Order. Although Abraham Bishop and his allies had created a viable Republican opposition, Connecticut's elections remained dominated by a Federalist-Congregationalist autocracy. Church ministers, in consultation with party leaders, helped dictate policy and control Federalist nominations. Anglophilia was so intense and overt that in March 1815, immediately after the cessation of the war, the high society of Hartford—described by one writer as "the metropolitan see of Federalism"—warmly hosted British Vice Admiral Henry Hotham and his officers, fresh from serving the Crown in the waters outside New London.

Connecticut Federalism grew so reactionary that it wound up offending some Connecticut Federalists. Religious divisions ran especially deep, as Episcopalians, Baptists, and Methodists (along with smaller numbers of Unitarians, deists, and nonbelievers) chafed under persisting indignities, including the legal requirement that they deposit with the state a formal declaration of dissent. In 1801 and 1802, the sojourning Virginia Baptist John Leland denounced "the mischief of Connecticut religion," and he called on dissenters to demand a new constitution that secured religious liberty. Leland's appeal produced no rapid results, although, as in other states, Connecticut's Methodist and Baptist minority did ally with the new Republican Party. More strikingly, over the ensuing decade, large numbers of Federalist Episcopalians also gravitated to the Jeffersonians.

Connecticut's evolving political economy produced additional political rifts. Between 1800 and 1815, a manufacturing sector began to emerge in the eastern and southern portions of the state, aided by the embargo, the Non-Intercourse Act, and the wartime cessation of trade. In 1820, only Rhode Island could claim an appreciably larger percentage of its population engaged in manufacturing. The new manufacturers, in turn, had closer affinities with the Republicans than with the Federalists. Federalist leaders did not oppose early industrial development, and some even encouraged it. But the combination of Federalist Anglophilia and mercantile priorities conflicted with the interests of the state's manufacturers, who wanted to block imports of British manufactured goods. Alert Republicans appealed for the manufacturers' support (as well as for the support of their employees) by backing special protective legislation and by celebrating them as the creators of a new form of national economic independence—"truly gratifying," one Republican paper noted, "to every true American."

The Federalists' antiwar politics, which had culminated in the Hartford Convention, also raised questions about the Standing Order's patriotism. Even some nominal pro-Federalists regarded the convention as "synonymous with *treachery and treason*." Members of the stiff-necked clerical wing of the state's Federalist party, led by Governor John Cotton Smith, aggravated matters by claiming that the prestige of the delegates' names alone vindicated the convention's proceedings. Republicans hit back hard, denouncing the Hartford gathering as "the foulest stain upon our escutcheon."

In February 1816, a meeting of Republican and Episcopalian citizens from around the state assembled in New Haven to unite all elements opposed to the Federalist-Congregationalist establishment. Several issues arose, including the state's obsolete suffrage laws, but the participants united behind challenging religious intolerance. In an effort to reinforce the group's credibility, the meeting unanimously nominated the impeccable ex-Federalist Oliver Wolcott Jr. for governor in the upcoming state elections, under the banner of the American Toleration and Reform Ticket.

The patrician Wolcott was an improbable tribune for democratic reform, which helps explain why he was so effective. Alexander Hamilton's successor as Treasury secretary, and a tormentor of President John Adams, Wolcott had made his national reputation in the 1790s as a stalwart conservative Federalist, a "representative of Mr. Hamilton," in one admiring Hartford editor's words. But Wolcott became estranged from the Federalists over foreign policy, and he broke with the party completely when he backed the war effort in 1812. On religious questions, he had become more broad-minded as he grew older. Having invested in a cloth manufactory, he was also sensitive to the interests of Connecticut's manufacturers. Wolcott's mellowed moderate conservatism made him a pariah in the state's Federalist press, which turned him into something of a hero to reformers.

In the May elections, Wolcott garnered an impressive 47 percent of the vote, while his Tolerationist running mate, ex-

Federalist Judge Jonathan Ingersoll, won the race for lieutenant governor. A year later, Wolcott won the governorship by a razor-thin margin, and in the autumn legislative elections of 1816, the Tolerationists took control of the lower chamber, the General Assembly. Although they still controlled the upper house, the Federalists were in retreat, and the Tolerationists broadened their attack to include a wide range of antiquities and defects in the state's political structure. Under the new name of the Constitutional and Reform Party, the reformers forced a repeal of the Stand-Up election law and broached the question of calling a state constitutional convention.

Grassroots agitation emboldened the insurgents, pushing them well beyond the moderate reformism favored by Governor Wolcott. In conservative Litchfield County, one "Solyman Brown" bid his "benighted section" to at last face up to democratic realities. A widely publicized essay, "The Politics of Connecticut," by the ex-Federalist Republican George H. Richards of New London, demanded a new constitution that would establish political as well as religious equality. "The Charter of King Charles II contains principles obnoxious to a Republican government," the town meeting of Wallingford declared in a memorial to its state representatives. At least sixteen other town meetings issued similar memorials between November 1817 and April 1818, and thereafter a deluge of petitions hit Hartford from towns all across the state.

Wolcott responded to the protests evenly, praising the old charter as sound for its time, but acknowledging the need for a more precise definition of government power and a declaration of the people's rights. Conservative Federalists vehemently counterattacked. Jonathan Edwards Jr. proclaimed the existing charter the best constitution in the world. Lyman Beecher fretted that the reformers intended to install a dictatorship of the dissenting sects and the rest of the hoi polloi. But the conservatives were now outnumbered. (To make matters worse, some New Haven Federalists defected to the opposition, attracted by a Reform Party proposal to alternate General Assembly meetings between their city and the state capital in Hartford.) After enacting a number of new reforms—including a suffrage act that granted the vote to free adult white males who paid taxes or served in the militia—the Reform Party legislators secured a call for a statewide election, to be held under the expanded suffrage law, that would select delegates to a constitutional convention. Even before the results were known, the tumultuous scenes at the polls on election day, July 4, were enough to cause Federalists to despair. ("The Universal suffrage law is horrible," the Reverend Thomas Robbins of Scantick wrote in his diary.) The reform coalition won a majority at the convention of nearly two to one.

The final draft of the new constitution, hammered out in Hartford over three weeks in late summer, was a moderate document that displeased some Republicans almost as much as it did the hard-liners of the Standing Order. Now led by the outspoken lawyer, Jeffersonian organizer, and customs collector of Middletown, "Boss" Alexander Wolcott (a cousin of the governor), the state's Republicans formed only a left-wing minority within the larger reform alliance. At the convention, the Republicans pressed for provisions that would have weakened the independence of the state judiciary, ended at-large voting for state senate representatives in favor of districted voting, and reapportioned town representation. All were democratic reforms; all would have enhanced the electoral prospects of Republican candidates; but all were turned aside by a centrist coalition of restrained Republicans, liberal Federalists, and cautious reformers like Governor Wolcott. "Boss" Wolcott, along with several of his allies, wound up voting against the final draft, saying it was "founded on no basis of republican equality."

One reform that stirred only passing debate but would later have great significance outside the state was the complete disenfranchisement of black voters. The numbers of free blacks had been negligible in eighteenth-century Connecticut, and the numbers of black freeholders even smaller—and no effort had ever been made to exclude otherwise qualified blacks from voting. By the close of the War of 1812, however, small but concentrated black communities had grown up, especially in and around the port cities of New Haven and New London, and were causing some consternation. In 1802, one self-styled "White Freeman" in Wallingford noted that his town included two black freeholders, "both democrats and free," and wondered whether, if they were ever elected to the legislature, they would actually be permitted to take office. In 1814, the Federalist-dominated legislature passed a law restricting freemanship to free white males. When the Reform Party legislators passed their expanded suffrage law four years later, they retained the racial exclusion.

The constitutional convention moved back and forth on the issue. An early resolution came out of a drafting committee restricting the vote to "white male citizens of the United States" with minimal property requirements. The aging Federalist judge Stephen Mix Mitchell proposed an amendment striking the word *white*, but after what was reported simply as "some debate," the amendment failed, and the draft language was approved by a vote of 103 to 72. From this distance and given the spotty sources, the politics behind the exclusion are difficult to discern. Federalists as well as Republicans appear to have been on both sides of the issue, yet the debate in the constitutional convention also appears to have been brief and to have stirred little interest outside the convention hall (apart, no doubt, from the state's black communities). What is clear is that when the opportunity first presented itself, the majority of the state's moderate political leaders thought it prudent to exclude the state's small but growing free black population from the polity—making Connecticut the second of the original northern states, after New Jersey, to draw a racial line in its suffrage laws. The action would provide an important precedent.

Too tame for some, and regressive for the state's free blacks, the new constitution nevertheless brought substantial reform to Connecticut—a belated end to old colonial structures and a local completion of the American Revolution. One key shift involved property and the suffrage. Connecticut Federalists still clung to the traditional argument that wage earners and other nonfreeholders, no matter how industrious, were so dependent on their employers and patrons that they should not be permitted to vote. Moderate reformers as well as Republicans rejected this argument out of hand, and countered that payment of taxes was sufficient economic proof of an individual's qualifications as a virtuous citizen. In slightly modified form, the convention upheld the legislature's earlier rule, opening the vote to white men "of good moral character" who had resided in their towns six months and were either freeholders worth seven dollars, militiamen, or state taxpayers.

Most dramatically, the new constitution overthrew the Congregationalist establishment by securing to all Christian denominations equal powers, rights, and privileges. Federalists fought the change furiously at the convention and gained some minor concessions regarding tithing responsibilities of church members, but could not prevent the majority from winning what, for two years, had been their chief raison d'être. With their insistence on religious toleration, the reformers guaranteed themselves sufficient popular support to carry the ratification vote in October. Moderate though the new constitution was, the fracturing of Connecticut's union of church and state would be long remembered as an overdue but momentous revolution—and, in the state's former ruling circles, as a catastrophe, when Connecticut, one minister asserted decades later, repudiated "[t]he ancient spirit which had . . . linked her . . . to the throne of the Almighty for almost two hundred years."

A similar political dynamic—involving democratic agitation, divisions within Federalism, and restrained reform—appeared in the less oligarchic commonwealth of Massachusetts. As in Connecticut, an unlikely figure led the reformers. Josiah Quincy was a former congressman and self-declared "raving Federalist" whose extreme anti-Jeffersonianism in Washington had led Henry Clay to declare that he "shall live only in the treasonable annals" of American history. After he quit Congress in 1813 and returned home to a country estate outside Boston, Quincy emerged as the leader of a third force in the city's politics, still hostile to the Republicans but also alienated from the old-line Federalist Central Committee because of its unshakable disdain for popular politics. Within Boston, Quincy aligned himself with a "Middling Interest" of artisans and petty merchants, led by the self-made printer Joseph T. Buckingham, who had been hit hard by the Panic of 1819 and were now seeking reform of laws governing debt and militia service. Elsewhere, especially in the old country democratic counties of Hampshire and Berkshire, reformers agitated for reapportionment of the state legislature and continued changes in the state judiciary. In 1820, the district of Maine's decision to seek separate statehood necessitated an overhaul of Massachusetts representation. And so, in a move instigated by Quincy (who had won election to the state legislature), voters approved a state referendum calling for a new convention in Boston, to suggest revisions of the 1780 constitution.

The convention's dramatic highpoint involved an extremely subtle but significant clash—not between reformers and antireformers but between two Federalist delegates, the aging antimajoritarian John Adams and the young conservative Daniel Webster. At issue was a plan devised by democratic reformers to apportion both houses of the state legislature, and not just the lower house, on the basis of population and not property. Adams, pallid and shriveled at age eighty-five, arose to deny that all men were born free and equal, to announce that government's "great object is to render property secure," and to denounce any effort to end property-holding qualifications for voters and officeholders. Government by "mere numbers," Adams argued, would lead the many to pillage the propertied few in scenes reminiscent of the French Revolution. Webster broadly agreed with Adams— "We have no experience that teaches us, that any other rights are safe, where property is not safe," he declared—but he believed that the majority actually held property and respected property rights. While for the present he would keep the existing arrangements for the upper house, Webster also urged government to encourage a wide diffusion of property "as to interest the great majority of society in the protection of the government." To

Adams, imprisoned in his eighteenth-century orthodoxies, democracy directly threatened property. To Webster, property ownership could be sufficiently widespread among the many, and opportunity to gain additional property sufficiently wide, that democracy and property rights were compatible. Over the years to come, Webster's more benign and dynamic vision would expand and encourage a genuine revolution of American conservatism.

The political agility of the Massachusetts conservatives, young and old, spared them from any sweeping changes for the moment, but could not fully defeat reform. In the contests for convention delegates, the Federalist Central Committee gained a majority for its own loyalists, along with friendly moderate and conservative Republicans who were wary of the most determined democrats. The coalition of antireformers and moderate reformers repeatedly thwarted what Joseph Story later derided as "a pretty strong body of radicals" inside the convention. As in Connecticut, the reformers made their greatest gains in proposing expanded religious liberties, recommending an end to the existing religious test for officeholders and equalization in the distribution of local tax monies to Unitarians and Congregationalists. The convention also proposed abolishing the existing freehold suffrage and giving the vote to all adult male taxpayers who had been resident in the state for twelve months and in their towns or districts for six months. Concerning the structures of government, the convention recommended stripping public prosecutors of the common-law right to indict citizens on their own, revising the structure of the governor's advisory executive council, and providing for the future amending of the constitution by approval of the legislature and a public referendum. The voters duly approved most of the proposed reforms, including the liberalized suffrage and the elimination of the test oath.

Compared to what had happened in Connecticut, the Massachusetts revisions seemed minor, if only because Connecticut's existing colonial-era charter had demanded much more reform than Massachusetts's revolutionary constitution of 1780. Compared to what the most emphatic Massachusetts democrats had hoped to achieve—universal manhood suffrage, complete separation of church and state, senate representation based on population not property, substantially diminishing the independence of the state judiciary—the convention's reforms looked negligible. "What has the convention done?" the frustrated Boston Middling Interest leader Joseph Buckingham asked. "Nothing—absolutely nothing." Among Federalists, the mood was one of quiet satisfaction. "We have got out as well as we expected," Webster confided to a friend. Still, the convention had reformed the old connection between property and power with regard to voting. More important, with its amendment provision, the revised constitution created the means for approving reforms without having to reconsider the entire constitution, thereby creating the possibility of more dramatic changes in the future.

DEMOCRATIC STRUGGLES IN NEW YORK

Months after the Massachusetts movement ran its course, a more consequential uprising overhauled New York's constitution, in the greatest reform convention held anywhere in the country during the decade after 1815. New York's existing constitution of 1777, with its elaborate two-tier property qualifications for voting and its highly centralized arrangements for appointing state officials and vetoing legislative acts, was nearly as obsolete as Connecticut's old royal charter.* But because New York's society and

---

* Under the 1777 state constitution, renters of tenements worth 40 shillings annually, freeholders worth £20, and freemen—merchants, prominent artisans, and like citizens—of the cities of New York and Albany could vote for members of the state assembly, but only freeholders worth £100 could vote for members of the state senate and for governor. Under the 1804 statutory revision for New York City, voting for the assembly was revised to enfranchise adult men who rented a tenement worth $25 per year. The £100 freehold requirement for senator electors had been translated into a $250 requirement by the time of the 1821 convention.

politics were more complex and fractious than those of any New England state, the combination of democratic agitation and constitutional reformism achieved far more.

Popular pressure for reform arose quickly after the conclusion of the War of 1812, focused on liberalizing the state's stiff property requirements for voting as well as on altering the appointment process. In New York City and in Albany, where the number of workingmen and laborers excluded from the franchise was growing rapidly, newspapers reported on developments in Connecticut and Massachusetts, as well as on the suffrage agitation as far away as Britain. In the state's rapidly growing western and northern rural areas, large-scale emigration from New England—where even before the latest round of reformism, the newcomers had enjoyed suffrage requirements more liberal than New York's—increased the pressure for constitutional revision. A growth in rural tenancy, whereby farmers remained ineligible to vote until they had paid off in full their installment mortgages, added to the ferment in the countryside. In 1817 and 1820, reform conventions assembled in Washington County and Montgomery County; another reform meeting, called by a group of "Republican Young Men," convened in Saratoga in January 1821. By then, following the constitutional conventions in Connecticut and Massachusetts, New York had come to look like an undemocratic oddity, its politics dominated by provisions like the freehold suffrage that were relics of British feudalism. "In this enlightened age, and in this republican country," one critic declared in the early summer of 1821, the rights of free citizens "should not be tested by the refinements and subtleties of Norman jurisprudence."

Factionalized party politics, exacerbated by the imperious leadership of DeWitt Clinton (who was elected governor in 1817), also helped turn constitutional reform into a potent issue. Clinton's dalliance with the Federalists in 1812 had stretched the personal loyalty of some upstate Republicans almost to the breaking point. (That point had already been passed in New York City, where anti-Clintonians, calling themselves City Democrats, had seized command of the local Republican organization and its Manhattan headquarters, Tammany Hall.) As governor, Clinton's unreliable patronage policies, support for various Federalist projects (including a Federalist bank charter, obtained through legislative bribery), and arrogant, almost patrician style led to a full-scale revolt. The anti-Clintonians took as their distinguishing political insignia the bucktail worn by New York City's Tammany democrats. And from the upstate Bucktails' ranks emerged a capable and disciplined new leadership, headed by Clinton's erstwhile ally, Martin Van Buren.

Ideology as well as political self-interest propelled the Bucktails. Clinton's collaboration in the temporary revival of New York Federalism after 1812 struck the Van Buren Republicans as nearly treasonous. The new Clintonism, which effaced the Jeffersonian principles of the 1790s, needed purifying. Once approved by the Republican caucus, party decisions had to be upheld to the letter. "The cardinal maxim . . . ," one Bucktail legislator said in 1824, "[should be] always to seek for, and when ascertained, always to follow the will of the majority." Any who wavered would be cut down as a matter of practical expediency and in deference to what Van Buren called "the democratical spirit." And while they preached party regularity, Van Buren's Bucktails accommodated to the electorate's will. On some issues—support for reform of the militia system, for example— they took up matters that appealed strongly to their own urban artisan base as well as to small farmers. On others, they learned how to tack with the prevailing winds. In his successful run for governor in 1817, Clinton had struck a strong popular chord with the latest version of his visionary proposal to build a canal across almost the entire breadth of the state, connecting the port of New York with the agricultural riches of the Great Lakes region. The Van Buren Republicans initially rejected it as a neo-Federalist attempt to align the established rich and wellborn behind Clinton's political fortunes. When Van Buren learned of the proposal's popularity upstate, he switched his position at the last minute and brought along enough anti-Clintonian votes in the state senate to pass the canal bill. Clinton won the election for governor anyway—a signal defeat for Van Buren—but the switch was a sign of the Van Burenites' growing pragmatic flexibility.

Clinton managed to retain enough popularity to win re-election in 1820, but the tightly organized Bucktails took control of the state legislature and of New York's peculiar Council of Appointments, which was empowered to select scores of state and local officials, high and low. (The Bucktail legislature also elected Van Buren to the U.S. Senate.) Van Buren's men wielded power ruthlessly, replacing Clintonians with their own loyalists throughout state government in what one newspaper called a "bloody inquisition." The Bucktails also looked for ways to forestall any Clintonian recovery. One sure method—that, paradoxically, might threaten the appointive weapons they now exercised freely—was to back the popular demands for constitutional reform. A convention bill had come before the legislature in 1818, but Clinton and his supporters had blocked it. A year later, amid rising popular protests, Clinton agreed to hold a convention limited strictly to changing the appointment power, but the Bucktails refused to take the bait. A bill calling for an unrestricted convention finally passed in 1820, after the Bucktails had captured the legislature, but the Council of Revision, controlled by Governor Clinton, vetoed it—delaying matters by claiming (perfectly correctly) that only the people at large had the power to call a constitutional convention. Unfazed, the Bucktails passed yet another bill early in 1821, creating a convention contingent on approval by a popular referendum. The Clintonians, not wanting to look like enemies of popular sovereignty, grudgingly went along. In a special election, with a widened suffrage that allowed virtually all adult males to vote, the convention proposal passed by a three to one margin.

The convention delegates, elected by the same widened suffrage, were, as a group, more diverse, more rural, and more liberal than their earlier counterparts in Connecticut and Massachusetts. Over half of the New York delegates were farmers, ranging from large landholders in Dutchess and Columbia Counties to small producers from the northern and western parts of the state. Nearly half were migrants from other states, chiefly in New England. Above all, the vast majority—98 of the 126 delegates—were either Bucktails or men friendly to Van Buren. Although a few old-line Federalists and Clintonians, including the eminent jurist Chancellor James Kent and the great patroon Stephen Van Rensselaer, made their presence felt on various issues, their numbers were marginal. The major lines of conflict pitted a feisty band of radical Bucktails, including the popular George Clinton Republican and antislavery man Erastus Root and Samuel Young of Genesee County—chiefly representing small farmers and rural townsmen from west of the Hudson—against a large and at times uneasy coalition of liberal and moderate Bucktails led by Van Buren.

Van Buren's side prevailed on every important issue. Easily overcoming Kent and the conservatives, the convention toppled the existing two-tiered freehold voting arrangement—yet replaced it not with universal white manhood suffrage, as favored by the radicals, but with a modest taxpaying requirement, which could also be met with membership in the militia or work on public roads. The convention eliminated both the Council of Revision (which controlled legislative vetoes) and the Council of Appointments (regarding patronage offices), giving much of the latter's power to county-court judges and new county boards of supervisors (which, not coincidentally, Bucktail Republicans controlled). The delegates made thousands of formerly appointive offices, ranging from sheriffs and county clerks to militia officers, open to popular election. Radical efforts to remake completely the state judiciary stalled, and the respected high conservative Kent was allowed to keep his job as chancellor of the old court of chancery—but the convention created a new supreme court to replace the existing Federalist-dominated body and established a new system of circuit judges. Senatorial representation, now to be based on persons not property, was altered to create eight senatorial districts instead of the existing four—a defeat for the Federalists and Clintonians, who had wanted even more districts in order to favor their little pockets of strength in Albany and Columbia Counties.

The moderate and liberal Bucktails also carved out a victory on black suffrage and representation. New York was home to the largest number of blacks of all the northern states, including nearly thirty thousand "free persons of color" and some ten thousand slaves, due to be freed in 1827 under the state's gradual emancipation law. The concentration of blacks, slave and free, in the five counties of what is now New York City and in the lower and mid Hudson Valley represented the largest such concentration anywhere in the country outside Charleston, South Carolina. (One-third of the state's free black population lived in Manhattan.) Black adult males, enfranchised on equal terms with whites under the 1777 constitution, were overwhelmingly loyal to the Federalists, in part because of alienation from the party of the slaveholders Jefferson and Madison and in part because of Federalist influence in the Hudson Valley small towns and countryside. In close elections, the black vote, although a small portion of the total, could swing key districts and even (or so it was alleged in 1813) decide the balance of power in the state assembly. For surviving Federalists, scrambling for whatever voting blocs they could find, black support was a vital resource. Now, with the imminent enlargement of the free black citizenry, the numbers of black voters would increase by about one-third. Moreover, if blacks were counted as part of the population on which the legislature would be apportioned, new advantages would go to New York City and its neighboring counties. Even more than in Connecticut, white fears of enlarged black political power pervaded the New York convention.

On the representation question, rural radical Bucktails like Samuel Young and Federalists like Rufus King could agree that direct representation was meant to be restricted to free white citizens, to the exclusion of blacks as well as paupers and white unnaturalized immigrants. "It was not the intention of the committee," King reported for the Committee on the Legislature, "to have free people of colour, or aliens, taken into account." Limiting the political power of New York City and its supposedly degrading influence was the ostensible reason for the exclusion, but so, too, most delegates appear to have assumed that only resident citizens deserved representation, and that free blacks were not truly full citizens. The delegates finally settled on a provision whereby "persons of color" (but not aliens) who paid taxes would be counted for purposes of representation and apportionment.

The suffrage issue was more divisive. In their reports to the convention on the legislative committee's recommendations, Nathan Sanford of New York City and John Ross of rural Genesee County declared that only resident white male citizens should be eligible to vote. This quietly affirmed the exclusion of unnaturalized immigrants who, under the 1777 constitution, had been permitted to vote if they met the stringent property requirements. The patrician Federalist Stephen Van Rensselaer then offered an amendment to exclude what he called "the wandering population," but his amendment's language, by accident or design, omitted the word "white." The radical Bucktail Young immediately moved that the word be added. Like Connecticut, presumably, New York would eliminate property requirements for white male citizens while also eliminating the black electorate. The proposal sparked a heated debate.

Federalist conservatives, including Chancellor Kent and Abraham Van Vechten, supported a motion by their antislavery colleague Peter Jay to strike the word *white*, while they also hoped to retain the $250 freehold qualification for all voters, white and black, in elections for state senators. Whatever their partisan motives may have been, these conservatives believed that class and property superseded color as a qualification for voting. "The landed interest of the state, on account of its stability and importance," Van Vechten told the convention, "is . . . entitled to distinct weight in the choice of at least one branch of the legislature."

A minority of the Bucktail radicals, most vociferously a firebrand physician from Delaware County, Robert Clarke, dissented and insisted on universal suffrage for black and white men alike in all elections. (Denying blacks a vote in a government they were bound to obey, the Jeffersonian Clarke said, was "repugnant to all the principles and notions of liberty, to which we have heretofore professed to adhere, and to our declaration of independence.") Most of the radical Bucktails, however, demanded democracy for white men only and the disfranchisement of all blacks—reversing the conservative idea by insisting that color, and not property, should govern suffrage qualifications. "The minds of the blacks are not competent to vote," Samuel Young, the most outspoken, asserted. ". . . Look to your jails and penitentiaries. By whom are they filled? By the very race, whom it is now proposed to cloth[e] with the power of deciding upon your political rights."

Partisanship and rural distaste for New York City cannot fully explain the vehemence of Young's racism. Among the conservatives, lingering patrician ideas of hierarchy placed all of the middling and lower orders in a naturally subordinate position, regardless of color—a subordination to be marked by property distinctions in political rights. (The exceptions were a group of even more conservative delegates who voted both to ban black voting and to sustain the freeholder requirement for whites in senate elections.) But for some of the most vocal Bucktail democrats, Young above all, the political equality they sought could not be squared with social inequality—and the conservatives' effort to oppose the first while glossing over the second was infuriating. For the racist democrats, as for most white Americans, free blacks were an inferior people who did not fully share in the burdens of the state. "The distinction of colour," Young said, "is well understood": relatively few free blacks were taxpayers; all were barred, by federal law, from militia service; a disproportionate number were illiterate and thus, Young charged, easily manipulated. To recognize these and other obvious inequalities in everyday life but to ignore them in politics was, to the racist democrats, a sinister absurdity, one that cheapened the franchise they were fighting to enlarge and that played into the hands of the white aristocratic few. Noting that Connecticut had recently banned black voting, Young insisted that "[w]e ought to make a constitution adapted to *our* habits, manners, and state of society." For Young and his allies—one of whom explicitly affirmed his own antislavery convictions—black disenfranchisement was the corollary of emancipation.

The majority of the convention took a more temperate anti-black position. Van Buren was loath to disenfranchise all proper-tied, taxpaying blacks who had heretofore voted. He thus joined with a coalition consisting of moderate and radical Bucktails and most of the Federalists to support Jay's proposal, and the conven-tion by a narrow margin reinstated black suffrage. But neither could Van Buren, who himself had owned a slave as a young man, imagine keeping blacks on the same footing as whites. He backed a compromise put together by a select committee of thirteen that limited black male suffrage for all elections to those who owned freeholds worth $250—the same property qualification the con-servatives wanted to retain for the entire electorate in senatorial contests. (Black voters would also have to meet a special three-year residency requirement, three times longer than for whites.) The compromise left the existing minuscule electorate for gover-nor and state senators intact, but it disenfranchised the over-whelming majority of free blacks previously eligible to vote for assembly candidates, as well as adult male slaves who would be free after 1827. Van Buren insisted that the principle of black suffrage had been sustained and added with bland condescen-sion that the property restrictions "held out inducements to industry." New York's racial exclusions were less severe than Con-necticut's. But the New Yorkers still affirmed that the conserva-tive idea of a responsible freehold franchise, obnoxious to white male voters, made sense regarding blacks.

Politics prevailed at the New York convention—not simply the opportunistic politics of Bucktail supremacy, but a vision of party democracy that foreshadowed later developments at the state and national level. With their constitutional revisions, Van Buren and his allies all but ensured their command of New York politics for nearly a generation, under the semi-ironic title of the Albany

Regency. In shifting a great deal of the appointive power to the county level, where his forces were strongest, Van Buren also candidly acknowledged that political parties were not only compatible with but necessary to an orderly democratic regime. "The republican party [was] predominant in the state," Van Buren told the convention, according to one recorder's notes, "and he did not believe that magnanimity, or justice, required that they should place themselves under the dominion of their opponents. While they continue to be in the majority, it was no more than right that they should exercise the powers of the government. That the majority should govern, was a fundamental maxim in all free governments."

To portray the New York convention only as a partisan affair, though, run by and for merely operational democrats, is to miss the deeper ideological issues at stake and to slight the convention's democratic achievements. At the time, the more cynical view prevailed among archconservative delegates like Abraham Van Vechten, who charged that the push for reform had "arisen more from violent party collisions, than from any real dissatisfaction" with the existing constitution. Later historians have endorsed Van Vechten's claim. Yet popular agitation to revise the constitution had begun before the "collisions" Van Vechten described, and had taken on a life of its own before 1821. After repeated rebuffs by the Clinton Republicans, pro-reform sentiment carried the popular referendum on calling a convention by a huge majority. Van Buren and his allies exploited this sentiment, but they also created a polity and state government that, for white male citizens, were far more democratic in spirit and in form than anything New Yorkers had ever known.

In trying to protect the status quo, conservative delegates turned to two contradictory lines of argument about what Chancellor Kent called the terror of democratic principles: either the poor would, as Kent said, "share the plunder of the rich," or the propertied few would manipulate the masses. By defeating these chimeras—contemptuous, they believed, of ordinary citizens—the Bucktails won a major victory against what they saw as a resurgent Federalism in a political war that dated back to the 1790s. As Van Buren put it in a private letter before the convention to Rufus King—not a man to be impressed by populist claptrap—the war pitted the "yeomanry of the State" against a "nefarious band of speculators" that had "preyed upon the very vitals of government." If the War of 1812 had vindicated American independence and the Revolution of 1776, then, in the eyes of the Van Burenites and their followers, the convention of 1821 vindicated, in New York, the Jeffersonian revolution of 1800–01.

The vindication was substantive as well as symbolic. True, the Van Burenites shied away from backing universal manhood suffrage, even for whites; and for most black voters, the convention of 1821 was a disaster. In opposing those delegates whom Van Buren derided as the "Map-caps among the old democrats," the Bucktails could sometimes sound as conservative as James Kent. But more than any other group of reformers in the older states in the years after 1815, the Bucktails also won dramatic democratic victories. They reduced the term of the governor from three years to two, making the chief executive more responsible to the electorate as well as to his party. Under the new constitution, most state positions were elective, while the rest were appointed not by the now-defunct Council of Appointments but by order of the governor and the state senate. Above all, the number of New Yorkers eligible to vote for the state assembly rose from roughly 200,000 to roughly 260,000, and those eligible to vote for governor and state senate rose from roughly 100,000 to roughly 260,000. Whereas previously about two-thirds of all white males could vote in assembly elections and only about one-third could vote as well for governor and state senators, now more than 80 percent could vote in all elections. No revision of an existing state constitution had enfranchised anywhere near so many citizens in a single stroke. It was close enough to universal white manhood suffrage that, a mere five years later, New York amended its new constitution to remove the last, difficult-to-enforce taxpaying requirements for white male voters.

DEMOCRATIC STRUGGLES IN THE WEST
AND THE SOUTH

Between 1816 and 1820, four western states—Indiana, Mississippi, Illinois, and Alabama—joined the Union. The conclusion of the War of 1812, by removing the threat of the woodland Indians in the North and the Creeks in the South, accelerated both the white settlement of these areas and the alacrity with which Congress acted to incorporate them as states. Formally, their constitutions were democratic in comparison to most of the original state constitutions back East. But contrary to persisting myth, developed most powerfully by Frederick Jackson Turner, no "wind of Democracy" blew from the Mississippi Valley back to the long-settled regions of the seaboard. In fact, the West borrowed heavily from eastern examples. And although the arrivistes who settled in the West chose—and in some cases were forced to adopt—democratic institutions, their actions did not spring from democratic mores unique to a frontier setting. They arose out of a combination of self-interest on the part of the more prominent settlers and political pressure from below.

Westerners did exert some indirect democratic influences in the East when eastern reformers asserted that unless they heeded democratic pressures, capable residents would migrate west in droves. "By rendering it the interest and happiness of our population to stay at home," the Republican editor of the New York *Columbian* wrote in 1817, "is the only way to check the [emigration] rage." Western constitution makers, meanwhile, relied heavily on the precedents of neighboring states from which the majority of new settlers had come, which in turn had built on earlier precedents. Thus, Illinois and Indiana drew on the constitutional structures of Ohio, which had earlier drawn on the examples of Kentucky, Tennessee, and Pennsylvania. One Massachusetts newspaper, reviewing the Mississippi constitution of 1817, remarked that it was so similar to those "of many of the other states that its perusal does not excite much interest." Alabama took Missis-

sippi's constitution as its model when it framed its own constitution two years later.

The wealthier and more politically connected residents of the
new states certainly sounded more democratic than many of their
eastern counterparts. In Alabama's plantation-dominated black
belt, Georgia émigrés from the Tidewater Broad River region
established themselves early as a social elite but espoused
broadly democratic ideas for the white male citizenry. "[T]he fundamental principle of all our institutions," John W. Walker of the
Broad River group wrote on the eve of Alabama's first constitutional convention, "supposes [the Constitution] to be an act of
the People themselves." Yet self-interest, as well as democratic
idealism, had shaped westerners' views well before statehood was
in the offing. Under the fifty-acre freehold requirement for voting
in the territories established by Congress, only a tiny proportion
of western settlers qualified—including many who actually
owned sufficient land but had difficulty establishing their titles.
In Mississippi in 1804, only a little more than two hundred out of
a total of nearly forty-five hundred residents were entitled to
vote. Similar circumstances in Indiana led to petitions calling the
voting requirements, as one put it, "subversive of the liberties" of
the people at large. Congress reluctantly gave way in a series of
reforms that eventually established a small taxpaying suffrage
requirement for adult white males.

Territorial leaders, particularly in the Old Northwest states,
saw liberalized voting laws as an important incentive to attract
enough new settlers to qualify for statehood. Thereafter, leading residents in sparsely populated areas saw even further liberalization as a means to encourage settlement, raise land
values, hasten economic development, and expand the tax
base. In the southwestern states, full citizenship and enfranchisement of all white men enlisted in the militia would
ensure full participation in policing patrols, which would help
minimize the possibility of slave revolts. It would also, in time,
become a powerful means of blurring the class lines between
slaveholders and nonslaveholders, by appealing to their basic

equality as white citizens regardless of property—creating a Master Race democracy.

Self-interested sagacity, however, goes only so far in explaining the trend toward expanded democracy in the new states. In some places, notably Alabama, plain settlers and their champions pushed more conservative men further than they wanted to go. At the 1819 Alabama constitutional convention, an exclusive Committee of Fifteen offered a draft constitution that included the absence of any property or taxpaying qualifications for voting and officeholding. Overall, the Alabama Committee's draft plan offered the new state's white male adults the most liberal state constitution in the country. But even that was too limited for the delegates from the "upper counties" in the northern part of the territory, populated mainly by nonslaveholding yeomen. With timely aid from a few of the more prominent delegates—including the convention's president, Princeton-educated John W. Walker—the upper-county delegates forced the convention to base representation in both the upper and lower houses of the legislature strictly on the basis of white population. The upper-county men also secured a provision abolishing imprisonment for debt, and they defeated efforts to prevent the popular election of county sheriffs, the most important state officials at the local level.

In other western states, the more democratic forces prevailed from the outset. The election of delegates to the Indiana state constitutional convention in 1816 was thrown open to all adult white male citizen taxpayers. The convention, dominated by farmers and lawyers who had resettled from the Virginia backcountry, in turn approved a constitution that provided white manhood suffrage and voting by written ballot, and established a decentralized judiciary with term limits of seven years for judges. Soon after Alabama completed its constitution, Mississippians began raising the issue of revising their own constitution in order to catch up. In Illinois, no taxpaying requirement was required at any stage.

The major obvious difference among the western state constitutions concerned slavery, although the politics behind that difference were complicated. In Indiana, a faction of resident slave-holders known as the Virginia Aristocracy, backed by William Henry Harrison and his so-called Vincennes Junto, was losing its sway to an antislavery faction, called the Parvenues, concentrated in the southeastern parts of the territory. When the constitutional convention met in 1816, antislavery opinion mobilized itself, and the Parvenues and their allies got the upper hand. After a bitter debate, the convention adopted a provision which declared that "the holding of any part of the human creation . . . can only originate in usurpation and tyranny" and outlawed slavery and involuntary servitude in perpetuity—but the delegates also excluded blacks from the franchise. The Illinois constitution of 1818 likewise banned both slavery and black suffrage. But under pressure from the state's large southern-born white population, it also sustained existing black employment indentures on terms close to slavery. In 1819, the new Illinois legislature would pass a series of draconian black codes strictly regulating black settlement and employment, and in 1822 the antislavery governor Edward Coles—a native of Albemarle County, Virginia, and protégé of Thomas Jefferson—would have to organize furiously to stave off an effort to introduce slavery. In Mississippi and Alabama, egalitarianism for whites became in part a means for protecting slavery. In Illinois and Indiana, it helped to prevent slavery from taking root—although not without a fight and not without the total exclusion of blacks from the polity. As in Connecticut and New York, political rights for men in the new northwestern states would stop sharply at the color line.

The stongest resistance to any egalitarian trends, including those that purportedly enhanced slavery, appeared in the seaboard South. South Carolina's broad suffrage and quasi-aristocratic governance, installed in 1808, sustained the state's basic conservative character, and neither North Carolina nor Georgia (where white manhood suffrage had been established in 1789) generated significant reform activity between 1800 and 1820. By contrast, in Virginia, the largest and economically most diverse of the southern states, the slaveholding Tidewater political establishment confronted demands for constitutional revision quite similar to those that arose in New England and New York. But conservative Virginians killed off calls for a new state convention, partly by granting piecemeal concessions and partly by remaining united.

Much as in the northeastern states, Virginia's democratic movement originated from below. On June 21, 1815, a meeting of nonfreeholders assembled in Harrisonburg in Piedmont Rockingham County to protest "the inhibitions to the elective franchise," chiefly Virginia's fifty-acre freehold requirement. The group also appointed a committee to draft a petition that would be circulated throughout the state, signed by other nonfreeholders and their supporters, and forwarded to the legislature in Richmond. Issued on July 4, the petition demanded that militiamen recently "coerced into military service" as well as all male taxpayers be given the franchise, and that the state assembly call "a CONVENTION of the PEOPLE" to revise the 1776 constitution.

Signed copies of the circular poured into the legislature from the western counties, populated mainly by nonslaveholding small farmers and commercial wheat growers. The legislature, dominated by eastern slaveholders, took no action, which prompted a new round of formal western protests during the summer of 1816, now led by moderate gentleman reformers. In early August, delegates from eleven western counties met in Winchester to demand equalized representation in the state legislature. An even larger meeting, consisting of men from thirty-five counties, assembled later that month in Staunton—and, when taken over by more insistently democratic reformers, issued a call for a state convention with an unlimited scope that would consider suffrage reform as well as equal representation. The democrats' passion left even some of the genteel western reformers worried that "the idle and vicious & worthless" were about to overthrow the rights of property.

From his Albemarle County aerie, Thomas Jefferson viewed the agitation with approval. In June 1816, he received a pamphlet from its author, one H. Tompinkson—actually Samuel Kercheval, a freethinking Piedmont writer and reformer—endorsing the convention movement, along with a note inquiring about his reactions. Begging that his opinions be kept out of "the gridiron of the public papers," Jefferson delivered a lengthy affirmation that actually went much further than the radical Virginia democrats had dared to go. Jefferson supported a "general suffrage" (that is, giving the ballot to all taxpayers and militiamen) as well as equal representation, but he also proposed a complete overhaul of the county court system and a revamping and democratization of local government to resemble more closely the townships of New England. "I am not among those who fear the people," Jefferson emphasized. "They, and not the rich, are our dependence for continued freedom."

Among the great majority of Virginia's Republican landed gentry, however, Jefferson's democratic views were anathema. Schooled in the traditional conventions of advancement through honor, talents, and connections, slaveholders of all partisan persuasions had little use for the rude democracy being foisted on them by the nonfreeholders. If few were as allergic to democracy as John Randolph—who, in his acidulous way, would later remark that Jefferson had no authority on any subject, even "in the mechanism of a plough"—most believed that apart from electioneering days, politics ought to be left in the hands of virtuous gentleman-masters like themselves, and that men of property, especially slaveholders, deserved a larger voice in the legislature than others.

An instinct for political self-preservation did open the way for some concessions to the more moderate of the westerners. Thomas Ritchie, a friend of Jefferson's and now the editor of the influential *Richmond Enquirer*, gave considerable coverage to the reformers' activities. At Ritchie's urging, a few eastern Republicans pushed a convention proposal through the lower house of the legislature in 1816. Thereafter, a coalition of western Republicans, Federalists, and eastern moderate Republicans passed legislation extending internal improvements and new bank charters to western areas and reducing the disproportional representation of the eastern counties in the senate—thereby conciliating the more temperate and well heeled of the western reformers. But the senate killed the convention bill. "Enough was done at the last session," one conservative wrote, hopefully, after the legislature adjourned, "to quiet the Western counties and to prevent any mischief at the next." Virginia's Republican old guard had, for the moment, thoroughly contained the democratic challenge.

The reformers' defeat in Virginia affirmed emerging patterns in the state-level efforts at constitutional liberalization after 1815. Several factors contributed to the pressure for change— religious tensions, the search for partisan advantage, economic self-interest, as well as the growth of portions of the population either ineligible to vote or badly underrepresented under the existing rules. But in no state did reform come easily, or without agitation and pressure from below. In the older states, the task of calling state conventions proved extremely difficult, resisted by establishment leaders until they had no choice but to accede. Once assembled in conventions, conservatives and moderates proved highly capable of limiting reform. The greatest exception, outside the new states, came in New York, and even there, moderate and not radical reformers prevailed. Local political elites, as in Virginia, might forestall major reforms with concessions, but in no instance did reforms occur simply because of the calculations of the existing ruling groups. The success of the state movements depended, in turn, on the solidarity, homogeneity, and political will of the respective local elites, leaving the southeastern slave states the most impervious to change.

The result was a highly uneven pattern of democratization. By the end of 1821, twenty-one of the twenty-four states had approved something approaching a divorce of property-holding and voting—a major shift since the nation's founding. But of the four original states that lay below the Potomac, two, Virginia and

North Carolina, still had significant property restrictions on the suffrage, and a third, South Carolina, placed severe property limits on officeholding that helped keep political power firmly in the hands of the slaveholder elite. Only six states, all but one of them in the free North, had approved manhood suffrage, regardless of property, for blacks as well as whites; conversely five of the original thirteen states—Connecticut, Delaware, Maryland, New Jersey, and New York—had either withdrawn or sharply curtailed black voting rights. The new states admitted to the Union after 1789, from Maine to Louisiana, had generally liberal constitutions, but outside the New England states and Tennessee, they too excluded blacks from the polity. In the only state where women had enjoyed the franchise, New Jersey, that right had been removed. And in every state but four, aliens were formally banned from the polls.

Democracy for white men had come a long way since the Revolution, but it had also had to overcome resistance, sometimes intense, in much of the country—and it still had far to go in most of the older portions of the South. For those white men left out, as well as for free black men newly excluded, the sight of democratization for others stoked deep resentments. The full ramifications of these trends, and of the passions that lay behind them, would not, however, become fully apparent until the mid-1820s. By then, two national political crises, both of which began in 1819, had destroyed the optimistic spirit of patriotic unity proclaimed by President James Monroe and had greatly altered the context of democratic reform. The first crisis involved the sudden collapse of the economy—a catastrophe caused, many believed, by the reborn Bank of the United States.

THE PANIC OF 1819

James Monroe was a model of dignified and somewhat dim perseverance—an unlikely promoter of vigorous postwar economic expansion and improvement. A son of Virginia's lesser tobacco gentry, he had studied law with Jefferson, attached himself to his mentor's political fortunes, and doggedly risen the political ladder to the highest reaches of national affairs, winning appointment (at Jefferson's urging) as Madison's secretary of state. Fluent in French but less than brilliant—"a mind neither rapid nor rich," William Wirt noted in one widely quoted remark—Monroe was by nature more of an ideological purist than either Jefferson or Madison, and he remained one well after 1801. In 1808, when some doctrinaire Virginians bridled at Jefferson's selection of Madison as his successor, Monroe let it be known that he would allow himself to be advanced as an alternative—backing off only at the last minute, and thereby saving his political career. Under Madison, Monroe directed the State Department with admirable energy. He displayed particular fortitude during the British destruction of Washington when, while the rest of the administration scattered into the Virginia night, he organized what meager defenses he could. The Republican congressional caucus duly gave him its presidential nomination in 1816, and he won the election handily over Rufus King, losing only in the die-hard Federalist strongholds of Delaware, Massachusetts, and Connecticut. Yet Monroe came to the presidency generating a sense of solid and unexciting entitlement—a gray-haired worthy of fifty-nine, at the tag end of the Revolutionary generation, whose penchant for wearing old-fashioned knee breeches and silk stockings on ceremonial occasions signaled a certain strangeness in the rapidly rebuilding capital.

Monroe turned out to be more of a combination of old and new than a throwback to the 1790s. Catching up with the Republican mainstream, he had shifted toward nationalist views since 1808, a shift that became more pronounced during the war. "The nation has become tired of the follies of faction," the Philadelphia ex-Federalist and man of letters Nicholas Biddle wrote with relief to an associate shortly after Monroe won the White House, "and the ruling party has outgrown many of the childish notions with which they began their career 20 years since." For Monroe, ending factionalism also meant fulfilling Jefferson's old dream of incorporating the remnants of Federalism into a grand national party. He did not appoint Federalist hold-outs to office, lest his own friends denounce him for treachery, but he made a point of reaching out to the surviving Federalists in Congress and generally won their backing. As for rejecting old dogma, Monroe began his presidency by vigorously supporting government encouragement to industry, trade, commerce, and national defense—sentiments that led the newly selected attorney general, Richard Rush, to wonder if Mr. Monroe had moved too far in the Federalists' direction.

Other observers, with longer memories than Rush, also viewed Monroe's embrace of consensus and nationalist improvement with misgivings. Although the new president had no visible enemies in Washington, he also had no fervent friends. He was an old man's young man, whose career had thrived thanks to alliances with his elders, above all Jefferson, now all but passed from the political scene. Moreover, Rufus King wrote in 1818, "strong passions" lurked just beneath the surface of nationalist amity on Capitol Hill, "waiting only for an occasion to show themselves." By the end of Monroe's first term, those passions had men shouting all across the political nation—the result, in part, of the moderate nationalist Republicans' rejection of the formerly preternatural Jeffersonian hatred of a national bank.

Republican reconciliation with Hamilton's bank idea had taken place by fits and starts, and was never monolithic. In 1811, when the charter for the Bank of the United States (BUS) came up for renewal, the Madison administration, goaded by Secretary of the Treasury Gallatin, supported it. (Madison, the anti-BUS scourge of twenty years earlier, allowed that "expediency and almost necessity" now required rechartering the bank.) In Congress, a coalition of Republican southerners and westerners, seeing the bank as an instrument for economic development in their respective regions, led the recharter effort. But they were checked on three different fronts, which led to the bank's downfall by a single vote in both the House and the Senate. Old-line Jeffersonians, ranging from the Virginia planter William B. Giles to the veteran city democrat Michael Leib of Pennsylvania, resurrected the constitutional antibank arguments originally advanced by Jefferson and Madison. More interestingly, some of the most commercially oriented Republicans, including Henry Clay, opposed recharter on the grounds that the national bank unfairly constrained the operations of state banks, which had proliferated throughout the country (rising in number from three in 1791 to eighty-eight in 1811). Finally, some of the nation's leading capitalists—above all, in New York City, John Jacob Astor, the immigrant mercantile magnate, and the speculator Jacob Barker—had fallen out with the national bank's directors and (with plenty of state bank stock in their coffers) lobbied hard to kill the recharter bill.

Five years later, the disasters of wartime, plus the intervention of leading financiers, turned the tide yet again. In 1813, the Treasury Department, facing imminent federal bankruptcy due to military expenditures and the wartime loss of revenue, floated sixteen million dollars' worth of government paper. Astor and Barker invested heavily, along with Secretary Gallatin's fellow Pennsylvanian, the longtime pro-Republican financier Stephen Girard, in concert with Hamburg-based merchant David Parish, who represented European capital. No one in this tiny group, including Secretary Gallatin, had been born in the United States, yet they could claim, justly, to have patriotically rescued the nation's credit at a perilous moment.

Patriotism was not altruism. The bonds promised the investors a triple profit, and in 1814, Girard, Astor, and Parish, looking to guarantee their investment, tendered an undisguised Hamiltonian proposal to the Madison administration—to enhance the value of their investment by making government bonds exchangeable for stock in a new BUS. The proposal faltered when Treasury Secretary Gallatin, privy to the deal, departed for Ghent as part of Madison's peace commission. When Pennsylvania's senators, Michael Leib and Abner Laycock, blocked the appointment of their nemesis (and Gallatin's favorite) Alexander Dallas as Gallatin's replacement at the Treasury Department, the bank plan looked dead. But after the burning of Washington, and following direct intervention by what Dallas called an anonymous "deliberate concert among the Capitalists," the Pennsylvanians gave way, Dallas was confirmed, and the bank proposal was back on track. After a few legislative false starts, the pro-bank forces in Congress, now led by the repentant Speaker of the House Henry Clay and his nationalist comrade John C. Calhoun, won enough support from hitherto wary southerners and westerners to prevail in April 1816.

Monroe fully supported the bank's rebirth. As secretary of state during the darkest days of the war, he had come to understand the Hamiltonian imperatives of wartime finance, and he extended those imperatives to the postwar situation. A national bank, he wrote to Madison in May 1815, would "attach the commercial part of the community in a much greater degree to the Government; interest them in its operations. . . . This is the great desideratum of our system." Monroe's change of heart was eased by the fact that some of the most prominent figures in the "commercial part" were now self-made Republican parvenus, exemplified by Astor and Girard.

As immigrant outsiders-made-good, both Astor and Girard found the Republicans more socially and politically congenial than the Federalists. And their expanding influence added a fresh dimension to Republican politics to go along with the young national Republicans of the South and the West: an eastern monied group that strongly advocated the creation of a stable and efficient national system of money and credit. Their idea was to Republicanize Hamiltonian bank policy—understanding, as their congressional ally Calhoun boasted, that the Republicans had the support of "the yeomanry, the substantial part of our population," who would now "share in the capital of the Bank."

The chief financial rationale for re-creating the BUS was to ensure that this democratized expansion proceeded soundly. Under the financial stresses of the war, state-chartered banks had suspended specie payments, which meant that they could issue the equivalent of paper money in bank notes to borrowers without regard to the amount of gold or silver coin the banks actually held in their vaults. The suspension continued after peace returned, allowing established banks to make large dividends by extending loans and note issues far in excess of their specie reserves, and permitting new private banks to open with only tiny amounts of borrowed specie on hand and indulge in profligate lending of their own notes. With so much bank paper of dubious value forced into general circulation, the nation's economic health was threatened by a large and growing bubble of speculation. A new BUS, however, serving as the federal government's depository, could curb the inflation by reinstating specie payments—that is, by regularly presenting the state bank notes it received back to the state banks and demanding specie in return, thereby compelling the banks to reduce their vastly inflated loans and note issues. Acting as a financial balance-wheel, the national bank would, in principle, keep currency values and capital markets stable, and prevent national economic expansion from turning into an orgy of overspeculation and runaway inflation.

The main office of the Second BUS opened in Philadelphia on January 7, 1817, with Girard and four other Republicans serving as its government-appointed directors, and with another Republican, Dallas's friend William Jones, serving as its president. In the short run, all went swimmingly, despite some initial resistance from state and private banks. "We oppened here our office and agreed to take Bills on Baltimore Virginia & Phila," Astor wrote to Gallatin from New York, in his still-unsteady English, of the resumption of specie payments on February 20. "[I]n half an hour all was at par & on a level." By enforcing discipline over state and private bank emissions of paper, Astor and his friends had seemingly created what Astor called "a national blessing." Yet February 20, 1817, would prove the zenith of the "Era of Good Feelings" as far as the bank and American enterprise were concerned. A year later, Astor warned Gallatin that redoubled speculation, goaded by the BUS, now threatened "a general Blow up" among the state banks. A year after that, the American economy collapsed from top to bottom.

The bank's directors were both financially and morally culpable, but their offenses involved making a bad situation worse. The downfall originated in much larger shifts in the Atlantic economy, initiated in 1815 by Napoleon's final defeat at Waterloo. Britain's warehouses were bulging with manufactured goods, which, with the coming of peace, the British dumped on the American market, overwhelming the protectionist tariff measures enacted by Congress in 1816 and threatening American manufacturers who had sprung up in the hot-house wartime economy. Those difficulties were masked by a dizzying climb in agricultural export prices, sparked by European crop failures and by a seemingly limitless British demand for American short-staple cotton, now easily grown throughout the American South. A speculative boom in American land and cotton ensued, fueled by the riotous proliferation of new state-chartered banks prior to the national bank's reinstallation. Unnoticed at the time, however, was a growing shortage in available specie due to political unrest in Mexico and Peru, the major sources of supply for gold and silver, which in turn put a downward pressure on wholesale commodity prices. That pressure, coupled with the recovery of European agriculture and increased British imports of East Indian cotton, sent prices of American goods tumbling in 1818 and burst the speculative bubble. American staple prices and land values dropped by anywhere from 50 to 75 percent; and backward the dominos fell, from ruined speculator to merchant to farmer.

The national bank badly exacerbated the situation. At direct fault was its president, William Jones. A deft political self-promoter, Jones had won the confidence of both Monroe and Madison as well as Alexander Dallas, even though his Philadelphia mercantile firm had recently limped through bankruptcy proceedings and despite his uneven record in government service at the Navy and Treasury Departments. Stephen Girard, now a bank director, scorned Jones as an adventurer, and Gallatin was so aghast at Jones's elevation that he never thereafter spoke to

Alexander Dallas. But Jones had the support of the majority of bank directors as well as of the White House, and his style of cheery indifference came to dominate the bank's policies, both in Philadelphia and at its branch offices. The original BUS, Jones wrote to Secretary of the Treasury William Crawford in July 1817, had been too conservative in its credit operations, "circumscribed by a policy less enlarged, liberal, and useful than its powers and resources would have justified." Backed by his board, Jones would Republicanize the bank by feeding the postwar rage to get rich quick.

Rather than force state banks to curtail their inflated emissions of notes and loans, Jones approved lavish lending, especially by its new branches on the western urban frontier. By putting so many BUS notes into circulation, Jones abdicated the leverage he had had over the state banks early in 1817—for no longer could the national bank demand specie payments without being pressed for such payments in return. Compounding the problem, the Baltimore branch directors, with Jones's connivance, forced other BUS branches to redeem notes they had issued to themselves and various insider friends, expecting that the speculative boom would know no end. By 1819, the fraud netted the Baltimoreans three million dollars, half of which was never recovered. Finally, in 1818, Jones sharply reversed course, and began calling in loans—but too late to save his own skin. Early in 1819, pushed by Astor and Girard, the bank's directors finally dismissed Jones and replaced him with the South Carolinian Langdon Cheves. The new president further tightened the screws, reducing the bank's liabilities by more than half, sharply cutting back the total value of bank notes in circulation, and more than tripling the bank's specie reserves.

Without question, Cheves's decision to contract instinctually made sense, both in halting the runaway inflation and in doing right by his stockholders. Not only had Jones accelerated the speculation he was supposed to control; he had allowed the Baltimore swindlers to create what Nicholas Biddle (who joined the BUS board of directors in 1819) called "that solecism—a monied institution governed by those who had no money." For reversing that trend and restoring the bank's credibility, many historians have given Cheves high marks. Yet for the national economy, his timing and the extent of his actions could not have been worse. By the time Cheves took over the BUS, Jones's all-too-late contraction had already begun to right the situation. In clamping down even harder through 1820, Cheves accumulated a huge horde of specie in the BUS—and, in the process, contributed to turning what might have been a sharp recession into a prolonged and disastrous depression. Just as the bank intensified its deflationary pressure, commodity prices for American staples on the world market collapsed. Coupled with the bank's brutal deflation, the free fall of agricultural prices prevented state banks from either collecting from their debtors or meeting their obligations to the BUS—leading to a tidal wave of bank failures, business collapses, and personal bankruptcies. As the financial writer and bank critic William Gouge later observed, "[T]he Bank was saved and the people were ruined."

The panic appeared, at first, to hit hardest in the nation's cities. New England bore the least suffering, in part because its conservative state banks had resisted the bubble and retained their specie reserves, and in part because postwar competition from British manufacturers had checked speculation. But farther South and West, from the older seaboard ports to the growing commercial centers in the newly settled interior, the effects were catastrophic. In New York, the public almshouse, already under strain, could not handle the hundreds of new cases. In Philadelphia, three-fourths of the workforce was reported idle in 1820, and hundreds were imprisoned for nonpayment of debts. The larcenous Baltimore commercial firm Smith and Buchanan fell, John Quincy Adams recorded in his diary, "with a crash which staggered the whole city," causing the failure of more than a hundred major merchants and throwing thousands out of work. From Pittsburgh, Lexington, and Cincinnati came dolorous dispatches of unremitting commercial annihilation. (Lexington, briefly the center of Kentucky's cordage manufacturing, would never really recover, and the lion's share of Cincinnati's commercial real estate wound up in the hands of the forecloser of last resort—the Second BUS.)

The panic was just as damaging—and its effects would last longer—in rural America. "[A]ffairs are much deranged here . . . ," one British traveler wrote from Jeffersonville, Indiana. "Agriculture languishes—farmers cannot find profit in hiring labourers. . . . Labourers and mechanics are in want of employment. I think that I have seen upwards of 1500 men in quest of work within eleven months past, and many of these declared, that they had no money." Back in Virginia, the aged ex-president Jefferson reported that "lands cannot now be sold for a year's rent." Among the victims was Jefferson himself, who, having cosigned a number of bank loans for his friend Wilson Carey Nicholas, was overwhelmed "by a catastrophe I had never contemplated." Right away, he wrote a "Plan for Reducing the Circulating Medium," in which he called for "the eternal suppression of bank paper," the transfer to a specie currency, and a prohibition on bank charters by any government, state or federal. He asked his friend William C. Rives to introduce the proposal to the Virginia legislature without disclosing the author, but it got nowhere. Jefferson would spend the few remaining years of his life scrambling to keep his beloved Monticello from defaulting into the hands of his and Nicholas's creditors.

In Washington, responses to the disaster ranged from denial to rumblings about restricting bank credit. In his annual message in 1819, President Monroe took only passing notice of currency problems and the downturn in manufacturing, and said that the difficulties were lifting on their own accord. A year later, when the crisis had worsened, Monroe noticed that "an unvaried prosperity is not to be seen in every interest of this great community," but generally saw "much cause to rejoice in the felicity of our situation." Secretary of the Treasury William Crawford, on the contrary, issued a report that lamented the BUS's expansion of credit, criticized the excess number of state banks, and called for a sharp curtailment of the paper-money system, including the prohibition of small-denomination note issues.

In the immediate crisis, however, with the BUS charter not due to expire until 1836, banks and finance as well as debt laws were mainly state responsibilities—and the political fury over the panic shook state politics even more broadly and severely than the continuing campaigns for constitutional reform (and sometimes precipitated new ones). In Boston, the hardest-hit city in New England, popular anger at an alarming rise in imprisonment for debt helped consolidate the Middling Interest and pave the way for the calling of the 1820 Massachusetts convention. Debtor-relief laws were enacted in Vermont and Maryland, and came close to passage in North Carolina, Virginia, Delaware, and New Jersey. New York and Rhode Island approved milder forms of debt relief. More dramatically, several eastern states intervened to restrict state banks. New York State's Bucktail reformers, their constituents reeling from the panic, included a provision in their new constitution requiring a two-thirds' legislative majority to approve any new state banking charter. In 1820, the Pennsylvania legislature commanded all state banks to resume specie payments. Vermont passed similar legislation and forced the closure of every bank in the state. Other eastern states tightened regulations governing existing state banks. In the West, Ohio, Indiana, Illinois, Kentucky, Tennessee, Louisiana, and Missouri passed debtor-relief laws, while Illinois, Missouri, and Alabama issued state paper money aimed at aiding small debtors. And more radical popular outrage against commercial banking— sometimes directed against banks generally, sometimes simply against the BUS—spread like wildfire. "All the flourishing cities of the West are mortgaged to this money power," exclaimed Thomas Hart Benton of the nation's newest state, Missouri, inventing an antibank phrase that would loom large in national politics over the decades to come. Virtually every western state passed legislation restricting bank charters and credit; only Louisiana and Mississippi escaped the antibank wrath.

Some of the attacks on the BUS came from the same state bankers that state legislatures were trying to regulate. These banks had always resented the BUS's power to restrain their operations, and their solution to the crisis was to expand greatly the issuance of state bank paper in order to end what they called a scarcity of money. But across the country, the antibank revulsion also brought appeals, similar to Jefferson's, for the partial or total elimination of the paper-money system—what, in future years, would become known as a "hard-money" politics. By facilitating the spread of credit, the argument went, both the BUS and the state banks had created a dangerous new speculative economy, prone to illusory breakneck booms followed by busts that left the great mass of the population strapped or destitute. To correct matters, hard-money advocates demanded the virtual elimination of bank paper except for certain kinds of commercial transactions, and for its replacement with metal currency, whose value would not wildly fluctuate. Numerous antibanking schemes appeared from the pens of newspaper editors (including Thomas Ritchie of the *Richmond Enquirer*), legislators and political leaders (including the Grand Sachem of New York City's Tammany Hall), fledgling political economists, and committees of local citizens. The greatest political effect was to reinvigorate the city and country democracies, with a renewed focus on economic and financial issues.

The revived city democracy appeared most dramatically in the eastern seaports, above all in Philadelphia. Although no longer the nation's largest city, and with its mercantile sector in decline, Philadelphia had begun experiencing rapid new growth as a manufacturing center at the end of the eighteenth century. The growth accelerated during Jefferson's embargo, the War of 1812, and after. Philadelphia master craftsmen and merchants began investing in scores of new enterprises, running the gamut from highly mechanized gun manufactories and printing firms to small outwork proto-sweatshops turning out cheap shoes and clothing for the expanding western and southern markets. Along with this diverse urban manufacturing base emerged a new and polyglot class of manufacturing wage earners, ranging from highly skilled overseers to poor, barely skilled women and children pieceworkers.

The early industrialization of Philadelphia—similar, if less dramatic transformations also unfolded in Boston, New York, and Baltimore—had, by 1819, already brought to America class tensions of a sort familiar in the Old World. The established customs, hierarchies, and solidarities of craft—based on the presumption that all honest and sober skilled tradesmen would some day earn their independent competence—crumbled under the rearrangement of work and a spreading permanent dependence on wages. The surest sign of new troubles was the evolution of journeymen's friendly associations into something closer to trade unions, a step first taken by the city's shoemakers in 1794. An especially bitter shoemakers' strike over the winter of 1805–06—initiated when master shoemakers tried to cut wages—concluded in the conviction of the union leaders on common-law restraint-of-trade conspiracy charges and signaled a sharpening of class lines. Something, it seemed, had gone terribly awry amid the city's rapid industrial progress. "[T]he time before long will come," one local petty craftsman observed, dolefully, "when we shall tread in the steps of Old England."

Leading the charge against the new industrial inequities was the editor of the venerable *Aurora*, the indefatigable William Duane. Duane's red hair, close-cropped in front in the "radical" French style known as the Brutus cut, had faded to light amber—but his devotion to Paineite radical democratic principles remained undiminished. Virtually alone among Philadelphia's democrats, Duane defended the striking shoemakers in 1805, claiming that were their union suppressed, then "the constitution is a farce and the bill of rights is only a satire upon human credulity." He bitterly opposed the effort to recharter the BUS in 1811. More generally, Duane brought his English experience to bear in warning that America was, indeed, treading the same path as its former imperial ruler—allowing "the *paper money*, the *mercantile*, and the *banking* system" to enrich the few, while creating an Anglicized society where "poverty, stupidity, disease, and vice have superseded industry, intelligence, health, and innocence."

Pennsylvanians did, of course, enjoy political rights only dreamed of by British radicals, and Duane clambered into the electoral arena to help rally the city's working classes. In addition to his work at the *Aurora*, he organized Republican election committees, public meetings, and reading groups, mobilizing the artisans' autodidact pride and their renewed sense of injury against both the Federalists and the pro-banking Republicans. Yet through the prewar boom years, Duane's radical Republicans (who included a newcomer, an idealistic young army veteran and ex-clerk at the BUS named Stephen Simpson) found that good times had fractured the workingmen's vote. By 1810, the moderate Republicans had gained a decided edge even in the Duanite's city stronghold, the plebeian Northern Liberties district. The patriotic demands of wartime in turn inspired an uneasy truce between the major Republican factions. In 1813, Duane, serving as adjutant general of the state militia, organized thousands of workingmen to serve as volunteers manning the city's rickety defense works.

After the war, a combination of political estrangement and an uneven economic boom that bypassed manufacturing, followed by the devastation of 1819, reinflamed the Duanites. A new, even more aggressively pro-business group of "New School" Republicans had, in the meantime, emerged from among the moderate Republicans. Buoyed by the nationalist promise of the Era of Good Feelings, and devoted to rapid expansion of banking facilities, the New Schoolers won the governorship for their most prominent leader, William Findlay, in 1817. Knit closely by kinship and business ties—so much so that they also became known as "the Family Party"—the New Schoolers took a firm grip on the machinery of Pennsylvania politics, largely thanks to their control of the state Republican caucus. But they acted too swiftly in trying to remake the party in their own image, which led to grumbling about how the state was under the thumb of "a few lawyers of *questionable* character" and "a host of bank stock holders and bank directors." And Findlay hurt himself when he quietly joined in various shady operations, including an extortion scheme involving the awarding of auctioneers' licenses.

Writing for the *Aurora* under the pseudonym "Brutus," Stephen Simpson became the scourge of the New Schoolers, moving beyond the old radical democratic politics with fresh explications of political economy. The caucus system, long a blight to the Duanite radicals, came in for fresh attack. But Simpson also ripped into the favoritism and oppression of the New Schoolers' banks. He demanded not just reform but "the total prostration of the *banking* and *funding* system" by the elimination of all bank charters, the reliance on specie as the circulating medium, and the confinement of paper to commercial operations. The Panic of 1819 turned the protests into an uproar. Duane's son, William John Duane, who had won election to the state legislature, joined an officeholders' revolt in Harrisburg in 1820. After calling for a constitutional amendment to ban the BUS, the reformers managed to pass a law requiring forty-two so-called village banks that had been chartered all at once in 1814 to return to specie payments by the first of August or forfeit their charters. Reviving the old country-city alliance, Duanite sympathizers in rural counties as well the cities circulated mass petitions declaring that (in the words of one circular from Huntingdon County) "the industrious are impoverished whilst the speculating part of the community are growing daily more wealthy." The younger Duane chaired a special investigative committee whose official report confirmed that "[d]istress is general," and then thwarted Governor Findlay's efforts to relieve public distress by expanding paper-money loans. Findlay's attempts to obstruct the return to specie payments worsened the political crisis.

The depth of the *Aurora* group's antibank, hard-money fervor marked the culmination of a gradual ideological and political switch of considerable importance. Early in Jefferson's presidency, Duane, like other city democrats, had considered commercial banking a useful tool for general prosperity so long as it was not concentrated in a few private hands and so long as ordinary mechanics and farmers had access to its loans. But Duane's own overly optimistic use of bank credit over the following years had nearly ruined him, and he shifted toward the idea of a national paper currency issued by the federal government, which would serve as a check on irresponsible bankers and provide a sound currency. By 1819, he had shifted again, taking Simpson's position that only a carefully administered, specie-based currency system, free from the baneful influence of chartered commercial banks, could spare the country an entrenched plutocracy and mass misery. The chartering of the Second BUS in 1816 had increased his worries that privileged private investors had once again seized control of the public interest, and that the new mammoth institution would "overdo the system of banking." The New Schoolers, in Duane's eyes, had created a rage for paper money and easy credit that could only bring moral and financial catastrophe. And amid the panic, Duane's supporters, now known as the Old School faction, came generally to regard the banking and paper-money system as a monstrous engine of oppression.

The immediate political results of the Old School upsurge were mixed. Statewide, the backlash following the panic cost William Findlay reelection in 1820, but the New Schoolers were able to regroup and retake the governorship in 1822 with a compromise candidate acceptable to both urban and rural dissidents. Duane, Simpson, and the reborn city democracy, meanwhile, fared far less well in Philadelphia than they did, briefly, statewide. Factionalism plagued the radicals: in 1820, Philadelphia voters were presented with a baffling list of candidates claiming Federalist, moderate Federalist, Old School, New School, and a variety of no-school family allegiances—"a perfect chaos of small factions," Nicholas Biddle wrote. The Old Schoolers ran weakly even in the workingmen's wards. Although William Duane still emanated charisma, the most effective Old School officeholder, Michael Leib, was on his last legs (he would die in 1822, the same year that Duane, saddled with debts, finally abandoned the *Aurora*). The up-and-coming radicals and reformers, including Simpson and the younger Duane, lacked the connections, electoral shrewdness, and practical skills of their elders. Still, Philadelphia's Old Schoolers (some of whom had taken up the name City Democrats) had begun to establish themselves as a political force. And, thanks to the *Aurora* and especially to the writings of Simpson (soon to begin his own paper, the *Columbian Observer*), they had emerged as an intellectual force as well, promoting a workingman's critique of the banking system and the early industrial order.

Country dissidents in other states also generated their own antibanking political ideas. The most developed rural critiques appeared in the writings of surviving southern Old Republicans, notably John Taylor. After the depression hit, Taylor's *Inquiry* of 1814 began to look prophetic. The entire "paper system" of bank notes, bonds, bills, and stocks that Taylor had claimed was robbing honest producers seemed, amid the foreclosures and bankruptcies of 1819 and 1820, to be fulfilling its appointed piratical role. Worse, in Taylor's eyes, that system won a unanimous official endorsement in 1819 from Chief Justice John Marshall and the Supreme Court in the case of *McCulloch v. Maryland.*

The *McCulloch* decision was the latest in a series of Supreme Court rulings that struck down state laws interfering with corporate charters and protecting bankrupt debtors—and there would be many more to come. Marshall, Jefferson's old nemesis, had outlasted his state-rights critics and, in a concerted campaign, had talked dubious Republican associate justices into joining a judicial phalanx to enlarge federal power and enhance its instruments of economic development. The *McCulloch* ruling was especially rich in neo-Hamiltonian implications. Maryland had passed a law levying a severe—some said prohibitive—fifteen-thousand-dollar annual tax on the operations of the Baltimore branch of the BUS. In upholding a suit by Baltimore bankers protesting the Maryland law, Marshall and the Court also pronounced an interpretation of the Constitution that seemed to explode what was left of Jeffersonian restraint of federal power. Declaring that "[t]he power to tax involves the power to destroy," Marshall's opinion basically rephrased Hamilton's broad interpretations of Article I, Section 8 as the law of the land. "Let the end be legitimate, let it be within the scope of the constitution, and all means which are appropriate, which are plainly adapted to that end, which are not prohibited, but consist with the letter and spirit of the constitution, are constitutional." The bank, in short, was fully constitutional—and the states could do nothing to impede its operations.

Taylor responded with a hastily written tract, *Construction Construed and Constitutions Vindicated*, probably the most influential thing he ever wrote. Recapitulating his earlier attacks on exploitative "artificial" property, Taylor ripped into the rechartering of the BUS and the *McCulloch* decision as the final corruptions overthrowing the American Revolution. The heretic Marshall and his fellow justices had at last enshrined the federal government as a new "sovereign power," completing an effort first undertaken (but, originally, thwarted) in 1787 and then doggedly advanced by Hamilton and his successors in an unholy genealogy of oppression: "The great pecuniary favour granted by congress to certificate-holders, begat banking; banking begat bounties to manufacturing capitalists; bounties to manufacturing capitalists begat an oppressive pension list." All of that had created "a perfect aristocracy, exercising an absolute power over the national currency."

Taylor's was a voice from the past, reflecting the deepening anxieties of the old Chesapeake Tidewater planter elite amid the devastation that followed the Panic of 1819. Never a democrat (in sharp contrast to William Duane), Taylor had no use for the kinds of constitutional reforms advocated by his nonslaveholding fellow Virginians. *Construction Construed* was as much concerned with preserving slaveholders' rights against a potentially intrusive federal government as it was with resisting the BUS. Yet if detached from its pro-slavery moorings, Taylor's arguments on capitalist consolidation and federal complicity carried force with more thoroughgoing egalitarians. In Philadelphia, Duane, a committed antislavery man who also detested the *McCulloch* decision, echoed and even printed the relevant anticapitalist portions of Taylor's writings, simply ignoring the portions on slavery. Elsewhere, alliances of up-and-coming planters and country democrats turned Taylor's arguments against the resident gentry and their banker friends as well as against the BUS.

One of the loudest of the rural movements—and, in the end, the most consequential—arose in Tennessee. After Tennessee gained statehood in 1797, an ambitious entrepreneurial gentry, led by the affluent lawyer, speculator, and jurist John Overton, emerged in and around Nashville, controlling, among other assets, the state's two banks. Unlike Henry Clay and his Bluegrass friends in Kentucky, who came to welcome the rechartering of the Second BUS, the Overton forces continued to regard the national bank as a threat to their local interests. When the panic struck in 1819, Overton's men moved rapidly to protect those interests, passing what they billed as a relief act that was actually designed to shield the two state banks and the state's large debtors. The blatant favoritism aroused the public against what one editor called the banking "horse-leeches of the country" who had "produced a monied aristocracy." On the defensive, the legislature, goaded by the tempered ex-radical Felix Grundy, established stay laws, began a program for the cheap sale of public lands, and established a new loan-office "bank" to lend state paper to poor debtors—moves that mitigated the suffering, but mainly in middle Tennessee and not in the poorer regions. They did not calm the growing revolt. Representatives from mountainous, yeoman-dominated East Tennessee, in particular, denounced Grundy's loan office as an "untried and dangerous experiment" and called all paper institutions disastrous for the nation's well-being.

The insurgency soon found a leader from among the younger self-made heroes of the War of 1812. William Carroll, an unschooled migrant from rural Pennsylvania, had joined Andrew Jackson's state militia staff in 1812, risen quickly to succeed Jackson as general of the Tennessee militia, and played a major role at the Battle of New Orleans. Returning to Nashville after the war, Carroll also returned to his mercantile pursuits, made a good deal of money, and established a popular reputation above and beyond anything the Nashville grandees had to offer. In

1821—having been nearly ruined in the depression and having decided that the banks and their gentry friends were responsible—the ex-shopkeeper challenged the Overton candidate for governor, the planter Henry Chase (who took a somewhat milder pro-specie position), and crushed him. Soon after Carroll took office, his backers in the state legislature—including another veteran of Jackson's command, the semiliterate rifleman David Crockett—opposed the stay laws and loan bank as biased and forced the old state banks out of business by demanding that they resume specie payments. Carroll would go on to become (save for his old commander) the most popular politician in Tennessee, winning reelection to five more terms as governor.

In Tennessee, as in the rest of the shaken country, commercial banks, and especially the Second BUS, became the scapegoats for the nation's economic ills. The charges against the BUS were not completely justified. If before and after the panic the bank looked to some like a grasping and devouring monster, its policies were in fact a sign of weakness as well as strength. The bank could not be blamed for the drastic modifications in the Atlantic economy that occurred after the end of the Napoleonic Wars. Nor could it be blamed for initiating the reckless proliferation of unsound chartered and unchartered banks around the country, especially in the South and West, and for the unwise borrowing by investors. As an official inquiry by the Pennsylvania state senate concluded, the problem lay *"first* in the excessive number of banks, and secondly in their universal bad administration." Yet many of these same state and local bankers had no trouble evading their responsibilities and joining in the public condemnations of the BUS.

The BUS, mismanaged from the start, played an important role in hastening and then deepening the economic crisis, loosening credit when it should have been tightened and then tightening credit for far too long. The incompetence (and, in some instances, larceny) of its directors understandably made the bank the focus of public anxiety at a fundamental turning point in American life, with profound political repercussions. Americans may always have been an enterprising people, but amid the transforming spread of commerce that accelerated after 1815, the structures and rules of enterprise were changing dramatically. As the business historian Bray Hammond, no enemy to banks and banking, once observed, "[A]n economy in which barter has been important and financial transactions had been wholly subordinate to the exchange of goods was giving way to an economy concerned more and more with obligations, contracts, negotiable instruments, equities, and such invisible abstractions. . . . Later generations that contemplate an America which is miraculously productive in a myriad of ways, from sea to sea, can understand only with an effort the terrible cost to their progenitors of settling and improving it." Countless small farmers, tyros in this new economy, had relied on unending credit only to be undone by plunging prices, rising costs, and implacable creditors. Countless urban artisans and shopkeepers had either been thrown into complete idleness or seen the value of their wages and incomes plummet amid a flood of notes no longer worth the paper they had been printed on.

For these ordinary Americans at the bottom of a chain of debt that they only vaguely understood, the panic and depression cracked open huge questions about who was to be the chief beneficiary of the new business order—and about its implications for political democracy. Would those who actually produced useful goods, ordinary men like themselves, accumulate the full fruits of their labor and enterprise? Or would their fruits be stolen, as they saw it, by unelected monied men and their political allies who had promised, falsely, to provide prosperity everlasting? And would those men continue to be permitted to wield such enormous power unchecked by the sovereign people?

THE BUBBLE BURSTS

The Panic of 1819 and the ensuing depression came as little surprise to some older political heads. "[T]he paper bubble is then burst," Thomas Jefferson wrote in November 1819 to his old foe John Adams, with whom he had reconciled in recent years. "[T]his is what you & I, and every reasoning man, seduced by no obliquity of mind or interest, have long foreseen." Always distrustful of the paper system, even when he had deferred to Albert Gallatin over the first BUS, Jefferson took no pleasure in the suffering the panic caused—he was among the sufferers—but did feel a measure of vindication.

What remained to be seen was who, in national politics, might turn the politics of depression and the democratic outrage it inspired to his advantage. Nationalist Republicanism had been dealt a severe blow, but neither the southern Old Republicans nor the city democrats nor the country democrats appeared capable of creating a credible national alternative. Under the stress of economic collapse, the regnant Republican coalition looked increasingly fractured, yet with no one national figure an obvious claimant to the presidential succession after Monroe (who, lacking a serious challenger from either his own party or the Federalists, won reelection without opposition in 1820). And by the time political leaders began adapting to the effects of the panic, its implications had been clouded by a distinct though related political crisis over slavery that also began in 1819—a crisis originally confined to Washington City but that quickly assumed national significance.

2

SLAVERY, COMPROMISE, AND DEMOCRATIC POLITICS

Despite the compromises at the federal convention in 1787, conflicts over slavery had never completely disappeared from national politics. Hardly a year passed without some discussion that touched on the matter. The First Congress argued over whether to include a special tariff on imported slaves, and whether to accept petitions for regulating the "debasing" and "abominable" slave trade and for gradual emancipation. (Both proposals were scuttled.) In 1798, there was a sharp contest over outlawing slavery in the newly formed Mississippi Territory, followed six years later by a failed effort, led by the Federalist James Hillhouse of Connecticut, to ban slavery in the newly acquired Louisiana Territory. The movements to abolish slavery in New York and New Jersey helped prompt James Sloan, a New Jersey Republican, to propose unsuccessfully in 1804 the gradual abolition of slavery in the District of Columbia. Slavery, and southern slaveholders' fears over its future, were also latent concerns in foreign policy questions from the adoption of the Jay Treaty to extending diplomatic recognition to the black republic in Haiti. In 1807, with President Jefferson's firm support, Congress formally abolished the transatlantic slave trade, at the earliest possible date under the Constitution, but only over the stern objections of both Federalists and Republicans from the Deep South.

Sectional divisions worsened after 1815. Contrary to the enlightened hopes of the Revolutionary generation, including slaveholders such as Jefferson, slavery flourished in the South, even as it died in the North. Southern defensiveness over slavery as an unfortunate burden gave way to assertions of the institution's basic benevolence. Northerners, including egalitarian Jeffersonian Republicans as well as surviving Yankee Federalists, grew increasingly embittered at having to make repeated political concessions to the unapologetic planters. The rapid inclusion of new states carved out of the Louisiana Purchase lands raised the critical question of whether the nation would permit human bondage to expand even farther or would begin, once and for all, to commence its elimination. Between 1819 and 1821, with Americans already reeling from economic catastrophe, congressional debates over that question focused on the future of the Missouri Territory and boiled over—further dissipating illusory invocations of an Era of Good Feelings and creating a fearsome specter of the nation's collapse.

BACKGROUND TO CRISIS

The recurrent struggles over slavery during the decades preceding the Missouri crisis indicated some important political facts and shifting dynamics that lay just beneath the surface of the early republic's politics. First, contrary to the tangled ambivalence of many Jeffersonian slaveholders, lawmakers from the Deep South, Republicans and Federalists alike, expressed a powerful commitment to slavery during the new nation's earliest days. Their justifications anticipated almost every theme of what would later be called the "positive good" pro-slavery argument. Southern slaves, the Republican senator James Jackson of Georgia declared in 1789, had exchanged African barbarism for American ownership by masters "bound by the ties of interest and law, to provide for their support and comfort in old age or infirmity." William Loughton Smith, the South Carolina Federalist, addressed the House a year later and called slavery the ideal status for blacks— a race deficient in intellect, "indolent" and "improvident," but well suited physically for labor on southern plantations. "If, then, nothing but evil would result from emancipation," he concluded, "why should Congress stir at all in the business, or give any countenance to such dangerous applications."

Through Jefferson's first administration, the pro-slavery southerners could usually count on the support of conservative northern Federalists. Although several leading Federalists were conspicuously involved in manumission societies and other antislavery efforts, Federalism showed its more traditional face in Congress, intent on sustaining party solidarity across sectional lines against the common Republican foe. Vaunting, as ever, the inviolability of private property, Federalists were swift to denounce antislavery agitation as a threat to social peace, derived from the vicious French egalitarianism advanced by Jefferson and his party. To the Massachusetts Federalist Senator George Cabot fell the honor of introducing the fugitive slave bill in 1793, which implemented the Constitution's guarantee that masters could cross state lines to retrieve their runaways. Harrison Gray Otis declared, typically, in 1798 that he would not "interfere with the Southern states as to the species of property in question" and that "he really wished that the gentlemen who held slaves might not be deprived of the means of keeping them in order."

Virginia Republicans, by contrast, sometimes aligned with moderate northern Federalists and northern Republicans against the Deep South on matters relating to slavery, at least through 1800. Well into the post-Revolutionary era, the assumption prevailed among many Virginians, slaveholders and nonslaveholders, that human bondage was a moribund abomination. Thomas Jefferson had famously written, in his *Notes on the State of Virginia* of 1785, that "[t]he whole commerce between master and slave is a perpetual exercise of the most boisterous passions, the most unremitting despotism on the one part, and degrading submissions on the other. . . . I tremble for my country when I reflect that God is just." Jefferson would never tremble enough to free more than a handful of his own slaves. Neither he nor most other first-rank southern political leaders took up the antislavery cause too publicly or too vociferously. When pushed hard by the Deep South slaveholders—as they were in 1790, over a House committee report giving Congress wide powers over slavery—the Virginians chose expediency over idealism. Still, the Enlightenment and religious humanitarian impulses that helped bring emancipation to the northern states were there in Virginia and the upper South. Manumissions rose markedly after 1790. (A greater number of Virginia slaves were freed between the Revolution and the War of 1812 than at any time until 1865.) A persistent glut and depressed prices in world tobacco markets further augured a shift in southern agriculture toward wheat production, highly profitable without slave labor. To some Virginians, including Jefferson, it appeared as if morality and self-interest might actually converge in the not-too-distant future.

That future never came, and by 1815, the politics of slavery had acquired an entirely different political charge. The closer Congress verged on legislation concerning the institution directly, the more southerners recoiled, and the more pro-slavery views hardened. More important, slavery experienced a renaissance after 1790 that forever changed the course of southern history—and American history. A rapid rise of world demand for sugar and, even more, for cotton; the decline of many Caribbean plantation economies in the wake of the Saint Domingue revolution and the reduction of the Spanish empire during the Napoleonic Wars; the expansion, with the Louisiana Purchase, of American territory suited to plantation-based economies; the boom in short-staple (or upland) cotton production enabled by the introduction of Whitney's cotton gin—all gave Americans extraordinary advantages in reviving their own plantation system. For some southerners, the combination of new opportunities and revived fears of slave revolts led to a new vision of an American slavery spreading steadily westward, no longer dependent on freshly imported (and possibly troublesome) slaves from Africa but on a growing domestic slave population, beautifully situated to cash in on the production of sugar and cotton.

Suddenly, the liberal blandishments of the post-Revolutionary years either faded away, fell on the defensive, or turned, ironically, into their opposites. In border states like Henry Clay's Kentucky and in portions of the lower South where slavery was scarce, the Jeffersonian view of slavery as a necessary evil— degrading to master and slave alike, but not amenable to any safe and practical immediate solution—still held powerful sway. But elsewhere, pro-slavery opinion became more widespread and bolder. Some Deep South slaveholders paradoxically came to support antislavery efforts to end the transatlantic slave trade in 1807, seeing in western expansion a more secure basis for slavery's future. More generally, the lower South became even more outspoken in its view of slavery as benevolent. In a speech to the House late in 1806, a young, ardently pro-slavery Republican, Peter Early of Georgia, revealed how southern sensibilities were changing. Noting that he had earlier described slavery as an "evil," Early begged to explain that he had only meant to say that "[r]eflecting men" in the South apprehended slavery as a "political evil" that might "at some future day" cause great troubles, but "that few, very few, consider it a crime." As if affirming that former heresy was becoming southern orthodoxy, Early then added, "I will tell the truth. A large majority of people in the Southern states do not consider slavery as even an evil."

Northern hostility to slavery grew apace, for opportunistic as well as principled reasons. With the decline of southern Federalism after 1800, northern conservatives had less reason to attach themselves to Deep South slaveholders—and additional political reasons to try to restrict slavery's expansion while attacking the three-fifths clause and other pillars (as they saw them) of Jeffersonian power. Now it was the Republicans who had the most to worry about in preserving intersectional party unity, leading some northern Republicans to back southern positions. Yet northern Republicans still formed a core of antislavery opinion in Congress. In one telling House vote during Jefferson's first term, rejecting the proposed abolition of slavery in the District of Columbia in 1804, southern Republicans voted with the majority by a margin of 40 to 1, as did northern Federalists by a margin of 13 to 5. Northern Republicans voted in favor of abolition, 25 to 16.

The sectional cleavage deepened after 1815, as cotton became the most valuable staple commodity in the Atlantic world. The end of the war with Britain and the reopening of the cotton trade with the Lancashire mills vastly stimulated the American cotton boom, and with it the spread of slavery. Between 1815 and 1820, the amount of baled cotton produced by the southern states doubled, and it would double again between 1820 and 1825. Before the war, the boundary to cotton cultivation ran as far north as the backcountry of South Carolina and as far east as central Georgia; thereafter, cotton slavery swept into Alabama and then into Mississippi and Louisiana. In the older states of the upper South, the Deep South cotton boom sent the price of redundant slaves soaring, giving slaveholders there a strong material incentive to support slavery's expansion. In the North, however, despite the mercantile fortunes to be won by shipping cotton across the Atlantic, there arose a new determination to check any further westward expansion of slavery, especially when evidence began to mount that smugglers were successfully evading the ban on the transatlantic slave trade. Northern concern about expansion—and disgust at the southerners' truculence over slavery—heightened when the acquisition of Florida from Spain under the terms of the Adams-Onís Treaty of 1819 raised the issue of admitting another new slave state.

Five days before the treaty was formally signed in Washington, the House of Representatives completed debate over a bill approving admission of the territory of Missouri to the Union.

Given that the territory was already home to thousands of slaves, most observers might have safely assumed that it would enter with slavery intact. But two alarmed northern Republicans would take nothing for granted—and, drawing the line at Missouri, they revealed how forceful northern antislavery opinion had become.

THE MISSOURI CRISIS IN CONGRESS

James Tallmadge caught his fellow congressmen off guard on February 13. A Poughkeepsie, New York, lawyer and former secretary to Governor George Clinton, Tallmadge had served in Congress for just twenty months (and would leave the House, by choice, after serving a single term). He had, so far, made two mildly auspicious congressional contributions: joining an unsuccessful effort to obstruct Illinois statehood because its new constitution was "insufficiently" antislavery; and giving an eloquent speech in defense of General Andrew Jackson, who stood accused of exceeding his authority and executing civilians in connection with his postwar military command in East Florida. Mainly, Tallmadge was considered an ambitious, personable, odd-duck backbencher, nominally a Clintonian (and therefore detested by Van Buren's Bucktails), but also distrusted by DeWitt Clinton as well as the surviving Federalists.

Tallmadge's behind-the-scenes ally in his surprise attack, his fellow New York congressman John W. Taylor of Ballston Springs, was very different, a well-known Clintonian and shrewd politician who, in 1820, would succeed Henry Clay as Speaker of the House. Taylor had an established record as an antislavery man, and in that same session of Congress, he led a narrowly defeated effort to ban extension of the institution into Arkansas Territory. Tallmadge, too, was staunchly antislavery—before coming to Congress, he had helped craft and enact New York's final emancipation law in 1817—but his personal political motivations for initiating the crisis remain a puzzle. It is equally puzzling why the unknown Tallmadge instead of Taylor took the lead on the Missouri issue. What is certain is that the two New York Republicans—working on their own—started an uproar that would rattle the already strained Jeffersonian coalition.

At stake, formally, were the terms of Missouri's admission to the Union, but the implications were much graver. In the flurry of state admissions since 1815, the numbers of new states that allowed slavery and those that did not had been equal, leaving the balance of slave and free states nationwide, and thus, in the Senate, equal as well. But that balance was deceptive. Prior to Illinois's admission to the Union in 1818, antislavery forces, fortified by the exclusion of slavery in the territory under the Northwest Ordinance, found themselves challenged by downstate settlers from the South. The antislavery men managed to gain a state constitution that formally barred slavery, but at the cost of including an apprenticeship system regulating the lives of free blacks—the focus of Tallmadge and others' effort to block Illinois's admission—as well as the selection of two southern-born pro-slavery senators. In practical terms, there was an argument to be made that by admitting neighboring Missouri as a slave state, the pro-slavery bloc in the Senate would enjoy not a two-vote majority but a four-vote majority. And among some northerners, there was a mounting determination to prevent Missouri from having a constitution as bluntly racist as Illinois's.

Southerners saw the situation completely differently. With discussions already underway for the creation of Maine as a new state, Missouri's admission as a slave state was essential to preserve the sectional balance. Moreover, Missouri was to be the second state carved out of the Louisiana Purchase, and the first whose land lay entirely west of the Mississippi River. The precedent for Purchase land, though slight, was pro-slavery. Although Missouri, unlike Louisiana, was not suited to cotton, slavery had long been established there, and its western portions were promising for growing hemp, a crop so taxing to cultivate that it was deemed fit only for slave labor. Accordingly, southerners worried that if slavery were banned in Missouri—with its ten thousand slaves, comprising roughly 15 percent of its total population—there would be a precedent for doing so in all the states from the trans-Mississippi West. When the territorial citizens of Missouri applied for admission to the Union, most southerners—and probably, at first, most northerners as well—took it for granted that slavery would be allowed. All were in for a shock.

Tallmadge rose in the House near the end of the week's business and offered a resolution containing two amendments to the Missouri enabling bill then pending before the Committee of the Whole, banning further introduction of slavery into the new state and freeing all slaves born in the state after its admission when they reached the age of twenty-five. The ensuing debate in the House lasted but a few days—the Fifteenth Congress would expire on March 4—but it was blistering. Opponents of the amendments, including the territorial delegate from Missouri, harshly attacked them and threatened disunion were they ever approved. Let it come, Tallmadge spat back: "Sir, if a dissolution of the Union must take place, let it be so!" ("I hope that a similar discussion will never again take place in our walls," wrote one shaken representative from New Hampshire.) Northern House members, strikingly, united across party and factional lines to support Tallmadge. Despite virtually unanimous opposition from the slaveholding states, the lopsided margins in favor of the amendments by free-state congressmen—84 to 10 on the first amendment, 80 to 14 on the second—were sufficient for Tallmadge's proposals to prevail narrowly in the House. In the Senate, five northern members, including both senators from Illinois, provided the margin to defeat the amendments, but the House antislavery northerners (now called restrictionists) would not cower. By a twelve-vote margin, the House, voting once again on sharp sectional lines, reapproved Tallmadge's proposals, thereby killing the statehood bill and handing the dispensation of Missouri over to the Sixteenth Congress, which was not due to assemble for another nine months. And when the new Congress met, the divisions proved to be just as deep as before.

The debate over Missouri in both Congresses stimulated northern Federalists as well as Republicans. Senator Rufus King of New York expressed the Federalist view with a special wintry eloquence. At sixty-four, King was the last of the original Federalists still on the national stage, a point that rankled the Republican southern delegations. At Philadelphia in 1787, King had argued strongly against the three-fifths clause as an ignominious sop to the slaveholders. Now, more than thirty years later, he warmly supported keeping slavery out of Missouri, restating the persisting Yankee Federalist fear of southern political dominance. The issue, for King, was not chiefly moral, at least not in his early speeches on the matter. Asked by a southerner, at one point during the crisis, about his views on slavery, he replied that he was only imperfectly informed on the subject, and was interested in it only as it had a bearing on "great political interests." For King, that meant protecting the free white majority, objecting once more to the three-fifths rule, and rejecting state rights—securing what he called "the common defence, the general welfare, and [the] wise administration of government." In his early pronouncements on Missouri, the embers of northern Federalism flared one last time.

Southern Republicans saw all this as a deliberate and desperate power play on behalf of discredited Federalist heresy. To Thomas Jefferson, the Missouri controversy amounted to a reckless effort by the Federalist "Hartford convention men" to resurrect their political fortunes by seizing on the slavery issue and then salvaging Federalism by creating a new northern sectional party. Andrew Jackson called Tallmadge's maneuver part of the "wicked design of demagogues, who talk about humanity, but whose sole object is self agrandisement regardless of the happiness of the nation." John Taylor of Caroline, at work on his refutation of *McCulloch v. Maryland*, added a closing section on how the Missouri debates foreshadowed the unlawful assumption by a neo-Federalist general government of the power to abolish slavery. And fair-minded northerners could understand the southerners' fears, even if their sympathies about slavery lay elsewhere.

Restriction, John Quincy Adams wrote in his diary, "disclosed a secret," unanticipated by its proponents, that the North could be united upon halting any further extension of slavery: "[H]ere was a new party ready formed, . . . terrible to the whole Union, but portentously terrible to the South—threatening in its progress the emancipation of all their slaves." Yet contrary to what Jefferson and others charged, the "new party," in the House, were not the Yankee Federalists and crypto-Federalist Clintonians, but a bloc of between forty and fifty northern Republicans.

Like every other party to the Missouri controversy, the Republican restrictionists were a mixed lot in almost everything except their sectional origins. But unlike the others, they boasted no great figure who had achieved the celebrity of their Federalist ally King, or their numerous Republican opponents from the South. They included experienced ex-Federalists such as Joseph Hemphill of Pennsylvania and Clifton Clagett of New Hampshire (who first came to Congress in, respectively, 1800 and 1803), as well as Jeffersonian veterans such as Peter Hercules Wendover of New York City—a successful artisan who, in 1799, had won the first of his two terms as president of the city's Republican-friendly General Society of Mechanics and Tradesmen. They also included younger men such as William Plunkett Maclay of Pennsylvania, the nephew and namesake of the prickly country Republican member and diarist from the First Congress, William Maclay; and Marcus Morton of Massachusetts, an idealistic lawyer who had become a Jefferson devotee. Roughly two-thirds of the antislavery Republicans came not from Federalist New England but from the middle Atlantic states, although their leading spokesmen on the House floor included the little-known but forceful Republican lawyers Arthur Livermore of New Hampshire, Timothy Fuller of Massachusetts, and John Wilson Campbell of Ohio. Their contentions in favor of restriction advanced an antislavery Jeffersonian reading of politics and the Constitution that overlapped but was quite distinct from the antislavery arguments of King and the Federalists. That reading prefigured arguments that in later years would become the foundations of the political antislavery platforms of the Liberty, Free Soil, and Lincoln Republican Parties.

At the heart of the Republicans' reasoning was their claim that the preservation of individual rights, and strict construction of the Constitution, demanded slavery's restriction. The claim was rooted in humanitarian morality, not expediency—the firm belief, as Fuller declared, that it was both "the right and duty of Congress" to halt the spread "of the intolerable evil and the crying enormity of slavery." Individual rights, the Republicans asserted, had been defined by Jefferson himself in the Declaration of Independence—"an authority admitted in all parts of the Union [as] a definition of the basis of republican government." If all men were created equal, as Jefferson said, then slaves, as men, were born free and entitled to life, liberty, and the pursuit of happiness under any truly republican government. The Constitution had, in turn, explicitly made the guarantee of republican government in the states a fundamental principle of the Union. Thus, the extension of slavery was, by any strict reading of the national compact, not only wrong but unconstitutional.

The Founding Fathers, the Republicans conceded, had permitted slavery to persist as a purely local, not a national, right. Given the social and political practicalities of 1787, they had had no other choice, as no feasible plan existed for ending slavery in the southern states without creating even greater evils. But the local exception, the Republicans argued, should not be confused for a permanent national rule. The Founders, as Tallmadge pointed out, had not committed the "original sin" of inventing slavery. Rather, as Hemphill claimed, "a certain kind of rights" had "grown out of original wrongs"—a set of rights that the Founders expected would fade away, not proliferate. Not only did the Constitution studiously, even tortuously avoid the words *slave* and *slavery*. The Founders had also taken steps, as William Plumer Jr. of New Hampshire put it, "leading gradually to the abolition of slavery in the old States," above all by explicitly allowing for the eventual abolition of the foreign slave trade and by prohibiting slavery in the Northwest Territory under the Northwest Ordinance. Furthermore, the Republicans insisted, Article IV, Section 3 of the Constitution authorized Congress to admit new states as it saw fit, without any stipulated limitations. "The exercise of this power, until now, has never been questioned," John Taylor charged in debate. Once again, the Republicans averred, the proslavery side was attempting to rewrite the explicit letter of the Constitution, as well as to denigrate its spirit.

As all southerners immediately understood, these were intensely dangerous arguments. Bits and pieces of them had turned up earlier, in Congress as well as in the speeches of Republicans like Tallmadge advocating emancipation in the northern states. As early as 1798, the Massachusetts Republican Joseph Varnum declared his hope that "Congress would have so much respect for the rights of humanity as to not legalize the existence of slavery any farther than it at present exists." The democratizing forces unleashed in the northern states, privileging persons over property, also rendered the Constitution's three-fifths clause ever more an anachronistic, quasi-aristocratic embarrassment—one which if spread to new states would mean, contrary to the Framers' intentions (a Pennsylvania Republican remarked), that "[t]he scale of political power will predominate in favor of the slaveholding States." But it took the cotton boom and the Missouri crisis for northern Republicans to mount a truly threatening Jeffersonian antislavery critique in national affairs. By making Jefferson's Declaration, as one antislavery proponent called it, the great "national covenant" from which the Constitution proceeded virtually as a legal and spiritual instrument, the pro-restrictionist Republicans affirmed a new form of nationalist loyalty. Firmly planted in Jeffersonian writ, this nationalism would not seek to expand the powers of the federal government one whit beyond the strictest construction, yet neither would it endorse the idea, dear to John Taylor and the Virginia Old Republicans, that the Union was a mere compact of the several states. It would not fall into the Federalist trap of inventing a new national good; rather, it would restrict an old national evil.

The nation, said the antislavery northern Republicans (in agreement with the Federalists), preceded the states as a historical fact. Therefore, preserving the self-evident rights of equal individual citizens—which they took to be the essence of republicanism—must take precedence over honoring the rights of individual states. The aim of that federal Union had been eventually to remove the injustice of slavery, not to perpetuate it. The Constitution, strictly interpreted, gave the sons of the founding generation the legal tools to hasten that removal, including, in the case of Missouri, barring the admission of additional slave states. Republican principle—what one antislavery representative called "the good old Republican doctrines"—as well as constitutional mandate gave them no choice but to keep slavery out of Missouri.

To do otherwise would bring the condemnation of future generations—and, John W. Taylor suggested, even worse condemnation still. "History will record the decision of this day as exerting its influence for centuries to come . . . ," Taylor declared in the first set speech of the House debate; then he delivered an extended sentence-long blast:

> If we reject the amendment and suffer this evil, now easily eradicated, to strike its roots so deep in the soil that it can never be removed, shall we not furnish some apology for doubting our sincerity, when we deplore its existence—shall we not expose ourselves to the same kind of censure which was pronounced by the Saviour of Mankind upon the Scribes and Pharisees, who builded the tombs of the prophets and garnished the sepulchres of the righteous, and said, if they had lived in the days of their fathers, they would not have been partakers with them in the blood of the prophets, while they manifested a spirit which clearly proved them the legitimate descendents of those who killed the prophets, and thus filled up the measure of their fathers' iniquity?

Not only did the pro-slavery men lack patriotism—they were pharisaic blasphemers.

The slave-state representatives reacted to the charges by banding together with a unity even more impressive than the northerners'. Most of their arguments took a straightforward state-rights position: as Congress had no power to interfere with slavery in the states where it already existed, so it was powerless to do so in new states just gaining admission. "Can any gentleman contend," John Scott, the delegate from Missouri asked, "that, laboring under the proposed restriction, the citizens of Missouri would have the rights, advantages, and immunities of other citizens of the Union? Have not other new states, in their admission, and have not all the states in the Union, now, privileges and rights beyond what was contemplated to be allowed to the citizens of Missouri?" Precedent, as well as constitutional principle, demanded that Missourians decide the slavery question for themselves. States were the essential units in federal affairs, and each new state possessed the same power to decide its own constitution as the original thirteen states had enjoyed. Equality for all meant, in this instance, allowing Missouri to retain slavery as it wished to do.

Had Tallmadge and the restrictionists merely followed their Federalist allies' reasoning, the sectional argument might have remained pitched at this abstract legalistic and constitutional level. But the antislavery Republicans also attacked slavery head-on as an immoral institution, whose very existence in any new states would deny those states a truly republican government. By condemning slavery while abjuring broad construction of the Constitution, the Republicans lessened their vulnerability to charges, plausible enough when delivered against the Federalists, that they were using the slavery issue as a pretext to enlarge federal power and their own political advantage. And they exposed the southerners to countercharges that *they* were simply twisting constitutional issues as a means to expand slavery.

The result was a rupture within the Republican camp, between antislavery northerners who embraced egalitarian Jeffersonian ideals and hard-core, pro-slavery southerners who rejected those ideals—leaving in the middle Republican nation-alists such as Henry Clay, who like Jefferson considered slavery a necessary evil. As debate wore on, the southern antirestriction-ists, particularly in the Deep South, found it difficult to cling to the antislavery shibboleths that had prevailed among the enlight-ened slaveholders of Jefferson's generation. Some did so, like the Georgia representative Robert Reid, who called slavery "a dark cloud which obscures half the luster of our free institutions." But increasingly, in and out of Congress, these high-minded pro-nouncements sounded ritualistic and pale beside angry southern objections that only fanatics would seek to eliminate or even check slavery anytime soon.

The soft antirestrictionist line, voiced most eloquently by Speaker Clay and a young Virginia congressman named John Tyler, held that diffusing slavery across a wider geographic area would actually benefit the slaves and encourage the institution's eventual demise. "Slavery has been represented on all hands as a dark cloud [and] . . . in this sentiment I completely concur . . . ," Tyler told the House. "How can you otherwise disarm it? Will you suffer it to increase in its darkness over a particular portion of this land until its horrors shall burst upon it?" This had become Jefferson's and Madison's view as well—that a disper-sion of the slaves would reduce racial anxieties and the threat of slave revolts, dilute the institution of slavery, and afford the slaves better food, clothing, and shelter than if they remained confined to the existing slave states. Defeating Tallmadge's pro-posals, Tyler contended, would "ameliorate the condition of the slave, and . . . add much to the prospect of emancipation and the total extinction of slavery."

At one level, the diffusion argument was a rhetorical fallback for the tortured enlightened slaveholders of the older generation who genuinely believed slavery an evil but who could not imagine getting rid of it peacefully except by highly deliberate and time-consuming means. At another level, diffusionism was in line with efforts by younger men concentrated in the border states—above all, those of the American Colonization Society, founded in Washington in 1816 with Clay presiding—to promote the voluntary colonizing of free blacks to Africa and provide a spur for humane and gradual emancipation. "No man is more sensible of the evils of slavery than I am, nor regrets them more," Clay would write a few years after the Missouri crisis. To restrict slavery's spread would only hurt the chances for eventual tranquil emancipation—or so Clay and many of his southern colleagues had convinced themselves. Yet even the soft antirestrictionists insisted that the North had no business at all interfering with slavery. And they sometimes cast aspersions on the northern Republicans' egalitarianism, likening it (in Tyler's words) to the radical leveling doctrines of the Jacobins, who proclaimed liberty and equality "at the very moment when they were enriching the fields of France with the blood of her citizens." Behind these attacks lay the ever-present fear that too much talk of equality might cause the slaves to revolt.

A harder southern line also emerged during the Missouri crisis, expanding on the contention, long-established in the Deep South, that slavery was essentially benevolent. As sectional bitterness spiked, so did the southerners' militancy over slavery—as well as their threats that if decided wrongly, the Missouri controversy would have cataclysmic results. Thomas W. Cobb of Georgia allowed, but only for the sake of argument, that slavery might involve "moral impropriety." But he would not bother to dignify with a direct reply the "slander" heaped on "the character of the people of the Southern States in their conduct towards, and treatment of, their black population," and warned that unless the slandering ceased, a fire of southern resistance would arise that "could be extinguished only in blood!" In the Senate, the esteemed Old Republican Nathaniel Macon of North Carolina, as orthodox a Jeffersonian as could be found anywhere, not only defended slavery but also denied that the egalitarian sentiments once written down by his gloried mentor had any binding force whatsoever. "A clause in the Declaration of Independence has been read," Macon said, calmly and simply, "declaring that 'all men are created equal;' follow that sentiment and does it not lead to universal emancipation?" Macon would not have it so: just as the Declaration "is not part of the Constitution or of any other book," so there was, he proclaimed, "no place for the free blacks in the United States."

The most passionate defense of slavery, by Old Republican Senator William Smith of South Carolina, actually annoyed many of Smith's fellow southerners in its frankness, but it showed where hard-line southern Republican thinking was headed all along. The "venerable patriot" Jefferson had been wrong, Smith said, to claim in *Notes on the State of Virginia* that some basic antagonism pitted master against slave: "The master has no motive for this boisterous hostility. It is at war with his interest, and it is at war with his comfort. The whole commerce between master and slave is patriarchal." Likewise, northerners were completely wrong to say that slavery was sinful. Had not "the only living and true God" specifically condoned slaveholding in the laws He gave to Moses, as recorded in Leviticus? By substituting their own religion of nature for the Bible, the antislavery restrictionists were endorsing the same intoxicating pagan beliefs "preached up in the French Convention in the days of Robespierre" that had led to the Reign of Terror. By maligning slavery as a moral and political evil, ambitious rabble-rousers, "like the praetorian guards of the Romans," hoped "finally [to] take the Government in their own hands, or bestow it on the highest bidder." Stirred by misguided humanity, the traducers of the South were in fact the traducers of benevolence, order, and all that was holy, led by reckless partisans who would unleash on the nation a torrent that none but the Lord could quell.

Harsh though they were, these congressional thrusts and counterthrusts did not necessarily mark a general national political crisis. When the first stage of the Missouri debates ended in deadlock in March 1819, hopes had run high among moderates, led by Henry Clay, that after the recess, a new Congress would take up the matter with greater detachment—a possibility that filled Tallmadge and other restrictionists with "fearful anxiety."

Yet those hopes and fears proved illusory, for antislavery northerners decided to take their cause to the people, in the first American antislavery political campaign of its kind. By the next winter, of 1819–20, that campaign, and southern reactions to it, had turned the controversy in Congress into a desperate situation, demanding every bit of shrewdness that Speaker Clay and his moderate allies could muster.

THE DEBATE OVER SLAVERY: AGITATION, COMPROMISE, REPERCUSSIONS

The northern agitation leading up to the Sixteenth Congress began in late August 1819. Public meetings, organized by local luminaries, assembled in virtually every major town and city from Maine to New Jersey and as far west as Illinois, to cheer pro-restrictionist speakers, pass antislavery resolutions, draft circular letters demanding a free Missouri, and instruct their representatives to stand fast. On November 16, more than two thousand citizens gathered in New York City, headquarters of the movement, where they established their own committee of correspondence and arranged for the printing of an antislavery circular for wide distribution. By December, according to William Plumer, it had become "political suicide" for any free-state officeholder "to tolerate slavery beyond its present limits." The agitation cut across partisan lines. Some of the most prominent organizers of the popular protests were Federalists and Clintonians, and the crusade began with a meeting in Burlington County, New Jersey, a traditional Federalist stronghold—all of which lent superficial credence to the southerners' charges of a political conspiracy. But antislavery fervor gripped northern Jeffersonian supporters as well. "[Slavery's] progress should be arrested, and means should be adopted for its speedy and gradual abolition—and for its ultimate extinction," William Duane wrote in the Philadelphia *Aurora*. One prominent Maine Republican noted that "in most of the states which contend for restriction, federalist and republican are scarcely known."

Nearly as striking as the bipartisanship of the northern opposition was the virtual absence of any similar agitation in the South. "The people do not yet participate in the unhappy heat of zeal and controversy, which has inflamed their Senators and Representatives," the *Baltimore Patriot* remarked at the height of the crisis. The economic devastation of the Panic of 1819 seems to have cast a greater pall on the planters and farmers of the South than did the debates about Missouri. More important, in the unreformed court-dominated southern polities, there was little to be gained and much to be risked by stirring up the populace over slavery issues. That populace, after all, included a white majority with uncertain loyalties to slavery, and a large black minority that, as far as the South's rulers were concerned, would be better off hearing as little as possible, even secondhand or thirdhand, about the lunatic Yankee agitators in Congress. "Our people do not petition much," Nathaniel Macon remarked, "we plume ourselves on not pestering the General Government with our prayers. Nor do we set the woods on fire to drive the game out." The wisdom of that restraint, from the slaveholders' viewpoint, would be confirmed during the years to come.

James Tallmadge did not return to Washington for the new Congress in December (having already decided to seek a state senate seat in Albany), but the ruckus he kicked up resumed even more intensely than before. Maine was now officially applying for admission to statehood, separate from Massachusetts. Antirestrictionists were quick to assert that if Congress had the power to ban slavery in Missouri, so it had the power to make Maine's admission contingent on Missouri coming in as a slave state. ("The notion of an equivalent," Speaker Clay agreed, had guided commonwealths and states "from time immemorial.") The House passed a new Maine statehood bill after a bruising debate, only to have the Senate Judiciary Committee add an amendment admitting Missouri without restriction. After decisively rejecting efforts led by the Republican Jonathan Roberts of Pennsylvania to recommit the bill to committee, the Senate united the Maine and Missouri statehood bills, then heard an additional amendment from one of the Illinois antirestrictionists, Jesse B. Thomas—the germ of a possible compromise. As newly amended, the Senate bill would admit Maine as a free state and Missouri as a slave state, and bar slavery from all additional states carved out of the Louisiana Purchase territory that lay north of latitude 36°30'. Sectional balance would be sustained: the North would give way on the admission of Missouri as a slave state and be rebuffed in its meddling, but the South would give way on the principle that Congress had the authority to regulate slavery in the territories, something southerners had successfully resisted since the ratification of the Constitution.

On February 17, the Senate passed compromise measures with the Thomas amendment, 24 to 20—only to have the House, which had been debating its own Missouri statehood bill, dismiss the Senate proposals in a sharply sectional vote. John W. Taylor, now the sole leader of the antislavery congressmen, offered a strengthened version of the Tallmadge amendments that freed all children of slaves at birth, and as amended, the bill passed the House by a wide margin. The Senate remonstrated with the lower house, demanding passage of its own bill—and, once again, the House flatly refused.

The political will and parliamentary skill of the compromisers, most conspicuously Henry Clay, finally broke the impasse, or so it appeared. Clay's major weapon as Speaker, apart from his rhetorical skills and stamina, was his power over committee appointments. On February 29, the House consented to hold a joint conference with the Senate over the outstanding issues, and Clay chose reliably pro-compromise members for the conference committee. Keeping the restrictionists momentarily happy, Clay, the next day, allowed the House to pass its own Missouri bill, even as the conference committee met. The day after that, the Senate returned the House bill once more, with the restrictionist amendment stricken and the Thomas amendment restored—and at virtually the same hour, the conference committee issued a quickly drafted statement urging passage of the Senate version. Clay knew that he could never get a majority in the House if he presented his compromise in a single bill, so the House considered Missouri statehood and the 36°30' questions separately. With the South voting as a bloc and with eighteen northerners either going along or absenting themselves, the House agreed, by a mere three votes, to remove its slavery restriction provision. The outcome was touch and go until the final tally was counted. ("One hour before & one hour after, we should have lost the vote," the pro-compromise Maine congressman John Holmes remarked soon after.) With Missouri now opened to slavery, the House approved the Thomas amendment, over strong opposition from seaboard southern Old Republicans, centered in Virginia, and Deep South hard-liners who rejected any federal interference with slavery. On March 6, President Monroe signed the Missouri statehood bill.

It all happened so quickly that it seemed to have been scripted in advance, a script that has never been and may never be recovered in full. Certainly Clay's wizardry, formidable as it was, cannot completely explain what transpired. Pressure for compromise in fact came from many imposing sources. At the White House, even before Thomas offered his amendment to the Senate, President Monroe, who fervently favored allowing slavery in Missouri—and believed that the controversy was a power play by his old foe DeWitt Clinton—kept close tabs on the Virginia delegation. He also quietly conferred with friendly northern congressmen, using patronage promises to seal their loyalty. ("[T]he influence of the Palace, which after all is heavier than the Capitol," Representative William Plumer Jr. wrote his father at the end of February, "[has] produced a considerable change here.") John C. Calhoun, on solid nationalist grounds, publicly calmed southerners' fears—expressed most vociferously by the influential Richmond editor Thomas Ritchie—that compromise over Congress's power to ban slavery in the territories was capitulation. Outside of government, Monroe mobilized influential allies—chief among them the banker Nicholas Biddle—to line up support. "Rely upon it you have nothing to fear at home," Biddle assured one wavering Pennsylvania congressman, who eventually voted with the pro-compromise side.

One ferocious antirestriction participant, John Randolph, crowed soon after the vote that the southerners had so frightened their antagonists that the compromisers could have rounded up as many northern backsliders (whom he dubbed "dough faces") as they needed to admit slavery into Missouri. As was his custom, he wildly exaggerated. It would be just as accurate—and in some respects more accurate—to say that the southerners, led by the border South, gave way over the Thomas amendment, in their frustration at the antislavery northerners' obduracy. "[I]t has been ascertained by several votes in the House of Representatives that a considerable majority of that body are in favor of restriction as to all the country purchased from France under the name of Louisiana," a weary Senator Montfort Stokes of North Carolina wrote as the compromise took shape. "All that we from the slave holding states can do at present is to rescue . . . a considerable portion of Louisiana, including all the settled parts of that extensive country." Better to settle for Missouri (and probably, in the more distant future, Arkansas Territory) than for nothing at all. Of far greater consequence numerically to the outcome than northern defections over slavery in Missouri was the compromisers' effort to seize on this sense of angry frustration and rally southern support for both ends of the compromise. In 1819, when Tallmadge proposed his amendment, thirteen southern congressmen were absent. A year later, all but three southerners were present and voted against restriction (as did the representative from the newly admitted slave state of Alabama). This eleven-vote pickup from the South represented the lion's share of the fourteen votes added to the antirestrictionist column between 1819 and 1820. But the hard part was winning enough southern votes to pass the Thomas amendment, which Clay managed by holding onto a majority, albeit slender, of 39 to 37 among House southerners, the great bulk of the votes in favor coming from the border states. In the end, the compromise involved winning over a tiny minority of northerners and a small majority of southerners.

At the critical margins, a deficit of solidarity and of leadership did show up on the northern antislavery side. John W. Taylor, in charge of the antislavery restrictionist cause, lacked Speaker Clay's power and presence. Many in Congress perceived the New Yorker, who harbored higher political ambitions, as growing more tepid the longer the fight continued. Additional difficulties for the northerners stemmed from the always intricate factional fighting in New York. Martin Van Buren's Bucktails remained lukewarm about restriction, suspicious that their archenemy DeWitt Clinton stood to profit politically from a restrictionist victory, and vulnerable to patronage pressure from the Monroe administration. The Bucktails were also, in general, more hostile than other northern Republicans to the idea of racial equality, as they would soon affirm at the New York State constitutional convention. One of the six northern freshmen who voted to open Missouri to slavery was Henry Meigs, a Bucktail close to Van Buren, and three of the absentees, including the erstwhile pro-restrictionist Caleb Tompkins, were also Bucktails. Although no evidence of any prearrangement has come to light, those four New York votes, colored by local considerations quite distinct from the slavery issue, did represent the antirestrictionists' miniscule margin of victory. The compromising Bucktail votes bespoke Van Buren's willingness to ignore northern antislavery opinion (and, some would say, truckle to the slaveholders) in order to reach political accommodation with the South—something that would come to typify Van Buren's politics over the next twenty years.

Still, responsibility for opening Missouri to slavery cannot be placed solely or chiefly on the Van Buren Bucktails, let alone on northern acquiescence. Northern support for nonrestriction and compromise in 1820 came from a small, motley group from various states, Federalists as well as Republicans. The great majority of New York Republicans, including Bucktails as well as Clintonians, voted for restriction in 1820. Only one of the northern representatives who voted for restriction in 1819 voted against it a year later. Compared to the southerners' close vote endorsing the Thomas amendment, the northern vote against slavery in Missouri—a division of 87 to 14—was unyielding.

Unfortunately for Clay and the compromisers, die-hard anti-slavery northerners and the pro-slavery citizens of Missouri proved less malleable than the House of Representatives. Over the late winter and spring of 1820, Federalist and Republican restrictionists in Pennsylvania and Ohio—joined by a radical Irish immigrant editor in Washington, Baptist Irvine—urged northern congressmen to reject the compromise by refusing to approve Missouri's new constitution when Congress reassembled. Then the Missourians, faced with the seemingly straight-forward task of writing a pro-slavery state constitution in compliance with the statehood bill, gratuitously inserted a clause requiring the new state government to enact legislation that barred "free negroes and mulattoes" from entering the state. An apparent violation of the U.S. Constitution's guarantee that the rights of citizens in any state would be respected by all states, the clause deeply offended northerners, who proclaimed that the compromise was now dead. Compounding the difficulty, Clay had retired as Speaker, prefatory to retiring from the House, and was succeeded (after a lengthy sectional struggle) by John W. Taylor. By the time Clay arrived in Washington in January 1821 for what he had hoped would be a brief second session, the House was in chaos. While northerners declared that Missouri was still a territory, southerners insisted that Missouri was now a state and that no additional conditions could be attached to its admission.

The making of the so-called second Missouri Compromise was even more convoluted than the making of the first—and it demanded even more of Clay. The Senate adopted a resolution accepting the Missouri constitution with a proviso that withheld congressional consent to "any provision" that contravened Article IV, Section 2 of the Constitution. Revived restrictionist House Republicans, however, defeated a resolution admitting Missouri—only to fail to pass a subsequent resolution, offered by Republican William Eustis of Massachusetts, that would have struck the offensive clause from the Missouri constitution. Like punch-drunk brawlers, the contestants threw rhetorical haymakers at each other for weeks to come, in one wild round after another, each side standing its ground, neither side able to put the other away. Clay, now working through a chastened Speaker Taylor, did his best to stack committees, undermine the southern hotheads and northern hotheads alike, and cajole a compromise out of the House. Finally, in late February, a joint House and Senate committee, headed by Clay, hammered out the wording of a resolution admitting Missouri provided that the state legislature solemnly pledge not to pass any law in violation of the U.S. Constitution. By a six-vote margin, the House assented; two days later the Senate approved the measure; and on August 10, 1821, President Monroe officially proclaimed that Missouri was the Union's twenty-first state. "I was exhausted," Clay later recalled, "and I am perfectly satisfied that I could not have borne three weeks more of such excitement and exertion."

It has been said that had the Civil War broken out over the Missouri controversy, it would have amounted to a brawl on the floors of Congress, with the rest of the nation looking on perplexed. Certainly by 1821, the nation, in its second year of unprecedented hard times, welcomed the end of the congressional quarreling over slavery and the preservation of the Union. So did virtually all of the major figures who would dominate national politics over the coming two decades: Henry Clay, John C. Calhoun, John Tyler, William Crawford, John Quincy Adams, Nicholas Biddle, Martin Van Buren, and Andrew Jackson, all of whom either helped achieve the compromise or supported it with varying degrees of enthusiasm. Divided over other important issues—especially the questions of banking and economic development raised by the Panic of 1819—they would prove effective at keeping the slavery issue out of national debates, at least until the early 1830s.

The issues debated, and the charges leveled, from 1819 to 1821 were, however, of far more than passing interest. Once a resurgent southern slavery had been attacked and defended as directly as it had been during the Missouri crisis, it would prove impossible to restore completely any fiction of sectional amicability, either in Washington or around the nation. Even Thomas Jefferson, normally the sanguine apostle of reason, grew pessimistic. "This momentous question, like a fire bell in the night, awakened and filled me with terror," he wrote in a famous letter to Congressman John Holmes of Maine in April 1820, at a moment when it seemed, mistakenly, that the controversy had been settled. "I considered it at once as the knell of the Union." Jefferson, who had no use for the emerging pro-slavery ideology expressed by the likes of William Smith, would never abandon his belief that the Missouri affair had been manufactured by a failed Federalist monarchical plot. (It must have pained him to hear northern Republicans cite his beloved Declaration and southern Republicans slight it, although characteristically he left no direct comment on the matter.) Yet Jefferson also apprehended that the inflammatory issues at hand would outlast any political cabal.

Clay's brokered bargain bought national political peace, but the Missouri crisis hardened northern and southern positions on slavery, in and out of Congress. What occurred in 1820 and 1821 was not a genuine compromise so much as it was a cleverly managed political deal, patched together by moderate leaders frightened by the depth of sectional antagonisms, yet unable to achieve genuine sectional accord. By pushing the two halves of the compromise through the House on separate votes, Clay helped to create an exaggerated sense of amity. Antislavery Republican representatives had not at all been cowed by a recalcitrant South, as John Randolph claimed, and neither had their constituents. Whereas virtually all of the Republicans who voted for the original Tallmadge amendments voted against opening Missouri to slavery a year later, the majority of those northern congressmen who either voted against restriction or absented themselves in 1820 found themselves out of office after the next election in 1822.

In the South, meanwhile, opinion moved in the opposite direction. Missouri had been opened to slavery, but the Thomas proviso affirmed in law the northern antislavery Republican argument that Congress had the power to interfere with slavery's expansion, and to set aside forever a large portion of national territory as free soil. This, the pro-slavery Republican Nathaniel Macon wrote, was "acknowledging too much." Clay was fortunate to get a bare majority of southern congressmen to back the 36°30' restriction. Those who went along with him were not quite as fortunate: more than two-thirds of the congressmen who took a hard line and voted against the Thomas proviso won reelection in 1822, compared to about two-fifths of those who supported it. And reinforcing southern fears and resentments was a very different kind of agitation, one that followed the Missouri upheaval by more than a year but that was closely linked to it in the public mind.

In 1781, a slave ship captain, Joseph Vesey, had carried a young slave, perhaps born in Africa, from St. Thomas in the Danish Virgin Islands to work in the sugarcane fields of Saint Domingue. Captain Vesey bought him back after a year, renamed him Telemaque, and, in 1783, settled in Charleston, South Carolina, where he arranged to have the young slave trained as a carpenter. The slave, with another new name, Denmark, grew into a powerful man, married a slave woman (and, thereafter, took at least one other wife), and fathered at least three children. His life changed forever in 1799 when he won a fifteen-hundred-dollar jackpot in the East Bay Charleston lottery—enough to buy his freedom, though not his family's, and establish his own carpentry shop. Thereafter, Denmark Vesey became a mainstay of Charleston's rapidly growing free black community—a class leader in the much-harassed local African Church whose shop on Bull Street became an informal meeting place for freedmen and slaves alike.

On June 16, 1822, white Charlestonians awoke in panic. Some weeks earlier, a slave had told his master's family that the city's blacks were planning an insurrection—improbable, and therefore all the more frightening for the city's slaveholding families, who prided themselves on the relative mildness of their local variant of human bondage. Governor Thomas Bennett, whose own trusted house servants were implicated, had investigated and, to his great relief, heard one slave after another scoff at the reported conspiracy. But on June 14, another slave stepped forward to confirm an imminent uprising, which he said was due to begin at midnight the following Sunday, when slaves from outlying plantations would be crowded into the city to sell their masters' produce. Bennett ordered the military to secure the city, then proceeded prudently, tracking down the origins of the latest scare while trying to keep his fears under control.

Claiming they were fed up with Bennett's caution, Charleston city authorities led by the mayor, James Hamilton Jr., stepped in, arrested scores of suspected conspirators, and extracted information from them in secret special court sessions. The tales the authorities uncovered were blood-curdling—of a plot involving up to nine thousand slaves and free blacks from Charleston and its hinterlands who would seize the city arsenal, exterminate the white male population, and ravage the white women, before escaping by ship to the black republic of Haiti. All roads from the confessions and testimony seemed to lead back to the African Church, to an associate of Vesey's named Gullah Jack Pritchard (who had concocted a mystical faith and had supposedly given recruits amulets to ward off bullets), and to Vesey, the plot's alleged mastermind. With a minimum of judicial safeguards, the authorities duly convicted and hanged Vesey and five of his confederates on July 2. Gullah Jack, apprehended on July 5, was hanged one week later. Nearly two dozen more convicted rebels were put to death in a mass execution on July 26, and over the next two weeks eight more blacks were convicted and one executed. Finally, their thirst for revenge and deterrence slaked, the local judges halted the carnage and, in August, published an official account of the proceedings as an exemplar of fair-minded slaveholders' justice.

The surviving evidence, most of it obtained under coercion, forms an interpretive house of mirrors. Read one way, it shows a sophisticated and widespread conspiracy, the largest insurrectionary plot ever by U.S. slaves, that was detected only at the

last minute. Read another way, it shows a frantic white population manipulated by ambitious politicians, obtaining false or
greatly exaggerated testimony before sending innocent men to
their deaths—leading to the largest number of executions ever
handed out by a civilian court in the nation's history. Much
depends on the reader's preferences for seeing slavery as an
institution that did more to stir the revolutionary passions of the
oppressed or the cruel and even murderous passions of the
oppressors. Apart from what might have been idle boasting (or
frightened invention), there is little to support the idea that
thousands had been recruited for an uprising, and various inconsistencies in the testimony suggest that some of it was fabricated
to suit the captors' suspicions and their intentions to inflame
white fears. Yet there is also sufficient evidence of a plot—not
least the words of the original betrayer blacks—to conclude that
something dangerous was afoot in Charleston in the summer of
1822.

In a more important sense, the mere fact that most of white
Charleston, and then the rest of the country, believed there had
been a slave conspiracy was enough to make the Vesey affair a
major event. Charleston commanded attention—the premier
southern city in that part of the South where the density of the
black population was the greatest, a seaport vulnerable to the sort
of uprising that appeared to have been in the works. It was made
all the more vulnerable by the access its black population had to
easily diffused newspaper reports and pamphlets about the Yankee troublemakers and the Missouri crisis. For white
Charleston—and in turn, the white South—few passages in the
official account were more chilling than the reported confession
of the slave Jack Purcell just before he was hanged:

> If it had not been for the cunning of that old villain
> Vesey, I should not now be in my present situation. He
> employed every stratagem to induce me to join him. He
> was in the habit of reading to me all the passages in the
> newspapers that related to Santo Domingo, and appar-

ently every pamphlet he could lay his hands on, that had any connection with slavery. He one day brought me a speech which he told me had been delivered in Congress by a Mr. King on the subject of slavery; He told me this Mr. King was the black man's friend, that Mr. King had declared that he would continue to speak, write, and publish pamphlets against slavery as long as he lived, until the Southern States consented to emancipate their slaves, for that slavery was a disgrace to the country.

Simply allowing public airing of antislavery views seemed to provide fodder for bad elements like Vesey and his friends, who would rise up and slit their masters' throats. "Our Negroes," the Charlestonian Edwin C. Holland reflected, "are truly the *Jacobins* of the country." The fears of slave rebellions aired during the congressional debates over Missouri appeared to have been alarmingly accurate.

And so the repercussions of the Missouri controversy spread into the deepest recesses of the institution of slavery, opening up the possibility (or, just as important, a specter of the possibility) of a popular uprising at the regime's foundations. Those repercussions inflamed sectional arguments that, over the next four decades, would sear the American political system—a dialectic of northern outrage and southern repressive self-protection that proved every bit as destructive as Thomas Jefferson had feared it would. And Missouri had an additional, more immediate repercussion that went utterly unnoticed at the time—the passing presence, in Vesey's own church, of a free black migrant from North Carolina named David Walker, who would in time make his own fateful revolutionary plans.

Still, the bargain over Missouri achieved its immediate goal of pushing aside the slavery issue under a deceptive nationalist truce so that Americans could concentrate on even more pressing matters of economic survival. For all of the portents provoked by the Missouri crisis and resulting sectionalism, the politics of panic, depression, and democracy proved even more riveting in the early 1820s, dividing against each other the national political leaders who had rallied to the compromise over slavery. A permanent realignment of congressional politics along North-South sectional lines—welcomed by some, feared by most—had failed to materialize, thanks to Clay and the compromisers. A different realignment was underway, one strongly affected by sectionalism but influenced even more by the hard times and democratic ferment of Monroe's second term—a realignment that would revive, with new labels and updated ideas, the party divisions of the 1790s. The first indications of this political transformation surfaced during the contest to decide which Republican would succeed Monroe to the White House—a contest from which the least likely of the contenders, Andrew Jackson, emerged as the most popular of all.

JACKSON REEMERGES: THE ELECTION OF 1824

For nearly a quarter-century, one or another Virginia gentry Republican with his political roots in the American Revolution had occupied the American presidency. That tradition, everyone knew, would end after the election of 1824. A new generation of political leaders had come to the fore, many of whom were born after Thomas Jefferson drafted the Declaration of Independence. The leading presidential prospects hailed not from the Old Dominion but from more energized areas of the country, including reinvigorated commercial New England, the cotton-enriched slave states of the lower South, and the rapidly expanding West. All but one could point to long and distinguished careers of service in Congress, the cabinet, or the diplomatic corps. Their respective chances would hinge on the factional fallout from the prolonged depression, the Missouri debates, and the wave of democratic reform that had swelled since 1815.

John Adams's son John Quincy was in many ways the most remarkable of the lot. His public service stretched back to 1781, when at age fourteen, thanks to his father (and with a fluency in

French), he traveled to St. Petersburg as secretary of the American legation. After service as the American envoy to the Netherlands and then Berlin, he was elected to the U.S. Senate in 1802, where he broke with his father's party over Jefferson's embargo, resigned his seat in 1808, and instantly became Federalism's best-known apostate. Under President Madison, Adams served as minister to Russia and, in 1814, as commissioner (and calming influence over Henry Clay) at the Ghent treaty negotiations. Above all, as Monroe's secretary of state, he moved from triumph to triumph, arranging with England for the joint occupation of the Oregon country, obtaining from Spain the cession of the Floridas, and formulating the basic principles of what became known as the Monroe Doctrine—accepting the balance of power in Europe and British dominance on the high seas while committing the British to accept American dominance of the Western Hemisphere. Given the past Republican practice of having secretaries of state succeed their presidents, Adams had a strong presumptive claim to the White House.

The economic depression and, even more, the Missouri crisis clipped Adams's wings. His comparatively limited experience in domestic affairs proved increasingly disadvantageous amid the nation's economic difficulties. Many thought him a pampered novice in the cut-and-thrust of congressional politics. Although he publicly supported the Missouri Compromise as the only possible solution under the constraints of the Constitution, privately he regretted not having pushed harder for restriction. Adams had friends and admirers outside New England—among them Andrew Jackson—but the debates over Missouri turned southerners against any nonslaveholding candidate, much less the son of the very last Yankee Federalist president. Adams's candidacy would rise or fall on the basis of how well he could run in the free states outside his New England base, above all in New York and Pennsylvania with their large blocs of electoral votes.

Two southerners presented themselves as a possible alternative to Adams. Secretary of the Treasury William Henry Crawford of Georgia was the main beneficiary of the Old Republican revival provoked by the panic. A gregarious, outsized political intriguer and successful cotton planter, Crawford was not a Quid ideologue, having cultivated a strong alliance with the Second Bank of the United States and having come to endorse moderately protectionist tariff legislation. But when the economy collapsed in 1819, Crawford turned the Treasury Department into the headquarters for neo-Jeffersonian efforts to slash federal expenditures and curb the alleged financial profligacy of the postwar nationalists. Calhoun, whose War Department suffered more than most, despised him; John Quincy Adams called him "a worm preying upon the vitals of the Administration within its own body." Crawford and his so-called Radical supporters took the slurs as a badge of honor and waged war from within the Monroe administration and in Congress, cutting federal expenditures and hoping to sweep into the White House in 1824 by re-creating a sense of rectitude among the Republican faithful. "He is called the '*radical*' candidate, by way of derision," one of Crawford's northern admirers wrote. "Jefferson was called the democratic or jacobinical candidate in '98 & '99 & by the same sort of people who now talk about 'radicals.'"

Jefferson himself thought Crawford the best choice, as did Madison, although they would not declare themselves openly. The Georgian also had some important and influential younger friends from New York, Van Buren and the ascendant Albany Regency. Elected to the Senate in 1820, Van Buren took his seat in the session after the second Missouri Compromise, determined to purge national politics of the factionalism rampant in his own state and the sectionalism that had erupted over Missouri. He blamed Monroe's consolidation policy, above all, and worked tirelessly in Washington, he wrote, "to commence the work of a general resuscitation of the old democratic party" with "a radical reform in the political feelings of this place." Reviving the Jeffersonian New York–Virginia political axis was Van Buren's first goal, which prompted him to help House allies unseat the Clintonian John W. Taylor from the Speaker's chair in favor of the more reliable Virginian Philip Barbour. Then, by joining Virginia and New York's votes in the Republican congressional nominating caucus to those of Crawford's base in Georgia and North Carolina, Van Buren hoped to create an unstoppable momentum on the Georgian's behalf. With Crawford in the White House and "regular" Republicans elected nationwide, Van Buren calculated, Clintonian-style treachery and its crypto-Federalist abettors would crumble.

Bad feelings and worse fortune, however, haunted Crawford's campaign. In September 1823, he succumbed to what appears to have been a massive stroke, which left him a partially paralyzed, semi-blind hulk who had to be hoisted out of bed in order to make occasional public appearances. Crawford's friends, including Van Buren, gamely insisted that he would recover, and in a fierce act of will, Crawford forced himself to return to his duties at the Treasury Department in time for the 1824 elections, despite a relapse in May. But Crawford's political recovery was hampered by the late-in-the-game candidacy of a second southern presidential contender, Secretary of War John C. Calhoun. Until the summer of 1821, the South Carolinian might have seemed most likely to support his friend and fellow nationalist in the cabinet, John Quincy Adams. But a political sojourn through the northern states had convinced Calhoun that although Adams could not win outside New England, a broad-minded slaveholder could save the Republic from the clutches of the retrenchment Radical Crawford. Never one to slight his own abilities, Calhoun entered the lists, concentrating his initial efforts on converting the business-friendly, pro-BUS, New School Republicans of Pennsylvania to his cause.

Henry Clay, putatively the western candidate, also enjoyed widespread celebrity as "The Great Compromiser" who had saved the Union in 1820 and 1821. Urged by friends and political cronies to return to the center of political action, he abandoned his lucrative retirement (spent in part collecting fees as the BUS's favorite lawyer), regained his House seat in 1822, and was triumphantly reinstalled as Speaker the following year.

Back in power, he assembled ideas about vigorous federal action to bolster internal economic development, which he had been musing over and speaking about for several years, and integrated them as a comprehensive program to combat hard times and sectional divisions. "Is there no remedy within the reach of the Government?" he asked the House. "Are we doomed to behold our industry languish and decay yet more and more? But there is a remedy, and that remedy consists in . . . adopting a genuine American system." Federally sponsored internal improvements, combined with responsible sale of the public lands and a high tariff wall to protect American manufacturers would, Clay proclaimed, benefit all Americans and strengthen the bonds of Union. Quickly dubbed "the American System," it was a western enterpriser's agenda of federal aid— but it was also, Clay insisted, a national vision of improvement and unity.

Clay's gregarious personality and legislative record distinguished him immediately from the rest of the field. In the Eighteenth Congress, he built on those advantages, pushing successfully for the General Survey Bill to plan federal internal improvements and, in 1824, for the first explicitly protectionist tariff in the nation's history. But Clay had his weaknesses, not least his unswerving faith in his own greatness. According to John Quincy Adams (admittedly no friend to the Kentuckian), Clay in conversation would become "warm, vehement, and absurd upon the tariff," making it "extremely difficult to preserve the temper of friendly society with him." In fact, as Clay the brag artist knew well, his political situation was tricky. Adams had sewn up New England, and either Crawford or Calhoun would almost certainly carry the Southeast. To succeed, Clay would have to pick up a bloc of electoral votes from either New York or Pennsylvania, while carrying Ohio, Illinois, Indiana, Missouri, Kentucky, and Tennessee—too little to win outright, but enough to deprive any other candidate of an electoral majority and throw the election into the House of Representatives, where his personal influence would prevail. All of which seemed eminently possible, except for the curious candidacy of another western slaveholder with virtually no presidential credentials whatsoever.

Andrew Jackson, although still a national idol, had receded into a knot of resentments. During the winter of 1817–18, an incident along the border of Spanish Florida had led the Monroe administration to unleash the man now lionized as "the Hero of New Orleans," and still major general of the U.S. Army, against the Spanish authorities. Jackson, familiar with the area from his Pensacola campaign during the late war, proved as ruthless as ever, pursuing across the border Seminole Indians who stood in his way, summarily executing two British citizens whom he found among the Indians, and (greatly exceeding his orders) expelling the Spanish from Pensacola and installing an American government there. A diplomatic row ensued, along with a humiliating formal congressional investigation into Jackson's behavior. In time, Jackson survived the charges of insubordination and witnessed an infuriated but enfeebled Spanish Crown give way in negotiations with the United States and cede the Floridas to American control. But Jackson could not forgive those in the administration and Congress—virtually everyone of importance, as far as he knew, other than Calhoun and Adams—who had criticized his Florida exploits. Crawford became his special nemesis when the Radicals in Congress cut the army in half and forced Jackson's resignation as the junior of the nation's two major generals. Jackson took little comfort when President Monroe, in 1821, named him governor of the new Florida territory. After eleven tempestuous weeks mainly spent fighting departing Spanish grandees, he quit the post and returned to the Hermitage, where he would brood and nurse his latest hurts.

Most of official Washington hoped that the old soldier would now finally fade away, and except for several ironic twists of fortune, he might have. His comeback began in Tennessee, supported by the bank-friendly Overton faction. After turning aside an offer to run for governor, Jackson acceded to his stalking-horse nomination for the presidency, solely as a means to keep Tennessee's Radicals, led by his old protégé Governor William Carroll, in check. Few, including Jackson, took his presidential aspirations seriously, given his small experience in elective office. (Jackson himself actually favored Adams, his most outspoken friend in the cabinet during the Florida contretemps; most of his Tennessee backers actually favored either Adams or Clay.) Had everything proceeded as planned, Andrew Jackson might be remembered today as a minor footnote to presidential history.

Strangely, however, Jackson's candidacy, made formal by his nomination by the Tennessee legislature in the autumn of 1822, elicited interest not only in neighboring Alabama and Mississippi but as far east as North Carolina and New Jersey. More ominously, Jackson, no obedient pawn, began thinking and acting for himself on the issues related to Tennessee banking. His alliance with Overton and opposition to the Tennessee Radicals had not led him to abandon his distrust of banks and bankers, dating back to his near ruin due to bad paper two decades earlier. In 1820, at the height of the state's postpanic banking controversy, he had helped draft a memorial that denounced Felix Grundy's paper-money loan office bill and blamed the depression on "the large emissions of paper from the banks." (Indeed, it had been temporary endorsement by some of the Radicals of inflated state-issued paper money, as well as their friendliness with Crawford, that convinced Jackson to keep his distance from them.) Yet if, at the time, he stayed loyal to his old patrons, the Overton machine's efforts to protect large debtors and the state banks had always offended Jackson—and the offense deepened when, in 1823, Overton and his allies got the legislature to pack the state supreme court with justices favorable to expanded land speculation. Jackson, enraged, began putting it about that he opposed all banks on principle, which prompted Overton to demonstrate Jackson's political weakness by secretly backing the reelection of one of his (and Jackson's) old enemies to the Senate by the state legislature in 1823. Jackson's friends, awakening late to the scheme, hurriedly nominated their man, and with the candidate himself showing up outside the legislature the night before the balloting, he won by a scant ten-vote margin. Senator-elect Jackson's presidential campaign was very much alive.

An even greater shock came over the following autumn and winter from Pennsylvania, thanks principally to William Duane, Stephen Simpson, and the revived antibanking Philadelphia city democracy. As soon as John C. Calhoun had begun courting the state's New School Republicans and emerged as almost certain to win the state's backing, Duane and company began casting about for a candidate of their own. Adams, Clay, and Crawford were out of the question, not least because each was connected to the discredited incumbent administration. But Simpson had served under Jackson at New Orleans and thought he was one of the greatest living Americans—a second George Washington and a reformist leader who would create a genuinely democratic party, free of corrupt old uses like the caucus system, to protect what Simpson called "the productive classes."

In January 1822, Duane's *Aurora* floated the long-shot Jackson's name for the presidency. Simpson then started his own pro-Jackson weekly, the *Columbian Observer*, and a pro-Jackson movement began making headway all across the state. Calhoun's lieutenants and pro-Calhoun New Schoolers dismissed Jackson's supporters as an agglomeration of "giddy young men," "the dregs of society," and "grog shop politicians of the villages & the rabble of Pittsburgh and Philadelphia"—only to discover at the state party's nominating convention in March 1823 that the rabble was numerous enough to thwart them. Sensing an impending Jacksonian rout, the New Schoolers managed, just barely, to postpone the nomination process for a year, but disaster delayed was not disaster averted. During the autumn and winter of 1823–24, Old School Jacksonians held mass meetings and rallies across the state, deploying all of the methods of public agitation that Duane's and Michael Leib's City Democrats had inherited from the Democratic Society of the mid-1790s and refined in support of Jefferson. In Philadelphia, Simpson, Duane, and the *Aurora* democrats at last managed to rip control of the local party machinery away from the New Schoolers. With the city's delegation secure for Jackson, the New Schoolers, facing certain defeat, gave up on Calhoun and grudgingly backed the Tennessean. Calhoun's backers managed to win him the convention's nomination for vice president, which Calhounites elsewhere now focused on securing.

The Pennsylvania outcome left a presidential field of four. It also bolstered Jackson's supporters in North Carolina, where pro-Crawford Quids had alienated popular support in the interior of the state by opposing a campaign for democratic reform of the state constitution. Anti-Crawford sentiment had initially gravitated to Calhoun, but by the spring of 1824, the North Carolina "People's Ticket" switched to Jackson. Suddenly, even in Washington, Jackson's presidential bid had genuine credibility. After visiting John Quincy Adams, Congressman William Plumer Jr. wrote to his father that "I was surprised to find that he (& I find many other people talk in the same way) considered Jackson as a very prominent & formidable candidate. And what was more, he not only considered him as strong, but also as meritorious—He had, he said, no hesitation in saying that he preferred him decidedly to any other candidate—." Jackson's chances improved even more when Crawford's political lieutenants, led by the political magician from New York, Martin Van Buren, played by the old rules and gained their man an orthodox victory that proved disastrous.

Since 1796, all Republican presidential and vice presidential candidates had secured the backing of their respective party's congressional caucus, a practice that had always struck some democratic writers as open to abuse. In 1816, Crawford had refrained from allowing his name to be placed before the caucus, and in 1824, Senator Van Buren believed that this earlier forbearance had earned Crawford the nomination, which a revived New York–Virginia axis could secure. But a forced display of party discipline, of the sort Van Buren found so appealing, proved to be political poison. The early challenges to the caucus system, notably George Clinton's in 1808, had obvious personal motivations, augmented by the desires of northern

Republicans to break the Virginians' domination of the party. But after 1812, Federalists (who had abandoned the system in favor of conclaves of state party leaders) as well as Republicans charged that the caucus embroiled presidential politics in *aristocratic* intrigue, cabal and management." In 1817, with the Federalist threat virtually gone, local anticaucus stirrings began in earnest, most conspicuously in Pennsylvania. Republicans of all stripes wondered whether the caucus system—originally designed to keep the party leadership in touch with the wishes of its rank and file—had become a usurping anachronism. In 1820, amid the Missouri crisis, the caucuses met but then adjourned without even going through the formalities of making nominations, and President Monroe was reelected virtually without opposition. The elder William Plumer, among many others, approved of how the caucus system had reached "a low ebb," and complained that it involved "too much regard for private, & too little respect for the public interest."

Four years later, the end of the system was nigh—and the harder that Van Buren cracked the caucus whip for Crawford, the less it hurt his adversaries. Adams told associates that, on principle, he would never consent to receive a nomination for any office from a congressional caucus; Jackson and Clay likewise stayed on the sidelines; and on the eve of the meeting, all but eighty congressmen, fewer than one-third of the total, had publicly pledged not to attend. Van Buren insisted on going through with the gathering, but only sixty-six actually showed up, to hand Crawford a lopsided and thoroughly Pyrrhic victory. Less than a month later, the Senate debated, without coming to a vote, what Rufus King attacked as the "self-created central power" of the caucus, and the system was quietly buried. Poor Crawford, insensibly bearing the onus of the last official caucus nomination, lost whatever slim chances for the presidency still remained.

Pennsylvania proved to be Jackson's breakthrough. With Calhoun now knocked out of the contest, Jackson inherited his large following in New Jersey and Maryland as well as in both of the

Carolinas. In Washington, where he unexpectedly found himself in the Senate, he played the charming, socially correct gentleman, putting the lie to his reputation as an impetuous barbarian. Without compromising the protocol of appearing not to be actively campaigning, he also reassured supporters from clashing parts of his embryonic alliance. His Tennessee friends Major William Lewis and Senator John Eaton arranged for Stephen Simpson's *Columbian Observer* to publish a series of letters—signed "Wyoming" but written by Eaton—spelling out the case for Jackson as a virtuous keeper of the Revolutionary heritage against corrupt privilege, and as a genuinely national candidate in a field of sectional favorites. On specific issues like the tariff, Jackson carefully explained his position to his close advisers and the public alike. To a protectionist Pennsylvanian (in a letter he was fully aware would be published), he claimed that "*a fair protection*"— which he believed the pending tariff bill did too little to provide— "would place the american labour in a fair competition with that of [E]urope." The letter matched his position in the Senate, where he consistently voted against amendments that would have lowered rates. But when an antitariff North Carolinian expressed his concern, Jackson replied (in another letter he knew would be published) that he favored a "judicious examination and revision" of the tariff, not an oppressive one.

Jackson's opponents leapt on the statements and charged him with being two-faced. (In response to the North Carolina letter, Henry Clay is reputed to have said, "Well by——, I am in favor of an *in*judicious tariff.") In fact, the statements were perfectly consistent, if artfully constructed. Instead of trapping himself by taking a dogmatic stance one way or the other, Jackson stuck to a middle ground, singling out certain products (like Pennsylvania iron) as articles of our "national independence, and national defence" in need of protection, while he refrained from naming others (including New England cotton goods). He also found a way to link tariff protection to the cause of populist Jeffersonian simplicity, arguing that tariff revenues were required to eliminate the accursed national debt that, if left standing, would "raise around the administration a moneyed aristocracy, dangerous to the liberties of the country."

Jackson's shifts in tone and unorthodox combinations of ideas were astute political moves, designed to solidify his disparate coalition. He had become a politician for whom, as for any army general, there is nothing without victory. But by confounding expectations—another military virtue—Jackson also defied what were becoming the pat categories of political thinking on specific policies while offering his own synthesis, and tying it to the people's cause. It was a trait that would become more pronounced as Jackson's political experience grew. Older Republicans—including the man Jackson called his political hero, Thomas Jefferson—could not fully grasp the appeal of the violent, passionate Old Hickory. (Jefferson, reportedly, thought he was "a *dangerous man*.") But younger Republicans who knew him, including the convert John Quincy Adams, understood that what many mistook for Jackson's intellectual confusion and emotional rashness hid what Adams called his "profound calculation."

Jackson's managers were single-minded in promoting their candidate as a national and not merely a sectional figure, a crucial appeal in the aftermath of the Missouri struggles and the Vesey affair. "The union is no longer activated by one soul, and bound together by one entirety of interest," the Pennsylvania Jacksonians declared at their Harrisburg nominating convention: Jackson would correct that, an Alabama paper proclaimed, by being "the President of the whole people, the enlightened ruler of an undivided empire, and not a sectional magistrate devoted to the 'universal Yankee nation' of the East or the mixed, mingled and confused population of the South." The other aspirants tried to build similar messages—Crawford by stressing his orthodox Jeffersonian loyalties, Adams by stressing his long and distinguished record in the nation's service, and Clay by playing up his ideas for national economic improvement—but none was as persuasive as the Hero of New Orleans.

The Jacksonians also invited mass participation in the campaign. Voters and spectators turned out on short notice for frequent rallies and parades, staged to invigorate the faithful and display that Jackson was the outsider candidate whose legitimacy could only come from the people at large, and not from any club of Washington fixers. Jackson benefited from other campaign innovations, including taking straw votes at militia musters and grand jury meetings. No doubt the pro-Jackson press inflated the enthusiasm these efforts generated—but more conventional observers, used to a smaller deployment of treating and stumping during campaigns, were shocked and dismayed at the Jacksonians' display. Some called the shows meaningless stagecraft. "Mere effervescence . . . can accomplish nothing," one pro-Calhoun New School Pennsylvanian sniffed, before Jackson knocked his man out of the race. Others sounded genuinely worried, as if these audacious tactics would carry away the thoughtless multitude, and they questioned the very legitimacy of Jackson's campaign.

With Jackson's candidacy surging, the center of intrigue moved to New York, one of only six states where the state legislature still chose presidential electors. As ever, the place was a hornet's nest. Van Buren and the Albany Regency, loyal to Crawford to the bitter end, had decided to resist public sentiment in favor of popular choice of electors in order to ensure that the Bucktail-controlled Albany legislature would hand Crawford the state's bonanza of thirty-six electoral votes. New York business interests friendly to John C. Calhoun tried to take the high ground, demanding that the Regency allow the people at large to choose the state's presidential electors—and portrayed Crawford and his friends as democracy's foes. When Calhoun's campaign collapsed in Pennsylvania in March 1824, so did his friends' efforts in New York—but Van Buren's Clintonian enemies, already organizing a reform crusade, rallied to what they called the People's Party and campaigned hard for the new Election Bill, which would give to the voters the direct power to select presidential electors.

Van Buren had badly outsmarted himself. To accede to the new bill would mean placing his slaveholder candidate, Crawford, at the mercy of New York's manifestly antislavery voters—a risky proposition in the wake of the Missouri Compromise. Worse, it might actually open the way for the hated Clinton himself to run as a favorite-son candidate, a contest Clinton would almost certainly win. Over the previous half-dozen years, work had proceeded steadily on the astounding canal-building project that Clinton had first proposed in 1808. With the new Erie Canal now nearing completion (and with Clinton serving as unpaid chief of the Canal Board), the ex-governor "Magnus Apollo" had become a hero all over again in the western part of the state. Even his political enemies had to grant that the canal was a marvel. Were Clinton to win New York, he could easily jump to the front of the presidential pack as the one man who could unite the anti-Crawford forces outside the South—a prospect that frightened Martin Van Buren even more than the prospect of being labeled undemocratic.

One Bucktail blunder led to another. As the price for suppressing their democratic principles on the Election Bill, radical Bucktails demanded that the Regency inflict some sort of punishment on Clinton. On the very last day of the legislative session, without consulting Van Buren (who was away in Washington), Regency bosses led by one aging Judge Roger Skinner gave the go-ahead, and Clinton was summarily removed, for no stated reason, from his Canal Board post. Van Buren exploded with rage, understanding immediately that the gratuitous disgracing of Clinton would give his enemy, as he put it, "what he had never before possessed—the sympathies of the people." ("[T]here is such a thing in politics," Van Buren later snapped at Judge Skinner, "as *killing a man too dead!*") Clinton, for his part, did not miss a beat. Unable to break the Regency's lockhold over the Election Bill, he wrapped himself in the populist garb of the People's Party, ran for governor, and, in October, swept back into power. Three-quarters of the new state assembly would be anti-Regency men.

Luckily for Van Buren, it would be the lame-duck legislature that would allocate the state's electoral votes, but for once he seemed to have lost his touch. After a prolonged series of

Byzantine negotiations, the battered Bucktails mustered only four electoral votes for Crawford—three fewer than Clay received, with the rest going to Adams. Van Buren, one Adams supporter exulted, "looks like a wilted cabbage, and poor Judge Skinner has quite lost his voice." Yet Van Buren managed to salvage a victory of sorts from the Regency's sorry performance.

By the time the New York legislature assembled formally to choose its electors, the popular rush for Jackson had secured sixty-six electoral votes; Adams had fifty-one votes, Crawford thirty-nine, and Clay thirty-three. The election seemed destined, as Clay had hoped, to end up in the House of Representatives. But the Twelfth Amendment to the Constitution, approved in 1804 after the Jefferson-Burr deadlock, stipulated that only the top three candidates would be considered, and Clay was running fourth. If Clay's backers fared as expected in the New York machinations, Clay might have gained hope that he would make the short list and then, in all likelihood, win the White House. But as the New York electors prepared to meet and cast their ballots, Van Buren maneuvered to suppress Clay's total. One elector pledged to Clay, under great pressure, switched to Jackson; two other Clay electors failed to appear and were replaced by Adams men; and the Regency persuaded one Adams elector to vote for Crawford. The final revised New York total was Adams twenty-six, Crawford five, Clay only four, and Jackson one. Had the original New York totals stood, the Electoral College result would have left Crawford and Clay in a tie for third place—but Van Buren, having failed to win his state for Crawford, at least made sure that his man, and not Clay, made it to the next round. The Great Compromiser was finished, in this election anyway, and New York had made the difference.

The biggest story of the election, however, unfolded in Pennsylvania and New Jersey (where the voters, and not the legislatures, now chose presidential electors) as well as in North Carolina, Illinois, Indiana, and the new states of the Southwest. Jackson won them all and, except in New Jersey, did so by landslide margins. In several states where he did not win—Maryland, Ohio, Missouri—Jackson finished a strong second. All told, he won 42 percent of the vote in the eighteen states that allowed voters to choose presidential electors—nearly 10 percentage points better than his nearest competitor, Adams. Outside Adams's New England base (where he and Clay were completely shut out), Jackson was the plain preference of the large majority of the voters. If those states where he ran second to Clay added their congressional votes to those of the states Jackson won outright, Jackson would have had the backing of fourteen congressional delegations—two more than necessary to win the election in the House of Representatives. (John C. Calhoun, meanwhile, had prevailed overwhelmingly in his quest for the vice presidency, having won the support of both the Adams and the Jackson forces.)

Considering where Jackson had stood only two years earlier, it was an extraordinary achievement, the sharpest ascent by any man in the young republic's political history. Out of the depths of his postwar difficulties, Jackson, a man of humble origins and minimal formal education, had risen to capture the imagination of a broad cross-section of the electorate. "The Giant Augean Stable at Washington wants cleansing," a group of Stephen Simpson's Old Schoolers had proclaimed over the winter of 1822–23, "and we know of no other Hercules." Tapping into the democratic frenzy unleashed by the Era of Bad Feelings, Jackson had become that frenzy's great symbol.

Now, only two rivals stood between him and the presidency, one a purported political lightweight, the other a virtual corpse. Yet despite all that Jackson had accomplished, his fortunes hung on the deliberations of the resourceful also-ran, Henry Clay, who was not quite finished after all.

"SOMETHING RADICALLY WRONG"

Late in May 1820, two of the most learned public men of their time boarded a carriage in Washington, took a long ride into the

Maryland countryside and conversed freely about politics. Secretary of War John C. Calhoun was gloomy about what he called "a general mass of disaffection to the Government, not concentrated in any particular direction, but ready to seize upon any event and looking out anywhere for a leader." The alarming Missouri question and the tariff debates, he said, were "merely incidental" to the crisis—one born of "a general impression that there was something radically wrong in the administration of the Government." His companion, Secretary of State John Quincy Adams, although more sanguine, was inclined to agree that the long-time "scourge of the country . . . speculations in paper currency," coupled with political demagogy, had hurt the Monroe administration. Unfortunately, Adams reflected, although "the disease is apparent, the remedy [is] not discernible." All he could do was to place his faith in Time, Chance, and Providence. "I have but one formula suited to all occasions—," he wrote in his diary, "'Thy will be done.'"

Five years later, Adams would have reason to believe that a merciful deity had answered his prayers. But as the campaign of 1824 proved, the disaffection ran far deeper than either Adams or Calhoun had feared. Worse, some of the ambitious men whom Adams loathed helped change the fundamentals of national politics forever—and, in the process, secured for their leader, Andrew Jackson, a powerful claim on the presidency.

The panic, as Adams perceived, was pivotal. Not only did the hard times of 1819 and the early 1820s revive, in new forms, the city and country democracies, they also raised fundamental questions about the nationalist economic policies of the new-style Republicans under Madison and Monroe, and focused inchoate popular resentments on the banks, especially the Second BUS. The critics were diverse, socially as well as ideologically, ranging from local monied interests, planters, and enterprisers angry chiefly at the BUS, to radicals like Stephen Simpson, for whom all commercial banking was a crime. The hostility was far from universal, as the strong northwestern popular vote for Henry Clay amply proved in 1824. But the panic persuaded a large portion of the electorate that something was terribly awry in the national government, and that (as one Pennsylvanian, appalled by "moon-struck madness" of the Jacksonians, observed) there "must be a new order of things."

The Missouri controversy, meanwhile, proved far more important than a "merely incidental" outburst. All four of the presidential contenders in 1824 (as well as Calhoun, before he backed out) publicly supported the congressional compromises. The northern restrictionists could not force the national debate their way, but neither could the southern die-hards. Each man tried to depict himself as the only true national candidate, with broad patriotic appeal, while disparaging his opponents as sectional favorites. Yet resentments over slavery did not disappear. John Quincy Adams, the sole nonslaveholder in the race, managed to win some support, but was badly beaten in the South and South-west. William Crawford, the candidate of the southeastern slave-holders and Van Buren–style northern "regulars," ran poorly outside of his southeastern base. Henry Clay, the western slave-holding compromiser, lost the support of southerners who thought him too hard on slavery and from northerners who thought him too soft. He wound up winning, barely, only one state, Ohio, apart from his native Kentucky and a grateful Missouri.

Both the panic and the Missouri debates underscored in different ways the overriding question of democracy as Americans perceived it. In economic matters, the questions arose primarily as a matter of privilege. Should unelected private interests, well connected to government, be permitted to control, to their own benefit, the economic destiny of the entire nation? Or should the manifest public good, for rich and poor alike, be pursued no matter what the majoritarian democrats believed and demanded? Regarding slavery, the questions were a matter of justice. Did the federal government have the constitutional power to control the expansion of slavery? Were blacks as well as whites endowed with certain inalienable rights that slavery destroyed? Should settler-citizens, slaveholders and nonslaveholders, have the right to decide slavery's fate for themselves? Should the nation's leaders abide by the Missouri Compromise's spirit and keep slavery issues out of national politics? Or did justice demand a sectional showdown over slavery?

Amid these debates, politicians tried to adapt to the broader shift in political sensibilities that emerged out of the War of 1812. At the state level, that required either accommodating, co-opting, or (as in Virginia) squelching surging demands for expanding democracy. At the national level, it required at least appearing to be in league with an enlarged popular sovereignty. "We must be democratic, we must be on the side of the people," one New York Clintonian wrote to another in 1821. "[I]f our adversaries are republicans, we must be democratic; if they are democratic, we must be jacobinal." The debacle over the nominating caucus in 1824 symbolized all that had changed. Those who heeded convention—above all, Martin Van Buren and his pro-Crawford Radical allies—painted themselves into a political corner. The more one did not play by the old rules, the better.

All of which accounts for the phenomenal emergence of Andrew Jackson. As a newcomer to national politics, Jackson had none of the insider connections with Van Buren–style "regular" northern Republicans that Crawford had; as a westerner (like Clay) and as a slaveholder (like Calhoun and Clay), he was unable to build an independent following east of the Hudson River. But elsewhere, Jackson's outsider status and his military glory made him the exceptional man, the only candidate untainted by the Monrovian political establishment in Washington, the only one who could convincingly portray himself, outside New England, as a national figure, the only one who could win credible followings outside his regional base. Only Jackson, as his backers insisted, seemed to possess the combination of heroism and independence required to offset sectional prejudices, prevent the entrenchment of what he called a "moneyed aristocracy," and, in the pro-Jackson Pennsylvania convention's words, vindicate "the durability of our free institutions."

Jackson became, in sum, the leader whose ascendance Calhoun had predicted in 1820. According to the later reflections of one of his supporters, Thomas Hart Benton, Jackson should therefore have been elected president in 1824, in line with what Benton called "the *demos krateo* principle." But as the events of the following winter proved, the meaning of *demos krateo* was far from self-evident, at least in Washington City.

3

THE POLITICS OF MORAL IMPROVEMENT

As Congress assembled in January 1825 to select a new president, Henry Clay reveled in the machinations. Having finished fourth in the Electoral College voting, he knew he would not be elected. But none of the other candidates had anything close to the simple majority of state delegations in the House required for election under the Twelfth Amendment. Clay, having carried three states and with a toehold in New York, could come close to deciding the matter. The Speaker played along with delight as representatives of Jackson, Crawford, and Adams buttonholed him, paid him florid compliments, and then pleaded the case for their man. "How can one withstand all this disinterested homage & kindness?" Clay wrote wryly to his Kentucky neighbor Francis P. Blair. Clay knew the choice was virtually his to make, and that Adams would be his beneficiary.

Clay had disliked Adams ever since Ghent, and later the two had disagreed sharply over the Spanish treaty that obtained Florida, but they shared broadly nationalist views. Crawford was impossible, a retrenchment Radical who seemed to be at death's door. Jackson was even worse, a backwoods Napoleon who, in Clay's view, had proved his unfitness to lead during the Florida affair. Jackson's election, Clay told friends, would "be the greatest misfortune that could befall the country" and "give the strongest guaranty that the republic will march in the fatal road which has conducted every other republic to ruin." So Clay would support Adams, an intention he announced to his closest associates in mid-December, nearly nine weeks before the House was scheduled to gather. In Washington, on the evening of January 9, the two met privately, at Clay's instigation, mainly, it appears, to smooth over their personal differences. It was all over but the shouting, although there would still be plenty of that.

Less than two weeks before the House gathered, Stephen Simpson's *Columbian Observer* published a sensational anonymous letter, from Washington, claiming that "the friends of Mr. Clay have hinted that they, like the Swiss, would fight for those who pay best," and charging that they had struck a secret deal to make Adams president. The price? "[S]hould this unholy coalition prevail," the letter said, "Clay is to be appointed Secretary of State." Clay whipped off a reply published in the quasi-official Washington *National Intelligencer*, pronouncing the author, whoever he was, a liar, and challenging him to a duel. Two days later, also in the *Intelligencer*, George Kremer, a flamboyant, democratic House backbencher from Pennsylvania unmasked himself as the accuser and declared he was ready to prove his charges.

Embarrassed to be entangled with the eccentric Kremer, Clay backed away from his challenge but demanded that Kremer offer proof. Kremer dodged. Finally, on February 9, the House began selecting the president of the United States. The three states Clay had won—Ohio, Missouri, and Kentucky—had already announced they would vote for Adams, leaving the New Englander two states short of his goal. Maryland, too, would back Adams, but only on the first ballot; after that, all bets were off. New York, split down the middle, became the key to victory. Adams and Daniel Webster went to work to secure the crucial vote of the old patroon Stephen Van Rensselaer, and the squire congressman came through, handing New York's vote to Adams.

"May the blessing of God rest upon the event of this day!" the president-elect wrote in his diary.

Henry Clay then committed one of the greatest errors in American political history. During the weeks leading up to the House vote, Adams and his lieutenants had given what they discreetly called "assurances" to various potential supporters in Congress. Among the least questionable of these understandings was reached with Clay. Both Adams and Clay were too sophisticated to strike any explicit bargain, either during their private meeting on January 9 or at any other time. None was needed. Clay brought with him congressional influence, charm, and geographical balance, all things that the New Englander required. Two days after the House voted, President-elect Adams duly informed President Monroe that he had offered the State Department to Clay; three days later, he returned to the White House to tell Monroe that Clay had accepted. Washington exploded. Suddenly, George Kremer's bluff looked like prophecy. "So you see," Andrew Jackson roared in private, "the *Judas* of the West has closed the contract and will receive the thirty pieces of silver. His end will be the same." Clay would never rid himself of the taint of this alleged "corrupt bargain" for the rest of his long public life.

If, in politics, a blunder is worse than a crime, then Clay, along with Adams, was guilty indeed, of a complete failure of political intelligence and imagination. That Clay only gradually came to understand what went wrong only proved the failure's magnitude. By his own lights, he had acted with patriotic correctness, even statesmanship. The Constitution's stipulations about procedures had been followed to the letter. By joining his supporters to those of the national candidate most like himself, Clay was promoting what he considered a credible divination of the democratic will as endorsing nationalist programs. The only display of bad faith had been the smear campaign mounted by the low Kremer and company, which he, the Speaker, had manfully foiled.

Clay disregarded the cardinal political maxim that the appearance of wrongdoing can be just as damaging as actual wrongdoing. More important, while playing by the established patrician rules of high politics, Clay did not comprehend how much and how quickly the rules were changing in the 1820s along majoritarian lines. To Clay, there was nothing wrong with commandeering for Adams the congressional vote of his home state of Kentucky (where he had trounced Jackson by nearly a three to one margin), even though Adams had won not a single popular vote in Kentucky and even though the state legislature had pointedly instructed its congressmen to vote for Jackson. Clay dismissed the national popular vote (which Jackson had won decisively, and in which the combined total of Jackson and Crawford was more than 50 percent), the Electoral College plurality (which Jackson had also won decisively), and the combination of first- and second-place finishes in the states (by which Jackson would have won easily in Congress). Adams, supposedly the lesser political calculator of the two, actually understood the situation far better than Clay, noting some months later in his diary that the election had not transpired "in a manner satisfactory to pride or just desire; not by the unequivocal suffrages of a majority of the people; with perhaps two-thirds of the whole people adverse to the actual result."

On March 4, Adams, after two sleepless nights, took the oath of office at the Capitol. John C. Calhoun, deeply offended by what he saw as Clay's selfish maneuvers, was sworn in as vice president. Clay, flushed with success, won a hotly contested confirmation as secretary of state from the Senate. Andrew Jackson suppressed his fury, graciously attended Adams's inauguration, voted against Clay's confirmation, and returned to a hero's homecoming in Nashville. But on the day that Adams was sworn in, a pro-Tammany New York City newspaper published a letter that Jackson had written days earlier to a local supporter, blasting Henry Clay for his insults and intrigues of recent months:

> To him thank god I am in no wise responsible, there is a purer tribunal to which in preference I would refer myself—to the Judgment of an enlightened patriotic &

uncorrupted people—to that tribunal I would rather appeal whence is derived whatever reputation either he or I are possessed of.

In October, with the Adams presidency only seven months old, the Tennessee legislature in a nearly unanimous vote advanced Jackson's name for the presidency in 1828, the earliest such nomination by far in any presidential season to that time. Jackson gratefully accepted and retired from the Senate, lest he be seen as using his office "for selfish consideration."

President Adams's morally inspired, ambitious vision of the nation would help set the terms for the battles of the next four years. But far from Washington, popular movements, old and new, with their own moral, religious, and political concerns, complicated local and, eventually, national politics—some in broad agreement with Adams's views, others in sharp contrast. Always there was the certainty that in 1828 Andrew Jackson would fight to reclaim what he believed was rightfully his. The Era of Bad Feelings had entered a new and furious phase.

A "SACRED" DUTY AND TRUST: JOHN QUINCY ADAMS IN THE WHITE HOUSE

"You come into Life with advantages which will disgrace you, if your success is mediocre," Vice President John Adams wrote his son in 1794. ". . . [I]f you do not rise to the head not only of your Profession, but of your Country, it will be owing to your own *Laziness Slovenliness* and *Obstinacy*." The younger Adams, at age twenty-seven, had already achieved much at the time, most recently as an essayist and orator defending the Washington administration and attacking the "political villainy" of Edmond Genet. Left to his own devices, he would have preferred a tranquil, bookish life as a Boston lawyer or, perhaps, a Harvard scholar. But his father's monumental expectations, as ever, overruled young Johnny's preferences, filling him with the mixture of determination and corrosive self-doubt that would torment him for most of the rest of his life.

Few Americans of such great accomplishment and distinction have left behind so revealing a record of inner affliction as Adams did in his great lifelong diary. Alongside the notations of his diplomatic triumphs, there are constant self-beratings. He repeatedly fretted that he suffered from "imbecility of will," a tendency to distraction that he feared would drive him mad. Even after his demanding father and his meddlesome mother, Abigail, were dead, their spirits haunted Adams, feeding his drive for eminence but also chastising him lest he fall prey to the sin of pride. Adams devoted mind, body, and soul to keeping his demons at bay. As president, he followed a strict daily regimen, awaking well before dawn, walking up and down Pennsylvania Avenue for two hours no matter the weather, and swimming in the Potomac during bathing season. To soothe his nerves he drank quinine and valerian root tea. For spiritual uplift, he read two or three chapters of scripture each morning, along with the corresponding sections in biblical commentaries. After hours, he enjoyed billiards as "a resource both for exercise and amusement." His diary was his greatest refuge, except when fatigue or distraction kept him from writing, which left "another chasm in the record of my life."

Among those he trusted, Adams was witty, chatty, and passionate, but he preferred solitude to most forms of Washington socializing. With strangers and most acquaintances, he adopted a protective reserve, masking his emotions with an austere gravitas. Behind the mask, Adams was a man of enormous learning, piety, and ambition, all of which shaped his political outlook. No president, including Jefferson, contributed more to American scholarship. Fluent in seven languages, sometime Boylston Professor of Rhetoric at Harvard, Adams was conversant in current debates in mathematics and the natural sciences, as well as in theology. With his translation of Christoph Martin Wieland's romance *Oberon* (completed while he served his father as ambassador to Prussia), he established the serious study in the United States of German language and literature. His religious devotions, described constantly in his diary, were of the liberalizing post-Calvinist Unitarian stamp, blending rationalism and enthusiasm in a creed of human elevation. "Progressive improvement in the condition of man," he would observe many years later, "is apparently the purpose of a superintending Providence." As Adams did God's will by improving himself, so he would improve the nation.

Adams harnessed his intellectual and emotional drives—and kept himself from going to pieces—with an intensely competitive political resolve. His adversaries underestimated him as a spoiled, book-smart dauphin; his maneuvers to win the presidency over the winter of 1824–25 amply showed him as a resourceful politician. (Many years later, Ralph Waldo Emerson would shrewdly describe Adams as "no literary gentleman" but "a bruiser," "an old roué who cannot live on slops, but must have sulphuric acid in his tea.") Yet Adams, like Clay, followed political rules that, in the 1820s, were quickly becoming outdated. A throwback, in some ways, to his father's generation, he imagined that national politics was an arena for the resolution of regional differences by like-minded men of virtue and education. He disdained public display of competitive striving as undignified. He despised mass party politics of the sort now associated with Andrew Jackson, and firmly favored government of and by the best men—"the most able and the most worthy," he told Henry Clay. He was a partisan who hated what was coming to be known as partisanship, a Federalist-turned-Republican who thought nominal affiliations counted for little and personal integrity counted for nearly everything—a politician who was not so much without a political party as he was opposed to the very idea of a political party.

As president, Adams hoped to usher in an era of great spiritual and intellectual as well as material improvements. His first annual message to Congress, delivered in December 1825, spelled out his goals exactly. He would have Congress fund the construction of extensive new roads and canals; he wanted to complete an old proposal of George Washington's and establish a great university in the city that now bore Washington's name; he would build at public expense an astronomical observatory, of which Europe could boast more than one hundred but of which in all of the Western Hemisphere there were none. "In assuming her station among the civilized nations of the earth," Adams declared, "it would seem that our country had contracted the engagement to contribute her share of mind, of labor, and of expense to the improvement of those parts of knowledge which lie beyond the reach of individual acquisition."

Adams's vision was moral as well as political—nothing less, he said, than a "sacred" duty and trust. Although his means would be very different from theirs, Adams wanted to mobilize the resources of the federal government to increase what the old Democratic-Republican societies had championed as "social virtue." Henry Clay, like other Republican nationalists, had described the ethical and patriotic benefits of active government and the American System as a by-product of economic expansion. Adams took a larger view. What was the use of popular sovereignty in a post-Federalist world, he asked, if government lacked the authority to advance the spiritual as well as the material conditions of the nation at large, for the weak and the middling as well as the strong? Must the nation be forever hamstrung by its old fears from the 1790s—fears, he explained, that had been scattered in a new era where "[t]he spirit of improvement is abroad upon the earth"? Who could call the federal government's energetic use of its enumerated powers a return to monocracy, so long as it aimed to work directly "for the benefit of the people themselves." Had not Jefferson himself laid aside the neat formulas of antigovernment convention when he believed strong executive action necessary to the public good, above all in the Louisiana Purchase? Might reflexive suspicion of government power disable such action, making us a lesser and not a greater nation than we could be?

Adams was neither an old-fashioned Federalist nor, strictly, a Republican economic nationalist. Neither, however, was he a "positive" liberal prophet of the modern democratic state. His energetic view of government, summarized in his first annual message's famous declaration that "liberty is power," held that only the federal government had the authority and the resources required to undertake his grand improvement projects. Yet through his presidential years, there was nothing democratic in the actual politics of Adams's liberality. Although he celebrated what he called, in his inaugural address, "a confederated representative democracy," he detested even the limited ideas of party and party loyalty that had arisen from the crises of the 1790s. He portrayed his administration as a patrician return to the rule of "talents and virtue alone." Especially in the aftermath of the corrupt-bargain episode, Adams's more attractive side was occluded by his utter failure to adjust to the democratic ferment of the 1820s. He appeared as if he wanted to impose his benevolent will on the people, instead of heeding the people's will. More than any other prominent American leader, he resembled a cosmopolitan liberal aristocrat, a type far more common in Britain and Europe than in America, his politics resembling those of his admirer, Alexis de Tocqueville.

Which is to say that Adams's program was doomed from the start. The specious allegations that he had struck a sordid gentleman's deal with Henry Clay hurt Adams badly even before his inaugural. Once in the White House, his antiparty stance on federal appointments, and his determination to unite all factions, including those that wished him ill, would have crippled him even had his policies proved popular. More important, those expensive federal policies were anathema to most Americans—and most of their elected representatives—who were still recovering from the economic and political crises of the Monroe years. While they were trying to make ends meet, the president wanted to spend the people's money to build a university and an observatory—an extravagant waste, it seemed, proposed by a Harvard elitist who had connived his way into the presidency. For southerners, there was the special fear, in the wake of the Missouri crisis, that the Yankee Adams's idea of improvement also meant renewed attacks on slavery and its expansion.

The new president certainly had the courage of his convictions. Instead of cloaking his overriding purpose, Adams at the conclusion of his first message to Congress, dared the representatives not "to slumber in ignorance or fold up our arms and proclaim to the world that we are palsied by the will of our constituents." Yet for all its bravery, that majestic line—delivered by a president who had run a clear second in the popular vote—survives as one of the most politically ruinous in the history of American presidential rhetoric. Adams took what encouragement he could from a few friends (including Edward Livingston, the former New York Democratic Society member, now a congressman from Louisiana) who told him they agreed with the message's every word. But the advance private reviews from his own cabinet members, including Secretary of State Clay, were negative. The intramural warnings appear only to have hardened the pugnacious Adams's resolve, but the public's jeering proved devastating. Alternatively mocked as an effete dreamer and denounced as a would-be Caesar, Adams suffered through what he called in his diary a "protracted agony of character and reputation." Less than a year into his presidency, he began to realize that Congress would enact none of his improvement projects.

Foreign affairs, Adams's forte, proved no happier, and for reasons that had much to do with domestic politics. The major debacle involved the spread of republicanism in Latin America, and the elaboration of the Monroe Doctrine barring European interference in Western affairs, of which Adams, as secretary of state, had been the chief author. By 1825, revolutions in the Argentine, Chile, Peru, Colombia, and Mexico had changed the face of Atlantic politics, and raised new concerns. Belligerent factions in newly independent Colombia and Mexico harbored designs on wresting the slave colony of Cuba away from the tottering Spanish government as soon as the last traces of Spanish rule departed from their own shores. Adams and Clay persuaded the Mexican and Colombian governments to back off, but Adams, with his penchant for ambitious projects, and with Clay's support, also wanted to foster stronger commercial and political ties among all of the Western republics. In his first annual message he announced plans to dispatch ministers to a conference scheduled to be held the following year in Panama, "to deliberate upon objects important to the welfare of all." Three months later, the Senate consented to Adams's plenipotentiary nominations—but the American mission, like the conference itself, was doomed.

In light of the recent abolition of slavery in Chile and Central America, and its impending abolition in much of the rest of formerly colonized Latin America outside Brazil and Cuba, southern Republicans feared that the Panama conference would raise the specter of emancipation. They were also repelled by the idea that American officials would have to mix as equals with a black Haitian envoy. Northern Republicans aligned with Senator Martin Van Buren of New York (who was still a Crawford-style Radical) saw an opportunity to build southern support and harass the administration by objecting to a possible surrender of American sovereignty in any agreements made in Panama. Debates on the matter became intensely personal, at times turning the House of Representatives into what one member called "a perfect Scene of Confusion," with "no one addressing the Chair, the Chairman crying out Order Order, Order, hurly burly, helter skelter, Negro states and yankies." John Randolph, still the most stinging voice of southern Old Republicanism, delivered a rambling speech in the Senate insinuating that Secretary Clay had forged the invitations to the Panama meeting, and denouncing the president and his Kentucky ally as a sordid combination "of the puritan and the black-leg." (Randolph's remarks prompted a duel with Clay, which drew no blood.) More costly, to the administration, was the fuss kicked up by the publication, with Adams's approval, of a pseudonymous letter attacking Vice President Calhoun for failing to speak up during Randolph's rant. Calhoun assumed, mistakenly, that Adams himself was the author and he sent a bristling pseudonymous reply. The clerk who actually wrote the first letter anonymously fired back, and the Adams administration's Panama policy looked like it had degenerated into warfare between the president and the vice president.

The denouement was pathetic. Apart from the United States,

only four other countries wound up sending officials to the Panama meeting, which gathered in June 1826. The two American delegates never actually arrived: John Sergeant, the Pennsylvania Federalist, refused to suffer through the Panamanian summer; and Richard Anderson of Kentucky died of a mysterious tropical disease en route. The actual conference was reduced to drafting hastily some common defense treaties, none of which would ever come into effect. Another grand design shattered.

On a different diplomatic front, dealing with the surviving Creek and Cherokee tribes in Georgia, the Adams administration became embroiled with the state government in what would prove to be a momentous shift in southern politics, and responded in a way that ultimately looked pusillanimous. Politics in Georgia since 1819 had pitted established planter and financier interests from the coast and piedmont, in a faction led by the pro-Crawford Radical governor George Michael Troup, against backcountry small farmers and debtors led by a semiliterate former Indian fighter, John Clark. Georgia's backcountry democrats, having elected Clark governor in 1819 and 1821, fought for constitutional reforms, most auspiciously in a campaign that, in 1824, transferred election of the state governor from the legislature to the electorate. But Troup, who had displaced Clark in a close vote in the legislature in 1823, managed to hold the governor's mansion in the first popular election and staved off democratic opposition by harping on issues designed to unite the planters and the backcountry. Clark and his supporters had generally agreed with the planters on Indian removal. And so, as John C. Calhoun, still a leading nationalist, saw it, Troup, like other "mad and wicked" Crawford men, began blending "the Slave with the Indian question, in order, if possible, to consolidate the whole South" as a sectional political force under the Radicals' command.

Of special interest to land-hungry Georgians, planters and backcountry farmers alike, were nearly five million acres of rich cotton lands, lying between the Chattahoochee and Flint rivers in the northwestern part of the state, legally occupied by Creeks and Cherokees. Since 1802, the Indian tribes had lost huge tracts of land in extortionate federal treaties. By the 1820s, the Indians were fed up, and the Monroe administration, led by Secretary of War Calhoun, agreed to let them stay put. But Governor Troup, working with a part-Creek cousin of his named William McIntosh, arranged for a total cession of Creek lands with paltry compensation in the so-called Treaty of Indian Springs, signed on February 12, 1825. Amid the confusion following Adams's election as president, the Senate quickly approved the treaty, and Adams agreed to it—but after learning about its fraudulence, he suspended the cession. Governor Troup forced a crisis by ordering a survey of the lands in question preparatory to their distribution by lottery. On the Indian question, Troup insisted, the federal government was now powerless to interfere with the State of Georgia.

The Creeks reacted to the Indian Springs cession by closing ranks and executing the traitor McIntosh and his Indian co-conspirators. The Adams administration was more uncertain. Secretary Clay, in contrast to Calhoun, thought the Indians ineluctably inferior to Anglo-Saxons. Adams agreed, remarking that there was "too much foundation" for Clay's assertion that the Indians were "destined to extinction" and "not worth preserving." Embarrassed by the Indian Springs treaty, the administration tried to save face by negotiating a second agreement, the Treaty of Washington, which restored to the Creeks a tiny portion of their original lands and which the Senate duly ratified. But Governor Troup and the Georgia legislature, smelling blood, refused to recognize the new agreement, then ordered the commanders of two Georgia militia divisions to prepare to repel a hostile federal invasion.

In an inflammatory declaration sent to Secretary of War James Barbour, Troup scorned federal authority:

> From the first decisive act of hostility, you will be considered and treated as a public enemy; and, with the less repugnance, because you, to whom we might constitu-

> tionally have appealed for our own defense against inva-
> sion, are yourselves the invaders, and, what is more, the
> unblushing allies of the savages whose cause you have
> adopted.

Troup's constitutional presumptions were veering toward what would soon be an even more radical theory of undivided state sovereignty. "The governor's roughness and violence," the nationalist Niles' *Weekly Register* observed, amounted to a "desperate effort to . . . bring about a political scramble," reminiscent of the Hartford Convention and contemptuous of the Union. Yet after the White House announced it would, if necessary, meet force with force, first the Senate and then President Adams yielded to the Georgians and allowed them to regain the entirety of the Creek lands and commenced the Creeks' final expulsion. In the first menacing assertion of what came to be known as southern state-rights sectionalism, Adams permitted the nation to surrender to a state.

The ironies of the situation—and for Adams, the political humiliation—deepened over the months to come. Vice President Calhoun, who had seen his "civilizing" Indian policy rejected, hastened his own dramatic shift from nationalism to southern sectionalism, under political pressure from South Carolina's equivalents of the Troup Radicals. Emboldened by their victory, Troup's men, having narrowed the breach between themselves and the backcountry, turned their sights against the Cherokees, hoping to remove them as well. Adams, although now formally as well as personally committed to Indian removal, did not follow up with any practical plan to achieve it, which only hardened the surging Radical South against him.

From a long-term perspective, the debacle offers a glimpse at a political process that would soon dominate southern politics. In Indian removal, Troup and the Georgia planters found a winning issue that, by appealing to land hunger, racial antagonisms, frontier fears, and suspicion of Yankees, undercut the backcountry forces led by John Clark. By then attaching to that issue the slogan of "state rights," and pitting local prerogatives—"the sovereignty of Georgia," Troup proclaimed—against a meddlesome, outsider federal government, the planters consolidated local support. State and sectional loyalty, buttressed by racism and desire for land, supplanted the democratic agitation that had been exacerbated by the Panic of 1819—and raised troubling implications about the nation's future.

One of the planters not at all impressed by Troup's state-rights vehemence was Andrew Jackson. Watching the affair from the Hermitage, still furious at Adams and Clay, Jackson fully approved of Indian removal. On the Georgia matter, however, he thought the president was acting in good faith, if weakly, while Troup and his accomplices were demagogically abetting their personal ambitions. Troup's behavior, he observed in 1825, "has afforded evidence of derangement from some cause." The entire affair, he wrote, was "produced by designing Whitemen" who wanted to distract attention from the fraud used to extract the "fictitious" original Indian Springs treaty from the Creeks. "State rights and military despotism are themes where eloquence can be employed, and the feelings of the nation aroused," he added some months later, but he hoped that "both these themes will slumber for some other occasion." Jackson had no respect for the administration's empty threats—nobody was silly enough, he wrote, to believe that men like Adams and Clay "who so oft have denounced mil[itary] chieftains" would "raise the sword against a sover[e]ign State"—but his contempt for the administration did not change his mind about the limits of state sovereignty. In due course, he himself would battle against even more extreme versions of the themes he wished would slumber, as developed by the transformed ex-nationalist, John C. Calhoun.

More immediately, the developments in Georgia dramatized the dangerous drift of the administration's policy. Had Adams summoned the nerve to call Troup's bluff and send troops to Georgia, it is likely that the other southern states (save, perhaps, South Carolina) would have supported or at least acquiesced in federal action. Instead, Troup's triumph encouraged Alabama and Mississippi to adopt extreme state-rights positions regarding Indian tribes within their own borders, and set the stage for new and even more worrisome collisions between the federal government and the states over the tariff of 1824. Adams, who displayed little enough concern for the Indians, bears responsibility for allowing the southern bullies to have their way.

Adams's weakness must be understood not as a personal failing—in politics, he was normally anything but weak—but in the context of his deteriorating political situation. He well might have called up troops to force Troup to back down, but would have thereby risked the outbreak of a bloody civil conflict. And he would have done so in the teeth of intense opposition from within his own cabinet, above all from Henry Clay, as well as from the Senate, where one committee advised him to complete the Creeks' relinquishment of Georgia land. Trapped, Adams bowed to political circumstances, which only made those circumstances grimmer.

The consequences of Adams's political slide would not become fully apparent until the final year of his presidency. Until then, events in Washington—and, indeed, conventional political events—receded in importance. As Adams failed to revive national harmony, popular movements redirected public loyalties and unleashed fresh ideas and programs. Many of these movements emerged from outside electoral politics, but they would all have dramatic political effects on both the theory and the practice of American democracy. The most profound of them involved the greatest explosion of evangelical religious fervor yet in the nation's history.

RAPTURES OF JOY AND DEVOTION: PIETY, POLITICS, AND THE SECOND GREAT AWAKENING

In 1771, when the Regulator country democrats of North Carolina squared off against the royal governor William Tryon, a

backwoods Prebysterian minister, David Caldwell, tried unsuccessfully to mediate between his plebeian flock and the imperial
British government. Caldwell became an active patriot in 1776
and, after independence, a leading participant in North Carolina
politics. He left legacies in both politics and religious life. His
grandson, John Caldwell Calhoun, would become one of the
leading American nationalists—and then the leading southern
sectionalist—of his day. And at the turn of the nineteenth century, several young ministers whom Caldwell had helped train
headed west to sanctify the newly settled farmers and planters of
Kentucky.

Among the most successful of Caldwell's students was a tall,
awkward Pennsylvania-born minister of Scots-Irish extraction,
James McGready. What McGready lacked in elegance he made
up for with eloquence and homiletic fervor. In 1797 (and thereafter for three years running) his sermonizing sparked a remarkable excitement and religious revival in the still-raw settlements
of Logan County, in southwestern Kentucky near the Tennessee
border. Then, in August 1801, in a clutch of cabins called Cane
Ridge in Bourbon County near Lexington, another of David
Caldwell's pupils, Barton Stone, hosted an ecumenical three-day
communion service that turned into a week-long explosion of
ecstatic devotion, involving more than twenty preachers (Presbyterian and Methodist, white and black) and upwards of twenty
thousand worshippers. The roar of raucous piety at Cane Ridge
sounded like Niagara: "Sinners dropping down on every hand,"
one participating minister wrote, "shrieking, groaning, crying for
mercy, convoluted; professors [of religion] praying, agonizing,
fainting, falling down in distress, for sinners, or in raptures of
joy!"

One year after Cane Ridge, hundreds of miles away in New
Haven, Connecticut, a more sedate but still remarkable revival of
religion gripped the undergraduates of Yale College. In 1795,
Timothy Dwight, grandson of the great New England evangelist
Jonathan Edwards, had ascended to the presidency of Yale in
place of Thomas Jefferson's friend Ezra Stiles, hoping to rid the

place of its reputation for irreligion and pro-French radical politics. Dwight's stern hand did not work immediate wonders—in 1800, there was only one church member in the college's graduating class—but in 1802, a revival hit the campus. "Wheresoever students were found," remarked one participant, the future minister Noah Porter, "in their rooms, in the chapel, in the hall, in the college-yard, in their walks about the city—the reigning impression was, 'surely God is in this place!' The salvation of the soul was the greatest subject of conversation, of absorbing interest."

Fifteen more revivals would break out at Yale over the next forty years. Under Dwight's spur, Yale became the intellectual seedbed of the so-called New Haven Theology, formulated by Dwight's student, professor of theology Nathaniel W. Taylor, which recast and energized received Calvinist doctrine. And although "Pope" Dwight could not save the Connecticut Standing Order (which finally collapsed one year after his death in 1817), his students, above all the great organizing cleric Lyman Beecher, spread revised versions of the New Haven revival out into the rest of New England, and then into upstate New York, Ohio, and points west—wherever New Englanders and their children settled in large numbers.

The concurrent events at Cane Ridge and Yale were in no way the result of a coordinated effort. Their differences—in denominational origins, liturgy, and social setting—outweighed their similarities. Likewise, the so-called Second Great Awakening—of which these revivals were harbingers, and which would last into the 1840s—was a diverse movement, generated by impulses too unruly and doctrines too contradictory to be contained by any one organization. It was a movement that, at its outermost edges, saw farmers and factory workers talk directly with Jesus Christ, angels appear in remote villages bearing wholly new dispensations and commandments from the Lord, and women of all ages and backgrounds commune with the spirits of the dead. Closer to its core, the Awakening saw rival denominations (especially Methodists and Baptists) denounce each others' beliefs and practices nearly as much as they denounced sin and Satan.

A few recurring and overriding themes are detectable through the furor. First, the sheer scale of religious conversions was astounding, in every part of the nation. Although the figures are sketchy, it appears that as few as one in ten Americans were active church members in the unsettled aftermath of the American Revolution. The evangelizing that ensued proceeded, at first, in fits and starts, but gathered tremendous momentum after 1825. By the 1840s, the preponderance of Americans—as many as eight in ten—were churched, chiefly as evangelizing Methodists or Baptists (in the South) or as so-called New School revivalist Presbyterians or Congregationalists (in the North). What was, in 1787, a nation of nominal Christians—its public culture shaped more by Enlightenment rationalism than Protestant piety—had turned, by the mid-1840s, into the most devoted evangelical Protestant nation on earth.

Second, although it is better understood as a movement of the heart and the spirit than of the mind, the Awakening asserted a hopeful, crisis-driven, post-Calvinist theology. The awakeners' devotions contrasted sharply both with the hyper-Calvinism of the Edwardseans and the Old School Presbyterians (with their strict belief in predestination and God's inscrutable will) and with the laxity about salvation promoted by well-heeled Unitarians and more plebeian Universalists. The degree of departure from Calvinist orthodoxy varied: whereas the Methodists and New School churches largely abandoned the central Calvinist doctrines of election and predestination, the Baptists, at least formally, retained them. (Some Baptists, objecting to what they perceived as even the slightest backsliding, formed their own more fiercely traditional Calvinist connections.) But in all of the largest denominations, there was a fresh emphasis placed on individual rejection of personal sin and on the struggle to attain God's merciful grace, through His Son, the Redeemer Jesus Christ—an intense process that culminated in a wrenching moment of spiritual rebirth.

Emotional display reached a deafening intensity in the camp-meeting style that prevailed in the South. Drawing heavily on the "new measures" of the Wesleyan Methodists, the camp-meeting phenomenon shattered the unity of the largely Presbyterian clerisy of the southern and southwestern backcountry, prompting some church leaders to back off in disapproval and others (including the Cane Ridge preacher, Barton Stone) to reject their own Calvinist orthodoxy. The communal camp-meeting uproars (commonly attended, on their outskirts, by scoffers, drinkers, and prostitutes, drawn by the mere presence of a throng) in turn solidified the believers' faith that they truly had gained redemption and a holy discipline that set them apart from the rest of the world (not least from the sinners at the edges of the crowd). For the preachers, meanwhile, the camp meetings' aftermath helped institutionalize the revival, binding the fresh harvests of souls into local congregations that could be linked to other congregations, within regular, regionally organized denominations.

Socially and spiritually, the southern revivals paradoxically challenged and confirmed existing structures of authority. In contrast to the Episcopal and old-line Presbyterian connections, and the smaller but influential deistic currents among the enlightened gentry, the revivals bred a devotional upsurge from the lower and middle strata of southern life that can only be described as democratic. In place of refined, highly trained ministers, young Methodist circuit riders and unschooled Baptist farmer-preachers became cynosures of religious life, preaching a gospel of holiness open to the most degraded and forlorn of God's children. Simplicity and directness in all things were signs of grace, in contrast to ornament and artifice. Among the truest believers, restraint in all but love of Christ was the only way to escape hellfire. "Therefore avoid the allurements of Voluptuousness," one self-reproving Methodist preacher wrote in his diary, "and fly every temptation that leads to her banquet as you would the devil himself."

Most unsettling of all, in the southern revival's opening stages, was the announced indifference of some evangelicals to race and their outright hostility to slavery. Methodist circuit riders were particularly aggressive in seeking out black converts, slave and free. In the 1780s, conferences of Methodists and Baptists condemned slaveholding as, in the words of one Methodist assembly, "contrary to the laws of God, man, and nature, and hurtful to society, contrary to the dictates of conscience and pure religion." (In 1784, the Methodists actually moved to excommunicate slaveholders, although they quickly retreated into less coercive methods of moral suasion.) At least one black minister preached to a separate throng of blacks at the Cane Ridge meeting in 1801. In the first wave of conversions, African Americans accounted for as much as one-third to one-quarter of the membership in individual evangelical churches. And into the 1820s, evangelical egalitarianism among whites helped make the mountainous areas of the upper southern states, notably Tennessee, home to the largest number of antislavery societies in the nation.

By 1830, however, the more egalitarian and antislavery implications of the southern revivals had adapted to the resurgent slaveholders' regime. Middling evangelical farmers who cashed in on the cotton boom and became small slaveholders had little use for imprecations against African bondage. Established planters mostly ignored antislavery preaching with a cold contempt—although, from time to time, they took firmer action, as in Charleston where, in 1800, authorities publicly burned Methodist antislavery pamphlets. In 1816, the Methodists formally gave up on trying to end slaveholding, while still pronouncing it "contrary to the principles of moral justice." Over the next thirty years, southern evangelicalism, among whites, transformed itself into a doctrine of Christian mastery, no longer troubled by human bondage but providing slaveholders with a set of religious and moral imperatives to treat the slaves, as they would all subordinates, on the highest moral level, in accord with scriptural injunctions. While instilling order and benevolence, the churches also reinforced the slaveholders' claims to supremacy. "We who own slaves," the well-known South Carolina Baptist clergyman James C. Furman wrote to a master suspected of wrongdoing, "honor God's law in the exercise of our authority."

More broadly, the southern evangelicals' spiritual egalitarianism centered increasingly on inculcating personal holiness to the exclusion of all else—an ethos of individual sanctification that precluded wider secular campaigns or benevolent reform. Older social distinctions between elite nonevangelicals and plebeian evangelicals blurred, as successful Methodists and Baptists began striving for their own sort of refinement, signaled by the building of several denominational academies and colleges, like the Virginia Baptist Education Society of Richmond, all across the region. Simultaneously, the color line grew darker, creating a southern revivalist piety that, among whites, fully accommodated itself to the slaveholders' regime. Slaveholders did spearhead the spread of Christian devotion in rural areas, especially in the 1830s and 1840s, but did so with an eye to provide their property with the kind of moral uplift that would make them better slaves (and make the masters better Christian stewards). Black evangelical churches, with their own preachers and proselytizers, held their own services, most conspicuously in seaboard cities like Charleston with large free black populations. But these segregated houses of worship came under close scrutiny from officials as possible breeding grounds of sedition—scrutiny that intensified following Charleston's allegedly church-based Denmark Vesey affair in 1822. Among the slaves as well as free blacks, despite their masters' intentions and surveillance, Christianity became what they made it, a source of communal solidarity, pride, and endurance, with a millennial edge of impending liberation. But among whites, slaveholder and nonslaveholders, the Second Great Awakening became a pillar of the reborn slaveholding order.

The northern awakening involved dramatic adaptations by the declining patrician Yankee establishment. Pressured on one side by the passing popularity of anticlerical "Jacobin" skeptics and, even more, by dissenting evangelicals and liberalizing Unitarians who opposed their political privileges, the old-line Calvinist clergy had embraced Federalism with unsurpassed fervor. The election of the deist and secularist Jefferson in 1801 and the rise of a viable northern Republican party further sapped the clerics' dominance. But Timothy Dwight's reclamation of Yale from the infidels energized the orthodox by borrowing the evangelicals' voluntarist organizing methods—above all, the formation of the Moral Society to effect and enforce what one of his acolytes called a "reformation" among students and faculty. When Dwight's student Nathaniel Taylor loosened Calvinist doctrine and argued that salvation was a matter of individual regeneration as well as God's will, fresh opportunities opened to expand the flock of the faithful. Looking back, Taylor's accomplice, Lyman Beecher, would even call the Connecticut Standing Order's destruction in 1818, paradoxically, "*the best thing that ever happened*," because it forced the more complacent congregations to evangelize. "By voluntary efforts, societies, missions, and revivals," Beecher observed, "[ministers] exert a deeper influence than ever they could by queues and shoe buckles, and cocked hats and gold-headed canes."

Beecher was the most vigorous and ambitious of the Yankee missionaries. Born and raised in New Haven, well outside the local patriciate—both his father and his grandfather were blacksmiths—Beecher was an eminently practical and blunt man of God, more a polemicist and organizer than a theologian. Ordained a Presbyterian minister in 1799, he took up his first ministry in East Hampton, Long Island, where he gained notice in 1804 for a sermon, following Alexander Hamilton and Aaron Burr's fatal interview, that denounced dueling and its sinful code of "honor." In 1810, he moved to Litchfield, Connecticut, and burnished his reputation with Dwight-inspired sermons on the gloomy state of the nation's soul. Everywhere, Beecher charged, "[t]he name of God is blasphemed; the bible is denounced; the Sabbath is profaned; the worship of God is neglected; intemperance hath destroyed its thousands . . . while luxury, with its diversified evils, with a rapidity unparalleled, is spreading in every direction, and through every class."

Beecher's solution was to encourage circuit-riding ministers to spark revivals and establish local lay moral reform groups. In 1813, Beecher organized the Connecticut Society for the Promotion of Good Morals, which quickly boasted dozens of branches and several thousand members. Three years later, he helped launch the Domestic Missionary Society for Connecticut and Vicinity, sending young reformist Congregational and "New Side" Presbyterian ministers to convert the soaring numbers of Yankee migrants in upstate New York and northern New England. At about the same time, like-minded churchmen opened a branch of the New England Tract Society. By 1817, Beecher and his allies had established a mass-circulation religious magazine and, in Hartford, a charitable school for the deaf and dumb, the first of its kind in the country. Quicker than many of his colleagues, Beecher came to understand how the successful voluntarist innovations of the revivals had rendered formal state support unnecessary. "[T]ruly," he wrote, "we do not stand on the confines of destruction. The mass is changing. We are becoming another people."

Methodist circuit riders and Baptist exhorters also crisscrossed the North with growing success, but it was the allied front of evangelized Presbyterians and Congregationalists, the so-called Presbygationals, who left the strongest spiritual, cultural, and, in time, political mark in the northern states. The Presbygationals' influence redoubled in the 1820s when, backed by pious businessmen in the seaboard cities, they confederated various state and local efforts to form the American Sunday-School Union (claiming fifty thousand students), the American Tract Society, the American Home Missionary Society, and the American Society for the Promotion of Temperance (a special interest of Lyman Beecher's). And by the latter years of John Quincy Adams's presidency, Presbygationals were contemplating political efforts to shape public morality. Like their southern counterparts, Yankee evangelicals eschewed parties and formal electoral politics as profane and divisive. Yet far more than most southerners, the northerners believed that proper moral stewardship demanded direct participation in secular affairs, including the promotion of what the Philadelphia pastor Ezra Stiles Ely described in 1827, a bit rashly and vaguely, as a "Christian party in politics."

The first notable evangelical political campaign focused on ending desecration of the Sabbath. Despite local ordinances enforcing the restriction of commerce on Sundays, Sabbath breaking had increased across the country during the early years of the nineteenth century. Most egregiously, in the eyes of the pious, the Jeffersonian Congress, in 1810, had passed a postal regulation requiring postmasters to conduct business on Sunday whenever mail arrived on that day. Already perturbed by the Jeffersonians' adamant hostility to any merging of church and state, evangelicals saw the Sunday postal law as an assault, both real and symbolic, on proper Christian order. By compelling Sunday mail operations, the government not only forced thousands of postal workers to violate the Sabbath, but also invited townsmen and farmers from surrounding districts to defile the Lord's Day, which in turn invited local businessmen to do the same and encouraged local officials to ignore Sunday closing laws. That so many local postmasters (political appointees all) were also petty merchants and "greengrocers"—meaning that they sold liquor— only worsened the blasphemous rowdiness. Reestablishing the Sabbath was as "necessary to the health of the state," one evangelical observed, as enforcing "laws against murder and polygamy."

Sabbatarian efforts gained little notice until Lyman Beecher and his friends formed the General Union for Promoting the Observance of the Christian Sabbath in May 1828. Thanks to the financial backing of numerous, newly successful businessmen-converts with Yankee backgrounds—above all the flour merchant Josiah Bissell of Rochester, New York, and the silk merchant Lewis Tappan of Manhattan—the Union deployed all of the organizing and proselytizing techniques familiar to the northern revivalists, including tract distribution, public rallies, and prayer concerts. Bissell supplied the money to back a six-day, blue-law stagecoach service. A similar Sabbatarian boat line was established to travel (liquor-free) along the Erie Canal from Albany to Buffalo, but never on Sundays. Along with Tappan, Bissell toured the friendly Presbygational churches of the Northeast to drum up support for the cause. Over the summer and autumn of 1828, while most of the political nation was embroiled in a presidential campaign, the Sabbatarian machine promoted a national petition campaign directed at Congress. By year's end, Bissell was predicting imminent triumph, telling Tappan that the "petitions were flowing in well," and actually welcoming displays of anti-Sabbatarian opinion in the West as "just enough . . . to give a zest to the Sabbath measures."

With their new emphasis on inner sanctification, moral choice, and benevolent stewardship, the proponents of what came to be known as the New School transformed a staid New England Protestant devotionalism into a vital evangelizing creed, distinct from rationalist Unitarians and traditional Calvinists and from southern camp-meeting Methodists and Baptists. Agitation in turn created the institutional basis of what would become an entirely new kind of political power, democratic in tone and sophisticated in its organizational tactics, but very different from the main forms of democratic politics that had emerged since the Revolution. The full meaning of those efforts would only become clear when new coalitions in secular politics displaced the disarray of the 1820s. And those new political alignments would be shaped by yet another enthusiasm that arose from the Yankee areas of western New York during John Quincy Adams's presidency—one that began with an abduction and a rotting corpse.

ANTI-MASONRY AND "A SECOND INDEPENDENCE"

On October 7, 1827, in the settlement of Lewiston, a drowned man's body washed up at Oak Orchard Creek, where the creek joins Lake Ontario. Although the body was badly decomposed, many people in the neighborhood were certain that it had been one William Morgan, who had disappeared more than a year earlier after being snatched from the Canandaigua town jail. Morgan's widow came out to Lewiston and confirmed that the putrid mass looked like her vanished husband; Morgan's dentist inspected the corpse's teeth and affirmed the identity; and the body was duly buried with grand obsequies in Morgan's adopted hometown, Batavia. Others were not so sure. After several disinterments, and amid charges that certain interested parties had tampered with the body to make it look more like Morgan, the local coroner officially ruled that the dead man could not be named. But by then, the mysterious corpse had become a cause célèbre, deepening the popular outrage against Morgan's kidnappers—the members, allegedly, of a vast murder and cover-up conspiracy involving the Order of Ancient Free and Accepted Masons.

Morgan had been a perfect nobody until a few weeks before his disappearance. A native of Virginia, he had wandered around upstate New York as an itinerant bricklayer and stonemason. Upon settling in Leroy, New York, outside Rochester, he claimed membership in the Masonic Order, and his new neighbors admitted him to the local lodge. At some point in the early 1820s, however, Morgan relocated to nearby Batavia and was denied Masonic membership there by a lodge that took a dim view of his dubious social standing and inability to land a job. Enraged—and, quite possibly, seeing an opportunity to make some easy money—Morgan enlisted the aid of a Batavia printer, David Miller, and published a purported full-scale exposé of the lower-degree Masonic rituals and lore. Morgan's tract circulated widely around the country. Incensed loyal Masons tried to burn down Miller's printshop and harassed both Miller and Morgan with petty legal charges. Morgan was twice remanded to the Canandaigua jail, the second time for an alleged unpaid debt, but suddenly was released to two men who paid his debt, shunted him into a waiting carriage, and carted him off westward to Fort Niagara—where he disappeared forever.

Within a month of Morgan's disappearance, western New York State was awash in broadsides and newspaper articles describing the events, which touched off a wave of protest meetings. Governor DeWitt Clinton, himself a Mason, offered a reward for apprehending the kidnappers. Grand juries in five counties investigated suspect Masons, including the sheriff in Canandaigua, who was convicted for complicity in Morgan's disappearance. But most of the accused and the suspected escaped punishment, either by fleeing the state or by finding the charges against them summarily dropped by judges and juries believed to be dominated by Masons. At many of the trials that did take place—legal proceedings continued for four years after Morgan's disappearance—Masonic witnesses refused to testify, placing their obligations to the secret fraternity above those to society. The Masonic lodges, meanwhile, insisted on the Order's innocence and took no disciplinary actions whatsoever. Some Masons tried to blame Morgan for his own misfortunes because he had broken his oath of secrecy about Masonic rituals; a few even charged that Morgan had collaborated in his own kidnapping, to enlarge his notoriety and sell more pamphlets. The Mason's ripostes only deepened suspicions that Morgan had been murdered, and that the Order was conspiring to protect the evildoers. The appearance of the corpse in Oak Orchard Creek came as belated but positive proof to the growing Anti-Masonic movement that they had been correct all along. If not the murdered man himself, one leader of the agitation said, the body was "a good enough Morgan," unless and until he turned up alive.

The continuing intrigues of New York politics turned the affair into a major political event. Following the disputed presidential election of 1824–25, Martin Van Buren had switched his national allegiance to the cheated Andrew Jackson, and by the summer of 1827, Van Buren was cultivating a pro-Jackson alliance with his old enemy, Governor Clinton. But both Jackson and Clinton were high-degree Masons, and Jackson was a slaveholder to boot, which offended transplanted Yankees in the strongest Anti-Masonic districts—all of which caught the notice of Van Buren's political opponents. With Van Buren's allies shouting about phony issues, so-called Anti-Masons nominated candidates in the 1827 legislative elections who pledged to uproot the secret order's malevolent influence. The Oak Orchard corpse controversy was still raging when New Yorkers went to the polls and elected fifteen Anti-Masons from several western counties to the state assembly. A strange and unpredictable political movement had been born—one that would soon be afoot from Pennsylvania to Maine, and particularly in New England and areas, like western New York, settled heavily by migrants from New England.

The rise of Anti-Masonry has often been linked, at times facilely, to a species of extremist lower-class paranoia supposedly peculiar to American democracy. The Anti-Masons' claims that a gigantic conspiracy had seized control of the nation's institutions were, to be sure, overwrought and ripe for political manipulation. But fears of all-powerful conspiratorial secret societies—including, prominently, the Freemasons—were rife throughout the revolutionized Atlantic world at the end of the eighteenth and beginning of the nineteenth century. Those fears cut across class lines: prior to the Anti-Masonic outbursts of the 1820s, the greatest American conspiracy theory had come not from the easily deluded unwashed but from the highly educated New England Federalist clergy, who blamed both the French Revolution and the appearance of the Jeffersonian opposition on secret cabals, including the European-based, so-called Bavarian Illuminati. The Anti-Masons' thinking was perfectly in keeping with the broader American republican outlook, inherited from the Revolutionary era, which blamed social disorder on political corruption by select and malign factions or cabals. There was, moreover, justified outrage at the New York lodges' efforts to suppress Morgan's publication and reasonable suspicion that some sort of cover-up had taken place. The Masons' refusal to cooperate with public authorities threw fuel on the fire. That so many of the judges and other authorities were themselves Masons made Anti-Masonry an intelligible response to events.

The Morgan excitement fed long-growing popular resentments originating in the rapid commercialization of the northeastern states. The Masonic Order had enjoyed a long history in America when the outburst against it began. Especially popular in New England, Freemasonry flourished among upper- and middling-class men throughout the early republic, counting within its fraternity such patriots as George Washington, Benjamin Franklin, and at least eleven other Framers of the Constitution. Dedicated to spreading their own blend of latitudinarian Christian virtue and crypto-Enlightenment reason, Masons performed a panoply of ceremonial rituals and symbols, including the wearing of their famous white aprons, which offered members an elaborate, esoteric nondenominational aesthetic absent in most Protestant churches—and that was open to men of lukewarm religious devotion. The public appearance of the Masonic lodges in full regalia at civic events gave the Order an air of importance. The intense secrecy that shrouded other lodge rituals from view made Freemasonry all the more charismatic and high-minded among its brotherhood. "[E]very character, figure, and emblem, depicted in a lodge," Thomas Smith Webb, the early-nineteenth-century Masonic organizer, wrote in 1821, "has a moral tendency, and inculcates the practice of virtue."

Freemasonry's looming crisis was rooted in its success, as well as in its worldly, meritocratic ethos. At the end of the eighteenth century, the lodges had a distinctly Federalist air about them, a by-product partly of Freemasonry's popularity in New England. After 1800, however, increasing numbers of Jeffersonian and Republican partisans and officeholders gained admission to the Order—including, in New York, not a few of Van Buren's Bucktails—in keeping with Freemasonry's openness to successful men of influence and virtue, regardless of social background, religious affiliation, or political connections. The Order also grew phenomenally, especially in the middle Atlantic states, where the number of lodges rose from 327 to 525 over the decade from 1810 to 1820. In the developing cities and towns along the widening thoroughfares of northern commerce, above all the Erie Canal, young men of the commercial and professional classes, separated from their kin back East, gained from the lodges fraternal connections and an instant badge of social distinction and acceptance. These, in turn, bred a mixture of power, exclusiveness, and self-satisfaction that, to outsiders, could look like arrogance—the kind of arrogance that, as in the Morgan case, set itself above the law. "In the foundation of every public building we have beheld the interference of these mystic artisans with their symbolic insignia," one Anti-Mason complained, "in every public procession, we have seen their flaunting banners, their muslin robes, and mimic crowns." The Masons replied that they were, indeed, a special set of men, the natural leaders of the community.

The Morgan case ripped away that perceived complacency and exposed rising moral and political anxieties about Freemasonry's proliferation—and about how the Masons, with their unfair advantages, had established what amounted to a hidden unelected government, run by and for themselves, that could manipulate the government elected by the people. With men of power in their secret ranks, one Anti-Masonic article explained, the Masons could rule wherever and whenever they liked: "in the desk—in the legislative hall—on the bench—in every gathering of business—in every party of pleasure—in every enterprise of government—in every domestic circle—in peace and in war— among enemies and friends—in one place as well as another." To older, Federalist-oriented elites, Freemasonry seemed to have fallen into the hands of aggressive upstarts who, although successful in business, lacked the proper education and breeding required of civic leaders. To poorer, less-connected farmers and rural shopkeepers, the Masons looked like an incipient self-created nobility, based on mysterious principles known only to the favored few. What, they wanted to know, was going on behind the thick barred doors of those Masonic temples? What private business arrangements were being hatched; what political deals were being cut? Even worse: What debauched revelries did the Masons indulge in once freed from the obligations of the hearthside and the restraints of public scrutiny?

As the lurid speculation mounted amid the Morgan affair, propagandists and opportunists threatened to commandeer the Anti-Masonic movement. To compete with local newspaper editors—who included a substantial number of Masons and kept the excitement out of their columns—an Anti-Masonic "free press" appeared in every county of western New York. Former Masons organized mock lodges and performed the Order's secret rituals in public view. Hair-raising accusations and confessions, along with suspect solicitations on behalf of William Morgan's bereft widow, began circulating in cheap pamphlet form much like the religious tracts of the revivalists. Yet the men who made the most of the Anti-Masonic excitement were not profiteers but capable pro-Adams politicians with genuine Anti-Masonic allegiances. Their leader was the Rochester editor and printer, Thurlow Weed.

Born in 1797, in a log cabin near the town of Catskill, New York, Edward Thurlow Weed was a thoroughly self-made man. Raised in an economically marginal and peripatetic household, he had entered the printer's trade as a thirteen-year-old apprentice in Onondaga in central New York (whence his father, Joel, chronically in debt, had moved the family two years earlier). As a tramp journeyman printer, he held jobs in various localities from Cooperstown to Albany, joined an early trade union, the New York Typographical Society, eventually married, and acquired a little weekly newspaper of his own, which he called *The Republican Agriculturalist*, in the Chenango County town of Norwich. Weed made his name, though, farther west in Rochester, where, after selling the *Agriculturalist* in 1820, he became junior editor of the anti–Van Buren *Evening Telegraph*. A supporter of DeWitt Clinton and of the Erie Canal project that promised to make Rochester a boomtown, Weed coarsely lit into the Bucktails as a corrupt cabal of wire-pullers interested only in exploiting the spoils of office. ("Van Buren's pimps," he called them at one point.) In 1823, Weed was one of the local leaders of the Clintonian People's Party, and the following year (while supporting John Quincy Adams for the presidency and after lobbying with state legislators in Albany on behalf of local banking interests), he was elected state assemblyman on the People's Party ticket. A tall, darkly handsome young man, Weed cut an impressive figure in Albany, but he remained financially strapped. When his old *Telegraph* boss put the paper up for sale, though, he obtained a twenty-five-hundred-dollar loan from a wealthy Clintonite friend, snapped up part-ownership of the paper, energetically increased its paid advertising base, and, in September 1826—the month that William Morgan disappeared—shifted it from a weekly to a semiweekly publication schedule.

Like most of his anti-Bucktail neighbors, many of whom were Masons or familiar with members of the Order, Weed initially regarded the tumult over the Morgan affair skeptically. (Morgan had approached Weed about publishing his exposé, but Weed wanted nothing to do with it.) After visiting Lewiston early in 1827, however, Weed became persuaded that Morgan had been murdered, and he joined with those calling on the Masons to denounce the crime and help identify the perpetrators. The lodges' silence pushed him over the line. By the start of the autumn election campaign, Weed had allied himself with the Anti-Masonic crusade, even though, as a consequence, subscriptions to the *Telegraph* dropped sharply.

The Anti-Masons' surprisingly strong showing in the 1827 elections vindicated Weed's political shrewdness as well as his sense of outrage. In purely political terms, Anti-Masonry not only inflamed public sensibilities; it offered a wonderful solution to what had become several serious difficulties for the anti-Bucktail partisans. To their chagrin, DeWitt Clinton, hoping to improve his own future, had recommitted himself to Andrew Jackson's presidential candidacy, in alliance with Martin Van Buren. The Adams administration and its supporters, now known as National Republicans, already tainted by the alleged corrupt bargain, showed a singular ineptness in handling local patronage and seemed, on their own, a weak alternative to the Van Burenites. With the Erie Canal completed, there was a dearth of issues with which to inflame local anti-Bucktail voters. Suddenly, an independent popular movement arose, pledged to the protection of republican liberty against corrupt insiders—a movement, based in heavily Yankee western counties, that appealed, for different reasons, to evangelicals, temperance men, and ordinary farmers put off by eastern elitists and their smug imitators. Organized in politics, under Weed's careful hand, the Anti-Masons of 1827 preached democracy against the entrenched self-styled democrats, Van Buren's Bucktails, much as Clinton's People's Party had three years earlier.

After the 1827 elections, Weed traveled to Washington, where he opened negotiations to complete a quiet formal alliance between the administration and the politicized Anti-Masons. Upon his return to Rochester early in 1828, he did what he had done best, establishing a new paper, *The Anti-Masonic Enquirer*, while helping to found, with his Clintonian, anti-Bucktail friends, a formal Anti-Masonic party. The day before the *Enquirer's* first issue appeared, DeWitt Clinton suddenly died, clearing the way for a thorough reorganization of Clintonian voters under new leadership. Through the *Enquirer*, Weed became one of those leaders, as he stoked the fires of Anti-Masonry by ridiculing Masonic pretensions—holding off, for the moment, from backing Adams for reelection, but with every intention of doing so once the presidential campaign began in earnest later that year.

While Weed plotted, a passing acquaintance of his, William Henry Seward, was following a similar political course, attempting to ally the National Republicans and the Anti-Masons. Seward had first encountered the editor by chance in Rochester three years earlier, when, on an excursion to Niagara Falls, his wagon got mired in a patch of mud and Weed came to his assistance. The two men were strikingly different: Weed, the poor man's son, well over six feet tall, hard-bitten and calculating; Seward, a Phi Beta Kappa college graduate and lawyer, the son of an affluent Republican officeholder, red-haired, slight, and with a penchant for idealism. Their common interests were political. Seward, although raised in a Bucktail household, had broken ranks, along with his father, in 1824, persuaded that Van Buren and his allies had, as he wrote a friend, "sunk into cunning and chicanery." John Quincy Adams was far more to his liking, a man hobbled by what Seward described as "pedantry," but a champion of the moral, educational, and economic improvements that Seward thought essential to local and national development.

When Anti-Masonry spread to Seward's home in Auburn over the winter of 1827–28, Seward formally remained a National Republican, but also quietly helped draft Anti-Masonic speeches and proclamations. The Anti-Masons of Cayuga, after agreeing to form a coalition ticket with the Adams men, then nominated Seward for Congress without first notifying him. The nomination offended National Republicans, who thought Seward had become too clever by half; Seward, embarrassed, withdrew from the race, which ensured the election of the Bucktail candidate. Thereafter, convinced that National Republicanism was dead in the water, Seward threw himself into political Anti-Masonry, proclaiming it the true cause of the common man—all of which led him to renew and deepen his connection to the man who had helped pull him out of the Rochester mud years earlier.

Grafting Anti-Masonry to National Republicanism, as Weed and Seward were attempting to do as early as 1828, would require major political and ideological adjustments. The grassroots outrage and vulgar appeals of the Anti-Masons offended National Republican worthies, who preferred that government be left to gentlemen of education and virtue. The demonization of Freemasonry had no appeal at all for those self-made allies of the administration who had joined the Order on their way up the social ladder—most conspicuously Grand Master Mason Henry Clay. What one Adamsite called "this demon of Antimasonry" expressed a distrust of conniving politicians that in time would lead Anti-Masons to condemn Adamsites as well as Van Burenites. National Republicans, meanwhile, took numerous positions, above all supporting internal improvements, which, although popular in Anti-Masonry's western New York strongholds, had nothing to do with the Anti-Masons' one great cause. Still, in its raw, conspiracy-obsessed form, Anti-Masonry made fresh problems for Martin Van Buren and the anti-Adams Republicans. Picking up where the Clintonian People's Party had left off, but without the imperious DeWitt Clinton, the Anti-Masons revived the antiaristocratic animus that had stunned the Bucktails in 1823, especially in western New York, and invested it with greater authenticity and passion. The transition from the ranks of the people's men to Anti-Masonry was a smooth one for Yankee farmers—and for rising politicians like Thurlow Weed—who were thoroughly convinced that the Masonic Order threatened the rule of law.

More broadly, in terms fitted to the rapidly commercializing Northeast, Anti-Masonry revamped moralistic and egalitarian themes that had once been the mainstays of the old country democracy. Exactly fifty years after America had declared its independence of the British monarchy—a coincidence lost on nobody—new forms of privilege and exclusiveness now seemed to threaten the land. Insidiously, that threat had wormed its way into the very heart of the commercializing countryside, proclaiming its ethical and intellectual superiority, all the while plotting secret power grabs and protecting kidnappers and murderers. Masonry may once have included such great men as Washington and Franklin, but that legacy had been corrupted by a new class of power-hungry, virtueless men—a brotherhood of sharpsters sworn to aid each other, in business and politics, to the exclusion of the democratic majority. The fate of the republic hung in the balance, emboldening Anti-Masons to fight for what they called "a *Second Independence*," to "hand down to posterity unimpaired the republic we inherited from our forefathers."

MORALITY, DEMOCRACY, AND THE POLITICS OF IMPROVEMENT

At a glance, the evangelical revivals and the Anti-Masonic movement shared little, intellectually or spiritually, with each other, or with the rationalist sacred elevation proclaimed by President John Quincy Adams. Both the evangelicals and the Anti-Masons had a rougher, more democratic edge than the patrician Adams. Both deployed the kinds of direct emotional appeals that Adams found coarse. Neither particularly prized the bookish life of the mind or the men who pursued it. Some prominent evangelicals, notably the outspoken Philadelphian Ezra Stiles Ely, regarded Adams as a poor Christian or, even worse, a deist in disguise. And, although they railed against the Masons for their immorality and expressed sympathy for Sabbatarianism and other evangelical causes, Anti-Mason leaders like Thurlow Weed could not have cared less about saving anybody's soul.

Yet even as Adams suffered through his presidency, lines of convergence became visible, at least to political operatives like Weed and Seward. Anti-Masonry appealed, across denominations, to traditional Yankee moral virtue and mistrust of secular slackness, as well as to insistence on equality before the law—and the upright Adams happened not to be a Mason. Directed against the wily partisan Van Buren, and his new favorite, the slaveholding Mason Andrew Jackson, Anti-Masonry had enormous potential for reviving anti-Bucktail politics as a popular democratic movement. Evangelical religion had similar political potential in western New York and the rest of greater New England. With the Yankee revivalist rejection of Calvinist orthodoxy came a new emphasis on individual moral choices and stewardship of the fallen as the source of social as well as individual well-being. Out of the democratized spirituality of the revivals arose a panoply of voluntary efforts to spread the gospel—and to encourage others to live righteously and find Christ's salvation. Although based on religious precepts very different from Adams's—a difference that meant everything to the likes of Reverend Ely—those efforts to encourage self-improvement were in line with the idea of National Republicanism as, in Adams's formulation, a "sacred" cause, dedicated to using government power to uplift the nation in mind and spirit.

Events outside greater New England after 1825 made these potential convergences seem more striking—and, for men like Weed and Seward, made their success all the more imperative. Like the Anti-Masons, urban workingmen, led by the democratic radicals of Philadelphia, continued their agitation, raising issues that neither the Adamsites nor any other Republican faction were prepared to handle. Similar movements gathered strength in portions of the rural South and West, most strikingly in Kentucky. By the late 1820s, these reborn city and country democracies were politically active and vibrant as never before, with ideas very different from those of the Yankee moralizers, Anti-Masons, and National Republicans—and they were looking for a national leader very different from either John Quincy Adams or Henry Clay.

4

THE ARISTOCRACY AND
DEMOCRACY OF AMERICA

Andrew Jackson and his political supporters read President Adams's ambitious first annual message with indignant disbelief. As they saw it, a president whose election lacked democratic legitimacy had brazenly bid the Congress to disregard the will of the electorate, expand its own powers, and legislate on behalf of the favored few at the expense of the many. "When I view the splendor & magnificence of the government" that Adams proposed, Jackson wrote, "together with the declaration that it would be criminal for the agents of our government to be palsied by the will of their constituents, I shudder for the consequence—if not checked by the voice of the people, it must end in consolidation & then in despotism."

Jackson, already looking to a rematch in the 1828 elections, was confident that "the intelligence, and virtue, of the great body of the American people" would defeat Adams's plans. Instead of extravagant programs enlarging the federal government's authority, Jackson proposed that Congress should pay off the national debt and apportion whatever surplus remained to the states for the education of the poor. At such moments, when he stressed retrenchment, Jackson sounded much like his old foe William Crawford and the other state-rights southern Radicals. Although they had some things in common, Jackson's evolving politics were more complex. And although Jackson would welcome, indeed court, the state-rights Radicals, including Crawford, he knew that they provided an insufficient political base for a national victory.

The fragmented results of 1824 had shown clearly that success at the national level required building disparate coalitions that cut across the lines of class and section. To defeat Adams, Jackson needed to find a message that conveyed his thinking above and beyond state rights, and build a winning national combination. He needed, in particular, to expand beyond his connections to William Duane and Steven Simpson and impress city and country democrats who had not backed him in 1824. That would not be simple. Conceptions of American democracy were, as ever, in flux in the late 1820s, appearing in new variations to suit altered social circumstances. And by 1828, democratic movements were forming new minor parties and raising new issues about equality, the Constitution, and economic justice.

THE CITY DEMOCRACY REBORN

The sudden revival of Philadelphia's radical Old School Democracy in 1824, in support of Andrew Jackson, faded once John Quincy Adams became president. Even before Jackson lost in the House, the pro-banking and erstwhile pro-Calhoun New School Democrats had taken over the pro-Jackson movement and reconsolidated their command over Pennsylvania's political machinery. With William Duane's *Aurora* defunct, Michael Leib dead, and their supporters virtually locked out of office and influence, Philadelphia's Old School—and with it, America's city democracy, dating back to the Revolution—seemed to have reached the end of the line. Only three years later, however, early in 1828, it reemerged, transformed, as the Philadelphia Working Men's Party, based in the city's trade unions and dedicated to raising what its chief spokesman, the shoemaker William Heighton, called a new standard in politics, "the banner of equal rights."

Although closely connected to the Duanite democrats, the new party formed along fresh lines, taken in response to economic and social changes long evident in all of the northern cities, especially the major seaports, but that had accelerated after the recovery from the Panic of 1819. Manufacturers and master craftsmen, with widened access to mercantile capital, expanded the subdividing and rearranging of the work process in order to hire cheap, relatively unskilled labor (including women and children) and cut their own costs. Small master craftsmen, clinging to an insecure independence, found their prospects shakier than ever. Skilled journeymen, their job security and incomes threatened, faced becoming, as one of their number put it, "journeymen through life." Craft wage-earners began insisting that, as one printer's group put it, "the interests of the journeymen are separate and in some respects opposite of those of their employers."

Philadelphia, still the nation's leading manufacturing center, was home to the most prominent working-class dissent, from which the Working Men's Party would grow. Journeyman wage-earners in at least a dozen trades formed new societies, joining the eight surviving unions in other crafts. Strikes became increasingly common, numbering no fewer than ten in the year 1821 alone. In 1827, when the city's journeyman carpenters went on strike, demanding a limitation of their workday to ten hours, the other trade societies rallied to their support. After a series of public meetings in the working-class stronghold of Southwark, a new organization arose, the Mechanics' Union of Trade Associations (MUTA)—the first citywide organization of journeymen in America.

Echoing the opening paragraphs of Jefferson's Declaration of Independence, the MUTA turned its support for the carpenters into a broader assertion that "[w]hen the disposition and efforts of one part of mankind to oppress another, have become too manifest to be mistaken and too pernicious in their consequences to be endured," it was right and proper for the oppressed to organize for mutual protection. The membership left no doubt about the cause of their collective misery: "an unequal and very excessive accumulation of wealth and power into the hands of a few." Soon thereafter, the carpenters won their strike; the emboldened MUTA supported the creation of a new working-men's newspaper, the *Mechanics' Free Press*; and early in 1828, the MUTA established the Working Men's Party as its formal political arm. Looking to the autumn elections, the new party pledged to defend the unions and secure various reforms, from expanding public education to restricting bank charters, while electing "men of our own nomination, *whose interests are in unison with ours.*"

Heighton, the foremost organizer of both the MUTA and the Working Men's Party and later editor of the *Mechanics' Free Press*, is a mysterious, meteoric figure. Born around 1800, the son of a poor tradesman in the English Midlands, he emigrated to America with his family about 1812 and settled in Southwark. He appears to have been apprenticed to the shoemakers' trade in his native Northamptonshire town of Oundle, an early industrial shoemaking center; in any event he became a wage-earning shoemaker in Philadelphia, turning out cheap footwear for merchants and middle-man masters in exchange for meager pay. During the five years he led the city's labor movement, Heighton said a great deal about what he was thinking and what he had read, and in the taverns and meeting rooms of Southwark he was something of a celebrity. Yet when he departed Philadelphia sometime in the early 1830s, he virtually vanished. We do not even know what he looked like.

Heighton exemplified the self-taught working-class radical appearing all across the Atlantic world in the opening decades of the nineteenth century. Although his ideas were rooted in the democratic egalitarianism of Thomas Paine and the elder William Duane, Heighton also updated it to fit with the changed social circumstances of the early industrializing world, above all the fracturing of the urban artisan crafts. Borrowing heavily from the writings of other contemporary radical political economists—his favorites included the Englishman John Gray's *Lecture on Human Happiness*—he began with the proposition that the value of all property was based on the labor expended to produce it, the so-called labor theory of value. The theory was so expansive that it could justify the new industrializing order or condemn it. Critics like Gray and, later, Heighton, adopted a strict view of labor as the actual production of goods by human effort, and divided society into what Gray called the exploited "productive many" and the unproductive few, including landlords, moneylenders, merchants ("mere *distributors of wealth*"), and manufacturers. Only by suppressing the unproductive few and abolishing capitalist wage labor—what Gray labeled the "competitive system"—would the deserving many receive their just reward and gain "as much wealth as we have the power of CREATING!!!"

Inspired by Gray, Heighton adapted his radical critique to the social and economic antagonisms of working-class Philadelphia, and in 1827 he began proclaiming his ideas at mass public meetings in Southwark. A "system of competition," he declared, had ground down the mass of the city's producers while enriching a privileged elite. Heighton offered a taxonomy of the nonproducing exploiters, naming six distinct groups—legislative, judicial, theological, commercial, independent, and military—that earned their collective luxuries from the labor of the many. If these parasites were not overthrown, he charged, then the producers' prospects—"as a class," he wrote—would be "a gloomy one of endless toil and helpless poverty." To win what was rightly theirs, Heighton said, workingmen had to educate themselves and establish both libraries and "a POOR MAN'S PRESS," all "appropriated to the interests and enlightenment of the working class and supported by themselves." Duly enlightened, the workers would then have to organize.

The chief difference between Heighton's thinking and his British counterparts' concerned politics. In Britain, where large portions of the urban middle class, let alone workers, were disenfranchised, and where all species of plebeian radicalism had been routinely crushed since the French Revolution, political organizing seemed a hopeless enterprise—and, in any case, an irrelevant one. Reversing the eighteenth-century radical assumptions of Paine and the city democrats, Gray and others claimed that economics, and not politics, was the true matrix of exploitation. Heighton, building on work of the Old School democrats and writing in a country where the franchise for white men was expanding, took the opposite view, in line with ideas about the primacy of politics that Americans generally shared. "Surely we, the working class, who constitute a vast majority of the nation . . . ," he asserted, "have a right to expect an improvement in our *individual condition* will be the natural result of legislative proceedings." Class injustices enforced at law—the entire range of what Heighton called "monopolistic legislation"—could be undone at law as well. With the trade unionists organized into their own political party, Heighton saw nothing "which can materially impede their progress or prevent their success."

Heighton and other workingmen radicals built on other aspects of the Paineite legacy as well, above all in their religious beliefs. Although hardly uniform in its devotions, Philadelphia's old city democracy had always had strong connections with small but lively rationalist currents outside either the city's Quaker meetings or its Anglican or Presbyterian churches— skeptical about the divinity of Christ, dubious about human damnation and the existence of hell, and endlessly inquisitive about the mysteries of creation and nature. At the more radical end of this spectrum, deists (or, as they preferred to call themselves, freethinkers or free enquirers) dispensed with all clergy and upheld the frankly anti-Christian, Enlightenment benevolence elaborated most famously (and, among Christians, notoriously) by Paine's *Age of Reason*. Benjamin Franklin Bache, the elder Duane's mentor and one of the most prominent Philadelphia freethinkers, had, in the 1790s, distributed hundreds of cheap copies of Paine's tract from the *Aurora*'s printing shop, and the Paineite freethinking current persisted into the 1820s.

Slightly more conventional, and more numerous, were the artisans who dominated the congregation at the First Universalist Church on Lombard Street in the heart of Southwark, originally founded by the late ex-Baptist minister Elhanan Winchester in 1781. The Universalists were devout Christians who looked to the Bible for spiritual and moral instruction, but they also believed human nature inherently good and altruistic, not sinful and self-interested. Their God revealed Himself through the handiworks of nature, to be comprehended by humanity with scientific inquiry. And through Jesus Christ, their God had guaranteed salvation to all His children, poor and rich, lazy and diligent, drunken and sober. "GOD loves all his Creatures without Exception . . . ," the Reverend Winchester had taught, "his tender Mercies are over all his works." In the mid-1790s, nearly two in five of the subscribers to the First Universalist Church were also members of the Pennsylvania Democratic Society; thirty years later, numerous important trade union and MUTA leaders, including William Heighton, were also Universalists. Universalist clergy, in turn, opened their churches to mass meetings and other workingmen's activities, including at least one of the assemblies where Heighton delivered a major organizing speech prior to the MUTA's foundation.

These continued links assumed special importance alongside efforts by the evangelical sects and, in time, Presbygational revivalists and Sabbatarians to proselytize among the city's workers. Universalism directly rebuked the evangelical focus on individual sin as the sole source of workers' distress—a precept, they charged, that acclimated workers to inequalities rooted in politics and economics. The same view was pervasive among the leadership of the workingmen's movement. "When you have complained of oppression," one correspondent for the *Mechanics' Free Press* exclaimed, "they have told you that such was the dispensation of Providence, and you must be obedient." It was not (as some evangelicals contended) that the radicals encouraged libertinism: Heighton, in particular, inveighed against workers wasting their money and their minds in the city's taverns and gaming rooms. Instead, the MUTA sought to create an alternative to both the evangelical chapels and the dram shops, raising the moral and intellectual standards of the producers with rational enlightenment and not hellfire moralism.

There were some glaring limits to the radicals' inclusiveness. Although geared chiefly to the grievances of oppressed wage-earners, the reborn city democracy restricted itself almost entirely to men who worked in the bastardized artisan trades. Cartmen, shop clerks, dock workers, domestics, and day laborers—those who performed what Heighton described as "official" as opposed to "productive" labor—had no societies in the MUTA. The growing numbers of female wage-earners in the debased sweated crafts likewise were excluded—thought by some organized journeymen as more of a threat to their livelihoods than as class allies. Although it is possible that some of Philadelphia's black male workers in the trades, eligible voters all, took part in either the unions or the new party, neither Heighton nor others acknowledged their presence. Neither the MUTA nor the Working Men's Party endorsed the rights of blacks as producers or as citizens, nor did they remark on the expansion of southern slavery. The gaps and the silences, especially over slavery, would soon test the resolve of working-class radicals all across the North.

If, in 1828, the movement and its political party fell far short of proclaiming the cause of all Philadelphia's workers, it still offered a new and effective critique of the inequalities and injustices of the early industrializing city. What remained to be seen was how the Working Men, determined to establish themselves as an independent force, would align themselves in national politics and in the impending presidential election. In contrast to the early Anti-Masons, the transformed city democracy, with its assaults on bankers, manufacturers, and other nonproducers, looked like barren political ground for the pro-improvement, National Republican supporters of Adams and Clay. Despite the dominant New School's conversion to Andrew Jackson's presidential hopes, many MUTA and Working Men loyalists—notably Jackson's Duanite admirer Stephen Simpson—remained fierce Jackson loyalists as well. But like the Anti-Masons, the Working Men had to confront what role a small locally based party with a very specific following and agenda might play in the changing political environment. Would an alliance with Jackson, or any other national opposition leader, betray William Heighton's promise to create a fully independent party of the producers? Alternatively, would a refusal to back any presidential candidate inevitably place the new movement on the political margins in its very first election campaign? If the Working Men declined to throw their full support behind Jackson, might they dampen the anti-administration vote in Philadelphia, where Jackson had received crucial support in 1824, and, in effect, help President Adams? Finally, looking beyond the autumn elections, would Philadelphia's Working Men inspire workingmen in other cities and towns to form their own political movements, as Philadelphia's Democratic Society had inspired city democrats more than thirty years earlier? Or would the Philadelphians' new departure, for all of its innovations, prove the last gasp of the old city democracy?

COUNTRY POLITICS: RELIEF WARS AND STATE RIGHTS

While northern city democrats undertook new political ventures, country democrats in the slaveholding states of the West and South continued the struggles over banks, debt relief, and land policy that had broken out after the Panic of 1819. In the newest state, Missouri, panic produced a rebellion at the polls that brought the downfall of the old territorial political establishment just as statehood was gained. With that began a shift in the allegiances of the new state's most popular politician, Thomas Hart Benton. Expelled from the University of North Carolina over an incident involving theft, Benton had moved west with his parents, settled temporarily in Tennessee (where he and his brother Jesse were involved in a nasty tavern brawl and gunfight with Andrew Jackson), and eventually arrived in St. Louis in 1815. Amid the early-postwar boom, Benton prospered as a politician and newspaper editor as well as an attorney, and worked closely with fur-trading and mining interests. After the panic, in 1821, he was named one of the new state's first two U.S. senators. Three years later, he backed the presidential hopes of Henry Clay (who had married Benton's cousin, Lucretia Hart).

Yet Benton, who always thought of himself as something of an outsider, was in political transition. The panic had plunged him into debt, tempering his entrepreneurial enthusiasm. The popular outcry against eastern creditors from his farmer constituents made a powerful impression. And in Washington, Benton, a strong pro-slavery man during the Missouri admission controversy, had gravitated toward the Virginia Quids, especially John Taylor and John Randolph, and their denunciations of the Second Bank of the United States and the Hamiltonian "paper" system. Even as he supported Clay in 1824, Benton was devising a new agrarian policy for distributing the public lands of the West to poor settlers by drastically reducing the price once the lands had been on the market for five years, a proposal that appalled pro-development Clay supporters. In the final presidential showdown in 1825, Benton backed Jackson instead of Clay's anointed Adams, completing his break with the nationalist Republicans. Adding acerbic attacks on the national bank to his cheap-land proposals, he transformed himself into the spokesman for Missouri's small-farm settlers—and of western opposition to Clay's American System.

A greater battle—involving issues and personalities of singular importance to later national developments—unfolded in Clay's Kentucky, where disputes over legislative reforms led to a full-blown constitutional crisis over the state courts. Like the rest of rural America, Kentucky, once the richest state west of the Alleghenies, had been hit hard by the panic and rendered a virtual creditors' protectorate. The downturn's effects lingered into the early 1820s. A so-called Relief Party, after winning a commanding legislative majority in 1819, enacted several pro-debtor measures: abolition of imprisonment for debt, laws greatly extending the time granted to repay creditors, and, above all, replacement of the Bluegrass-dominated Bank of Kentucky with a special relief bank, the Bank of the Commonwealth, empowered to issue massive amounts of inflationary paper money. Creditor interests, aghast, appealed to the state judiciary, which, after the hard times lifted in 1823, declared the laws unconstitutional—moves that the aroused legislature denounced as both economically ruinous and an attack on the electorate, "subversive of their dearest and most valuable political rights." Relief issues dominated the 1824 state elections, in which another pro-relief majority was returned to the legislature. The pro-relief candidate for governor, an admired former officer from the War of 1812, Joseph Desha, trounced his pro-court opponent by a margin of nearly two to one. The new legislature, led by a rugged, self-made ex-congressman named John Rowan—who had once killed a man in a duel over who was the greater master of classical languages—passed a reorganization bill that created an entirely new court of appeals, friendlier to the state's hard-pressed small farmers. But the members of the established court refused to stand down, creating a dual court system and a constitutional crisis of the first order.

The political alignments over Kentucky relief and the court issue fit the basic patterns found throughout the South and West after 1819, pitting the more settled, economically developed areas against the rest of the state. Antirelief sentiment, and support for the old court, clustered in the commercializing Bluegrass areas in Lexington and the south-central counties. This was Henry Clay's Kentucky: pro-improvement, friendly to banking and financial institutions, home to Kentucky's finest plantations and largest manufacturing enterprises. The mountainous and knob-hill counties to the east, along with the western and southern portions along the Tennessee border of the state, were, by contrast, mainly pro-relief—dominated by smaller farmers, including many recent arrivals, unbridled by any established local elite. A clearer demonstration of the class divisions of rural America could not be found, articulated as battles between small farmer and planter-businessmen districts. Yet no section of the state was completely nailed down on the court question, which required both sides to canvass support from every corner of the commonwealth. The most influential arguments on behalf of the country democracy came not from some crossroads hamlet but from the state capital of Frankfort, and were written by a sickly Dartmouth graduate and ex-lawyer, Amos Kendall, who had moved to Kentucky barely a decade earlier.

Straight-laced, shy, and sallow, Kendall was a ferocious polemicist once he had pen and paper in hand. He had been born to a hardscrabble Massachusetts farming family in 1789. A bookish boy afflicted with asthma, he was sent to study at the academies at New Ipswich and Groton, then worked his way through Dartmouth, where he graduated first in his class in 1811. After studying law back in Groton with a Republican congressman, and seeing few opportunities in depressed wartime New England, he decided to move south and west, eventually settling in Lexington, Kentucky. There Kendall befriended a brother of Henry Clay's, which led to a job as tutor to the great man's unruly children, but Kendall, restless, took leave after about a year. With the backing of another congressman—the self-proclaimed slayer of Tecumseh, Richard Mentor Johnson— he decided to get into the newspaper business. In 1816, in Frankfort, he set up shop as part-owner and editor of the *Argus of Western America*, and leapt into the hard-knuckle world of Kentucky political journalism.

Over the following decade, Kendall gradually underwent a conversion not unlike Thomas Hart Benton's. Initially a reluctant supporter of the Second BUS, he changed his mind completely when the bank began contracting credit in 1819. He denounced the bank as an unconstitutional "monied aristocracy," excoriated "paper systems," and upbraided the Marshall Court's decision in *McCulloch v. Maryland*. Initially cool to the pro-relief cause, which he saw as endangering contractual obligations, Kendall turned about again in 1823, when the focus of the relief battle shifted to the courts. Convinced that the antirelief court's rulings embodied the "spirit of monarchy," he became a fierce advocate for the New Court Party formed out of the Relief Party, which led to tremendous strain with his old benefactor, Henry Clay, after the 1824 election. By then, Kendall was the chief articulator of the New Court Party's positions, not simply at the *Argus* but as Governor Desha's ghostwriter—honing a skill he would display to even greater effect in the future.

The New Court Party's other gifted writer, who in time would succeed Kendall at the *Argus*, was the lawyer and pamphleteer Francis Preston Blair. Reared in Frankfort, the son of Kentucky's longtime Republican attorney general James Blair, Preston graduated with honors from Transylvania College the same year that Kendall finished at Dartmouth. Blair, like Kendall, was initially a strong supporter of Henry Clay, only to distance himself after backing Clay for president in 1824. "I never deserted your banner," he wrote to Clay after the fact, "until the questions on which you and I so frequently differed in private discussion— (State rights, the Bank, the power of the Judiciary, &c.)—became the criterions to distinguish the parties, and had actually renewed, in their practical effects, the great divisions which marked the era of 1798." A skilled writer, Blair contributed pamphlets and several open letters (under the pseudonym "Jefferson") to the Relief Party efforts, actually surpassing Kendall in the sting of his invective. But he also took an active role as the clerk of the new court of appeals and (out of step with Kendall's hard-money views) as a director of the state-run, paper-issuing Commonwealth Bank.

While Kendall and Blair, the well-connected New Court supporters, did their utmost in Frankfort, their Relief Party instigated and coordinated activities across the state. Pro-relief leaders—including some, like Rowan and the chief justice of the new court, William Barry, with considerable experience and skill as stump orators—whipped up support for the cause. (Barry, another veteran of the Battle of the Thames who had risen to the top of Kentucky politics, traveled to pro-relief areas and denounced the citizens of his own hometown, Lexington, as "a vile aristocracy.") There was a sublime absurdity to some of the

drama, as the two courts jostled for legitimacy. Yet to Kentuckians, it was not a laughing matter but a crucial battle over legislative as against judicial supremacy as well as over economic
power. Kendall and his allies declared that they were *"republicans
of the Jeffersonian school,"* reclaiming the spirit of 1798. Their
opponents saw them as subversives. "We consider this not only
an unconstitutional and high-handed measure," an Old Court
Party manifesto proclaimed of the reorganization act, "but one,
which if approved, will prostrate the whole fabric of constitutional liberty; *we do consider it a REVOLUTION!"* Determined
to wrestle the legislature from the New Court Jacobin demagogues, the Old Court Party men built their own statewide
organization, enlisting printers and newspaper editors to circu-
late their diatribes, and matching the new court's supporters
stump speaker for stump speaker.

The fever finally broke in 1826, with the Old Court Party
forces victorious. An improving economy had taken the edge off
the relief cause's desperation, but equally important, the Old
Court Party, with more resources at its disposal, outorganized the
insurgents. Yet the results were not as clear-cut as they had been
in 1824, the Relief Party's banner year. Whereas the 1824 tally
had been a crushing triumph for the New Court men, the next
two elections were much closer, with the Old Court Party winning the house but not the senate in 1825, and only capturing
both houses the following year. The Old Court forces outlasted
their overmatched and exhausted opponents, but did not humil-
iate them. As the 1828 elections approached, the reforms
remained an important factor in Kentucky politics.

Compared to the new city democrats in Philadelphia, the
antirelief and pro–new court campaigns, mixing hard-money and
inflationist demands, produced little in the way of coherent critiques of the emerging economic order. Much more significant
were the Kentuckians' political complaints against the Old Court
Party's flagrant disregard of the people's will, as expressed in the
lopsided mandates of 1823 and 1824. Ironically, in retrospect,
Andrew Jackson was not among the movement's early admirers,

even though most of its constituents supported his presidential run in 1824. Jackson believed the insurgents' attacks on the duly-constituted judiciary were "alarming and flagi[t]ious," and initially he regarded pro-relief leaders as "the Demagogues of Kentucky." He would eventually change his mind about the "demagogues," if not about the court struggle. By standing up to Henry Clay's Bluegrass establishment, the New Court Party crystallized a popular majoritarianism attuned to Jackson's own developing democratic ideas. The hard-money currents within the party, expressed most powerfully in Kendall's writings, also converged with Jackson's views on money and banking. After 1826, the New Court men, most conspicuously Kendall and Blair, would expand their grassroots Kentucky democracy into a national political force. They would do so under Jackson's aegis.

Farther south, planter elites had greater success in establishing their political dominance and in creating a national force very different from either Henry Clay's or Kendall and Blair's. In Georgia, the planter faction headed by George Troup, combining state rights with Indian removal, had already broken the back of John Clark's backwoods democracy and embarrassed the Adams White House. For Troup, echoing John Randolph, virtually any increase in federal power was a danger to the South and especially to slavery, presaging the rise of "a combination of fanatics for the destruction of everything valuable in the southern country." In other slaveholding states, planter elites reconsidered their politics in the wake of these events—nowhere more dramatically than in quasi-aristocratic South Carolina.

In the 1820s, South Carolina politics took their own peculiar and dramatic twists and turns. The Panic of 1819, and a subsequent cotton market crash in 1825, crushed many of the state's enterprising planters who had moved up-country to cash in on the cotton boom. With short-staple cotton prices falling through the floor—from twenty-seven cents a pound in 1816 to barely nine cents in 1827—and with competition from large plantations in the Alabama and Mississippi black belts intensifying, thousands of slaveholders moved their families and their chattel westward. The downturn hit the sea-island cotton plantations of the low country hard as well, giving an additional boost to the sort of pro-relief sentiment that elsewhere emanated chiefly from small planters and nonslaveholders. The South Carolinians, however, aimed their criticisms at the Adams administration's high-tariff and internal-improvement policies. Planters perceived—incorrectly—that the tariff was the major cause of their misery, forcing them to sell their goods cheap but buy goods dear in protected markets. Additionally, more than $1.25 million in federal funds would be spent by decade's end on internal improvements in the northern states, but not a penny would be spent on South Carolina. Critics charged that South Carolina's pro-nationalist leaders, above all the ambitious Calhoun, were spending "the money of the South to buy up influence in the north."

Slavery, and the fear of slave insurrection, electrified the state's political climate just as dramatically. Lacking the imposing yeoman backcountry of other southern states, and with its formally democratic politics firmly in the grip of the planters, South Carolina was virtually immune from the kinds of powerful country democratic movements that emerged in Kentucky and Georgia after 1819. Any significant uprising from below would come from slaves and free blacks, not white voters—a threat that, after the Vesey insurrection panic of 1822, concentrated white South Carolinians' minds wonderfully. Legal crackdowns on transient free blacks went hand in hand with renewed panics over rumors of imminent uprisings, including a scare in Charleston late in 1825 that touched off six months of reprisals by white lynch mobs and police authorities. Amid the turmoil emerged a sustained body of pro-slavery polemics, defending bondage as an ancient and biblically sanctioned institution, "the step-ladder," one pamphleteer insisted, "by which civilized countries have passed from barbarism to civilization." Coupled with these arguments were claims that by expanding federal power even beyond what the antislavery Republicans had demanded during the Missouri controversy, Adams and his Yankee friends were paving the way to abolishing slavery.

The invigorated antinationalist and pro-slavery strains in South Carolina politics blended with particular power in the speeches and writings of the pro-Crawford Radical, William Smith. A former state circuit court judge, and later John C. Calhoun's fellow U.S. senator, Smith had distinguished himself during the congressional debates over Missouri as the most outspoken defender of slavery in either house, pronouncing it a blessing anywhere it took root. Denied reelection to the Senate by the state legislature, Smith immediately won election to the legislature itself, where in 1825 he revived a set of defeated resolutions directly attacking the tariff and the loose constructionism of President Adams and Vice President Calhoun as unconstitutional. In time, Smith declared, the tariff would either "rend your government asunder, or make your slaves your masters."

Smith and the Radicals gained the political initiative only gradually. As late as 1824, a state legislative committee, dominated by Calhoun's friends, rejected Radicalism outright and declared that any impugning by state authorities of federal laws—including, by implication, the tariff—would be "an act of usurpation." Congressman George McDuffie, Calhoun's follower and confidant, berated, on the House floor, "the extraordinary notion . . . that the State governments are to be considered as sentinels to guard the people against the encroachments of the General Government." But in 1825 and 1826, the South Carolina legislature, under powerful pressure from the planter elite, changed its allegiances, approved Smith's strict constructionist resolutions—and then reelected Smith to the Senate. Smith arrived in Washington to find Calhoun so receptive and pleasant that, he wrote a friend, "I could not hate him as I wished to do." Calhoun had quietly been perturbed by the ferocity of northern antislavery and its connection to expansive federal powers since the Missouri crisis. Now, pulled up short by political developments at home and in Washington, and above all by southern disgust directed at the Adams administration, Calhoun felt the pressure he said "[e]very prominent publick man" now felt, to "reexamine his new position and reapply principles." In time,

Calhoun would reapply his own principles so thoroughly that he would become the foremost pro-slavery antinationalist in the nation, surpassing even Smith in his sectionalist thinking. For when Calhoun changed his mind, he changed his whole mind.

The political upheavals of the 1820s, rooted in the Panic of 1819 and the Missouri crisis, left three major forces contending for power in the slaveholding states. Henry Clay and his American System continued to command support among enterprising elites and aspiring businessmen in the border states west of the Virginia Piedmont. A reborn country democracy, distrustful of the nationalizing elites, local and national, gained valuable political experience in the battles over debtor relief and related issues. And in the older eastern states, the antinationalist Radicalism of the disabled William Crawford became the ideological foundation of a planters' resurgence, hoping to reassert authority over the backwoods democrats and to lay the high-tariff nationalists to waste. As the Adams administration ended its second year, it was not yet clear which of these elements would dominate the politics of the slaveholding South and West, and whether any of them would coalesce behind Andrew Jackson's presidential campaign. Without question, however, the balance of forces in slaveholding America was stacked more heavily than ever against John Quincy Adams.

QUINCY ADAMS AT BAY

At ten past one on the afternoon of July 4, 1826, the fiftieth anniversary of the signing of the Declaration of Independence, Thomas Jefferson died at the age of eighty-three. President Adams heard the news two days later (and noted in his diary the "striking coincidence"), but only on July 9 did he learn that his father, too, had died on the Fourth, barely four hours after Jefferson. Although Madison lived on, a generation seemed, finally, to have passed, with providential omens—and for Adams all the signs were bad. In November, his opponents captured majorities in both houses of Congress, dividing the legislative and the executive branches against each other as never before in American history. In his third annual message, delivered to the hostile new Congress, Adams reported failure after failure in foreign affairs but included half-hearted offers for a moderation of land payment requirements and a vague reform of bankruptcy laws. He would not abandon his post without a fight, but privately he thought his position was hopeless. "General Jackson will be elected," he wrote in his diary two weeks later.

Adams's political prospects were so dim that even in Massachusetts an incipient pro-Jackson opposition arose—an unnatural coalition, and not enough to threaten Adams seriously on his home ground, but sufficiently prominent to raise a discomfiting clatter. David Henshaw, the chief Boston organizer of the group, was an unschooled former druggist's apprentice who had made a fortune as a wholesale drug merchant before branching out into banking and insurance. Turning to politics, he won election to the Massachusetts legislature in 1826, and started his own newspaper, the *Statesman*. Never accepted by the Brahmin worthies (whom he blasted as "nabobs" and "Shylocks"), Henshaw gravitated toward less haughty, self-made men (and self-proclaimed democrats) such as the former congressman and current state supreme court judge Marcus Morton. Together Henshaw and Morton formed a new political party, the Friends of Jackson, in anticipation of 1828. Among their fellow Jackson supporters, curiously, were a few of the notables whom Henshaw had found so disdainful, including the impeccable Federalists from Salem, George and Theodore Lyman, and the crusty old veteran of the Hartford Convention, Harrison Gray Otis. Deeply suspicious of John Quincy Adams ever since his apostasy of 1808, these gentlemen may have hoped that a Jackson victory would end the persisting Republican bar against appointing Federalists to office, and they may have found Adams's and Clay's economic nationalism too collectivist and pro-western an experiment. For John Quincy Adams, there seemed to be no completely tranquil political harbor, even in his native state.

The greatest storm brewed on Capitol Hill, where the Twentieth Congress organized itself into a virtual committee for the defeat of the president. On December 2, the House, by a ten-vote margin, replaced Speaker John W. Taylor of New York (of Missouri Compromise fame, who had been reelected Speaker in 1825 and was an Adams ally) with Andrew Stevenson, a Virginian aligned with Jackson. Stevenson duly packed the key standing committees with anti-administration men, including, as chairman of the Ways and Means Committee, the obstreperous John Randolph, whose political antics, among them his recent duel with Henry Clay, had so alienated southside Virginians that he had been turned out of the Senate seat he won in 1825. The Senate, meanwhile, selected as its official printer Duff Green, a Missourian close to Calhoun who had moved to Washington in 1825 and whose *United States Telegraph* had become the capital city's chief scourge of Adams and Clay. Tennessee's newly elected governor, Sam Houston, wrote mordantly to his old friend and military comrade Jackson about the administration's predicament: "[D]esperation is their only hope!!"

At the center of the presidential intrigues was Senator Martin Van Buren, on the verge of being selected by the New York state legislature for a second term. When he was not harassing the Adams White House over the Panama conference, Van Buren spent much of his time after 1825 licking his wounds over Crawford's defeat, reconciling with DeWitt Clinton, reconsolidating his Albany Regency political machine, and (beginning in 1827) fending off the Anti-Masonic uprising in western New York. Yet he was not too distracted to neglect presidential politics—and to undertake a quiet effort, detected by Adams in the spring of 1826, "to combine the discordant elements of the Crawford and Jackson and Calhoun men into a united opposition against the administration." At Christmas in 1826, on a southern trip, Van Buren struck an agreement with Calhoun to promote Jackson's election, with the South Carolinian to continue on as vice president. (Van Buren would keep the compact confidential until after his reelection to the Senate the following February.) In supporting Jackson, Van Buren hoped to build a lasting national party, drawing a line between themselves and Adams's supporters as sharp as the one that had once divided Jeffersonian Republicans from Federalists.

Van Buren understood better than most the imperatives of creating a victorious national coalition—and, more than most, he had both the energy and the political skills to build one. His maneuverings and negotiations over the winter of 1826–27 would prove crucial to the reorganization of national political alliances, and to the birth of what would become known as Jacksonian Democracy. But historians have badly misinterpreted both the intentions and the effects of Van Buren's efforts. Particular attention has focused on a letter Van Buren wrote, mainly to please Calhoun, to the Richmond editor and spokesman of the revived Old Republicans, Thomas Ritchie, on January 13, 1827. The letter solicited Ritchie's support for what Van Buren called a "party," reviving the old Jeffersonian coalition of "the planters of the South and the plain Republicans of the north," in order to squelch the "prejudices between free and slave holding states" that had produced, most dangerously at the time of the Missouri Compromise, a northern "clamour agt. Southern Influence and African Slavery." Here, supposedly, lay a blueprint for the entire political era to come—the formation of a truly professional national party, run by partisans, uniting North and South but fundamentally pro-slavery in its politics, standing in legitimate and enduring opposition to another party.

In fact, although Van Buren did speak (to Ritchie and many others, as early as 1826) about the formation of a new party, and although he observed that "we must always have party distinctions," he was not proclaiming, at this point, any major political innovations beyond a return to the party competition of the Jefferson and Madison years. His main objections were to the amalgamation policies of Monroe, which he believed had artificially admitted Federalists into the Republican fold, displaced loyalty based on principle with "*personal preference,*" and allowed what he called "local jealousies" to dominate national politics, most ominously in the Missouri crisis. Others had been making the same point for years, including Thomas Jefferson, who, having shifted his views since his presidency, wrote in 1822, "I consider the party division of whig & tory, the most wholesome which can exist in any government, and well worthy of being nourished, to keep out those of a more dangerous character." In devising his alternative, Van Buren chiefly looked backward. His focus was on reviving "the division between Republicans and Federalists" and returning to the "old" solidarities. Those alignments and allegiances, he said, had been papered over by Monroe, but they were never truly obliterated. Better, he said, to face that reality and reconfigure the old Jeffersonian party—with the clear presumption that, this time, the Republicans would stand by their principles and, unless careless, permanently sustain their domination instead of merging with their foes.

The idea that Van Buren was building a pro-slavery or pro-southern party fundamentally distorts his motives and his conception of politics. There was a rising pro-slavery impulse in the South, dating back to the Missouri crisis, and Van Buren certainly wished to incorporate its supporters into his new party— above all his friend Thomas Ritchie, whose blasts against the Missouri Compromise and expanded federal power in the *Enquirer* were among the harshest anywhere. When he approached these southerners, Van Buren naturally emphasized his opposition to the more vociferous antislavery northerners, Republican and Federalist, and blamed them for stirring up sectional trouble (which, in the case of the Missouri crisis, was accurate). But while Van Buren courted the pro-slavery southerners, he neither shared their pro-slavery views nor hoped to build a new party on them. Unlike Ritchie and the others, Van Buren had supported the Missouri Compromise and wished only that it had never been made necessary. As far as possible, he wanted to keep the slavery issue out of national affairs by supplanting sectionalism with party loyalty, a very different proposition from what the increasingly militant pro-slavery men were advocating. While deprecating the antislavery agitation in the North, Van

Buren was asking potential allies in both sections—in the South, most delicately, Thomas Ritchie—to honor national political compromise. The South, as well as the North, would have to eschew the politics of slavery.

Van Buren's southern strategizing was only one part of his larger, extremely demanding national effort to unify behind Andrew Jackson a collection of forces that had little in common except their opposition to John Quincy Adams. Personal as well as purely political divisions needed bridging. Relations between Jackson and William Crawford had been sour ever since Crawford's harsh response to Jackson's Spanish Florida expedition in 1818. Crawford passionately hated Jackson's new supporter Calhoun, still known as an ardent nationalist. In the North, there were some anti-Adams men, Bucktails included, who distrusted the South as much as some southerners distrusted the North and who, as one of them wrote to Van Buren, would never accede "the Executive authority to the Slave holding states." Other northerners, especially Bucktails, worried that Jackson would become a creature of Calhoun and DeWitt Clinton—the worst possible combination from a Bucktail point of view. At the end of 1827, it remained uncertain whether Jackson would choose Clinton instead of Van Buren as his chief lieutenant in New York, despite Van Buren's exertions on his behalf. Even worse, there was informed speculation that Jackson might designate Clinton as his favorite for the vice presidency. Reports, direct from the Hermitage, that Jackson was speaking highly of Clinton and was concerned about Van Buren's "reputed cunning" spread a wave of anxiety through the Albany Regency.

Van Buren's situation simplified when, on February 11, 1828, Clinton dropped dead. After the eulogies were over (Van Buren's was one of the most gracious), Regency men who had been put off by Clinton began gravitating toward Jackson's campaign, while Clintonians drifted toward Adams. In Washington, southern and western Jacksonians began praising Martin Van Buren. Gradually, the pieces were falling into place. Crawford, after a personal visit from Van Buren, agreed to back Jackson as vastly preferable to Adams (although Crawford tried, unsuccessfully, to get Van Buren to replace Calhoun with the Old Republican Nathaniel Macon in the ticket's second spot). In New York, Jackson's supporters, with the help of the Regency, swept the legislative elections in 1827 outside the western Anti-Mason districts, carrying New York City by four thousand votes—an excellent early indication that Jackson would win the all-important Empire State a year later. Early in his politicking travels in 1827, Van Buren stopped in Kentucky and made friends with Amos Kendall, who under pressure from local Jackson men had agreed to join Francis Blair and most of the rest of the New Court Party in support of Jackson's candidacy. Encouraged by Van Buren's firmly neo-Jeffersonian views—and later by his help in obtaining a personal loan—Kendall would throw himself into the campaign. Several of the most influential Virginians, including John Randolph's replacement, the newly elected senator John Tyler, also came out for Jackson. The chief remaining business for Van Buren and his allies was to solidify Jackson's support in Pennsylvania and Ohio—an effort that, over the winter and spring of 1828, became entangled with a bewildering congressional tussle over protectionist tariff policy.

While state-rights and pro-slavery advocates were finding their voice in the South, an equally determined school of protectionist writers and propagandists gained a sizable following among the farmers of the middle Atlantic and western states as well as among the manufacturers of New England. The movement had begun to emerge in 1816, as an assertion of patriotic solidarity. Following the Panic of 1819, its advocates agitated for higher tariffs as the best means to shelter American enterprise and bring recovery. After winning a signal victory with the enactment of the protectionist Tariff of 1824, the movement was emboldened even further by Adams's victory in 1825. Hezekiah Niles, the self-made printer and editor of the nationally distributed *Niles' Weekly Register*, held the largest audience of the protectionist writers. Matthew Carey, an Irish émigré, Jeffersonian, self-taught political economist, and tireless pamphleteer, organized the Pennsylvania

Society for the Promotion of Manufacturers in 1824. Lesser-known but more systematic political economists, above all Daniel Raymond, gave protectionist doctrine genuine intellectual heft.

The protectionists rejected individualist economic assumptions, already battered by the Panic of 1819, about the beneficence of individual self-interest and unfettered markets. Individual interest and the national interest, as Raymond wrote, "are often directly opposed." To augment the nation's wealth and spur what would now be called economic growth, the protectionists primarily looked to government to act for the benefit of the whole—"like a good shepherd, who supports and nourishes the weak and feeble ones in his flock," in one of Raymond's more famous lines. Shielding domestic manufacturers from foreign competition by erecting high tariff walls was, along with federal funding of internal improvements, the good shepherd's most pressing task.

Frustrated but unchastened by the Senate's rejection, by the narrowest of margins, of higher duties on woolen goods early in 1827, the protectionists and their friends in Washington (led by the administration's point man, Daniel Webster, who would soon win election to the Senate) planned an all-out campaign for the following year. In June 1827, Carey's Pennsylvania Society sponsored a national convention in Harrisburg of delegates from thirteen states—a remarkable group of editors, politicians, and political economists as well as businessmen—which hammered out a comprehensive protective program regarding the woolens industry and other manufacturers in need. The convention did not back either Adams or Jackson, hoping to exercise maximum leverage over both men. But the protectionists' pressure did put the Jacksonians—and especially the coalition builder Martin Van Buren—in a difficult political bind.

Jackson still held to the moderately protectionist line he had supported as a senator in 1823 and 1824, although he was beginning to think the importance of the tariff issue had been greatly exaggerated. But that middle position would not be good enough for some political blocs whose support Jackson badly needed. To southern Radicals, any sign of support for a protective tariff by Van Buren and his friends was a potential deal breaker in the coming presidential election. South Carolina slaveholders led meetings and petition drives throughout the state, warning that neither the federal courts nor national elections could protect the slaveholders' rights and interests over the protective tariff. Thomas Cooper, the ex-Jeffersonian radical turned state-rights ideologue, warned Van Buren, extravagantly, that passage of woolens protection would lead to instant secession by South Carolina. Northern protectionists, in New York as well as Pennsylvania and Ohio, were just as concerned that Van Buren's courting of the southerners would cause him to sell them out over the tariff issue. Those concerns deepened when, during the Senate vote over the woolens bill in 1827, Van Buren absented himself, opening the way for Vice President Calhoun (who denounced the bill as an attack on the South) to cast the tie-breaking, killing vote. All of Van Buren's coalition-building, it seemed, might come to nothing without a congressional deal over the tariff—the one issue over which nobody seemed willing to bargain.

The tariff bill that resulted in 1828 was more political than economic—connected, John Randolph remarked acidly, "to manufactures of no sort, but the manufacture of a President of the United States." Its author, Congressman Silas Wright from northernmost New York State, was one of Van Buren's brightest Regency lieutenants and thus, though only a freshman in the Twentieth Congress, a man of considerable consequence. Inside the House Committee of Manufactures, Wright drafted a bill that levied high duties not only on wool and hemp—appealing to growers and manufacturers in Kentucky, Ohio, and western New York—but also on pig iron and rolled iron, of utmost importance in Pennsylvania. Molasses, sail duck, and coarse wool—essential raw materials for New England rum distillers, sailmakers, and clothing manufacturers—likewise were burdened with heavy new duties, a direct attack on pro-Adams Yankees. The economic logic of Wright's bill was utterly whimsical, but its political logic was airtight: offer aid, above all, to the farmers and iron masters of the middle Atlantic and western states, while hitting New England hard. Antitariff southerners, aghast at the very idea of protection, added amendments that would hit the Yankees even harder, hoping to make the bill so obnoxious it would never succeed.

Jackson's friends wanted the protective bill to pass both houses, but could never admit as much to the southern Radicals. And so Van Buren and his agents pulled a bait-and-switch, assuring southerners that even if the House approved the bill, the Senate would kill it—thereby allowing the Jacksonians to tell the middle Atlantic and western state voters that they had fought to protect their manufactures and growers, but without actually forcing higher prices on southern consumers. The bill passed the House. In the Senate, old-line Crawford Radicals, led by Samuel Smith of Maryland, took up the fight to reject it. (It was Smith, speaking on the Senate floor, who gave the measure its notorious title, "a bill of abominations.") But united opposition from New England threatened to ruin everything, so Van Buren presented an amendment calling for upward revision of manufactured woolens duties. The maneuver swayed just enough New Englanders, including Daniel Webster, to get the bill through the Senate, on the presumption that a bad protectionist bill was better than no bill at all. President Adams, finding no constitutional basis for killing the tariff, signed it into law in mid-May, raising duties overall by about 30 to 50 percent.

In the short term, the tariff of abominations brought Van Buren and the evolving pro-Jackson coalition all they could have desired from what had looked like an impossible situation. Southerners, whose representatives voted almost unanimously against the bill, felt seduced and betrayed—furious Charlestonians lowered shipboard American flags in the harbor to half-staff, burned effigies of Clay and Webster, and organized protest meetings—but were too wary of dividing the ranks against Adams and Clay to vent their anger against the devious Jacksonians. Immediately after the vote, the South Carolina delegation caucused at Robert Hayne's lodging house, where blustery talk erupted about mounting dramatic protest. But at a second meeting, cooler heads—on instruction, almost certainly, from Vice President Calhoun—held sway, and the little rebellion subsided. Calhoun himself reacted philosophically, telling a New York friend that "truth will, in the long run, prevail." Under a Jackson presidency strongly influenced by Calhoun, Radicals consoled themselves, it would be easier to beat back the ignominious new duties; in any case, the southerners had to deal with first things first, namely, ousting Adams and Clay. Meanwhile, among Kentucky hemp growers, Pennsylvania iron makers, and New York wool farmers, the tariff greatly bolstered Jackson's cause, which had been Van Buren's objective all along.

Thoughts about the tariff's long-term repercussions were also taking shape inside John C. Calhoun's obsessive and (on the subject of nationalist politics) thoroughly changed mind. When the Twentieth Congress adjourned, Calhoun returned to his South Carolina plantation where he would spend the duration of the year, playing little part in the election campaign, confident that his election and Jackson's were foregone conclusions. Instead, he brooded over the tariff, and over the larger injustices done to the South. Publicly, he maintained a bland moderation, consistent with his commitments to Jackson and Van Buren. Privately, he filled his correspondence with ruminations about how an oppressive northern majority had gained a permanent ascendancy over the slaveholding states. The fallout from those ruminations would await the outcome of the presidential election. Only in November did Calhoun, at the request of a South Carolina state legislator, start refining his thoughts into a coherent protest.

"UNDER *WHIP & SPUR*": POLITICS, PROPAGANDA, AND THE 1828 CAMPAIGN

Although he looked like a distinguished old warrior, with flashing blue eyes and a shock of whitening steely gray hair, Andrew Jackson was by now a physical wreck. Years of ingesting calomel and watered gin to combat his chronic dysentery had left him almost toothless. (In 1828, he obtained an ill-fitting set of dentures, but he often refused to wear them). An irritation of his lungs, caused by a bullet he had caught in one of his early duels, had developed into bronchiectasis, a rare condition causing violent coughing spells that would bring up what he called "great quantities of slime." The bullet itself remained lodged in his chest, and another was lodged in his left arm, where it accelerated the onset of osteomyelitis. Rheumatism afflicted his joints, and his head often ached, the effect of a lifetime of chewing and smoking tobacco. He had survived near-total collapse of his health in 1822 and 1825, but for the rest of his life, he enjoyed few days completely free of agony. His outbursts of irascible fury, which sometimes shocked even his old friends and allies, owed partly to his suffering and to his efforts to suppress it. But after the debacle of 1825, they also owed to his determination to vindicate not just his own honor but that of the American people. For Jackson and his admirers, the two had become identical.

Willfulness did not mean rashness. In preparing to wreak his vengeance on Adams (whom he respected) and Clay (whom he despised), Jackson took care not to violate the accepted etiquette of presidential campaigning and appeal directly for the job. He was available to serve his country once more, but to look or sound less elevated than that would have been dishonorable (as well as onerous, given the state of his health). Jackson made only one major public appearance over the months before the election, at a public festivity in New Orleans on January 8, commemorating his great victory thirteen years earlier—an invitation, issued by the Louisiana legislature, that he could not refuse without seeming churlish. Yet while he stuck close to the Hermitage, Jackson threw himself into the fray as no other previous presidential candidate before him had, making himself available for visiting delegations of congressmen, giving interviews to interested parties, and writing letters for newspaper publication. When personal attacks on his character began, he became even more active, his sense of honor on the line. Some of his chief supporters, including Van Buren, asked that "we be let alone" and that Jackson "be *still*," but Jackson would command this campaign just as surely as he had any of his military exploits.

His positions on several key issues were moderate and flexible, replicating much of what he had said in 1824, in generalities that would not upset the national coalition his agents were assembling. On the tariff, the primary political issue in 1828, Jackson remained blandly middle-of-the-road, repeated his support for a "judicious" tariff, and allowed men of different views to imagine that his sympathies lay with them. On internal improvements, Jackson modified his stance somewhat to support a distribution of surplus federal monies to the states for any road and canal projects they wished to undertake, but generally he restated his cautious support for projects that were genuinely national in scope. On the Indian question, he remained persuaded that, for the good of white settlers and natives alike, orderly removal was the only sound solution, but he refrained from saying anything that might be interpreted as an endorsement of the more extreme state-rights removal position.

Instead of a long list of positions and proposals, Jackson's campaign revolved around calls for "reform," a theme broad enough to unite a disparate coalition without merely resorting to platitudes. At one level, "reform" meant undoing what Jackson considered the theft of the presidency in 1825, and ending the political climate that had permitted it. Sometimes, Jackson and his supporters proposed specific changes. Jackson himself said he would exclude from his cabinet any man who sought the presidency—one obvious way to help prevent any future "corrupt bargain." He also called for a constitutional amendment to bar any member of Congress from eligibility for any other federal office (except in the judiciary) for two years beyond his departure from office. Other Jacksonians spoke of the candidate's support for the principle of rotation in office, for limiting presidents to a single term, and for banning the executive from appointing congressmen to civil posts—all means to disrupt insider exclusivity and what Jackson called the "intrigue and management" that had corrupted the government. Otherwise, the Jackson campaign simply reminded the voters of what had happened in 1825—and went further, to charge that "Lucifer" Clay had, during the House negotiations, offered to throw his support to Jackson if Jackson promised he would name him secretary of state.

At another level, "reform" meant returning American government to Jeffersonian first principles and halting the neo-Federalist revival supposedly being sponsored under the cover of the American System. President Adams, Jackson and his men charged, had made the mistake of following his father's footsteps, balancing a "hypocritical veneration for the great principles of republicanism" with artful manipulation of political power. All of "the asperity which marked the struggle of 98 & 1800," Jackson wrote, had returned. Having "gone into power contrary to the voice of the nation," the administration had claimed a mandate it did not possess, and then tried to expand its authority even further. Illegitimate from the start, the new Adams regime raised what Jackson called the fundamental question at stake in the election: "[S]hall the government or the people rule?"

While Jackson and his closest advisors refined this message and called the shots from Nashville, his supporters built a sophisticated campaign apparatus unlike any previously organized in a presidential election, a combination so effective that it obviated the need for either a congressional caucus nomination or a national convention. At the top, Jackson's most capable Tennessee operatives, including John Overton, William Lewis, and John Eaton, concentrated their efforts in a central committee headquarters established in Nashville, where decisions about strategy and tactics could be taken efficiently, in rapid response to continuing events and with Jackson's approval. (A similar, smaller Jackson committee headquarters was established in Washington, to work closely with the pro-Jackson caucus in Congress that met regularly under Van Buren's aegis.) The central committee in turn dispatched its messages to (and received intelligence from) Jackson campaign committees established in each state. Finally, the

Jacksonians responded to the reforms in presidential voting around the country—reforms that, by 1828, had included, in all but two states, giving the power to choose presidential electors directly to the voters—by coordinating activities at the local level. The state pro-Jackson committees linked up with local Jackson committees, sometimes called Hickory Clubs, that stirred up enthusiasm with rallies and parades and made sure that their supporters arrived at the polls.

Even more extraordinary than the campaign committees was the dense network of pro-Jackson newspapers that seemed to arise out of nowhere beginning in the spring of 1827. Early in the campaign, Jackson's congressional supporters had caucused and pledged to establish "a chain of newspaper posts, from the New England States to Louisiana, and branching off through Lexington to the Western States." In North Carolina alone, nine new Jacksonian papers had appeared by the middle of 1827, while in Ohio, eighteen new papers supplemented the five already in existence in 1824. In each state, the Jackson forces arranged for one newspaper to serve as the official organ of their respective state committees, refining the broadcast of an authoritative message while promoting a cadre of prominent loyal editors, including Ritchie at the *Enquirer*, Amos Kendall at the *Argus of Western America*, Edwin Croswell at the *Albany Argus*, Isaac Hill at the New Hampshire *Patriot*, and, above all, in Washington, Calhoun's friend Duff Green at the anti-administration *United States Telegraph*.

Funding (as well as copy) for the campaign sheets came directly from Jackson's congressional supporters and their friends, who pioneered numerous fund-raising gimmicks, including five-dollar-a-plate public banquets and other ticketed festivities. More substantial sums, including money raised from local bankers and businessmen in the New York–Philadelphia region, were collected and disbursed by Martin Van Buren, who served as the campaign's de facto national treasurer. Some of these monies went to the newspaper editors; others were spent on printing campaign books and pamphlets and producing paraphernalia such as campaign badges. Much of this material made its way to supporters at government cost, thanks to Jacksonian congressmen's liberal partisan use of their personal postal franking privileges.

Jackson's friends made special efforts to solidify their connections to various popular democratic movements, urban and rural, while also winning over more established and politically influential men. The alliances ranged from complete mergers to testy but effective ententes. Kentucky was a special prize for the Jacksonians, having cast its congressional vote for Adams in 1825 at Henry Clay's insistence. The 1828 tariff's high protective rates for hemp growers and manufacturers helped Van Buren offset Clay's advantage among the Kentucky elite, recently aligned with the Old Court Party—but the Jacksonians mainly pinned their hopes on Amos Kendall, Francis Blair, and the revitalized New Court Party machine. In protection-mad Pennsylvania, where the tariff proved extremely popular among the state's ironmongers, the Jacksonians appealed to all of the elements of the old Jeffersonian coalition—including manufacturers, western farmers, and rural Germans—with a propaganda effort headed by the papermaking magnate Congressman Samuel Ingham. In Philadelphia, the presence of numerous New School candidates for state and local office on the Jacksonian ticket alienated the new Working Men's Party, but Jackson's friends reached out to the labor insurgents in various ways, including a direct fifteen-hundred-dollar contribution to rescue Stephen Simpson's financially strapped paper, the *Columbian Observer*. Ultimately, the Workies devised their own Jackson ticket, picking and choosing among the official nominees, offering joint nominations to those they deemed reliable, but running their own candidates for the other slots.

New York, which Jackson had lost in 1824, was a different and, as ever, more difficult story. Under the revised state constitution, voters now chose the state's presidential electors. Unlike in most other states, however, New York's electoral votes would be apportioned on a district-by-district basis, meaning that even if Van Buren's agents carried the overall popular vote, Adams was bound to win a portion of the state's Electoral College total. DeWitt Clinton's death resolved much of the early bickering within the New York pro-Jackson camp, leaving Van Buren in control, but it also raised the possibility that some pro-Clinton Jackson men, who had supported the Tennessean chiefly to promote Clinton, might now drift over to Adams. And then there was the perplexing Anti-Masonic uprising in western New York, an outburst of democratic outrage that could never be won over to Grand Master Mason Andrew Jackson. Even with all of the southern states plus Pennsylvania likely to support Jackson, it would not be enough to elect him president. New York's result would be crucial.

The outlook for Jackson improved when political operatives determined that the Anti-Masonic movement remained, for the moment, localized, and that its chief advocates, Thurlow Weed and William Henry Seward, were having difficulty merging it with the Adams campaign. The outlook improved even more when Jackson's operatives confirmed that Henry Clay was not only a Mason but, as one delighted Manhattan pol put it, "a Mason of rank." Van Buren, meanwhile, decided to make the most of his New York strongholds, above all New York City, where the old Tammany Society, after a history of recurrent factionalism, turned into one of the most united and reliable pro-Jackson organizations in the state. As early as January, Tammany began hosting giant public events touting Jackson, and after the death of DeWitt Clinton—who was hated by the Tammany braves—the way was cleared for an all-out effort to spike the city's vote. Hickory Clubs appeared in every ward, sponsoring hickory tree–planting ceremonies and barroom gatherings to toast the general's success. A clutch of partisan editors in the already well-established New York press churned out reams of pro-Jackson material. "The more he is known," one pro-Jackson paper boasted of its man, "the less and less the charges against him seem to be true."

Against this juggernaut, Adams's supporters—their candidate an awkward public figure who spurned involvement in campaign organization—were badly overmatched. But they tried their best and performed credibly as organizers. Henry Clay, ignoring advice that he resign and let Adams bear the full brunt of defeat, took charge of creating a national campaign and of stumping at dinners and celebrations around the country to make the administration's case. Daniel Webster pitched in as well, overseeing the canvassing of potential financial backers (fully exploiting his ample personal connections to New England capitalists), collecting substantial sums, and keeping track of accounts. Although they could not equal the Jacksonians, the Adamsites created a substantial pro-administration press, headed in Washington by Joseph Gales and William Seaton's *National Intelligencer* and Peter Force's *National Journal*. The Adamsites printed forests' worth of pamphlets, leaflets, and handbills, organized their own state central committees, and sponsored countless dinners and commemorations. In at least one state, New Jersey, the Adamsites probably outorganized their opponents. And everywhere outside of Georgia, where Jackson ran unopposed, there was a genuine contest under way, with both parties, as one Marylander wrote, "fairly in the field, under *whip & spur*."

Adamsite strategic and tactical errors at the state and local level repeatedly undermined whatever enthusiasm the administration's loyalists generated. High-minded stubbornness, linked to an aversion to what looked to some National Republicans like Van Buren–style wheeling and dealing, killed Adams's chances of carrying the middle Atlantic states. In upstate New York, the National Republicans insulted the Anti-Masons by rejecting their nominee for governor, a close friend of Thurlow Weed's, and then bidding the insurgents to show their good faith by adopting the pro-administration slate, ruining any chance of an alliance. In New York City, a protectionist movement, geared to halting the dumping of foreign manufactures on the New York market, arose in the spring; and, by autumn, it had gained a sizable following that cut across class and party lines. But the Adamsites, seemingly unable to believe that their protectionism might appeal to urban workers, held back from the movement. The protectionists ran their own ticket, and the opportunity was wasted. Similar shortsightedness prevailed in Philadelphia, where the Adamsites refused to make common cause with the surviving Federalist establishment, encouraging Jacksonian hopes of taking the city.

The Adamsites did excel in one area, the dark art of political slander. In 1827, a Cincinnati editor and friend of Clay's named Charles Hammond took a fact-finding tour into Kentucky and Tennessee, and unearthed some old stories about alleged legal irregularities in Jackson's marriage (supposedly he was a bigamist), along with charges that Jackson's wife, Rachel, was an adulteress and his mother a common prostitute. The charges were not simply mean-spirited: they evoked broader cultural presumptions that stigmatized Jackson as a boorish, lawless, frontier lowlife, challenging the Christian gentleman, John Quincy Adams. Clay immediately recommended his mudslinger friend to Webster, calling Hammond's paper "upon the whole, the most efficient and discreet gazette that espouses our cause," and suggested that the editor get direct financial support. Hammond, meanwhile, became a fountain of wild and inflammatory charges—that Jackson's mother had been brought to America by British soldiers, that she married a mulatto who was Jackson's father—all of which found their way into what may have been the lowest production of the 1828 campaign, a new journal entitled *Truth's Advocate and Monthly Anti-Jackson Expositor*. Jackson, enraged to the point of tears, held Clay responsible and sent John Eaton to confront the Kentuckian. Clay vehemently denied the charges, though his private correspondence with Hammond contains hints he was lying. Jackson continued to blame everything on Clay.

Character assassination in presidential politics was hardly invented in 1828—recall, for example, the lurid attacks on Thomas Jefferson and "Dusky Sally" Hemings—and Clay could easily and rightly complain of the Jackson campaign's unceasing attacks about the corrupt bargain as the basest sort of slander. But the Hammond affair, beginning more than a year before the 1828 electioneering commenced in earnest, marked the arrival of a new kind of calculated, mass cultural politics, pitting a fervent sexual moralism against a more forgiving, secularist, laissez-faire ethic. Hammond's attacks also ensured that a great deal of the campaign would be fought out in the sewer. The Jacksonians spread sensational falsehoods that President Adams was a secret aristocratic voluptuary who, while minister to Russia, had procured an innocent American woman for the tsar. Clay came in for merciless attacks as an embezzler, gambler, and brothel habitué. The Adamsites responded with a vicious handbill, covered with coffins, charging Jackson with the murder of six innocent American militamen during the Creek War, and labeling him "a wild man under whose charge the Government would collapse." The competition turned largely into a propaganda battle of personalities and politically charged cultural styles instead of political issues. A campaign slogan from four years earlier, coined in support of a possible Adams-Jackson ticket, assumed completely new meaning and summed up the differences, contrasting the nominees as "Adams who can write/Jackson who can fight."

And yet, for all of the vulgarities and slander, the campaign of 1828 was not an unprincipled and demagogic theatrical. Neither was it a covert sectional battle between a pro-slavery southerner and an antislavery New Englander; nor was it a head-on clash between pro-development Adamsite capitalists and antidevelopment Jacksonian farmers and workers, although strong views about slavery and economic development certainly came into play. The campaign pronounced a valediction on the faction-ridden jumble of the Era of Bad Feelings and announced the rough arrival of two distinct national coalitions, divided chiefly over the so-called corrupt bargain and the larger political implications of the American System. It was, above all, a contest over contrasting conceptions of politics, both with ties to the ideals of Thomas Jefferson.

For all of his setbacks and suffering, John Quincy Adams had never abandoned his moral vision of energetic government and national uplift. Protective tariffs, federal road and canal projects, and the other mundane features of the American System were always, to him, a means to that larger end. A fugitive from Federalism, Adams embodied one part of the Jeffersonian legacy, devoted to intellectual excellence, rationality, and government by the most talented and virtuous—those whom Jefferson himself, in a letter to Adams's father, had praised as "the natural aristoi." The younger Adams took the legacy a large step further, seeing the federal government as the best instrument for expanding the national store of intelligence, prosperity, beauty, and light.

Objections to the political ramifications of that vision united the opposition—objections rooted in another part of the Jeffersonian legacy, a fear of centralized government linked to a trust in the virtue and political wisdom of ordinary American voters. Jackson and his polyglot coalition contended that human betterment meant nothing without the backing of the people themselves. Lacking that fundamental legitimacy, Adams, Clay, and their entire administration had, the Jacksonians contended, been engaged from the start in a gigantic act of fraud—one that, to succeed, required shifting as much power as possible to Washington, where the corrupt few might more easily oppress the virtuous many, through unjust tariffs, costly federal commercial projects, and other legislative maneuvers. Were the Adamsites not removed as quickly as possible, there was no telling how far they might go in robbing the people's liberties, under the guise of national improvement, the American System, or some other shibboleth. Hence, the opposition's slogan: "Jackson and Reform."

Jackson himself laid out the stakes in a letter to an old friend, on the omens in what he called the Adamsites' exercise of "patronage" (by which he simply meant "power"):

> The present is a contest between the virtue of the people, & the influence of patronage[. S]hould patronage prevail, over virtue, then indeed "the safe precedent," will be established, that the President, appoints his successor in the person of the sec. of state—Then the people may prepare themselves to become "hewers of wood & drawers of water," to those in power, who with the Treasury at command, will wield by its corrupting influ-

ence a majority to support it—The present is an important struggle, for the perpetuity of our republican government, & I hope the virtue of the people may prevail, & all may be well.

Or as one of his New York supporters put it (presuming to speak on behalf of "the sound planters, farmers & mechanics of the country"), the Jacksonians beheld the coming election as "a great contest between the aristocracy and democracy of America."

The balloting began in September and, because of widely varying state polling laws, continued until November. Early returns from New England unsurprisingly gave Adams the lead, although not quite the clean sweep he had expected. (In Maine, a hardy band of ex–Crawford Radicals in and around Portland managed to win one of the state's electoral votes for Jackson.) The trend shifted heavily in mid-October, when Pennsylvania (overwhelmingly, including a strong plurality in Philadelphia) and Ohio (narrowly) broke for Jackson. It remains a matter of speculation how much this news affected the vote in other states, where the polls had not yet opened, but the Jacksonians took no chances, especially in New York, where the three days of voting did not commence until November 3. Holding back until the moment was ripe, the New York Jackson committee suddenly spread the word in late October that Jackson's election was virtually assured, in order to demoralize the opposition. In the end, Jackson carried the state's popular vote, although only by about 5,000 ballots out of 275,000 cast.

The state-by-state reporting of the vote, with news of one Jackson victory after another rolling in, heightened the impression that a virtual revolution was underway. The final tallies showed a more complicated reality. As expected, Adams captured New England, and Jackson swept the South below Maryland. But apart from Jackson's lopsided victory in Pennsylvania, the returns from the key battleground states were remarkably even. If a mere 9,000 votes in New York, Ohio, and Kentucky had shifted from one column to the other, and if New York, with an Adams majority, had followed the winner-takes-all rule of most other states, Adams would have won a convincing 149 to 111 victory in the Electoral College. In other races for federal office the Adamsites actually improved their position. Above all, in the U.S. Senate, what had been a strong six-vote opposition majority in the Twentieth Congress would be reduced to a Jacksonian majority of two when the new Congress assembled in December 1829. Despite all their blunders, and despite Adams's unpopularity, the friends of the administration had not lost future political viability.

These wrinkles in the returns were lost amid Jackson's overwhelming victory nationwide. Jackson won 68 percent of the electoral vote and a stunning 56 percent of the popular vote—the latter figure representing a margin of victory that would not be surpassed for the rest of the nineteenth century. The totals came from a vastly larger number of voters than ever before in a presidential election, thanks to the adoption of popular voting for electors in four states and the bitterness of the one-on-one contest in the middle Atlantic states. More than a million white men voted for president in 1828, roughly four times the total of 1824. Jackson alone won three times as many votes as the total cast for all candidates four years earlier. The magnitude of it all left Adamsites, including the normally sanguine Henry Clay, miserable, and Jacksonians jubilant.

Perhaps the only Jacksonian not thoroughly overjoyed was Jackson himself. Well before the voting was over, he had understood what the outcome would be, and the news confirming his election caused no particular stir at the Hermitage. After all the months of campaigning behind the scenes, and now faced with actually assuming the presidency, the victor reported that "my mind is depressed." Sadness turned to panic and then grief in mid-December, when Rachel Jackson, preparing for the move to Washington, suddenly collapsed and, after five days of violent heart seizures, died. Her husband, who sat up with her throughout her ordeal, would never really recover from the shock. His great biographer James Parton wrote that it henceforth "subdued his spirit and corrected his speech," except on rare occasions when, in a calculated effort to intimidate his foes or inspire his allies, he would break into his customary fits of table pounding and swearing. Yet Rachel's death also steeled Jackson for the political battles to come. Her health had been precarious for several years before she died. Jackson was absolutely certain that the slanders of the 1828 campaign had finally broken her. And for that cruel and unforgivable blow, he would forever blame, above all others, his nemesis, Henry Clay.

"JACKSON AND REFORM"

Jackson's victory marked the culmination of more than thirty years of American democratic development. By 1828, the principle of universal white adult male suffrage had all but triumphed—and accompanying that victory, much of the old politics of deference still left over from the Revolutionary era had collapsed. The country and city democracies of the 1790s had attained a legitimacy only barely imaginable a generation earlier. Once-impregnable political establishments—the Connecticut Standing Order, the Philadelphia Federalist regime, the planter and financier political elites of Georgia and Tennessee and Kentucky—had either fallen or been shaken to their foundations. Even where democratic reformers achieved the least—above all in the seaboard South, and there, above all, in South Carolina—local rulers granted cosmetic changes that permitted them to claim that they fairly represented the citizenry's will.

In building their impressive national organization, the Jacksonians had established once and for all the imperatives of coalition building and party organization following the collapse of the so-called Era of Good Feelings. Capitalizing on the long-term resentments from the Panic of 1819, and insisting on adherence to the Missouri Compromise, they had resolved much of the political confusion by consolidating a popular base that merged the urban mechanics and small farmers of the North with the yeomanry and much of the planter class of the South. Close examination of the 1828 local returns bears out the contention that the Jacksonian electorate, if not necessarily its leadership, was broadly drawn from the less well connected and from the lower (though hardly the lowest) rungs of the social ladder. The pattern was especially striking in the battleground states, where purely regional loyalties to the respective candidates did less to slant the totals than in New England or the South. Whereas Jackson ran strongest in the more isolated districts of small farmers from Pennsylvania on westward, as well as in the lower-class wards of New York City, Philadelphia, Baltimore, and Cincinnati, Adams ran strongest in the rapidly developing small towns along the new canals and transportation routes and in creditor-friendly districts like Kentucky's Bluegrass.

Yet if the Jacksonians' victory in 1828 clarified certain issues pertaining to democracy, it left others open—and opened up still others. Even as the Jacksonians celebrated wildly, the lucubrations of their southern Radical faction (and especially of the converted Vice President Calhoun) threatened one day to tear the alliance apart. In the rural North, the Anti-Masonic movement offered a democratic alternative to Jacksonianism that, in the hands of able men such as Thurlow Weed and William Henry Seward, might yet make its presence felt. In the seaboard cities, it remained to be seen whether the reborn city democracy of the Working Men's Party would spread beyond Philadelphia. Even if they did enlarge their following, the Working Men, along with the Anti-Masons, would have to resolve the place of minor parties in the emerging political order, and how they might advance their views without playing the self-defeating role of spoiler.

Many other open questions presented themselves. The great evangelical revivals and the Reverend Ely's proposed "Christian party in politics" had only barely begun to affect political debates with the Sabbatarian petition campaigns of 1828. What new turns might their politics of moral improvement take now that Andrew Jackson was in the White House? How would the pro-nationalist Supreme Court react to the Jacksonian ascendancy—the branch of the federal government least vulnerable to popular politics, led by an aging but forceful Federalist chief justice? Would Jacksonian party builders like Martin Van Buren and their opponents be able to sustain the Missouri Compromise? How would the defeated but hardly eradicated pro-Adams forces reorganize themselves, and with what new national coalition of their own?

Rather than settling these issues, the democratic triumphs that led to 1828 exposed them to further agitation, from the very top of the political system to the very bottom—even by men and women who stood completely outside the widened ambit of electoral democracy. Very quickly, all sorts of Americans would be wielding the tools of the new political democrats—a mass press, popular conventions, petition campaigns, and other means—to rouse support for demands that neither the Jacksonians nor their opponents were fully prepared to address, including such outlandish things as granting women the vote, banning liquor, restricting immigration, and abolishing slavery.

The antislavery campaign would prove the most unsettling. If the Panic of 1819 had galvanized the popular movements that led to Jackson's victory, the Missouri Compromise had established a shaky political middle ground on the issue that most threatened national unity, the future of what had become the South's peculiar institution. And behind that fact lay the hard, looming paradox of American democracy at the dawn of the Jacksonian age: that the democratizing impulse would in time threaten the very sectional peace on which the new political dispensation was founded. Only as long as Van Buren–style political managers kept alive the spirit as well as the substance of the compromise could they sustain political stability—but by expanding democratic possibilities, they all but guaranteed that their middle ground would come under attack. The nub of the matter was, as ever, political: either American democracy could tolerate slavery or it could not. Or as one Illinois politician—still a humble Indiana farmer's son and part-time ferryman in 1828, surrounded by pro-Jackson relatives but too young to vote—would later put it, "[T]his government cannot endure, permanently half *slave* and half *free*," a house divided against itself.

5

THE JACKSON ERA:
UNEASY BEGINNINGS

Anxious marshals had to stretch a ship's cable across the East Portico of the Capitol to keep Andrew Jackson's inauguration ceremony from being overrun. For weeks, people had been pouring into Washington from hundreds of miles around—job seekers, war veterans, state officials, ordinary Jackson admirers, and the curious, each seemingly determined to shake the new president's hand before inauguration day was over. Now they lined the route from Jackson's lodging house to the Capitol, where late arrivals wedged themselves into every possible space. Never before had an American ceremony of state turned into such a democratic and charismatic spectacle. Francis Scott Key declared the sight beautiful and sublime. But Supreme Court Justice Joseph Story, obliged to attend the swearing in and the reception that followed, thought that "[t]he reign of KING MOB seemed triumphant," and departed as quickly as protocol allowed.

Jackson, in deep mourning for Rachel, was dressed in the blackest black suit, tie, and coat, and looked all the more remarkable for it, his hatless head of now-nearly snow-white hair making him instantly recognizable to the crowds, even at a distance. One eyewitness reported the "electrifying moment" when Jackson appeared at the Capitol and "the color of the whole mass changed, as if by miracle," as all the men suddenly removed their own dark hats and looked upward, exultant. Jackson bowed, a courtly yet popular touch hard to imagine from John Quincy Adams. (Feeling slighted because Jackson had not paid him a courtesy call, Adams avoided the ceremonies, just as his displaced father had in 1801.) As was then the custom, Jackson delivered his inaugural address—a spare speech that took only ten minutes—before taking the oath of office. Jackson announced that his new administration would be dedicated above all to "the task of *reform*" in government. Then the chief justice of the Supreme Court swore Jackson in. Just as it was for Jefferson thirty years earlier, the first face that Jackson saw as president belonged to John Marshall.

The rest of the day's activities—especially the White House reception, where the outpouring of well-wishers, patronage hunters, and glory seekers got out of hand—are set pieces of American political lore, emblematizing, depending on the viewer, either the ebullience or the crass vulgarity of the president's admirers. An impenetrable mass of fancy carriages and country wagons followed Jackson down Pennsylvania Avenue. Thrown open to the public, the rooms on the lower floor of the White House were jammed with people of every age, class, and color, both men and women, and the crowd around the president was so thick and importuning that hundreds of visitors, including Amos Kendall, had to climb in the window of an adjoining room to get anywhere near him. Although not unduly perturbed by the chaos, Jackson had to beat a retreat down a back stairway and return to his lodgings. "What a scene did we witness!" remembered one caller, Margaret Bayard Smith, a fixture of Washington salon society. "*The Majesty of the People* had disappeared, and a rabble, a mob, of boys, negros, women, children, scrambling, fighting, romping. What a pity what a pity."

Jackson's inauguration was not the only sensational political exhibition and portent of 1829. On New Year's Day, Frances Wright, the Scots-born chestnut-haired "Priestess of Beelzebub," disembarked in New York Harbor, determined to capture the city, and especially its workingmen, for her own brand of radical free thought. She began her campaign with a series of lectures, delivered to mixed audiences of men and women numbering upwards of two thousand, denouncing, in brilliantly theatrical presentations, every kind of social inequality. Another sensation took shape in Boston, at the outermost fringes of American politics, where David Walker, a black dealer in used clothes, wrote down and published a mystical prophecy of American slavery's impending downfall. By year's end, Walker's pamphlet would make him, briefly, the most dangerous man in America.

Andrew Jackson, of course, exercised far greater political influence than Wright, Walker, or any other American over the next four years. As he began his administration, the new president said he would eradicate the privilege that had corrupted the federal government. If he had gained a mandate for anything from his rout of Adams, this was it. But exactly *how* Jackson would reform the government was unclear, just as his stance on numerous major issues, including the tariff and internal improvements, remained usefully flexible and, to some critics, singularly vague. By the end of his first term, many of these questions would be resolved, in conflicts involving everything from parlor intrigues in Washington City to Indian removal in the southeastern states. Yet the greatest conflicts, over the Second Bank of the United States and the South Carolina nullification movement, involved fights over money, slavery, the Constitution, and democracy more powerful than anyone could have foreseen in 1829. Their intensity arose in part from agitation by Frances Wright, David Walker, and other frustrated radicals for whom the boisterous democracy displayed at Jackson's inaugural was at best too limited and at worst an utter fraud.

SCANDALS: TREASURY RATS, SPOILSMEN, AND MRS. EATON

The first weeks of the Jackson presidency were marked by scandals—the first involving not the new administration, but the one that had just departed. Immediately, Jackson began clarifying what he meant by reform by investigating and clearing out the old order. Convinced that President Adams's higher civil service appointees had been awash in peculation, he appointed the trustworthy Amos Kendall as fourth auditor at the Treasury Department, with instructions to report directly to the president. Almost instantly, Kendall discovered that his own predecessor, one Tobias Watkins, a Clay man, had embezzled seven thousand dollars, and there were many more discoveries to come, involving fraud by more than a dozen of the former administration's Treasury and customs house agents. "Assure my friends," Jackson wrote to a political associate in April, "we are getting on here *well*, we labour night and day, and will continue to do so, until we destroy all the rats, who have been plundering the Treasury." By the end of the year, close to three hundred thousand dollars turned up missing at the Treasury Department alone. Additional fraud was exposed in virtually every executive department, down to a racket in the awarding of fishing bounties.

The discoveries formed the backdrop for what has become one of the most widely disgraced if also misunderstood of Jackson's political reforms, the implementation of rotation in office. The replacement of one party's appointees with another—so vexing in 1801, the last time control of the White House passed from one party to the other—had become a nonissue during the decades of the Virginia dynasty. John Quincy Adams's Olympian cross-factional approach to appointments disturbed his supporters, but raised no general debate. Now the issue reemerged, forcefully. During the campaign, Jackson's supporters had spoken of introducing rotation in office as a democratic innovation. Friends of Adams and Clay moaned about an imminent Reign of Terror that would replace experienced career government workers with inept, purely partisan appointees. With the revelations at Treasury and elsewhere, and with supporters from around the country pressing for jobs, Jackson was moved to implement quickly what he now called, simply, "rotation."

Rotation in office had some obvious partisan origins. After Jefferson's presidency, wholesale and heavily partisan replacement policies became common in the states, especially in Pennsylvania and in Van Buren's New York. "The old maxim of 'those who are not for us are against us,' you have so often recognized, that its authority cannot be denied," the Bucktail Jesse Hoyt warned Van Buren shortly after Jackson's inauguration. Jackson expanded on that maxim at the national level, rewarding and goading his supporters with the spur of self-interest as well as patriotic service. With his customary wariness, Van Buren himself (who had quit the New York governorship he had just won to serve as Jackson's secretary of state) actually counseled caution in replacing too many men too quickly, lest the administration look arrogant. But Jackson moved aggressively, approving batches of new appointments at a time.

Too often overlooked are the sincere reformist purposes that Jackson attached to rotation in office—part of the larger reform agenda to which he devoted considerable time and thought, and which would dominate his first annual message in 1829. Jackson hoped to destroy the insider political establishment that was responsible for what he believed had been the theft of the presidency in 1825. Stasis bred corruption in the executive, he thought, just as it bred the odious belief that ordinary men lacked the experience necessary to master the mysteries of government service. He wanted, instead, to ventilate and democratize the executive branch by making official duties "so plain and simple that men of intelligence may readily qualify themselves for their performance." Accordingly, he coupled rotation in office to proposals for what today would be called term limits, both for appointed executive officeholders (for whom four-year terminal appointments seemed to him about right) and for the presidents

who appointed them (who should be restricted, Jackson suggested, to a single term of either four or six years).

Although he would later face charges of executive despotism,
Jackson limited his major rotation reforms to the executive
branch. He did not call for terminal limitations for Congress,
where fraud or bribery could be punished by the voters, in the
most democratic of solutions. Wary of the constitutional separation of powers, Jackson did not propose terminating federal
judges, although he later envisaged replacing lifetime appointments with popular election to seven-year terms. Nor did he propose that rotation should be tied to partisan supremacy. Even if a
particular party were to remain in the White House year after
year, Jackson's rotation idea would have required a regular
turnover of executive employees. Its chief aim was to prevent the
formation of a permanent government in the executive branch,
an aim that won the approval of no less a political thinker than
Jeremy Bentham, who wrote Jackson enthusiastically that he too
supported rotation in office and had done so for many years.

Jackson's White House replaced roughly one in ten federal
appointees during his two terms as president, no greater turnover
than Jefferson had overseen. Still, the replacements were
unprecedented in their sweep. Among civil officers directly
appointed by the president, the removal rate was nearly one-half.
Jackson stretched the constitutional limitations on appointing
congressmen to civil posts (and broke with one of his campaign's
more specific proposals) by naming more than forty sitting members during his first four years. In 1829 and 1830, plummy postmasterships and deputy postmasterships changed hands by the
hundreds, particularly in the less politically reliable New England and middle Atlantic states. Especially outrageous to his foes
was Jackson's propensity to appoint loyal newspaper editors,
among them Amos Kendall, Isaac Hill, and (as commissioner of
the General Land Office) the Ohio editor Elijah Heyward—mere
"printers," one Virginian sneered—to conspicuous public office.
In the first two years of Jackson's presidency, the State Department moved nearly three-quarters of the contracts for printing

federal laws from opposition newspapers to pro-Jackson newspapers. To the fastidious—including Jackson supporters like Thomas Ritchie, himself an editor—the policy seemed to endanger the future of a free and independent American press.

Jackson's loftier democratic intentions widened the circle of executive talent and established a principle on appointments that all parties would adopt in decades to come. But democracy was never perfect. Rotation led to some humiliating disasters, as it became bogged down in politics and the president's own misjudgments. Not all of Jackson's confidants and supporters saw the rewarding of political office in the same reformist light he did, least of all the hard-nosed pols of the Albany Regency. When Van Buren's lieutenant, William Marcy, defended Jackson's policy in Congress and declared that "to the victor belongs the spoils of the enemy," he both twisted reform into a defense of the crassest sort of party patronage and handed Jackson's enemies a new rhetorical club—"the spoils system." Jackson's assessment of character, meanwhile, was sometimes flawed. Himself a man of absolute integrity, he too easily assumed the same about others whom he liked and admired. He had a special weakness for men who, sometime in the past, had gone out of their way to defend his honor—not the best standard for choosing civil officers.

A few of those appointees about whom Jackson felt most strongly proved disastrous. The Kentucky relief war veteran William T. Barry, who was appointed postmaster general when the incumbent, John McLean, refused to make patronage replacements, was singularly incompetent at preventing corruption in the awarding of department contracts and had to be replaced in 1835. ("No department of the government had ever before been subject to so severe an ordeal," Martin Van Buren later wrote.) And to Jackson's enduring shame, he made his worst appointment, New York City fixer Samuel Swartwout, to the most lucrative position of all, the collectorship of New York Port, a job rife with opportunities for larceny. Van Buren objected privately to the president, all but calling Swartwout a crook, but Jackson brusquely ignored him. After ten years on the job, Swartwout would abscond with over one million dollars—more than all of the Adams-appointed thieves combined.

To his credit, Jackson moved to end abuses once he became aware of their extent; and some of the worst embarrassments only came to light after he had left office. Initially, rotation in office distinguished the new administration from Adams's, changing the tone in Washington and providing Jackson's supporters the assurance that corruption was being uprooted and politically reliable men were getting appointed. More immediately trying for the president was the early jockeying for advantage within the administration, especially between Martin Van Buren and John C. Calhoun, both of whom hoped to succeed Jackson as president. The factional lines, based on substantive as well as personal differences, were already clear in 1829. The struggle commenced in a peculiar salon scandal involving the wife of John Eaton, an old political ally whom Jackson had selected as his secretary of war.

Margaret O'Neale Timberlake Eaton was a dark-haired, fine-featured, unashamed beauty who, at thirty, had risen to a dangerously ambiguous position in Washington society. The daughter of a local Irish immigrant tavern-keeper and hotelier, she had grown up amid the new capital's after-hours politicking and carousing at her father's I Street lodging house, a favorite with congressmen, senators, and visiting politicians from around the country. "I was always a pet," she later remarked. A prodigy of sorts (at age twelve, she was taken to the White House to dance for Dolley Madison), Margaret, by the time she reached womanhood, had little awe for the great and not-so-great lawmakers of Washington, and none at all for their spouses.

Margaret's first husband, John Timberlake, to whom she bore three children, was a naval officer and purser on the USS *Constitution*. The combination of Timberlake's prolonged absences at sea and his wife's close familiarity with so many public officials gave rise to risqué rumors. John Eaton was smitten by Margaret when he first came to Washington as a senator in 1818, and the two were spotted together all too often, in New York as well as in the capital. When, ten years later, Timberlake committed suicide aboard ship (distraught, the gossips said, at Margaret's infidelities), and Eaton, in part at Jackson's urging, promptly married her, the stage was set for a social uproar. Not only was the new Mrs. Eaton—known as "Peggy," affectionately by her friends, snidely by her detractors—an allegedly loose woman of low origins. She was a political wife's worst nightmare, an insider darling who had grown into a bewitching predator and who was now, shockingly, the wife of a cabinet member. To uphold their social honor, a group of administration wives, led by the imperious Floride Calhoun, worked up their indignation into a tempest and snubbed Margaret in every way they could, eventually boycotting any function she attended. The ladies' campaign brought social life in the White House to a virtual halt.

Jackson erupted. As a former guest at O'Neale's lodging house, he knew Margaret well and doted on her. The attack on her and her husband not only offended Jackson's paternalist pride; it was a perfect example of aristocratic contempt stoked by Washington's resident insider snobs. Whatever they might or might not have done that was improper, Jackson thought, the Eatons wound up doing the right thing by marrying. Still grieving over Rachel, he immediately likened Mrs. Eaton's persecution to his wife's during the 1828 campaign. He became consumed with the matter, devoting more than half his time to defending Margaret and railing at all who breathed a word against her. In one of the strangest cabinet meetings in all of American history, Jackson tried to quell the affair by making it the only item on the agenda, and thundered, "She is as chaste as a virgin!" The cabinet wives, unmoved, continued to ostracize Peggy.

There is no evidence that what some called "the Eaton malaria" had any factional origins. Calhoun might have seemed a likely protagonist, given his wife's initial prominence in the snubbing. Yet though he later praised the "great victory . . . in favor of the morals of our country, by the high minded independence and virtue of the ladies of Washington," he and Floride were not even in Washington for most of 1829, having returned to his plantation after the inauguration until Congress convened in December. At least in his correspondence, Calhoun paid little attention to the affair. Yet by the end of 1829, Jackson, who initially suspected Henry Clay, had become convinced that Calhoun was secretly directing everything through his Washington hatchet man Duff Green of the *United States Telegraph*—and the scandal opened a schism.

John Quincy Adams, dryly amused at Jackson's difficulties, reported that Washington was filled with rumors about "the volcanic state of the Administration." In what he called the "moral party" were Calhoun (whose wife became so aggrieved she refused to return to Washington for the winter of 1829–30), Attorney General John Berrien, Treasury Secretary Samuel Ingham, and Secretary of the Navy John Branch, as well as the wife of Jackson's nephew and private secretary, Andrew Jackson Donelson, who, in the absence of a first lady, organized the White House social calendar. All save Mrs. Donelson were Washington social mainstays. The pro-Eaton ranks—which Adams called the "frail sisterhood"—included the newcomer politicians: Van Buren (a widower and exempt from wifely pressures), William Lewis, William T. Barry, and Amos Kendall (who, though he found Mrs. Eaton unsavory, thought she had been slandered and found the continuing fracas absurd). At bottom, it was a cultural divide, pitting pious, self-important Washington fixtures against new arrivals and local commoners whom they deemed vulgar, loose in morals, and uppity. The cultural reverberations, reminiscent of the sexual scandalmongering and clashing masculine styles evident in the 1828 campaign, were powerful. But the Eaton matter also had direct political implications, as most of Eaton's critics were either southerners or close friends of the Calhouns, or both.

Van Buren made the most of the mess. After failing to persuade Mrs. Donelson to give way and invite the Eatons to something—anything—at the White House, he helped organize receptions and dinners for them elsewhere. The loyal secretary of state's stock with the president rose as quickly as the absent Calhoun's fell. Jackson and Van Buren were seen deep in conversation, strolling across the White House grounds and riding together on horseback around Washington. At year's end, Jackson, suffering from what he thought was dropsy and in fear of his life, privately affirmed that Van Buren—"frank open, candid, and manly . . . Republican in his principles"—and not the devious Calhoun should be his successor.

For John C. Calhoun to suffer politically because of a parlor scandal, instigated by his exasperating, politically uninterested wife, was one of the finer ironies of Jackson's early presidency. Although his sense of rectitude made him recoil at Peggy Eaton, Calhoun had little use for drawing-room triviality. Few politicians' letters even to closest friends and family are as devoid of rumor, whimsy, and small talk as Calhoun's. (An apocryphal story made the rounds that Calhoun once tried to compose a poem, wrote down the word "Whereas," and stopped.) There was, in fact, a great and widening divergence between Calhoun and Jackson over fundamental principles of American government, one that originated in the tariff debates of the late 1820s but that had far greater implications. In a world of Calhoun's choosing, those differences, and not the reputation of a cabinet wife, would have been the focus of political struggle. Soon enough they would be.

STATE RIGHTS AND AN ADMINISTRATION ADRIFT

Amid the continuing Eaton distraction, the annoyed Calhoun, once back in Washington, did stick to his last—although, as vice president, he worked behind the scenes, as he had under Adams, lest he appear openly disloyal. His most important work predated the scandal—the report on the tariff he had promised the South Carolina legislature and completed late in 1828, an assignment that Calhoun turned into a brief dissertation on constitutional theory. Released in December 1828 as a revised report by a special committee of the legislature, the document came to be known as the *South Carolina Exposition and Protest*, and offered, in slightly watered-down form, the first elaboration of Calhoun's doctrine of nullification. Over the decades since 1787, Calhoun argued, a hidden weakness in the Framers' design had surfaced: a national majority could, if built around a privileged sectional interest, oppress a sectional minority. The protective tariff, to Calhoun an unconstitutional perversion of Congress's power to set impost duties, exemplified the oppression, by exceeding the use of tariffs to raise revenues and aiding one sectional interest while exploiting another. To rectify the problem, Calhoun, alluding directly to Jefferson and Madison, insisted, as the Kentucky and Virginia Resolutions had in 1798, that individual states could weigh in on contested points of authority between themselves and the general government. But whereas Jefferson and Madison had appealed to the states in order to check the Federalists, whom they considered a repressive minority faction, Calhoun aimed to secure the interests of a slaveholding minority against the national majority. Although he would claim that he believed in majority rule, he also insisted that majority rights were not "natural" but "conventional"—and, as he explained in his draft of the *Exposition*, that "representation affords not the slightest resistence" to protect minority interests.

The only cure for majority despotism, Calhoun argued, was to recognize the undivided sovereignty of the individual states that, he asserted, was anterior to the Constitution. Just as the federal government could annul any state law ruled binding, so aggrieved states could void, within their borders, any federal law they deemed unconstitutional. Should three-quarters of the states then fail to revise the Constitution, under the amending power, to make the offending law constitutional, the nullifying state would have the option of seceding from the Union. Calhoun would always insist nullification was not secession, which was literally true. But in seizing on the theory of original state sovereignty, he offered a theoretical justification for both nullification and secession.

To Calhoun's chagrin, the *Exposition* actually adopted by the

South Carolina legislature sustained his practical steps for nullification but returned to the more traditional state-rights idea that the federal government and the states each enjoyed sovereignty in their separate spheres. The legislature also added a quotation from Thomas Jefferson at odds with Calhoun's thinking, to the effect that it was wrong to consider either the federal or the state governments as superior to one another. Unwittingly, the legislature indicated how Calhoun, although initially a backcountry Republican, had derived his ideas on nullification as much from conservative Federalist legal writings of the early nineteenth century, which he had imbibed at Tapping Reeve's Litchfield academy and Henry De Saussure's law office, as from Jefferson or Madison. In South Carolina, the low-country aristocrat Timothy Ford had anticipated Calhoun's concept of the minority veto as a check on democratic reforms. The first conceptions of a constitutional right to secession had come from Timothy Pickering and the New England plotters of 1804, and then swirled around the deliberations that led to the Hartford Convention ten years later. Both Calhoun's draft and the final exposition invoked Alexander Hamilton's authority as prominently as Jefferson's and Madison's. Out of this undemocratic political strain came Calhoun's defense of the slaveholders' interests in national politics—an innovative combination of Old Republican state-rights theory and Federalism's disdain for the popular majority. And although the *Exposition* ended with Calhoun's call for patience and conciliation given the change in national administrations, it also put the new administration on notice about what would ensue without a drastic reform of the tariff.

Calhoun's name appeared nowhere on the report, but political observers, including Jackson, suspected his authorship—an effort, some thought, to overcome old political rifts and get the Crawfordite Radicals to support his eventual bid for the presidency. Calhoun's direct influence showed, as well, a year later, when, amid a furious Senate debate over a bill to limit the sale of public lands, the vice president's ally, Robert Hayne of South Carolina, rose in opposition as Calhoun sat presiding over the scene in the Senate chamber. Hayne, trying to nourish an inter-sectional political alliance, argued that the Northeast was now trying to oppress the West over the land question much as it had the South over the tariff. Daniel Webster, in his famous second reply, linked Hayne's remarks directly to the nullifying "Carolina doctrine," charged that the doctrine threatened the Union, and launched into a formidable defense of the federal government, "just as truly emanating from the people as from the states." He concluded with a phrase once engraved in the memories of American schoolchildren: "Liberty *and* Union, now and forever, one and inseparable." Calhoun, the erstwhile nationalist Repub-lican, had melded undemocratic Federalism with state rights to defend a minority, the planters. Webster, the erstwhile Federalist, emphasized the idea of popular sovereignty and repudiated the idea of state sovereignty, while he proclaimed an emboldened democratic nationalism.

For once, the ex-Federalist Webster's thinking converged with the democrat Andrew Jackson's. However sympathetic he might be to state rights—far more so than Webster—Jackson, the national hero, could never countenance heresies like nullifica-tion, least of all over a tariff that, by his strict reading of the Con-stitution, was explicitly a matter delegated to Congress's control. His estrangement from Calhoun worsened when, during the Eaton scandal, the vice president let it be known that he intended to work hard for a sharp downward revision of the tariff, a move Jackson resisted. Push came to shove in April 1830, at a Washington politicos' banquet honoring Thomas Jefferson's birthday. The gathering had been called by southerners and west-erners sympathetic to Calhoun, and one toast after another pro-claimed state-rights slogans and attacked sectional favoritism by the federal government. Jackson, provoked beyond his careful preparation, raised his glass, glowered directly at Calhoun, and, as if issuing a dueler's challenge, gravely offered his own toast: "Our Union—it must be preserved." (He had planned to say "Our Federal Union," and so the phrase appeared in the newspaper reports the next day—but in the moment, he omitted the softening adjective.) Some in the thunderstruck audience thought they saw the vice president flinch, and though Calhoun's toast in reply was perfectly calm, its wordiness betrayed that he was on the defensive: "The Union—next to our liberty the most dear; may we all remember that it can only be preserved by respecting the rights of the states and distributing equally the benefits and burdens of the Union." The breach was now public, and within weeks would become bitter political warfare, overlapping the continuing struggle over the Eatons.

The cultural rifts apparent in the Eaton affair showed up in other political developments as well. Among them was Jackson's rejection of the Presbygational Sabbatarian movement that had arisen so swiftly in 1828. During the election campaign, Jackson and his strategists had courted the Sabbatarians, including the formidable Philadelphia revivalist Presbyterian Ezra Stiles Ely. When Ely, in 1827, called for "a Christian party in politics," his chief aim, in the short run, had been to round up Presbyterian support for Jackson, whom he preferred to the suspiciously rationalist John Quincy Adams. But Ely's overbearing appeal offended Baptists and Methodists, wary of connecting religion and politics, as well as those in Jackson's coalition with indifferent religious views. The Senate Committee on the Post Office and Public Roads, chaired by the pro-Jackson Richard Mentor Johnson of Kentucky, issued a blazing response to the Sabbatarian petition campaign as a gross intrusion on the constitutional separation of church and state, "fatal . . . to the peace and happiness of the nation." Jackson's loyalty to Margaret Eaton, in turn, infuriated the Sabbatarians. Ely began a personal crusade to uncover every salacious story he could about Margaret, which he then passed on directly to the president. Jackson's reply, though civil, was seething: "Truth shuns not the light; but falsehood deals in sly and dark insinuations, and prefers *darkness*, because its deeds are evil." As far as any alliance between Jackson and the Sabbatarians was concerned, that was that.

The divide between Jacksonians and Presbygationals ran deeper than the fight over Margaret Eaton. The resumption of the Indian removal battle in Georgia greatly exacerbated the conflict and further defined the character of Jackson's administration. Having outmaneuvered John Quincy Adams and cleared out the Creeks, Georgia's governor George Troup and his successors, John Forsyth and George Rockingham Gilmer, were eager to remove the remaining Cherokees. That goal became even more urgent when gold was discovered on Cherokee land in the summer of 1829. In December 1829, the state legislature declared the constitution and laws of the Cherokee Nation null and void as of the following June 1, 1830—leaving the White House and the Congress little more than five months to settle the issue and determine the Cherokees' fate.

The new controversy differed significantly from the earlier Creek removal. With the aid of missionaries from the Boston-based Presbygational American Board of Commissioners for Foreign Missions, the Cherokees had become a model of cultural assimilation—shifting from the hunt to settled agriculture, converting in large numbers to Christianity, adopting a written alphabet (credited to an ex-warrior, Sequoyah, who had fought with Jackson's forces against the Creek Red Sticks at Horseshoe Bend), and approving a tribal constitution that imitated the U.S. Constitution. Yet the Cherokees' adaptations, along with their insistence on constituting themselves as a sovereign nation within Georgia's borders, only heightened the state's resolve to remove them. And President Jackson, who was unashamedly for removal, would not back off from the situation as his predecessors had, even in the face of determined congressional opposition from northern moral reformers, led by Senator Theodore Frelinghuysen of New Jersey.

In his first annual message in December 1829, Jackson asked Congress for funds to remove the remaining southeastern Indians beyond the Mississippi, and touched off a furious reaction from the forces of Presbygational uplift. To the reformers, Jackson's efforts to make uprooting the Indians a federal matter marked the triumph of crass materialism over respect for humanity and the gospel of Christ. They were certain that Jackson, like the Georgians, had no interest in the Indians' welfare and wanted simply to open up valuable new lands for white speculators and settlers. "How long shall it be," one theology student protester, George Cheever, asked in the *American Monthly Review*, "that a Christian people . . . shall stand balancing the considerations of profit and loss on a national question of justice and benevolence?" Men and women, all across the country (including Georgia), joined in massive petition campaigns demanding that Congress defeat Jackson's plans and uphold the Indians' property rights. (In one of the larger campaigns, Lyman Beecher's daughter, Catharine, the head of the Hartford Female Seminary, initiated the nation's first women's petition drive, holding protest meetings in numerous towns and cities, and gathering thousands of signatures.) The American Board's secretary, Jeremiah Evarts, published an antiremoval legal treatise, *The "William Penn" Essays*, that became one of the most talked-about pamphlets since Thomas Paine's *Common Sense*. In their intensity and organizational sophistication—helped by the communication networks of the growing evangelical churches—the protests surpassed the antislavery "Free Missouri" outbursts of 1819. "A more persevering opposition to a public measure had scarcely ever been made," an amazed Martin Van Buren later wrote.

Jackson, unmoved, saw to it that the relevant House and Senate Indian affairs committees were stacked with pro-removal men—including George Troup, whose earlier extremist actions Jackson deplored but who had been elected to the Senate in 1828. The committees produced similar bills that gave the president the power to reserve organized American lands west of the Mississippi from which Indian tribes could "choose" parcels with perpetual title, in exchange for their eastern lands. In addition, Indians who had improved their existing holdings were eligible for individual allotments of eastern lands, which they could either use to stay in the East or sell to obtain funds required to resettle in the West. Although careful to avoid breaching previous treaties, and to appear as if the Indians remained protected, the vaguely worded bills gave the administration enormous power to dissolve tribal government and hasten removal. They spelled out the eastern Indians' doom.

Senator Frelinghuysen's six-hour speech in opposition to the removal bill was so eloquent that it earned him renown as "the Christian Statesman." Closely following the arguments in his friend Evarts's *"William Penn" Essays*, Frelinghuysen attacked the Georgians and their friends in the War Department for repeated violations of treaties with the Indians, and charged that racial prejudice combined with greed motivated the government's efforts to remove the Indians from their lands. ("Do the obligations of justice," he demanded, "change with the color of the skin?") Frelinghuysen's remarks, publicized widely by the American Board, were unavailing in the Senate, where the removal bill passed easily along party lines. But they did help embolden anti-removal forces in the House, especially among the Pennsylvanians who feared retribution from Quaker voters sympathetic to the Cherokees. Only on May 26, after a series of votes decided by tiny margins, did the House approve the bill.

Just as Jackson's rotation-in-office plans were once considered his administration's chief sin, so, in more recent times, has his insistence on Indian removal become the great moral stain on the Jacksonian legacy. Having stirred great public controversy before its enactment, but virtually none among historians and biographers over the ensuing century and a half, Jackson's Indian policy now stands, in some accounts, as the central drama not only of Jackson's first administration but of Jacksonian Democracy itself. The movement's first crusade, aimed, the critics charge, at the "infantilization" and "genocide" of the Indians, supposedly signaled a momentous transition from the ethical community upheld by antiremoval men to Jackson's boundless individualism. Jackson's democracy, for these historians—indeed, liberal society—was founded on degradation, dishonor, and death.

Like all historical caricatures, this one turns tragedy into melodrama, exaggerates parts at the expense of the whole, and sacrifices nuance for sharpness. Jackson truly believed that, compared to his predecessors' combination of high-minded rhetoric, treachery, and abandonment, his Indian policy was "just and humane," and would leave the Indians "free from the mercenary influence of White men, and undisturbed by the local authority of the states." Compared to some of his main political adversaries—notably Henry Clay, whose racist contempt for Indians had once prompted him to remark that their annihilation would cause "no great loss to the world"—Jackson was a benevolent, if realistic paternalist who believed that the Indians would be far better protected under federal jurisdiction than under state law. (Having adopted an orphaned Indian boy in 1813, he was literally a paternalist.) Complaints from northern humanitarians sounded, to him, hollow and morally convenient, considering the devastation and dispossession wreaked by their ancestors on the Pequots, the Narragansetts, the Delaware, and the rest of a long list of all but extinct northeastern tribes. The Pennsylvania Quakers alone could point to the alternative benevolent legacy of Jeremiah Evarts's hero, William Penn. Jackson, reflecting on the history of white abuse of Indians, said he wanted "to preserve this much-injured race."

Above all, the Cherokees' demand for full tribal sovereignty was, to Jackson, unconstitutional as well as unrealistic, a view he had developed long before his election. Article IV, Section 3 of the Constitution stated that "no new State shall be formed or erected within the Jurisdiction of any other State" without the approval of that state's legislature. Acceding to the Cherokees' claims, Jackson believed, would violate that clause, giving Congress the illegitimate power to dismember a state while imposing a burden on Georgia and Alabama that other states did not bear. If granted, tribal sovereignty would establish both congressional powers and an Indian *imperium in imperio* that would potentially threaten national integrity and security as much as the Carolina doctrine of interposition and nullification. And unless the Indians relocated to the federal territories, the federal government would be powerless, under the existing constitutional delegation of powers, to help them in any way. "As individuals we may entertain and express our opinions of [the states'] acts," Jackson observed, "but as a Government, we have as little right to control them as we have to prescribe laws for other nations." With clear discomfort, Jackson would follow precedent and negotiate treaties with the tribes to secure their removal, even though doing so contradicted his rejection of Indian sovereignty. The end justified the inconsistent means. To Jackson, removal was the only way to safeguard both the Indians' future and the Constitution of the United States.

Jackson was not a simple-minded Indian hater. His removal policy propounded views on the division of powers between the federal government and the states that fell between the state-rights extremism of Calhoun and George Troup and the nationalism of John Quincy Adams and Henry Clay. Neither was Indian removal, as proposed in 1830, a cornerstone of Jacksonian Democracy, especially among northern Jacksonians. Even Jackson's congressional loyalists were divided over the administration's bill. In the Senate, resistant northern Democrats joined with the opposition and nearly wrecked the bill with amendments. In the House, the Pennsylvania ex-Federalist Jacksonian Joseph Hemphill (who, a decade earlier, had helped lead the fight in the House against the extension of slavery into Missouri) demanded a decent concern for "the moral character of the country," and proposed delaying removal, appointing a commission to inspect the lands to which the Indians were to be sent, and shifting responsibility over the matter from the White House to the Congress. Hemphill closed his remarks with historical observations that blended hardheaded realism about the Indians' fate with a compassionate sense of tragedy:

> Against the aborigines who once possessed this fair country, what complaint have we to make? In what degree are their scalping knives and tomahawks to be compared to our instruments of death by which we have overthrown their once powerful kingdoms, and reduced the whole fabric of their societies, with their kings and queens, to their present miserable condition? How little

did they expect, three hundred years ago, that a race of human beings would come from beyond the great waters to destroy them.

Despite intense pressure from Jackson, twenty-four Jacksonians in the House—some angry at the White House over impending internal-improvement matters, others sensitive to the moral outrage of their constituents—voted "nay," while twelve others absented themselves. Sectional loyalties overrode partisanship: northerners broke two to one against the bill and, along with a handful of southerners, nearly defeated it. Only a solid turnout for the administration by Van Buren's New York delegation, along with the recovery of three Pennsylvanians who had begun to waver, saved the measure—a move that Van Buren later said was so unpopular with New York voters that it nearly killed the Albany Regency.

Nothing exculpates Jackson and his pro-removal supporters from the basic truths in the antiremoval arguments. Jackson's paternalism was predicated on his assumption, then widely but not universally shared by white Americans, that all Indians—although Jackson called them his "brothers," he also called himself their "great father"—were "erratic in their habits" and inferior to all whites. His promises about voluntary and compensated relocation, and his assertion that Indians who wished to remain near "the graves of their fathers" would be allowed to do so, were constantly undermined by delays and by sharp dealing by War Department negotiators—actions Jackson condoned. Consigning Indians who resisted removal to live under state law was itself coercive. Jackson tried to head off outright fraud, but the removal bill's allotment scheme invited an influx of outside speculators, who wound up buying up between 80 and 90 percent of the land owned by the Indians who wished to stay at a fraction of its actual worth. At no point did Jackson consider allowing even a small number of Georgia Cherokees who preferred to stay to do so in select enclaves, an option permitted to small numbers of Iroquois in upstate New York and Cherokees in western North

Carolina. Above all, Jackson, determined to minimize federal costs and extinguish the national debt, provided woefully insufficient funds for the care and protection of the relocated. Bereft of long-term planning and a full-scale federal commitment, the realities of Indian removal belied Jackson's rhetoric. Although the worst suffering was inflicted after he left office, Jackson cannot escape responsibility for setting in motion an insidious policy that uprooted tens of thousands of Choctaws and Creeks during his presidency, and would cost upwards of eight thousand Cherokee lives during the long trek west on the "Trail of Tears"—an outcome antiremoval advocates predicted in 1829–30.

The politics of Indian removal also reinforced those elements within the Jackson Democracy that presumed the supremacy of whites over nonwhites and interpreted any challenge to that supremacy as pretended philanthropy disguising a partisan agenda. True, Jackson's opponents, notably Henry Clay, seized on the issue and aided the antiremoval petition effort, whatever their earlier views of the matter. Noticing the divisions among Jacksonians over removal, especially in the swing state of Pennsylvania, Jackson's adversaries sought to exploit them fully, in preparation for the 1832 election. But to reduce all of the critics, as many of Jackson's supporters did, to "factious" politicians who were out to hurt the administration was to confuse the opportunists with sincere humanitarians like Evarts and Frelinghuysen, while making support for removal a matter of strict party orthodoxy. The attacks echoed those against Republican antislavery advocates as designing Federalists during the Missouri crisis in 1819 and 1820. Recast in the political fires of the 1830s and after, this turn of mind would complicate and compromise the Jacksonian variant of political democracy, by rendering all kinds of benevolent reform as crypto-aristocratic efforts to elevate blacks and Indians at the expense of ordinary white men.

Of more immediate importance, however, in the aftermath of the Indian removal debate was a very different conflict over state rights and federal power, involving Jackson's veto of an internal-improvements bill. Like Indian removal, debates over federal aid to road construction and other transportation improvements had a sectional dimension in the Twenty-first Congress's first session. In March and April 1830, Congress debated a bill, introduced by Joseph Hemphill, for a national highway of some fifteen hundred miles that would extend from Buffalo, New York, to New Orleans, via Washington, D.C. By proposing a north-south route connecting the Great Lakes region to the South, the plan envisaged a two-way, man-made alternative to the Mississippi River as a valuable military resource, a concourse for commerce and migration, and a further bond of Union. It also augured large federal expenditures funded by higher tariffs (and possibly a direct tax), while it extended federal power and, its critics charged, benefited certain areas of the country more than others—all anathema to the South. "National objects!" the pro-Jackson Virginian Philip Barbour exclaimed. "Where is the criterion by which we are to decide?" In a sectional vote, the bill was defeated.

More difficult was the fight over the so-called Maysville Road project. Unlike the Hemphill bill, this proposal called only for federal financing, not federal construction, of a road to connect Maysville and Lexington, Kentucky. Although the proposed road would lie entirely within a single state, its advocates claimed that it would one day be a crucial portion of a national road system, and hence deserved federal support. When both the House and Senate approved the bill late in the session, Jackson was torn: although southern Old Republicans were firmly against it, westerners, including Jackson's trusted allies Amos Kendall and Thomas Hart Benton, were friendly to it. Certain to disappoint at least a portion of his coalition, Jackson turned to his new confidante, Martin Van Buren.

In the spirit of Jeffersonian strict construction—but also displaying his propensity to placate the South, especially after the rancor over the tariff in 1828—Van Buren urged a veto. Extravagant federal spending on improvements, he reasoned, would turn elections into corrupt appeals to the voters' narrow self-interest, while opening up new opportunities for congressional logrolling at the public's expense. Jackson, who had been thinking along similar lines, decided to reject not just the Maysville project but a slew of other federal improvement bills. Yet in his Maysville veto message—written chiefly by Van Buren with the help of a young Tennessee congressman, James K. Polk—Jackson also defended the benefits of a "general system of improvement," praised state road and canal projects, and supported judicious federal spending on projects of clearly national importance. Having bolstered his Old Republican southern supporters, some of whom were leaning dangerously toward Calhoun's more extreme state-rights views, the president, his political circumstances precarious, made clear that he did not oppose all government-aided economic development. He would adhere to that position fairly consistently for the rest of his presidency.

"THINGS, THAT HAVE CORODED MY PEACE, AND MY MIND"

Coming at the very end of the new Congress's first session, the passage of the Indian Removal Bill and the announcement of the Maysville Road veto suggested that Jackson had begun to recover from the rocky first year of his presidency. By the middle of 1830, the influence of Calhoun and the incipient nullifiers was on the wane, while that of Van Buren and more moderate state-rights men had increased. The westerners, led by Thomas Hart Benton, although not yet accorded a major role, remained loyal to the president, as did the New Yorkers and (despite the Indian and national road bill debates) the Pennsylvanians, who had been so important in getting Jackson elected. In 1830, the president displayed a successful mixture of deftness and defiance in his dealings with Congress, as well as indifference to the moral objections of the anti-Indian removal movement. Amid persisting conflicts between different portions of the country, he started to chart his own political and constitutional path.

Jackson was not, however, out of the woods. The idea of reform he had announced at his inauguration had not proceeded far except with respect to rotation. The Eaton scandal continued to rage out of control. The alienation of Vice President Calhoun might well lead to the departure of a key element in his successful electoral coalition, the state-rights southern Radicals. Although Jackson got his way on Indian removal, the intense and well-organized public protests—far more impressive, while they lasted, than the Sabbatarian crusade—gave political momentum to his political adversaries and offended many of his northern supporters.

Finding and maintaining his own way, in defense of what he was starting to call "the great task of Democratic reform," was imperative. "[T]here has been, and are things, that have coroded my peace, and my mind, and must cease," he wrote after Congress adjourned, "or my administration will be a distracted one, which I cannot permit." But even as Jackson stumbled to find his footing, developments outside Washington were compounding divisions over slavery and economic development—and creating versions of democracy that sometimes complemented Jackson's, and sometimes attacked its very core.

6

RADICAL DEMOCRACIES

In June 1830, at the very moment that President Jackson pondered how to repair his corroded peace of mind, the free black David Walker, in Boston, put through the press the third and final edition of his *Appeal in Four Articles; Together with a Preamble, to the Coloured Citizens of the World, But in Particular, and Very Expressly, to Those of the United States of America*. Walker was a marked man, and he knew it. He persisted despite his friends' pleas that he flee to Canada.

In the fall of the previous year, Walker had begun sending batches of the pamphlet southward, some on consignment to scattered sympathizers, most smuggled by friendly sailors and ships' stewards, black and white, who on arrival in Charleston, Savannah, or some other southern port would distribute copies to local blacks. Before long, southern authorities began intercepting the *Appeal* and raising a storm. The mayor of Savannah instructed the mayor of Boston, the old Federalist Harrison Gray Otis, to put an end to Walker's mischief, but Otis refused. (Otis agreed that the pamphlet was an piece of "sanguinary fanaticism," but explained that he could do nothing, as Walker had broken no Massachusetts law.) Southern legislatures considered new laws banning "incendiary" publications like Walker's, and rumors circulated that enraged slaveholders had put a price of three thousand dollars on Walker's head—a sum that would rise to ten thousand dollars were he delivered to the South alive. Then, on August 6, Walker suddenly died. No physical evidence of foul play appeared, but word spread that he had been murdered.

The Walker controversy showed that no matter how much conventional politicians tried to abide by the Missouri Compromise, popular agitation over slavery could not be suppressed. Although cut short, Walker's activities would set in motion a chain of events that completely altered the context of American political conflict over slavery. And these events were only part of an efflorescence of reform movements outside the political mainstream—and intense reactions to those movements—that roiled the 1830s. "With this din of opinion and debate, there was a keener scrutiny of institutions and domestic life than any we had known . . . ," Ralph Waldo Emerson observed from the vantage point of the mid-1840s. "The country is full of rebellion; the country is full of kings."

THE BIRTH OF RADICAL ABOLITIONISM

David Walker's effort was the most ambitious black-led campaign in all of American history to incite a general insurrection of southern slaves. The scheme, and the controversy it provoked, marked the emergence of a new, and defiantly radical, abolitionist movement, at first composed almost completely of northern free blacks. Radical abolitionism—which came to be called "immediatism"—arose as a repudiation of the supposedly benevolent antislavery impulses among prominent whites that, in 1816, had led to the creation of the American Colonization Society (ACS). The brainchild of a New Jersey Presbyterian minister, Robert Finley, the ACS was founded in Washington at a meeting of influential national leaders in 1816, led by Henry Clay. It merged two distinct, and in some ways contradictory, points of view: first, a philanthropic antislavery reformism that aimed to eliminate slavery gradually and allow the ex-slaves the chance to return voluntarily to Africa; and, second, a growing fear among slaveholders that the nation's two hundred thousand free blacks were potential fomenters of slave rebellions.

Holding the group together was a deep pessimism about race relations—the long-standing assumption, as Henry Clay observed, that the "unconquerable prejudices" of whites about skin color doomed any effort at racial reconciliation and that blacks had better be sent back from whence their ancestors were stolen. Clay made clear that, as a slaveholder, he did not see colonization chiefly as a springboard to emancipation, but rather as a way to alleviate the racial tensions in America while providing those blacks who volunteered to go with a chance to start anew "in the land of their fathers." The ACS won a hundred-thousand-dollar grant from Congress in 1819, and in January 1820, the first group of emigrants set sail for Africa, headed for their new home in a settlement called Liberia. After the dispersal of the ad hoc antislavery movement that arose during the Missouri crisis, the ACS stood as the chief mainstream organization at all critical of slavery. Over the next forty-five years, the group would help transport approximately thirteen thousand free blacks across the Atlantic.

Some prominent free blacks, sharing in the ACS's racial pessimism, applauded the effort. But most northern blacks had no intention of leaving the country of their birth. Several mass meetings attacked the ACS campaign as the first step toward forcing them to do so—an opinion reinforced by the spectacle of forced Indian removal. Four separate gatherings in Philadelphia, from 1817 to 1819, denounced the colonizationists as tyrants. "Here we were born, and here we will die," a memorial from a group of New York City's free blacks declared. By the late 1820s, fear and loathing of the ACS had inspired the foundation of new, outspoken black antislavery benevolent associations in the major northern cities, as well as the appearance, in 1827, of the first black American newspaper, *Freedom's Journal*, edited by the New York activists Samuel Cornish and John Russwurm.

The outbursts emanated from a northern free black population too often slighted in considerations of the antislavery movement. Slavery had struck only shallow roots in much of the North, but there were specific locales, notably New York City and the middle and lower regions of the Hudson Valley, where the institution had been strong before the Revolution, and where, by the late 1820s, the numbers of free blacks were substantial. Joined by newly emancipated migrants from the countryside, urban free blacks formed coherent new communities along the seaboard from Baltimore (where slavery remained) up to Boston. Overwhelmingly poor, and held in contempt by the white majority, free blacks mostly occupied the lower rungs of the emerging seaport working class. But in each city, a critical mass of blacks succeeded in business (mainly in service trades such as hairdressing) and formed a small but vibrant and self-educated class. This class created and supported a variety of local institutions, sacred and secular, ranging from the first African Methodist Episcopal (AME) churches to the Prince Hall African Masonic lodge (named for the black Bostonian who helped found the world's first black Masonic lodge in 1775), to the antislavery benevolent societies. Having established themselves against long odds, propertied free blacks led protests over a variety of issues, including disenfranchisement in New York in 1821 and, later, impending disenfranchisement in Pennsylvania. They regarded the colonizationist movement with special anxiety—the "many headed hydra," as one black Boston abolitionist would describe it.

David Walker was a recent arrival to this northern black variation on the city democracy, having spent much of his young adulthood wandering the South. Born in Wilmington, North Carolina, about thirty years earlier to a slave father and free black mother—and hence, under the laws of slavery, born free—he probably obtained at a local AME church the religious instruction that would profoundly shape his later activities and writings.

He may also have heard stories of various rumored and attempted slave uprisings in the Wilmington area that had long disturbed local slaveholders. The possibility that Walker had some connection to the Vesey insurrection affair while he was briefly residing in Charleston early in 1822 is as elusive as everything else connected with that event—although by his own testimony Walker attended services at the African Methodist church where Vesey was a class leader, and which was allegedly one of the plotters' headquarters. After arriving in Boston around 1825, Walker quickly gravitated to the city's leading black institutions and to the interlocking directorate that ran them. An observant member of the May Street AME church (founded in 1818), Walker also rose to the position of secretary in the Prince Hall Masonic lodge and took a leading role in the antislavery Massachusetts General Colored Association. In March 1827, he became the chief Boston fundraiser and correspondent for *Freedom's Journal* and would later become an agent for a second paper, Cornish's *Rights of All*.

None of these engagements can fully account for the ferocity of Walker's *Appeal*. No doubt Walker read many antislavery proclamations and writings before and after he arrived in Boston. The apocalyptic imagery of his *Appeal* may have owed something to a fiery pamphlet, Robert Alexander Young's *Ethiopian Manifesto*, published in New York early in 1829—although there is little in the *Appeal* that Walker could not have also picked up himself from the Bible, particularly the book of Revelation. Certainly, Walker's work did not come out of the blue. It only seemed that way, hitting antislavery advocates and southern slaveholders like a lightning bolt.

The *Appeal* declared that the subjugation of American blacks—"the most degraded, wretched, and abject set of beings that ever lived since the world began"—could be blamed on four causes: slavery itself; fatalistic submissiveness to whites by blacks, both slave and free; the callousness and inattention of the so-called Christian churches; and the insidious colonization movement. Throughout, Walker indicted white Americans (using the terms *whites* and *Americans* virtually interchangeably) for their racism. Even Thomas Jefferson—the author of the egalitarian Declaration of Independence and, Walker wrote, "one of as great characters as ever lived among the whites"—had expressed hateful opinions about blacks in *Notes on the State of Virginia*. Only a thorough purging of America's heart and soul could, Walker said, redeem the country. To effect that cleansing, America's blacks would have to shrug off their despair-induced feelings of inferiority, improve their own moral condition, and themselves lead the fight for freedom and racial justice.

Written as if it were intended to be read aloud to illiterate blacks, with entire words capitalized and gaggles of exclamation points, the *Appeal* was a deeply alienated piece of work. Yet it still clung to American political principles and the possibility that they might be salvaged from racial oppression. Although Walker condemned Jefferson, he also regarded the Declaration, with its assertion that all men are created equal, as a model of human and political rights. And although Walker also condemned the Christian clergy (specifically exempting black preachers including Richard Allen, one of the founders of the AME church), his logic and his rhetoric were saturated in Christian faith. Walker held out hope that the whites would come to recognize their unrepublican, ungodly errors, repent, and open the way for a glorious new age of racial reconciliation. "What a happy country this will be," he wrote, "if the whites will listen."

Walker's hopes were slender. Even though the *Appeal* did not explicitly call for a slave insurrection, its preamble suggested that God might cause the whites "to rise up one against another . . . with sword in hand," causing slavery's downfall—clairvoyant lines, coming thirty years before the Civil War. And repeatedly, Walker alluded to an impending black rebellion led by some God-sent Hannibal that would overthrow the white oppressors. No strategist or tactician of revolution, Walker wrote more as if he were a Jeremiah or, perhaps, a John the Baptist, rousing his audience to set their sights on liberation and the coming of the Lord.

Walker's message—and his cleverness in actually smuggling it into the South—understandably shocked slaveholders who well remembered the Vesey insurrection scare of 1822. Even before Walker was dead, legislators in Georgia and Louisiana enacted harsh new laws restricting black literacy and rights to assembly. Similar legislation narrowly passed the Virginia House of Delegates but expired in the state senate; North Carolina adopted its own repressive literacy laws in the autumn of 1830. In Walker's hometown of Wilmington, white mobs harassed the free black neighborhoods. In Savannah, vigilantes and police confronted black sailors and prevented them from disembarking. It was bad enough that free blacks and slaves had learned of the loose talk by antislavery northerners during the Missouri debates. Now the idea of a godly slave rebellion was coming down directly from the North, written and published with impunity by the ever-dangerous free blacks, headquartered safely in New England.

Walker's work provoked a different sort of disquiet among the small bands of white antislavery advocates who had repudiated the colonization movement. During the years immediately preceding the Missouri crisis, a few isolated voices, notably the British émigré Reverend George Bourne, exhorted Americans to commence immediately the abolition of slavery. In 1824, the pamphlet *Immediate, Not Gradual Abolition*, by the English Quaker convert Elizabeth Heyrick, shook up antislavery opinion on both sides of the Atlantic. Otherwise, outside of the ACS, a scattering of white antislavery societies—most of them led by Quakers and unreconstructed antislavery Methodists and Baptists, and a majority of them situated in the nonslaveholding districts of the border states—were fighting a losing battle against slavery's revival. Although their presence was dwindling (especially in the upper South), these little groups did produce a few influential authors, editors, and activists. The most important of them was the peripatetic editor and exhorter Benjamin Lundy.

Slight of build and partially deaf, the indefatigable Lundy made his reputation chiefly from his newspaper, the *Genius of Universal Emancipation*. Born in New Jersey in 1789 to a struggling Quaker family, he had headed west at age nineteen to seek his fortune and spent four years apprenticed to a harness and saddle maker in Wheeling, Virginia. There, the sight of slave coffles so offended him ("the iron entered my soul," he later wrote) that he determined to fight the institution, and after moving across river into Ohio, he organized the Humane Society, intended as the first step toward a national abolitionist organization. He also began writing and working for a local Quaker antislavery newspaper, the *Philanthropist*; then, in 1821, he started the *Genius of Universal Emancipation*. After relocating his family once more to the rugged hill country of East Tennessee, Lundy assumed operation (using the *Genius*'s title) of one of the livelier border-state antislavery journals, the Quaker Elihu Embree's *Emancipator*. For the next fifteen years, Lundy traveled from New England to Texas like an itinerant preacher, giving lectures, organizing new antislavery societies, and, when a press was handy, printing new issues of the *Genius* (whose column rules, imprint, and heading he kept packed in a small trunk).

Lundy's antislavery program combined a practical sense of political and constitutional limits with the sense of urgency that had marked the "Free Missouri" stirring of 1819–21, and that the colonizationists utterly lacked. Under his plan, the federal government would abolish slavery only where he claimed it had the clear constitutional authority to do so, as in the District of Columbia. No more slave states would be admitted to the Union; the internal slave trade would be banned; and the three-fifths compromise in the Constitution would be repealed. Where slavery currently existed, Lundy favored moral appeals for gradual emancipation. Aid would be provided for free blacks who wished to depart the country (colonization efforts that Lundy himself pushed by trying to resettle blacks in Haiti, Texas, and Canada), but in the free states, free blacks who wished to remain would be accorded the same civil and legal rights as whites. Lundy's unyielding rhetoric as well as his proposals—slaveholders, he proclaimed, ranked among "the most disgraceful whoremongers on earth"—gained him admiration from free blacks, including David Walker, who singled him out for praise. It also impressed a young white writer and printer in Boston, William Lloyd Garrison.

Garrison, aged twenty-two, first ran across the *Genius of Universal Emancipation* early in 1828, on the exchange newspaper pile in the offices of the pro-temperance *National Philanthropist*, where he had been working since the start of the year. A lean, flinty young man, the son of an alcoholic Newburyport, Massachusetts, sailor and his devout Baptist wife, Garrison had been a working printer for nearly a decade, first as an apprentice in his hometown and then for two years as editor of his own paper, the *Free Press*, before he moved to Boston. Although his formal schooling was limited, Garrison had thrived in the world of the self-taught mechanics, gaining a love for literature and poetry as well as for politics. (While at the *Free Press*, he befriended the budding Quaker poet John Greenleaf Whittier and published some of Whittier's early works.) His opinions on public affairs tended toward the uplifting National Republicanism of John Quincy Adams, but Garrison grew impatient with electoral politics and enlisted in the temperance cause—"a great moral influence," he wrote. Under the sway of Lundy's paper—and of Lundy himself, who showed up in Boston on one of his tours in March 1828—Garrison then resigned from his job at the *Philanthropist* and threw himself into antislavery work.

Frustrated by white Bostonians' indifference, Garrison took a brief detour back into partisan politicking as editor of a pro-Adams sheet in Bennington, Vermont—but by the spring of 1829, he was back in Boston, sharing a room with his old friend Whittier and earning his keep with temporary printing jobs. Invited by, of all groups, the local branch of the Colonization Society to deliver a Fourth of July address at the prestigious, all-white Congregationalist Park Street Church, he made the most of the opportunity. Dressed with studied informality, open-necked and spread-collared in the Byronic romantic style, Garrison condemned the Fourth of July as a nauseating spectacle filled with "hypocritical cant about the rights of man." Imagine, he bid his listeners, if the oppressed slaves were ever to rise up in rebellion: would their justifications not fairly replicate Jefferson's Declaration? Was slavery not founded on absurd and immoral racial prejudice—the same prejudice that the slaveholder and charlatan Jefferson had expounded in *Notes on the State of Virginia*? "Suppose that . . . the slaves should suddenly become white," Garrison exclaimed. "Would you shut your eyes upon their sufferings and calmly talk of constitutional limitations?" He implored his audience: *"Let us not shackle the limbs of the future workmanship of God.* Let us, then, be up and doing."

It was as forceful a denunciation of slavery and racism as any white American had ever publicly delivered, and Garrison would soon be making even more radical assertions. Although the exact connections are obscure, there can be little doubt that Garrison's heightened radicalism owed a great deal to his widened contacts with black abolitionists—including, quite possibly, David Walker, who appears to have named a son after him. Garrison also discovered one of Reverend Bourne's old pamphlets, which impressed on him a maxim: "Moderation against sin is an absurdity." When, in August 1829, Garrison took up Lundy's invitation to join him in Baltimore (where Lundy had temporarily settled) as assistant editor of the *Genius*, he, unlike his mentor, had embraced the idea that slavery's demise must commence immediately.

Within weeks, Garrison became a target for repression. After the *Genius* condemned a Massachusetts merchant for allowing one of his ships to be used to transport slaves, Baltimore authorities, possibly at the instigation of pro-Jackson Maryland officials, tried and convicted Garrison on a seldom-invoked charge of "gross and malicious libel," and sent him to jail for six months. Dramatizing his role as a prisoner of conscience—in fact, he was kept in the kindly warden's own comfortable home—Garrison wrote a pamphlet on intellectual freedom, which Lundy published and which prompted the prominent New York evangelical Arthur Tappan to pay his fine. His notoriety growing, Garrison then lectured up and down the East Coast, drumming up support for a new weekly newspaper he planned to publish in Boston.

"I am in earnest—I will not equivocate—I will not excuse—I will not retreat a single inch—AND I WILL BE HEARD." With the now-famous lines of his first editorial, on January 1, 1831, Garrison announced that his new paper, the *Liberator*, would plant the standard for an uncompromising immediatism on slavery. The paper carried on the work of the *Genius*, collecting news of antislavery efforts and evil complicity with slavery from around the country. But the *Liberator* was pointed in its rejection of gradualism—"a sentiment," Garrison declared, "so full of timidity, absurdity, and injustice."

Garrison's continuing ties with black activists were crucial to his work. Most of the initial financial support for the *Liberator* came from blacks in Boston and other cities, above all the wealthy Philadelphia sailmaker and antislavery leader James Forten. Blacks constituted the majority of the newspaper's subscribers during its first year. Garrison, accordingly, opened the *Liberator*'s columns to black activists, male and female, covering black benevolent and political association activities and publishing work by such formidable figures as Forten and contributors like the former servant Maria Stewart. In July, Garrison published a twenty-four-page pamphlet based on speeches he had delivered to black groups in New York and Philadelphia, reiterating his newspaper's dedication to racial equality and inviting black support from outside of Boston. In his boldest move, Garrison also printed sympathetic appraisals of, and extensive excerpts from, Walker's *Appeal*, deprecating its violent passages but extolling its hatred of slavery and white supremacy. ("It is not for the American people, as a nation," he wrote of the *Appeal* in the second issue of the *Liberator*, "to denounce it as bloody or monstruous.")

In his newfound immediatism, Garrison also forever broke with mainstream American politics. Not surprisingly, in view of his Federalist–National Republican background, he assailed Jackson's administration in Washington—above all the slaveholder at its head who, Garrison declared as early as 1828, ought to be "manacled with the chains he has forged for others and

smarting under the application of his own whips." By 1831, however, Garrison had renounced all political parties as hopelessly
compromised. No political leader had earned greater admiration
from the young Garrison than Henry Clay, the great champion of
economic development and uplift. But Clay's support for colonization, and his political fraternization with the slaveholders of
his own party, betrayed his moral bankruptcy. Henceforth, Garrison would seek to redeem the nation's soul by agitating outside
the political system and renouncing the slightest complicity with
slavery and racial discrimination.

Apart from its black supporters—who hailed Garrison as the
greatest white man in America—the *Liberator* caused the largest
stir among southern slaveholders and their northern political
friends. It quickly became a favorite resource for the most outspoken southern pro-slavery papers, which would reprint Garrison's copy as proof positive that fanatics had overrun the
northern states. Nearly as contemptuous were northern papers,
Jacksonian and anti-Jacksonian alike, that lambasted Garrison as
a "mawkish sentimentalist" who was ranting against "imaginary
sufferings." But these attacks on Garrison and on radical abolitionism would come to seem gentle after August 1831, when a
cataclysmic slave insurrection struck Virginia.

Nat Turner was an unlikely rebel—which made the blood-
drenched rampage he helped to lead all the more chilling. Born
in rural Southampton County, Virginia, one week before Gabriel
Prosser was hanged in Richmond, ninety miles to the north, he
was thirty years old at the time of the revolt: shy of company and
physically unimposing, broad-shouldered but of medium height,
beardless, with thinning hair. As Turner himself would attest, his
latest master had treated him kindly, causing Turner, a field
worker, no complaints. Turner was a devout Christian, a sometime Baptist preacher who claimed to prefer "devoting [his] time
to fasting and praying." Yet it was apparently this piety that bid
him into battle.

In 1821, Turner ran away from his overseer, but returned after
thirty days. Like many runaways, he may simply have become

tired and hungry, and his hunger may have overcome his other senses; in any case, he later reportedly said that he received instruction from a holy vision to "return to the service of my earthly master." Four years later (after his sale to one Thomas Moore), Turner had another vision, of blood drops on ears of corn in the fields, and of hieroglyphs and blood-drawn pictures of men in the leaves in the woods. Three years after that, the heavens roared, and the Spirit appeared to Turner once more, telling him that the Serpent had been loosened, that Christ had laid down the yoke He had borne for men's sins, "and that I should take it on and fight against the Serpent, for the time was fast approaching when the first should be last and the last should be first."

In 1830, Turner was moved to the home of Joseph Travis, the new husband of Thomas Moore's widow. (Formally, Turner was the property of his recently deceased master's infant son, Putnam.) The following February, a solar eclipse signaled to Turner that the appointed time had arrived, and he began making preparations with four close friends for an uprising on July 4, only to fall sick, forcing a postponement. Finally, on August 13, a disturbance in the atmosphere tinctured the sun a bluish green. It was the Spirit's last sign. A week later, Turner and six confederates slipped off into the woods, barbecued and ate a stolen pig, washed it down with stolen brandy, and then made a whole new set of plans. At two the next morning, they hacked to pieces Joseph Travis and his entire household of five, including the baby Putnam Moore, before marching off with some pilfered rifles, old muskets, and powder.

Salathul Francis and his wife, asleep six hundred yards down the road from the Travises, were the next to die, followed by a Mrs. Reese and her son, followed by one household after another, upwards of a dozen, in a winding trail that left every white person who could be found (including the ten children at Levi Waller's place) axed, clubbed, or shot into mangled corpses, their blood sprinkled, according to one account, by Turner on the other rebels. At midday, the slaves—their force now numbering between fifty and sixty, most of them on horseback—headed south to lay to waste the town of Jerusalem, the closest settlement and the site of an armory. They may have intended to hide thereafter in the nearby and virtually uninhabitable Great Dismal Swamp. But the marauders never made it. Alerted to the devastation, a band of white militiamen confronted and scattered the killers only a few miles from their goal. After several skirmishes continuing into the next day, the rebellion was over.

Turner escaped the scene and avoided capture until the end of October. At least fifty-five whites had been slain, and a like number of slaves, including Turner, were tried for the crimes, of whom thirty-two were convicted, twelve transported out of the state and twenty executed (with their masters receiving due financial compensation from the Commonwealth of Virginia). Shortly before his death, Turner gave an extended interview to a profit-minded physician named Thomas Gray, whose rendition of Turner's account, published as *The Confessions of Nat Turner*, remains the fullest (if, perforce, highly questionable) piece of evidence about what transpired. Once he was hanged, Turner's body was dissected, as any eighteenth-century criminal's would have been. If there is any truth to the folk legends, the authorities then grilled down his flesh into grease and ground his bones into dust.

In strictly military terms, the Southampton insurrection amounted to a pinprick against the slaveholders' regime. Only a tiny portion of an isolated Virginia county had been affected. The terror lasted only a single night and a single morning. Some slaveholders reassured themselves (and tried to reassure others) that although the rebels had wreaked gruesome havoc, most slaves in the surrounding countryside did not rush to join them, and at least a few had helped their masters fight the rebels off—a moment of truth that supposedly proved slavery's basic soundness. One contributor to a Richmond paper saw the occasion as one to pay "tribute to our slaves . . . which they so richly deserve."

A very different perspective comes with the recognition that Turner's rebellion was the deadliest domestic uprising in the nation before the Civil War. If Walker's *Appeal* had offered a pretext for servile mayhem, and Garrison had helped disseminate Walker's ideas, the Virginia episode had made the mayhem real. A panic wave gripped most of the South, as slaveholders began wondering whether beneath the kindly deferent visages of their own bondsmen lurked more Nat Turners, just waiting to strike. Slaves in Virginia and North Carolina were rounded up as suspects in the plot, tried, and executed, while white mobs murdered (and, in some cases, tortured first) upwards of two hundred blacks. Southern editors lashed out at the seditious northerners and their free black southern accomplices whom they blamed for provoking the bloodshed. The *Richmond Enquirer*, quick to detect conspiratorial designs, asked its readers to send information about anyone circulating either Walker's *Appeal* or Garrison's *Liberator*. In Washington, the anti-Jacksonian, pro-colonizationist *National Intelligencer* called on the mayor of Boston to suppress the "diabolical" *Liberator* and punish "the instigator of human butchery" who ran it. The Georgia legislature offered a five-thousand-dollar reward to anyone who brought Garrison down from Boston to stand trial for seditious libel.

The chances that Nat Turner or any of his accomplices, in out-of-the-way Southampton County, knew anything about Walker's and Garrison's writings are unlikely. (By his own testimony, Turner had begun receiving divine instruction a decade before the *Liberator* even appeared.) Garrison, for his part, said that he was "horror-struck" at the first reports of the massacre, his pacifist soul shaken by a nightmare prediction turned "bloody reality." Yet as if to confirm the slaveholders' worst charges, Garrison also refused to condemn the Southampton rebels, noting that their oppression, and not his words, had inflamed the slaves' unholy vengeance. Garrison's stance—as one of a handful of editors to say anything on behalf of the uprising—redoubled the attacks against him, which only stoked Garrison's fury. By the end of 1831, he had increased both the sheet size and the page count of the *Liberator*. At the start of the new year, he was hard at work founding the first American organization of its kind dedicated to immediatist abolitionism, which he hoped would become a model to all righteous Americans, the New England Anti-Slavery Society.

The rise of the abolitionist radicals aggravated divisions within the North and the South as well as between them. The immediate impact was less severe in the North, where, as of 1831, abolitionism remained politically marginal. But in the South, the radical and violent turns in antislavery agitation instantly stirred up abiding differences over slavery—and over the desirability of democracy for white men. Although southerners had united, a decade earlier, around the proposition that slavery should not be barred from the new state of Missouri, there was no consensus over slavery's long-term future. The strains, evident in the Missouri debates, between pro-slavery men like the South Carolinian William Smith and more ambivalent, border-state diffusionists like Henry Clay persisted, as did political and social tensions between slaveholders and nonslaveholders, especially in the upper South. Walker's and Garrison's invective, punctuated by the Southampton massacre, forced a reevaluation on all sides and led to political struggles that quickly became entangled with continuing efforts by plebeian democrats to remove the remnants of patrician domination. In no southern state did these struggles erupt with greater force, or with greater significance, than in Virginia.

SUFFRAGE AND SLAVERY IN VIRGINIA

Democratic reform, for white men only, advanced unevenly in the South after 1825. At one extreme were the western cotton-kingdom states of Alabama and Mississippi, the most democratic in the region—defining the slave-based Master Race democracy. Alabama's constitution of 1819 underwent minor democratic revision in 1830, reducing the terms of state judges from life to six years. Two years later, Mississippians adopted a new constitution that established universal white manhood suffrage, as in

Alabama, but that also, surpassing Alabama, eliminated county courts in favor of boards of police (their members elected for two-year terms) and opened all state judgeships to popular election for limited terms of office. At the other extreme was South Carolina, where allied low-country and backcountry planters ruled virtually unchallenged through a centralized system buttressed by high property qualifications for officeholding and selection of the governor by the omnipotent legislature. Reform was almost hopeless in a state whose rulers candidly admitted that they held all power. "The people have none," John C. Calhoun's friend James H. Hammond would later remark, "beyond electing members of the legislature—a power very negligently exercised from time immemorial."

Virginia's Tidewater and Piedmont squirearchy, although nearly as adept as the South Carolinians at deflecting democratic rumblings, faced greater difficulties. The commonwealth's non-slaveholding counties west of the Alleghenies—particularly in the northern region around Wheeling—were expanding rapidly, thanks to continued migration from Pennsylvania, New Jersey, and Delaware. Between 1820 and 1829, the population of the western part of the state rose by nearly 40 percent, compared to a rise of only about 2 percent in the Tidewater counties. With its craggy terrain, ill-suited to slave production of cash crops, and with a populace consisting largely of Pennsylvania Dutch and Scots-Irish, the area was more an extension of the free-labor North than of the slave South. East of the Alleghenies and west of the Blue Ridge Mountains, in the Shenandoah Valley, slave-holder émigrés from eastern Virginia prospered. Overall, the percentage of slaves in the valley's population, although greater than in the far West, was about half that of the Piedmont and Tidewater counties east of the Blue Ridge. Virginia's borders contained two distinct social orders, with the valley serving as a buffer zone. As the western population continued to swell while the eastern population stagnated, efforts to throw off the East's political domination, secured by the freehold suffrage requirements and an increasingly malapportioned legislature, were bound to revive.

Additional pressure for political reform emanated from the growing cities of eastern Virginia, above all the state capital, Richmond. The city's nonfreeholders, including mechanics and shopkeepers, had long chafed at their exclusion from voting in state elections. By the 1820s, when their numbers had grown to include nearly half of the city's free adult males, they organized as never before to eliminate the freehold suffrage. ("We most earnestly wish that the state . . . would give us some practical proofs of that republican spirit and vigilance that she so much boasts of," said one editorial in 1821.) They were joined in their complaints by leading local editors from opposing political camps, most conspicuously Thomas Ritchie of the *Enquirer* and John Hampden Pleasants of the *Constitutional Whig*, who worried about losing the loyalties of western farmers.

A new round of reform agitation began in 1824, culminating in a popular convention of western counties, held in Staunton in August 1825, which demanded an end to the political monopoly of "the slave owning eastern aristocracy." Conservatives in the eastern-dominated legislature held their ground and rejected, in three successive sessions, bills that would have convened a state constitutional convention. Finally, in 1828, the general assembly approved putting the question to a popular referendum—and with one-fourth of the Tidewater vote (chiefly in the cities) and nearly half of the Piedmont vote breaking in favor of a convention, the reformers won a convincing victory. The old Tidewater and Piedmont regions still held the upper hand: in the subsequent legislative vote over the apportionment of convention delegates, easterners, a slender majority of the state's free population, wound up with two-thirds of the delegates. But the convention's political divisions proved complex, as roughly one in five of the ninety-six delegates ended up supporting reform of certain restrictions and not of others, creating ever-shifting coalitions and uncertain majorities.

The convention met at Richmond in early October, an event as rich in its political symbolism as it was stark in its sectional cleavages. The site, the house chamber of Jefferson's elegantly designed state capitol, was a monument to classical order, reason, and deliberation. The delegates included the greatest living eminences of two generations of Virginians, among them two former U.S. presidents (Madison and Monroe) and the chief justice of the U.S. Supreme Court, John Marshall. In their finery, the easterners, a mixture of Jacksonians, anti-Jackson National Republicans, and surviving Old Republicans and Federalists, looked every bit as imposing as they hoped to, in what would be their last great collective act as self-appointed guardians of the Revolution's wisdom. The westerners set a very different tone, their ill-cut homespun suits and mud-flecked boots summoning up a rough-hewn democratic future. Their foremost delegate, Philip Doddridge, won grudging admiration from some of the easterners for his breadth of knowledge and command of facts, but he also evoked derision as "a low thick broad shoulder'd uncouth looking man" who spoke with a Scots-Irish brogue and lacked "the bland and polished manner belonging to the South."

The debates themselves featured, from both sides, some of the most direct, informed, and intellectually engaging arguments heard anywhere since the Revolution about the pros and cons of democracy. The most spirited exchanges concerned representation and the freehold suffrage. The westerners argued for apportioning the lower house solely on the basis of white population, making the familiar claim that property owning was no measure of political virtue and that representation based on property was a tyrannical violation of natural rights. Their opponents, including an articulate forty-year-old judge from Northampton County, Abel Upshur, adapted the traditional "stake-in-society" justifications for patrician predominance, including the argument that the propertied, through taxes, did most to support the state. In terms familiar to any reader of Edmund Burke—an influential authority in Virginia—the easterners stressed solidity, permanence, tradition, and the unforeseen consequences of seemingly equitable change. They insisted that the possession of property helped temper the disruptive passions and weaknesses common to all mankind. They also candidly admitted that the struggle involved clashing interests as well as different philosophies, and they backed an amended plan basing representation on a formula that combined population and property. "If the interests of the several parts of the Commonwealth were identical, it would be, we admit, safe and proper that a majority of *persons only* should give the rule of political power," Upshur explained. "But our interests are not identical, and the difference between us arises from property alone."

"Property" was a dazzling abstraction. Everyone knew that it was the easterners' form of property in humans, as well as the greater value of their property, that set them apart from the westerners. Some delegates, including Upshur, forthrightly acknowledged the fact and expanded on it. Easterners agreed that what Upshur called their "*peculiar*" property, "exposed to peculiar impositions, and therefore to peculiar hazards," needed peculiar protection, but they disagreed over how best to achieve it. One faction argued that fairer representation was required to reinforce the westerners' (and nonfreeholder easterners') allegiance to slavery. Chapman Johnson, a Richmond lawyer representing a Piedmont county, said that proper apportionment would reinforce "a feeling of affection and sentiment of justice" between slaveholders and nonslaveholders, curbing any temptations to attack slavery. Others believed exactly the reverse, that adding to the westerners' power would badly undermine the slaveholders' regime.

The antidemocratic arguments held sway among the easterners. The majoritarian rule of "King Numbers," John Randolph insisted (in the last significant public appearance of his life), would create the sort of "Robinhood Society," promoted by the deluded Jefferson, that would lead to a plundering of the slaveholders' property through unfair taxation. Upshur said that easterners could not even count on the cooperation of slaveholders in the West "in any measure calculated to protect that species of property, against demands made upon it by other interests, which to the western slave-holder, are of more important and immediate concern." Others appealed more openly to class presumptions, while also contesting Jefferson's authority. Although intellectually and morally superior to black slaves, the clubfooted conservative Benjamin Watkins Leigh of Chesterfield County charged, the "peasantry of the west" had no more ability to govern than any other peasantry the world over. "I ask gentlemen to say, whether they believe," Leigh asked the convention, "that those who are obliged to depend on their daily labour for daily subsistence, can, or do enter into political affairs? They never do—never will— never can." So "large a dose of French rights of man" as the reformers demanded, Leigh claimed, would plunge Virginia into "fever, frenzy, madness, and death."

Similar divisions appeared over the freehold suffrage. One young reformer from the Piedmont, directly rebutting Leigh, invoked Jefferson and Paine ("whose immortal work, in the darkest days of our revolution, served as a political decalogue") and, with his western allies, attacked the property-based suffrage as a denial of popular sovereignty and free government. Others, from the East as well as the West, defended reform on pro-slavery grounds, citing the urgent need, as one westerner put it, "to call together at least every free white human being, and unite them in the same common interest and Government." Eastern conservatives scoffed at such "visionary" and "theoretical" proposals, and proclaimed their unswerving belief that voting rights belonged only to those who possessed what Philip N. Nicholas of Richmond called the "permanent interest and attachment" that came with owning land, a "durable," "indestructible kind of property." They also argued that expanding the white electorate to include large numbers of nonslaveholders might lead to emancipation, not least, Upshur said, because of the westerners' proximity to Ohio and Pennsylvania, whose "moral sentiment" against slavery would assuredly be felt. "Expediency" (a word the easterners used repeatedly) demanded an unequal suffrage as well as a property-based system of representation.

Defections by Piedmont representatives in the crucial convention votes prevented the eastern conservatives from prevailing outright, despite their disproportionate majority of delegates—but the old guard salvaged a great deal. After the population-property formula for representation was defeated, the conservatives regrouped and narrowly won permanent reapportionment on the basis of the obsolete 1820 census returns, thereby securing for the Tidewater and Piedmont a reduced but still substantial artificial majority in the lower house. The fifty-dollar freehold suffrage requirement was eliminated, but a twenty-five-dollar freehold survived in its place—enough to disenfranchise about one-third of the state's white freemen. The malapportionment of the state senate was left untouched, as was the power of the legislature to select the state's governor and the members of the state judiciary, thus preserving the county-court system that Jefferson had so despised. Westerners hated the results, and in the referendum on ratifying the new constitution, they rejected it by a 5 to 1 margin—but to no avail. Expediency, as understood by the most undemocratic slaveholders, had triumphed. Or so it seemed for a little over a year, when the Southampton insurrection suddenly forced Virginians to reassess what was expedient and what was not.

On January 16, 1832, Thomas Jefferson Randolph of Albemarle County—the dutiful and favored grandson of the departed great man—rose in the House of Delegates chamber and offered up a prophecy as lurid as David Walker's. To Randolph, it was obvious that were slavery perpetuated, troubles far worse than those that had recently hit Southampton County would befall future generations of Virginians. In time, he predicted, the Union would dissolve over the slavery issue. Northern armies, including black soldiers, would invade Virginia and arm the slaves. When the white men of the South marched off to repel the invaders, their women and children would be "butchered and their homes desolated in the rear." The only way to forestall the inevitable was to rid Virginia of slavery and blacks once and for all. And Randolph had a plan. All slaves born after July 4, 1840, would be freed upon reaching adulthood—women at age eighteen, men at twenty-one. All those freed would then be state property and shipped to Africa, their costs covered by the freed slaves themselves once they had earned enough as hired-out workers to finance their passage. By 1861, Randolph calculated, Virginia would be entirely free of slavery, and its population would be virtually lily-white.

Randolph's proposal gained instant approval from the state's leading newspapers, as well as, more surprisingly, from the state-rights extremist Governor John Floyd and some of the key slaveholders in the legislature. The "defenceless situation of the master and the sense of injured right in the slave," James McDowell Jr. from the Shenandoah observed, demanded emancipation and colonization. Western representatives, convinced that slavery was responsible for their continued political subjugation, rallied to the emancipation cause. Eastern defenders of slavery hastily drafted rebuttals, claiming that the dangers of insurrection were small given the overwhelming contentment of the slaves and that, in any event, the legislature had no power whatsoever to abridge slaveholders' property rights.

The two weeks of debate that followed proceeded within well-defined limits. Although a few of the pro-emancipationists talked of extending humanity and justice to the slaves, the majority took more self-interested and, often, racist positions. Slavery, some charged, had shackled the Virginia economy to an outmoded cash crop, tobacco, and hampered the economic diversification that would be the state's only guarantee of future prosperity. Slavery, said others, injured the manners and the morals of the white population, while leaving whites vulnerable to uprisings. Slavery, said still others, would only lead to the spread of what one delegate called the "slothful, degraded African" into the virtuous white western counties. The pro-slavery delegates, for their part, backed off from their endorsements of slavery as benevolent and stressed property rights above all. Even the redoubtable reactionary Benjamin Watkins Leigh remarked that the legislature had no business interfering with the "evil" of slavery.

The outcome of 1830 foretold the outcome of 1832. Rather than choose one of several emancipation proposals, including

Randolph's, the reformers drafted a more general proclamation that legislative action against slavery was—the word appeared once more—"expedient." The representatives from the trans-Allegheny West voted unanimously in favor, as did three-quarters of the representatives from the Shenandoah Valley. Had the constitutional convention a year earlier apportioned the lower house of the legislature on the basis of white population, the vote would have come down to the wire. Instead, thanks to the easterners' manipulated majority, the measure was comfortably defeated, 73 to 58—but the controversy was not nailed completely shut. When the pro-slavery men proposed tabling further discussion of emancipation, eleven eastern slaveholders joined with the nine who had backed emancipation to keep the debate roiling. The eastern moderates then helped the western emancipationists pass a resolution to commence slavery's demise by colonizing free blacks as a "first step," to be followed by colonizing slaves once a "more definite development of public opinion" had been achieved. A toothless measure, it gave the emancipationists a small symbolic victory.

With hindsight, historians commonly render the Virginia slavery debates as a thorough and stunning triumph for the most obdurate pro-slavery forces, and a turning point in the rise of pro-slavery politics in the South. Defeated in 1832, gradual abolition would never again be seriously debated in Virginia, and debated only briefly thereafter in Tennessee and Kentucky. Eastern resistance to democratic reform in 1829 and 1830 had helped ensure successful resistance to emancipation two years later. After the debates were over, influential Virginians, above all Thomas Roderick Dew of William and Mary College, chastised the legislature for its loose talk about emancipation and began hazarding more insistent pro-slavery arguments.

At the time, however, the Virginia debates described a much messier reality in which neither the slaveholders' domination over the Commonwealth nor white solidarity over slavery seemed completely certain. Some observers saw the debates as but a first step toward slavery's eventual removal. The outcome, the Richmond *Constitutional Whig* happily reported, was immediately "*deemed favorable to the cause of abolition*," which could proceed "when public opinion is more developed . . . and means are better devised." The breach between the state's western emancipationist country democrats and the eastern slaveholder gentry had widened. The old regime, with all its polished manners, had preserved itself only with bothersome political exertions and distasteful concessions. At crucial moments, the old regime had divided against itself and had failed to mount a powerful argument on slavery's behalf. It was a failure of discipline as well as of will that was incomprehensible to slaveholders in other parts of the South, especially the united slaveholders of John C. Calhoun's South Carolina. That failure toughened the South Carolinians' own resolve to resist all encroachments on their prerogatives, whether undertaken by the Yankee oppressors or by backsliding southerners.

The Virginia events also dramatized the growing differences—and, in some respects, similarities—between the slave South and the free North. Apart, perhaps, from Rhode Island, no northern state was ruled by a single class of property owners. The conservative antidemocratic views of John Randolph and Abel Upshur were quickly disappearing on the other side of the Mason-Dixon Line. Yet disputes about labor, property, and democracy also erupted in the burgeoning northern cities during the late 1820s and early 1830s. In part, these arguments arose from the consolidation of a new class of pious urban businessmen, caught up in the moralizing impulses unleashed by the northern version of the Second Great Awakening. They also arose from the spread of the transformed, working-class city democracy that the Philadelphia Mechanics' Union of Trade Associations and Working Men's Party had initiated in 1827—and from some short-lived but spectacular developments in the city of New York, which heightened conflicts over banks, monied power, and political justice. The religious revivals and labor radicalism of the North defined opposing ethics and social outlooks. Both would have deep and lasting effects on national politics.

REVIVALS AND LABOR RADICALISM IN THE NORTH

Nothing better signified the enormous surge of northern commerce and industry after 1815 than the growth of cities. Although the preponderance of the northern population remained rural, an extraordinary rate of urban growth, fed by immigrants and rural migrants—the fastest rate in American history—betokened the emergence of a modern, diversified commercial and industrial northern economy. The resulting stresses and strains astonished observers. New York impressed most of all, supplanting Philadelphia as the seaboard metropolis, its economy fattening off the Erie Canal traffic and the cotton trade connecting New Orleans with Britain and Europe. New York's wharfside forest of masts surrounded a sprawling pandemonium of rich and poor, native-born and newcomers. Two axes were quickly coming to define the distinctly charged poles of New York life: Broadway, slanting north-westward from the Battery, with its fine shops and hotels and churches; and the Bowery, slanting north-eastward, with its groggeries, cheap oyster houses and popular theaters creating what a later writer would call the city's proletarian pandemonium, "in such a condition that Christian men and women are disposed to keep shy." Clustered around these poles, and moving between them, was the most polyglot, minutely stratified population in America, including the nation's largest manufacturing and seaport working class.

Other, smaller cities ranged from the rough-hewn to the spectacular. Alongside the newly constructed roads and canals, settlements arose to process farmers' goods for shipment to the larger cities and abroad, and to distribute goods (from farm tools to ladies' finery) to the western hinterland. "The transition from a crowded street to the ruins of a forest, or to the forest itself, is so sudden" a British traveler noted of Rochester, New York, alongside the Erie Canal, "that a stranger, by turning a wrong corner in the dark, might be in danger of breaking his neck over the enormous stumps of trees." More imposing were the enormous power-loom cotton manufactories and adjacent boardinghouses constructed in East Chelmsford, Massachusetts (now renamed Lowell), by a consortium of capitalists called the Boston Associates, its workforce of young women recruited from the hard-pressed farms of New England. Inside of five years, the Lowell factories had outstripped the family-based Rhode Island cotton mills established by Samuel Slater in the 1790s, as well as the Boston Associates' inaugural venture in Waltham, and they struck visitors as one of the nation's great wonders. Lowell, the French-man Michel Chevalier remarked, was nothing like the gloomy factory towns of England but more like a huge brick New World version of "a Spanish town with its convents," where the girls, "instead of working *sacred hearts*, spin and weave cotton."

Lowell was an exception, painstakingly planned by its founders to provide the paternalistic necessities and virtuous monitoring that assured farmers and their wives their mill-worker daughters would be looked after well. Employers in other indus-trial settings attempted to adapt different kinds of benevolent paternalist regimes for millhands and their families. Most cities, however, large and small, arose with only the lightest of rules and oversight, thereby raising enormous challenges to supply the teeming new neighborhoods with adequate housing, sanitation, and policing. And among leading citizens of property and stand-ing, the pangs of growth posed moral and political dilemmas. How, in the boisterous new urban milieux, could they maintain their own authority as civic leaders? What could be done to instill a proper respect for public order among the growing hordes of poor and ignorant working people? Established secular benevo-lent institutions—the philanthropic soup kitchens and firewood handouts traditionally afforded the poor—had been over-whelmed by the urban influx since 1815. What, beyond prudent use of the billystick, could uplift as well as restrain those whom one New Yorker regarded as "the multitude of new comers amongst whom are a large portion of the lowest offscourings of Europe . . . improvident, careless, & filthy"?

For many propertied urbanites, above all in the areas newly

settled by New England émigrés, the answer appeared in the continuing Second Great Awakening, as recast by a new leader, the charismatic Presbygational evangelist Charles Grandison Finney. Born in Litchfield County, Connecticut, in 1792, but raised in what was then the frontier of Oneida County, New York, Finney had been trained as a lawyer and had professed an indifference to religion until 1821. Prompted by repeated references to the Mosaic code in the British jurist William Blackstone's *Commentaries*, he bought a Bible, started reading, and was suddenly overwhelmed by God's grace. "It seemed as if my heart was all liquid," he later recalled. The next day, he dropped his legal career and began preparing himself for his new calling as an evangelist. Finney soon began gathering ever-larger crowds in the little but growing upstate cities along the Erie Canal, from Troy to Utica, in what he later called his "nine mighty years" of revivals. The roar reached a crescendo in Rochester over the fall and winter of 1830–31.

Finney owed his phenomenal success to his evangelical style and down-to-earth bearing as well as to his liturgical and doctrinal innovations. Most of all, perhaps, he owed his success to his penetrating large blue eyes, set deep in a handsome angular head—eyes that seemed to radiate salvation. Finney was perfectly cognizant of his physical gifts and unapologetically used them to bring sinners to the bosom of Christ. For Finney, a religious revival resulted not from any miraculous visitation but from practical, voluntary human work—"the ordinary rules of cause and effect," he wrote—that, though blessed by God, could be systematized and then taught to other revivalists. Promoting prayer, comprehending (and not simply berating) thoughtless sinners, encouraging a full and unending moral stock-taking by each individual convert—by breaking down the job at hand, Finney was able to offer step-by-step guides on how to promote mass religious awakenings. Not least important, in his own ministry, was his adaptation of a variety of so-called new measures from other sects (notably the Methodists' prayer-inducing "anxious bench" placed directly in front of his pulpit), as well as the attention he paid to his own preaching style, down to divining the line of vision best suited to captivating his audience with his piercing gaze.

Finney's technical feats helped him propound the greatest liberalization yet in America of the doctrine of human agency in salvation. Lyman Beecher and the other pioneers of the northern Second Great Awakening had retained at least a kernel of traditional Calvinism, in their contentions that the ultimate bestowal of grace came only and directly from God. Although Finney would never eliminate God's agency, he pushed it into the background, as a setting of the stage, with the Almighty arranging events (including the appearance of the proper minister) so that sinners would be ready to recognize and receive the Holy Spirit. Otherwise, the preacher, his flock, and the sinners themselves were the true makers of a revival. "Men are not mere *instruments* in the hands of God," Finney declared, abjuring Calvinist orthodoxy more pointedly and thoroughly than his predecessors. "Truth is the instrument."

The fastest-growing city in the nation, Rochester was badly divided. Its rising men of wealth quarreled over politics and religion, and they lived in even greater estrangement from the flour-mill workers, canal boatmen, and immigrant laborers who had flocked to their boomtown. "Rochester was too uninviting a field of labor," Finney later recalled—until a force he referred to simply as "Something" told him that he was needed there all the more. His ministry galvanized the city's families of property as the surest means to restore moral order and unity. Installed at Rochester's Third Presbyterian Church, Finney preached three evenings a week and three times on Sunday, driving himself to the edge of physical breakdown. His sermons were spare and logical—"like a lawyer arguing a case before court and jury," one journalist attendee remarked—filled with everyday examples of how Satan worked his wiles and how all could remake their hearts and receive God's grace. He ended his stay in March 1831 with a five-day protracted meeting that brought the city's business to a halt and left him so exhausted his doctors feared he would soon be dead. In all, Finney had converted between eight and twelve hundred Rochester residents, including a disproportionate number of the city's leading manufacturers, lawyers, and other professionals, and especially their wives and daughters. The fire threw off sparks that lit revivals in nearby towns and villages, converting thousands more.

In capturing Rochester for Christ, Finney proclaimed a cluster of moral imperatives that soon helped the new northern urban middle class define itself. Finneyite theology did not rationalize success or instill complacency; on the contrary, it was a challenge to abandon selfish passions and convert—and then to work ceaselessly spreading the gospel and shepherding others into the flock. In rising to that challenge, the converted learned that life, and receiving life everlasting, was a matter of personal moral choices. Bad choices—intemperance, slothfulness, extravagance, dishonesty, violence—blocked the sinner from redemption. Good choices, coupled with prayer, opened the way to personal salvation and hastened the moral perfection of the world that, Finney taught, would precede Christ's Second Coming. That revival-drenched striving in turn sanctified what was becoming the northern middle-class domestic order and offered a way of understanding political discord and social confusion as essentially moral problems. Human suffering, by these lights, could and would be conquered once individuals set themselves sturdily on the road to Christ, one sinner at a time.

The potential political implications of the revivalists' message were enormous, even though politics was not chiefly on Finney's mind. The Finneyite excitement made its greatest stir in the rapidly developing portions of greater New England, and especially in the same so-called Burned-Over District of western New York that had spawned Anti-Masonry. The cities they transformed were boomtowns like Rochester, commanded by families of newfound prosperity searching for spiritual mastery for themselves and their neighbors. The revivalists preached a democratic gospel, at odds with the fatalism and hierarchy of the older Calvinist denominations, and at war with the secularism and indifference they saw closing in all around them. Finneyism offered its adherents a Christ-centered way of life that blamed disorder and degradation on individual decision, not political or social inequality. Here was the basis for yet another variation of the politics of moral improvement in the North—free of hierarchical presumption and overflowing with benevolence and Christian stewardship, but far more ambitious and better organized than earlier reform efforts stemming from the Second Great Awakening. Sabbatarianism had provided one largely failed model for moralistic politics—several of Finney's most prominent converts were also Sabbatarian leaders—but the evangelical impulse would soon find much sturdier and less narrowly pious political outlets. Among those who would tap into that impulse were anti-Jacksonians ranging from the Anti-Masons Thurlow Weed and William Henry Seward to the abolitionists organized by William Lloyd Garrison.

There were limits to the evangelicals' appeal, though, as Finney and his friends would soon discover. Following the upstate Pentecost, Finney moved his headquarters to Manhattan, where he would be based for three years and preach often thereafter, first in a reconstructed theater and then, beginning in 1835, in a spacious new church, the Broadway Tabernacle, built for him by local evangelical businessmen. Finney's New York years bore fruit, including a proliferation of evangelical missionary societies that turned Manhattan into the center for national evangelical reform. Yet New York, like the other great seaports, was too large, polyglot, and cosmopolitan, even cynical, to be turned upside down like the raw canal cities and towns to the west. Even among the faithful, Finney remarked, "the reason there is so little of the purest kind of piety in New York" was that so many "indulge in some kind of dishonesty, which eats out their religion." Apart from the city's sizable population of prosperous New England émigrés (of whom Arthur and Lewis Tappan were the most conspicuous examples), Finney's crusade made little headway among Manhattan's families of wealth. Equally important, New York's immense and variegated working class mainly evinced hostility for the evangelical crusaders and their mercantile backers—thoughts expressed with a special fierceness by a testy alliance of radicals who, in 1829, created their own version of Philadelphia's Working Men's Party. Although the New York Working Men's independent efforts would come to naught, their critiques of banking and the unrepublican power of concentrated wealth would gain a large following among workers and petty proprietors across the Northeast. Over the coming decade, those critiques would have an enormous influence among the more sympathetic of the Jackson Democrats, including President Jackson.

The freethinker Frances Wright's stormy arrival in January 1829 and her early lectures marked the beginning of the New York radical workingmen's insurgency. Deism and religious skepticism had claimed a small but vocal following in New York since the end of the eighteenth century, when the local skeptic Elihu Palmer made his newspaper, the *Temple of Reason*, the nation's leading exponent of free thought. In reaction to the evangelical resurgence, the movement enjoyed a small comeback in 1825, headed by a talented group of British radical émigrés including George Houston and George Henry Evans. But Wright, the daughter of an enlightened Scots merchant, and her companion Robert Dale Owen, son of the British utopian socialist Robert Owen, electrified the freethinkers' old-time irreligion. They relocated a newspaper they had founded at the Owenite community in New Harmony, Indiana, renamed it the *Free Enquirer*, and hired Evans as their printer. They also bought an abandoned church on the Bowery and turned it into what they called their Hall of Science, which housed their lecture hall, a reading room, a bookstore, a deist Sunday school, and a free medical dispensary. Wright herself took center stage, a scandalous celebrity preaching free love and abolitionism, and ridiculing Christian orthodoxy as the perfect model of mental and political thralldom.

Wright and Owen enriched New York free-thought radicalism intellectually as well as organizationally. There was a mustiness to the extant New York deists' attacks on aristocratic priestcraft, as if the freethinkers had slumbered through the Jeffersonian era of

religious disestablishment. Wright and Owen added more pertinent arguments for reform. Both were adherents to the radical
interpretation of the labor theory of value that had been proclaimed in Philadelphia by William Heighton. As a corrective to
America's plundering by the nonproducing few, they turned
chiefly to educational reform and what Owen called his state
guardianship plan. Based loosely on liberal schooling experiments in Europe, the scheme called for government-run secular
academies, where all children, rich and poor, would be instructed
with the most up-to-date methods and freed from sectarian
superstition. From these egalitarian barracks of enlightenment
would supposedly arise, Owen wrote, a "race . . . to perfect the
free institutions of America." Though not without an authoritar-
ian streak of its own, the plan at least recognized the new and
growing urban inequalities of the 1820s. "If the divisions of *sect*
have estranged human hearts from each other," Wright declared
at the Hall of Science, "those of *class* have set them in direct
opposition."

Other New York workingmen radicals agreed with Wright and
Owen on that point but thought their proposed solution was
worse than useless. The harshest and most consequential of
these critics was the machinist Thomas Skidmore. The son of a
struggling Connecticut farm family, Skidmore had left home at
eighteen and wandered along the East Coast as far south as
Delaware, picking up odd jobs as a tutor while immersing himself
in books on the mechanical arts and political economy. He settled in New York in 1819, set up a small business, and started
work on a project to devise an improved form of reflective tele-
scope—all the while continuing his self-education in political
theory. As a boy, he had been inspired by the city democratic writings in William Duane's *Aurora*; thereafter, he immersed himself
in the works of Locke, Rousseau, Joel Barlow, Jefferson, and
Paine, as well as more obscure recent works attacking the
competitive-wage labor system. Skidmore first turned up in politics in 1828 as a supporter of John Quincy Adams, drawn to the
incumbent president's support for protective tariffs and what

Skidmore would later call "necessary and useful Public Works." After Adams's defeat, Skidmore began writing a long treatise of his own, utterly out of step with the ideas of Adamsites and Jacksonians alike—an unremitting attack on the existing system of private property.

Skidmore's self-conscious title—*The Rights of Man to Property!*—placed his work in the Paineite urban democratic tradition but also noted that tradition's limitations. Whereas Paine's *Rights of Man* had blamed social oppression on political inequality, Skidmore blamed the unequal distribution of property, perpetuated from generation to generation by inheritance laws. Even radical interpretations of the labor theory of value were too meek for Skidmore, who charged that individuals' equal rights to property existed independently of human labor. All existing property holdings were illegitimate, based on a primordial violation of the self-evident principle, "engraved on the heart of man," that each had an equal claim on the Creator's endowment. Mocking the comparatively mild plans of "political dreamers" like Robert Dale Owen, Skidmore proclaimed that the rights of labor and the poor would be won only if "we rip all up, and make a full and General Division" of property.

Skidmore never abandoned his attachment to political democracy. His "General Division" would involve, first, the election by the enlightened masses of state legislatures that would call new state constitutional conventions, which would in turn enfranchise all men and women of all races. Thence would begin the process of expropriation and redistribution of existing property. All that could not be divided easily, in particular banks and manufactories, would be retained by the community at large and operated in its name. All else would be thrown into a common pool, with equal shares handed to everyone—men and women, of all colors—upon reaching adulthood. Thereafter, individuals would be permitted to labor as they chose, in cooperative independence. Men and women of superior talent, diligence, luck, and intelligence would, Skidmore allowed, inevitably produce more, to the greater benefit of all—and would therefore accumulate, rightfully, more property than others during their lifetimes. But so long as inheritance was abolished, and all property was returned to the community for redistribution when its owner died, natural differences would not be turned into permanent inequality. Gradually, class oppression would disappear, "till there shall be no lenders, no borrowers; no landlords, no tenants; no masters, no journeymen; no Wealth, no Want."

As political eschatology, Skidmore's tract was just as uncompromising as David Walker's vision of slavery's demise. In some respects, Skidmore was even more audacious than Walker, propounding a nonviolent democratic revolution that would not only abolish slavery but create a new egalitarian regime for all Americans. And as far-fetched as it appears in retrospect, Skidmore's scheme envisaged immediate political organization, to be led not by unreliable men "attached to the cause of a Clay or a Jackson," but by independent "friends of equal rights," chiefly the oppressed small producers and wage earners. Against the backdrop of continuing labor strife, that proposal led to the formation of the New York Working Men's movement.

Labor unrest had broken out repeatedly in New York after 1819. In the spring of 1829, journeymen reacted swiftly when rumors spread that large employers, in unspecified trades, were about to lengthen the workday from ten to eleven hours. At the urging of Skidmore (still at work on his manuscript), a large public gathering of wage earners pledged to refuse to work more than ten hours "well and faithfully employed." Five days later, an even larger crowd, estimated at between five and six thousand, attended a mass meeting in the Bowery, which affirmed the earlier pledge and appointed a committee of fifty small masters and journeymen to coordinate any strikes that followed. Soon after, the suspected employers renounced all plans to extend the workday, but the Committee of Fifty continued to meet and in midsummer decided to run its own independent ticket of candidates in the upcoming legislative elections. That autumn, the committee (joined, somewhat hesitantly, by Robert Dale Owen) announced its platform. The document showed Skidmore's influence, but it carefully avoided all mention of the General Division. Instead, it attacked private banking and chartered monopolies, and included demands for abolishing imprisonment for debt, reforming the coercive militia system, equal education, and a mechanics' lien law. Egalitarian to the last detail, the meeting then chose its candidate list by lottery, including, as a nominee for state assembly, Skidmore himself.

The 1829 campaign proved the acme of the New York Working Men's independent political efforts. At least one trade society, the painters', backed the movement. Owen, trying to capture the insurgency for himself and his state guardianship plan, assisted George Henry Evans in founding the weekly *Working Man's Advocate*, supposedly as a Working Men's organ. Pro-Jackson papers charged, with some merit, that pro-Clay mechanics and manufacturers, under the guise of "workingmen," were infiltrating and backing the Workies in order to divide the Democratic vote and elect National Republicans. The commercial press, including the Tappans' *Journal of Commerce*, denounced the new "sans-culottes," "Fanny Wright ticket," as a mad "anarchical" enterprise of poor men too ignorant to deserve the franchise. Finally, in November, the Working Men polled nearly one-third of the vote, more than twice the figure won by the National Republicans—enough to elect one of the Workies' state senate candidates and one of their assembly candidates (a journeyman carpenter named Ebenezer Ford), and nearly enough to elect Skidmore (who fell short by a mere twenty-three votes). Flushed with victory, Skidmore's followers formed new political debating societies in at least three workingmen's wards, and Skidmore produced a prospectus for a newspaper loyal to the Committee of Fifty.

Factionalism and manipulation quickly destroyed the fledgling party. As the Democrats had noticed, men friendly to the late administration and to Henry Clay had begun quietly to take over the Workie organization. Emboldened by the returns, they turned first to removing Skidmore, an effort in which they found willing allies among the naive Owenite freethinkers. At a mass meeting in December called ostensibly to debate the movement's future, the Owen and pro-Clay men packed the hall, forcibly prevented Skidmore and the committee from speaking, reconstituted themselves as the Working Men's Party, and purged the Skidmore faction. The next day, a pro-Clay paper rejoiced that the Workies had "wiped away every stigma" of Skidmore's crazed schemes. What had actually happened was that Clay's supporters, using the *Free Enquirer* radicals as their pawns, had seized the movement. Soon after, the Owenites and Clay men turned on each other. Ten months of bitter, at times violent, feuding ensued, after which the Jacksonians regained all of the wards won by the Workies in 1829. Although Owen, Evans, and the other free-thought radicals held out for another year under the name of the Workingmen's Political Association, the New York Working Men's political uprising was effectively dead by the end of 1830.

The New York radicals were not unique in their failings: Philadelphia's Working Men's Party experienced a similar mete-oric rise and fall, in a roughly parallel chronology. In 1828, the Philadelphia workingmen's candidates who ran on their own received only a scattering of votes—but all twenty-one Workie candidates who were also on the Jackson ticket were elected, an encouraging sign. A year later, the movement was flourishing. William Heighton's *Mechanics' Free Press* raised numerous specific demands, including the abolition of chartered monopolies, restriction of commercial banks, expansion of public education, and ending imprisonment for debt. Branches of a new Workingmen's Republican Political Association arose in the working-class wards, and city and county conventions, elected by general ward meetings, nominated twelve candidates for the fall elections, some of whom ran as Democrats and some as Adamsites. All of the Working Men's nominees won, leading the *Free Press* to boast that "[t]he balance of power has at length got into the hands of the working people, where it properly belongs." But support began to dwindle in 1830, when conservative papers started linking the movement to the Fanny Wright "infidels" and Skidmore "agrarians" of New York, and when the rank and file divided over whether they should restrict themselves to nominating actual workingmen. The movement's disappointing election totals that autumn, the Democratic *American Sentinel* rejoiced, "consigned *Workeyism* to the tomb of the Capulets; and there is no further nucleus for malcontents to form upon." A year later, the Philadelphia Workie vote was barely half of what it had been in 1829, and the organizers gave up the ghost.

Ironically, the deist and agrarian radicalism that galvanized the New York Workies in 1829 finally proved a fatal liability: it was too radical for most workingmen and provided a useful foil for more conventional politicians in both Manhattan and Philadelphia. Yet Workeyism's basic criticisms of economic and political inequality proved much more tenacious than the New York and Philadelphia parties did. Individual Philadelphia and New York radicals, including the irrepressible Manhattan editor George Henry Evans, continued their work long after the parties disappeared. Outside Philadelphia and New York, workingmen's parties sprouted up in smaller nearby ports and manufacturing cities, and the movement quickly spread into New England, Delaware, and Ohio. By August 1830, one Delaware paper reported that "not less than twenty newspapers" had "come out fearlessly in the advocacy of the principles of the *Working Men's Party*." Before the agitation was over, the list would expand to include at least fifty newspapers in fifteen states, from Maine to Missouri. Some of the new labor parties were so evanescent that they left mere traces in the historical record; others were pseudo-Workie parties organized by National Republicans. But a few of them, notably the New England Association of Farmers, Mechanics, and Other Workingmen, organized in 1832, became the foundations for even larger labor organizations. And the most important of the newspapers, Evans's *Working Man's Advocate*, lasted well past 1830, as a beacon for every variety of workingmen's reform.

These continuing efforts refocused Workeyism's energies on its more practical critiques of the developing commercial order. Above all, they sustained the radical arguments over monopolies, banking, and the currency that had emerged around the country after the Panic of 1819 and that both the Philadelphia and New York Working Men's movements had amplified. In 1828, the Philadelphians affirmed that the greatest evil they faced was "the legislative aid granted for monopolizing, into a few rich hands, the wealth creating powers of modern mechanism." The original New York Working Men's platform demanded abolition of the existing banking system and of all chartered monopolies. In the very first issue of his *Working Man's Advocate*, Evans promised to fight "the establishment of all exclusive privilege; all monopolies." Workies in the smaller cities seized on the banking issue, proclaiming (in the words of the General Executive Committee of the Farmers, Mechanics and Working Men of the City of Albany) that "at present the laboring classes create the wealth which the bankers and speculators pocket." Even Fanny Wright added currency and banking reform to the deist radicals' education plans as "indispensable" to labor's cause.

The most influential attack on banking appeared in Philadelphia in March 1829, at about the same time that the New York Working Men's movement was getting underway. A protest meeting of workingmen declared that hard times were the result of "too great extension of paper credit," and appointed a committee, not confined to workingmen, to write a report on the evils of the banking system. The committee included both of the Duanes and two trade union leaders, William English and John Robertson, who were also active in the Working Men's Party. It also included an editor and political writer named William Gouge. The report, apparently written chiefly by Gouge, admitted that banks had their uses as institutions of deposit and transfer, but charged that the existing commercial, paper-money banking system had laid "the foundation of *artificial* inequality of wealth, and, thereby, of *artificial* inequality of power," and needed radical reform.

The Workie uprising in turn got the attention of mainstream politicians. Andrew Jackson, who had announced his hostility to all commercial banks as early as 1820, had subscribed for years to the Philadelphia radical Stephen Simpson's *Columbian Observer*. Now Jackson called Simpson "his old friend," and through Thomas Hart Benton received word of Simpson's latest thinking on banking questions. The appearance of the independent Working Men's parties widened the radicals' audience among Jackson's supporters. Heighton's *Mechanics' Free Press* noted proudly in 1830 how the Philadelphia Working Men's campaign had brought "an open acknowledgement of the justice of working people's attempts to lessen the hours of labor." In New York, Democrats in the state legislature responded to the Workie challenge by abolishing imprisonment for debt and reforming the militia system, and the Tammany-dominated city council in Manhattan passed a mechanics' lien law. The lesson, for practical politicians, was clear: no party could succeed in the newly expanding cities—and, hence, could not expect to succeed nationally—unless it could appeal to the voters aroused by the Working Men and address their concerns. If that process of absorption killed off independent workingmen's politics, it also stimulated the more liberal and sometimes radical impulses within the Jacksonian coalition—which, for most of the Workies, quickly became their new political home.

"GET THE WORKIES TO BE UP AND DOING"

Three years after his inauguration, Andrew Jackson had begun asserting control over his own administration and clarifying its political direction, but Jacksonian Democracy had yet to come to pass. He had pressed hard, and successfully, for Indian removal and against expansive federal aid for internal improvements. The schism between Jackson and John C. Calhoun presaged the president's renunciation of state-rights extremism. Still, much remained to be sorted out, particularly over slavery, the limits of federal power, and the effects of rapid commercial development. In facing the last of these, Jackson and his closest supporters would confront the perennial question of how economic power ought to be distributed and exercised in a democratic republic. And they would find themselves forging an ever-closer alliance with the workingmen radicals, whose views on some crucial questions were converging with their own.

The Working Men's attacks on monopolies and banks failed, but far more powerful national Democratic leaders—aided and, in time, goaded further by the Workies and their friends—would not. One of those leaders, a former bank director, converted anti-monopolist, and crony of Martin Van Buren, New York Congressman Churchill C. Cambreleng, knew what to expect early in 1832 and where the former Working Men would fit in. "Get the Workies to be up and doing on the U.S.B. question," Cambreleng wrote to a Tammany Bucktail. "They are democrats in principle." The "U.S.B." Cambreleng referred to was the Second Bank of the United States—against which President Jackson, now recovered from his early political distractions, was arming for an all-out war.

7

1832:

JACKSON'S CRUCIAL YEAR

By 1832, President Jackson had forcefully resolved the internal disputes that had plagued his administration. The rift with Vice President Calhoun turned into a complete break late in the spring of 1830, after friends began sending Jackson incontrovertible evidence that Calhoun had secretly denounced him during the Florida expedition fracas in 1818—an episode that, like many long past, had never stopped mattering to Jackson. After confronting Calhoun and receiving a supercilious reply, Jackson cut off communication, raging that he had never "expected he would have occasion to say to you, in the language of Caesar, *Et tu Brute.*" After his summer vacation, Jackson returned to Washington, where the wearisome Eaton comic opera continued. Still livid over "[t]he double dealing of J.C.C.," he decided to end, once and for all, both the Eaton imbroglio and Calhoun's influence over his administration.

As a first step, Jackson established a reliable party newspaper in Washington to overcome the semiofficial *Telegraph*, edited by Calhoun's loyalist, Duff Green. Jackson summoned to Washington the Kentucky relief war veteran Francis Blair, who had taken over as editor of the *Argus of Western America*. Blair's new semiweekly paper, the *Globe*—soon to become a daily—would provide an effective counterweight to Green in the capital, while also helping to secure the disciplined attention and loyalty of Jacksonians down the party's chain of command. There would never be any doubt about its standing as, in Amos Kendall's words, "the friend of General Jackson and his administration, having no . . . political views other than the support of his principles."

Purging the cabinet of Calhoun's influence required more patience and finesse, lest it appear that Jackson was acting at the behest of the Eatons—and in retaliation not against Calhoun but against his wife. The pretext he needed finally appeared early in 1831, when Calhoun published a self-serving pamphlet containing his recent correspondence with Jackson, designed to make Van Buren look like an ambitious conniver. (The secretary of state, one overly abrupt opposition observer wrote, "is a gone dog. *he is done.*") For Jackson, this was the final affront, and he axed Calhoun's cabinet allies Samuel Ingham, John Branch, and John Berrien. To keep up political appearances, he also accepted Van Buren's resignation and forced Eaton out of the cabinet. But right away, he nominated Van Buren to serve as the American minister to Great Britain and arranged for Eaton to become governor of Florida Territory, where he and Margaret could settle in honorable exile from Washington's salons. Jackson had precipitously freed himself to start his troubled presidency anew.

The cabinet shake-up—involving the heads of five of the six existing executive departments, excluding only Postmaster General Barry (his incompetence not yet exposed)—was unprecedented. The new cabinet was more distinguished than its predecessor and, above all, untainted by Calhounism. Yet if the new men, particularly the nationalist-inclined Treasury secretary Louis McLane, promised to be personally loyal to the president, they would be cautious about pursuing his reforms. Accordingly, Jackson began to rely on the advice of his closest political friends outside the cabinet—Van Buren, Kendall, Blair, and his old ally from Tennessee,

William Lewis—an arrangement that his opponents disparaged as the president's "Kitchen Cabinet" government.

The twelve months following Congress's reassembly in December 1831 proved crucial, to both Jackson and his evolving coalition. The coming elections held everybody's attention. Less obvious were the continuing events in South Carolina that would lead to threatened secession. Jackson, meanwhile, was determined to press forward with what he had decided was the next item on his reform agenda—attacking the hated epitome of monied corruption, the Second Bank of the United States.

DEMOCRACY AND "A *FEW MONIED CAPITALISTS*": ORIGINS OF THE BANK VETO

Jackson's past political allegiances might have signaled that banking, currency, and finance would be near the top of his list of reforms. On the issues of banks and banking, his establishment loyalties had ended long ago. And during the 1828 election, he received word (which he believed) that the Lexington and Louisville, Kentucky, branch offices of the BUS had intervened on Adams's behalf. He then learned of similar charges against the New Orleans branch. Jackson's opinion of the BUS as a direct threat to American democracy was solidifying.

Banks and banking had not been issues in the 1828 campaign, in part because the debate over the federal tariff took precedence, and in part because raising the matter might upset Jackson's delicately balanced coalition. Jackson later claimed, however, that he had hoped to talk about banks in his inauguration address, only to be dissuaded by his more cautious advisers. And just two months after the inauguration, he was mulling over plans to do something dramatic about the BUS and erect a new institution for holding federal funds. Bringing the strict "hard-money" man Amos Kendall and then Francis Blair (now a hard-money convert) into his administration and giving them important duties was another sign of where Jackson was headed.

"Every one that knows me," he later wrote, "does know, that I have always been opposed to the U. States Bank, nay all Banks."

Jackson's complaints about the BUS reaffirmed his long-standing view that it fostered a "corrupting influence . . . upon the morals of the people." His major objections, however, were constitutional and political—objections that affirmed the primacy of politics and political institutions in how Americans thought about the state of the country. On strict Jeffersonian grounds, Jackson believed the bank was constitutionally invalid, an entity that Congress had created by asserting powers not ceded to it by the Framers. Just as important, Jackson perceived that the bank, by its very design, undermined popular sovereignty and majority rule. As a friend and adviser of Van Buren's, the New Yorker James A. Hamilton—ironically, Alexander Hamilton's son—put it in a key early memorandum to Jackson, the bank had concentrated "in the hands of a few men, a power over the money of the country." Unless checked, that power could be "perverted to the oppression of the people, and in times of public calamity, to the embarrassment of the government." But even when well administered, the bank was an enormity, which allowed, Jackson wrote, "a *few Monied Capitalists*" to trade upon the public revenue "and enjoy the benefit of it, to the exclusion of the many." No less worrisome, he added, was the bank's "power to control the Government and change its character," by influencing elections and, if need be, bribing representatives. Preventing a rechartering of the BUS, Jackson told the Tennessean Hugh Lawson White, was essential to his larger reform effort to vindicate "[t]he great principles of democracy."

President Jackson's early thoughts about how to handle the BUS are sketchy. From his correspondence and some recorded conversations, though, it is clear that he was thinking hard—and was receiving a great deal of contradictory advice. His initial preference was to replace the bank with a government-run institution that would serve as a bank of deposit only, severing any connection between public money and the issuance of bank paper. Jackson's partiality for a specie currency was as strong as ever. Yet

Jackson also became aware that the BUS performed some valuable services. Above all, the bank reduced the cost of government transactions, and, by checking emissions of state bank paper, restrained speculation. Offered numerous plans for a substitute to the BUS, Jackson showed a willingness to temper his views about how a reformed bank might operate, so long as those operations fell within the limits of his strict reading of the Constitution. By mid-1832, he would write, somewhat disingenuously, that he had always said he would favor "[a] Bank of deposit and Exchange, purely national, without stock holders."

Jackson announced his intention to strike at the BUS in his first and second messages to Congress, although he muted himself at the continued insistence of those advisers, above all Van Buren, who were worried about alienating too many important supporters too soon. In the first message, Jackson made clear that he strongly doubted whether the bank's existing charter was constitutional; he also believed the bank had failed to establish a sound currency. Jackson expanded his criticisms a year later, and proposed a possible replacement for the BUS: a wholly public institution with no private directors or stockholders, shorn of the power to extend loans or purchase property, but capable of restraining state banks from irresponsibly issuing paper. The bank question then receded in Washington for nearly a year, as Jackson recovered from the Eaton scandal and his initial clashes with Calhoun, battled against his recurrent physical ailments, and rebuilt his administration. Outwardly, the president managed to maintain a moderate mien. Privately, he wrote that, once his new cabinet was intact, the "great task of Democratic reform" would recommence—and the bank issue would be "fearlessly me[t]."

In assembling diverse anti-BUS forces, Jackson turned the issue into a matter of principle for his entire party. The major exceptions were inside the new cabinet, where more nationalist members, above all Secretary of the Treasury Louis McLane and Secretary of State Edward Livingston, held to a view that, Jackson wrote privately, "springs from convictions much more favorable than mine" to the bank. McLane and Livingston would prove useful as insider checks on unwisely precipitate actions and as signals to the public that the administration was considering a range of opinions. Otherwise, Jackson's hostility to the BUS meshed well with his reorganized administration party. Among the bank's strongest friends were certain pro-Calhoun slaveholders, including George Poindexter of Mississippi in the Senate and, in the House, the humorless, bombastic, but experienced South Carolina congressman George McDuffie, who had been a Calhoun family protégé since boyhood. Passionate sectionalists on the tariff and state rights, they also sustained parts of Calhoun's old economic nationalism and considered the Second BUS—whose chartering Calhoun had steered through Congress in 1816—as not only benevolent but essential to the nation's prosperity.

With the Calhounites thrown outside the administration, unequivocal antibank southerners, above all Jackson's new attorney general, Roger B. Taney of Maryland, enjoyed enlarged influence. A nearsighted lawyer with repellent features but a soft and persuasive manner, Taney had come to distrust large financiers during his years on the bench and as a state bank director. His anti-BUS animus was so strong that he was the only department head whom Jackson also admitted to his "kitchen cabinet" inner circle. There, Taney joined the Kentuckians Kendall and Blair, who were among the most ferocious antibank men in Washington and who urged Jackson to offer the bank no mercy. "It will come to this," Kendall wrote, "whoever is in favor of that Bank will be against Old Hickory." Both Blair and Kendall used the new *Globe* to denounce the BUS as an unconstitutional creature of "the monied power."

In Congress, Senator Thomas Hart Benton of Missouri—once Jackson's tavern assailant, now his ally—led the antibank forces. Like Kendall and Blair, Benton had completely rejected his early sympathies for Henry Clay's American System and the BUS. Early in February 1831, while Jackson was still grappling with Calhoun and the cabinet, he gave a scorching speech in the Senate on the bank and offered a resolution against renewing its charter, which still had five years to run. He called the bank too powerful for a government based on free and equal laws, an institution that worsened inequality by enriching the already rich and impoverishing the poor. In its place, he would institute a currency based on gold and silver, "the best currency for a republic." If, Benton added, he were "to establish a working man's party"— which was exactly what he wanted the Jacksonian coalition to become—"it should be on the basis of hard money; a hard money party against a paper party." The Senate defeated Benton's resolution, but by only three votes; the great preponderance of the Jackson men backed the Missourian. Blair's *Globe* reprinted Benton's speech in full; party newspaper editors and pamphlet printers around the country picked it up.

Benton's reference to "a working man's party" was purposeful. In the Northeast, former Philadelphia and New York Working Men and their emulators in other cities had strongly influenced and publicized the evolving antibank arguments. They were now primary targets of the Jacksonians' appeals. Apart from a handful of standouts, northeastern congressional support for Jackson's position on the bank was thin. But at the state and local level, particularly in New York, siding with Jackson on the bank question became a mark of party loyalty. (In New York, where Van Buren's men had initially been ambivalent, the state legislature resoundingly passed resolutions against rechartering the bank early in 1831.) And in the cities, large and small, where the Working Men had organized, the administration's antibank efforts won applause for attacking an unrepublican monopoly that, as George Henry Evans wrote, enabled "some men to live in splendor on the labor of operatives."

Benton, Kendall, and Blair, like the Workies, were more thoroughgoing critics of commercial banks and paper currency than were other antibank Jacksonians. The differences replicated those that had distinguished hard-money radicals from anti-BUS state bankers in the aftermath of the Panic of 1819. Taney, for example, although unsurpassed in his detestation for the BUS, objected primarily to the burdens it imposed on state banks. Other enemies of the BUS, including state and local bankers and would-be bankers, east and west, were interested in promoting cheap money, obtaining a share of the federal deposits held by the BUS, or taking over the national bank's functions themselves. David Henshaw, the Massachusetts parvenu, was the most energetic on the latter point. Rewarded for his efforts in the 1828 campaign with the appointment as collector of the port of Boston, Henshaw developed a scheme to replace the BUS with a new and even larger and more powerful bank—with him and his cronies of the so-called Custom House Party in control.

Given their prominence and power, the self-interested anti-BUS men easily created the impression—affirmed by later historians friendly to the bank and antagonistic to the Jacksonians—that the fight was merely one between rival groups of bankers and businessmen. Supposedly, the BUS was trying to uphold its responsible regime against grasping, entrepreneurial outsiders who (with the political aid of ignoramuses like Jackson) wanted to expand their own wealth and power. Jackson himself, so the argument ran, was motivated chiefly by the allegations that certain BUS directors had tried to thwart his election. In his outrage, Alexis de Tocqueville wrote, Jackson decided to "rouse the local passions and the blind democratic instinct of the country" against the bank and its directors. Not surprisingly, this view of the controversy, dismissive of the Jacksonians' political concerns, prevailed within the bank's imposing Greek Revival headquarters on Chestnut Street in Philadelphia. Its main proponent was the bank's president, the enormously capable and self-confident Nicholas Biddle.

Biddle was a wonder, only thirty-seven years old when President Monroe appointed him to run the BUS in 1823. His father, Charles Biddle, was a successful merchant whose own father, though of patrician lineage, had been ruined in business and died young. Charles, after boyhood stints at sea and as a merchant's apprentice, became a leading light in post-Revolutionary Pennsylvania politics. His rise, and his son's even loftier rise, was testimony to how, in the rapidly expanding early republic, the very highest reaches in America could be accessible to men of exceptional talent and drive. The Biddle saga also showed how some of these men, despite their family struggles, could come to think and act as if they had been to the manor born.

A brilliant, urbane graduate of Princeton (where he earned his B.A. at age fifteen), a former Federalist turned Pennsylvania New School Republican, Nicholas Biddle had served in the diplomatic corps (working as Monroe's secretary at the ministry to Great Britain), practiced law, edited a literary journal, and served in both houses of the Pennsylvania legislature—all before he began his career as a banker. Described by one English visitor as "the most perfect specimen of an American gentleman that I had yet seen," Biddle was no amateur dilettante, but a prodigy who seemed capable of mastering whatever vocation he chose. His chief flaws were his hubris and his excitability, both of which proved disastrous in national politics.

As the BUS president, Biddle favored interventionist policies, hoping to check the profligate tendencies of many state and local bankers and provide a sound currency. The bank's charter empowered it to act as the federal government's exclusive fiscal agent: holding its deposits, making interstate transfers of federal funds, and dealing with all federal payments or receipts, including taxes—all in exchange for an annual fee of $1.5 million. Yet although it was linked to the government (which owned one-fifth of its stock), and although it could use public funds interest-free for its own purposes, and although its branches were exempt from taxation by the states, the BUS was a private bank beholden to its directors and its stockholders, an elite group numbering four thousand. Like any other chartered bank, it had the power to issue its own notes and conduct normal commercial bank functions. In 1830, it was responsible for between 15 and 20 percent of all bank lending in the country and had issued upwards of 40 percent of all the bank notes in circulation nationwide. Its capital of $35 million was more than twice as large as the total annual expenditure of the federal government. Between 1830 and 1832, the BUS expanded further, increasing its notes and loans by 60 percent and its deposits by 40 percent.

By issuing orders either to constrict or relax the bank's twenty-five branch offices' demands on state and local banks for specie, Biddle and his bank could regulate the entire economy.

These were enormous privileges and powers for a private institution, beyond anything imaginable today. Biddle commanded his post expertly, salvaging the bank's credibility among business leaders and bolstering the rapid expansion of commerce after the panic depression lifted in 1822. Under Biddle, the BUS was vigilant about issuing notes, holding a specie reserve of one-half their value at a time when other banks held, on average, only between one-tenth and one-quarter of their note values in specie. In the process, Biddle transformed the BUS from a moderately profitable national branch-banking system into something more closely resembling a modern central bank.

Yet if Biddle's skills were unquestionable, the bank's regained prominence and heightened power also deepened misgivings about its anomalous position as a private institution with extraordinary public influence—and of its abuses of that influence, real and potential. Although the White House chose five of the institution's directors, the appointees were kept in the dark about the bank's operations. Biddle was very resistant to public supervision or even official inquiries. Beyond the naming of its five (largely ineffectual) directors, he insisted, "no officer of the Government, from the President downwards, has the least right, the least authority, the least pretense, for interference in the concerns of the bank." Biddle did extremely well by the bank's stockholders. But this fed concerns that Biddle's bank had become an all-powerful institution, accountable to no one but its owners—a monopolistic *imperium in imperio* of a new sort, an unelected fourth branch of government run by and for privileged insiders, exempt from the U.S. Constitution's checks and balances and in flagrant violation of democratic principles.

No argument in the world about the BUS's benefits would have convinced vested interests like Henshaw's crony consortium. At the other end of the ideological spectrum, hard-money men were unmoved by the bank's successes in steadying currency values and in driving worthless state paper out of circulation—for to them, all private commercial banks were suspect. (As Jackson himself told Biddle directly, his hatred was not reserved for the BUS: "I do not dislike your bank any more than all banks.") The bank's role as an engine of commercial development rendered it dubious to those who felt excluded from its power and also among workingmen, farmers, and others who had suffered amid the uncertainties and displacements that commercial development had wrought. The bank made its decisions behind closed doors, and these decisions were made by a man who declared himself beholden to no elected official in the land. Biddle, with his haughty bearing and his presumption that democracy was demagogy, personified the Jacksonians' charges that the bank threatened popular sovereignty.

Offended that anyone would impugn either his integrity or his public spirit, Biddle did not make life easier for himself. He thought nothing of approving dispersal of sizable sums in retainers, personal loans, or both to editors and elected officials, of both parties, in Washington—sometimes violating the bank's own regulations while reinforcing the impression, sensationalized by the *Globe*, that the bank was a fountain of political corruption. Nor, despite his literary skills, did he do a very good job at explaining either his bank or his running of it to the public. One of the main complaints of antibank congressmen concerned a useful reform, introduced by Biddle in 1827, that permitted the BUS to issue "branch draft" notes without their having to be hand-signed, laboriously, by the bank's president and cashier. The need for the notes was straightforward. Yet Biddle never convincingly demonstrated how the branch drafts facilitated the bank's operations, without creating what Senator Benton called an "illegal, irresponsible currency." Nor was Biddle politic. When asked, during public testimony, whether the BUS had ever oppressed any state banks, he replied it had not, but could also not help noting that "[t]here are very few banks which might not have been destroyed" had the BUS decided to do so. While he seemed to expect gratitude for his restraint and generosity, Biddle also sounded as if he assumed that all future BUS presidents would be just as skilled and benevolent as he. And there lay the heart of the matter for Jackson and his allies—that an office as powerful and unchecked as Biddle's was intolerable in a democratic republic.

THE POLITICS OF THE BANK VETO

The battle over the BUS was a personal clash between Biddle and Jackson as well as a constitutional struggle, but it began at a moment when a compromise actually seemed possible. In the autumn of 1831, Treasury Secretary McLane, the cabinet member friendliest to the BUS, proposed to the president a comprehensive scheme of fiscal reform that would at long last pay off the national debt but leave the bank standing, though greatly altered. Jackson, jumping at the chance to pay off the debt and also keep the bank issue out of the upcoming presidential election, bought the plan, so long as the changes removed his constitutional objections to the existing BUS, and so long as the rechartering was delayed until after 1832. McLane, elated, traveled to Philadelphia to assure Biddle that all was well. Jackson completed his part of the bargain in the third annual message, where he implied he was willing to go along with chartering a reformed bank and leave the matter up to Congress. But Secretary McLane overplayed his hand by calling explicitly in his annual report for rechartering the BUS.

Initially trusting in McLane, Jackson appeared unpersuaded, if defensive, when some of his supporters objected strenuously to McLane's "ultra federal" report—"a new version of Alexander Hamilton's," Cambreleng of New York declared. But when the implacably antibank *Globe* greeted the report by reprinting hostile reactions from other pro-Jackson newspapers, McLane threatened to resign, then geared up a conspiracy to arrange for Blair's ouster as editor. Disloyalty to Blair was, in Jackson's eyes, tantamount to disloyalty to Jackson himself, as well as to the larger cause of reform. McLane's influence with Jackson on the bank declined and Blair remained as the *Globe*'s editor. Compromise over the BUS was still possible but would depend on whether Biddle was willing to meet Jackson halfway and allow certain changes in the bank's charter, while also agreeing not to pursue the matter until after the election.

The National Republicans entered the fray in mid-December, when 150 delegates met in Baltimore and nominated Henry Clay for president. Three months earlier, a similar gathering had met in the same city to nominate William Wirt for the presidency on an Anti-Masonic ticket—the first national nominating convention in American history. Since 1828, Thurlow Weed and William Henry Seward had built their little protest party into a substantial organization in several northeastern states. As ever, Weed and Seward were trying to arrange for an alliance with the National Republicans, but the ascendancy of Clay, an unrepentant Mason, made that impossible. The National Republicans, however, were willing to imitate the Anti-Masons and call a nominating convention, in lieu of the congressional caucus of old. And their meeting concluded with a polemical, impossibly long address warning the nation that if Jackson was reelected, "it may be considered certain that the bank will be abolished."

Behind the scenes, Clay, along with George McDuffie, Daniel Webster, and other pro-BUS men, pressed Biddle to request rechartering of the bank before the election. Confident that a recharter bill would pass Congress, Clay and the others assured him that Jackson would not dare to veto it and face a disastrous public outburst. Such an executive veto of an institution already adjudged constitutional by the Supreme Court would be problematic under any circumstances; and Clay and Webster were also certain that the bank was popular with the voters. Initially, Biddle was more cautious, fearing, as another pro-BUS National Republican remarked, that if he forced "the Chief into a Corner he will veto the bill." But Clay and Webster (who, with their own political calculations in play, quietly hoped to provoke Jackson into a veto) were strong persuaders. In any case, Biddle convinced himself that he would have a stronger chance of winning a showdown with Jackson if it came before the election. Early in January, the nominal Jacksonian George M. Dallas, the son of Alexander J. Dallas, introduced a recharter bill in the Senate, while the South Carolinian McDuffie did so in the House. With Biddle's agreement, the proposals modified the existing charter by placing limits on the bank's powers to hold real estate and establish new branches. They also gave the president of the United States the power to appoint one director at each branch and Congress the power to prevent the bank from issuing small notes. But the reforms were too little, too late. As Biddle had originally feared, the alliance of the bank with Jackson's political opponents ended any hesitancy on Jackson's part to deny the BUS its new charter.

With New York's large congressional delegation divided and Pennsylvania's solidly behind rechartering, Congress's approval of the bank bill was foreordained. But the antibank men made themselves heard, if only for the benefit of the *Globe*. Sometimes they attacked the BUS's supporters as much as the bank itself— reaching out from Capitol Hill to build opposition around the country. ("Why this sudden pressure?" Thomas Hart Benton demanded. "Is it to throw the bank bill into the hands of the President . . . and to place the President under a cross fire from the opposite banks of the Potomac River?") Biddle, meanwhile, coordinated a public pro-BUS campaign and arranged, through his branch bank managers, for scores of petitions from state banks and citizens' groups to arrive on Capitol Hill and make it appear as if the BUS enjoyed massive grassroots support.

There was another drama during this congressional session, closely related to the political machinations surrounding the BUS—the Senate's confirmation vote on Van Buren's nomination as minister to Britain. Clay and Webster managed to maneuver the vote into a tie—leaving Vice President Calhoun, with mock solemnity and great delight, to cast the deciding vote to defeat Van Buren. (Benton later claimed he heard a scornful Calhoun say, "It will kill him, sir, kill him dead. He will never kick sir, never kick.") Having defeated Jackson's chosen successor, the opposition then went to work on outsmarting the president on the bank. When the BUS recharter bill finally came to a vote in July, it passed both houses comfortably. Nicholas Biddle, flushed with victory, appeared in the House to bask in the plaudits of his congressional backers, then hosted a raucous celebration in his lodgings, "sufficiently public," Taney later wrote, "to make sure it would reach the ears of the President."

On the evening of July 8, Van Buren, just returned from his aborted ministry, hurried to the White House and arrived at midnight to find a spectral Jackson, lying on a sick bed but braced for battle. "The bank, Mr. Van Buren, is trying to kill me," the president said quietly, almost matter-of-factly, grasping his friend's hand, *but I will kill it!*" Jackson's veto message was nearly complete, worked on by Taney, Donelson, Secretary of the Navy Levi Woodbury, and Jackson himself, but drafted and revised by Amos Kendall, whose slashing prose predominated. Signed by Jackson two days later, the document arrived at once at the Senate. It set off a political earthquake.

The bank veto message was a brilliant political document, crafted for wide circulation in order to reach over the heads of Congress, build public support, and unite the disparate Jacksonian factions opposed to the BUS. For the Workies and the western radicals, there were the message's angriest passages, ripping into the "opulent" bank as a despotic monopoly. To reassure Jackson's more moderate allies, the message conceded that "[a] bank of the United States is in many respects convenient for the Government and useful to the people," and remarked that other bank plans had been offered "on terms much more favorable" than the bank bill provided. State bankers, old-line Jeffersonians, and southern state-rights men—including some who backed Calhoun—would kindle to the message's claim that the bank's charter, as proposed, was not "subversive of the rights of the States and dangerous to the liberties of the people." For patriotic, and especially Anglophobic, Americans everywhere, there were discursions, tinged with demagogy, about foreigners who owned a substantial portion of the bank's stock and drained American prosperity.

The message also powerfully elucidated Jackson's political and social philosophy. Some of its strongest statements appeared in its comparatively staid middle section on constitutional issues. Contradicting those who charged that "[m]ere precedent" had settled the constitutionality of the BUS, Jackson beckoned to past congressional and state court opinions against the bank. The Supreme Court's decision in *McCulloch v. Maryland* did not, Jackson asserted, cover every aspect of the bank's charter. Moreover, he claimed, the executive, as a coequal coordinate branch of the government, had the sworn duty to uphold the Constitution as it saw fit, regardless of the Court. On various counts, the message depicted the bank as a privileged private institution that bypassed the authority of the state governments and enjoyed powers exceeding those granted the federal government. But surpassing all discussion of state rights was Jackson's assertion of rightful presidential power within the federal system, especially in relation to the Supreme Court.

The message's concluding passages combined Jackson's constitutional views with his larger democratic vision. "It is to be regretted that the rich and powerful too often bend the acts of government to their selfish purposes," Jackson observed.

> Distinctions in society will always exist under every just government. Equality of talents, of education, or of wealth can not be produced by human institutions. In the full enjoyment of the gifts of Heaven and the fruits of superior industry, economy, and virtue, every man is equally entitled to protection by law; but when the laws undertake to add to these natural and just advantages artificial distinctions, to grant titles, gratuities, and exclusive privileges, to make the rich richer and the potent more powerful, the humble members of society—the farmers, mechanics, and laborers—who have neither the time nor the means of securing like favors to themselves, have a right to complain of the injustice of their Government.

No agrarian leveler, Jackson nevertheless decried artificial inequalities of wealth and power—inequalities he blamed on the ability of privileged men to subvert the Constitution and turn political power, especially federal power, toward enriching themselves further, in defiance of popular sovereignty.

The message was more confused in its economic policy. Perhaps because of Kendall's influence—and apparently contrary to Jackson's own suggestions—it said nothing concrete about establishing a replacement for the bank. This omission fed fears, already rampant, that the president aimed simply to destroy the BUS without installing any substitute. The message's muddled reasoning on the BUS's connection to smaller banks worsened those fears. Early on, the message appeared to support the grievances of the state banks against the BUS monopoly. Yet in a later passage it complained that the BUS's redemption of notes presented by the state banks created "a bond of union" among the banking establishments of the nation that made them "an interest separate from that of the people." The latter remark was in line with Jackson's hostility to all commercial banks, but it contradicted what he had said earlier. The message also argued that the comparatively small amount of bank stock owned by westerners proved that eastern financiers were exploiting the rest of the country. Yet that exploitation consisted chiefly of loans extended by the BUS to western investors, hardly a show of pro-eastern favoritism. Perhaps Jackson was really objecting to western debt and (once again) to the banking system itself. But by refraining from saying so directly, and looking instead to build the strongest coalition against the bank, Jackson's argument was illogical. To uphold its constitutional arguments and democratic vision, and to buttress the antibank coalition, the veto message sacrificed consistency on economics and finance itself.

The National Republicans in Washington reacted sharply, emphasizing, as Jackson had, constitutional issues while proclaiming a very different social outlook. The anti-administration *National Intelligencer* called the veto a proclamation of presidential absolutism. Webster, addressing a packed Senate gallery, rebutted the message's claims about the executive's constitutional powers while charging that the message "attacked whole classes of the people, for the purposes of turning against them the prejudices and resentments of other classes." Clay likened Jackson to a European despot and alleged that an "electioneering motive" lay behind Jackson's act: true enough but risibly hypocritical, given Clay's own electioneering calculations. Back in Philadelphia, Nicholas Biddle, certain that the message would backfire on Jackson, detected the spirit of the French Revolution's Reign of Terror: "It has all the fury of a chained panther biting at the bars of his cage. It really is a manifesto of anarchy—such as Marat or Robespierre might have issued to the mob of the faubourgh St. Antoine." None of which mattered on Capitol Hill, where the bank charter bill again passed the Senate on July 13, this time by a margin of 22 to 19—five votes less than the original tally and far short of the two-thirds' majority required to override Jackson's veto. In the crunch, Jackson's antibank supporters stood up for the president more consistently than his National Republican opponents stood against him.

The veto message did, however, divide pro- and anti-BUS forces within Jackson's larger coalition around the country. In Boston, the horrified old-line ex-Federalists who had supported him in 1828 dashed over to the National Republicans. In New York, where businessmen's opinions about Biddle's operation were divided, the newly converted pro-BUS editor James Watson Webb assailed the president as a worn-out soldier manipulated by "political gamblers, money changers [and] time-serving politicians." Elsewhere, pro-BUS Jacksonians organized committees of "original Jackson men," heaping scorn on the veto but clinging to Old Hickory's name.

Henry Clay, his mind now completely on his presidential campaign, thought he had Jackson exactly where he wanted him. Told during the initial bank bill debate of Jackson's intentions, Clay had vowed, "Should Jackson veto it, I will veto him!" Now, with stunning éclat, Biddle and Jackson had turned the election into a referendum on the BUS—a contest that, with some timely financial and political help, Clay believed he could win. His friend Biddle threw enormous resources into the campaign, reprinting thirty thousand copies of the veto message—self-evident proof, as far as Biddle was concerned, of Jackson's unfitness for office. (When he learned that the public actually liked Jackson's message, Biddle hastily started printing copies of Webster's speech instead.) National Republican editors, pamphleteers, and cartoonists, making their first widespread appearance in presidential politics, hammered away at Jackson as either a corrupt would-be monarch, King Andrew I, or as the latest revolutionary manipulator. "The spirit of Jacksonianism is JACOBINISM . . . ," the *Boston Daily Advertiser and Patriot* screamed: "Its Alpha is ANARCHY and its Omega is DESPO-TISM." Although Clay, the Mason, denounced the Anti-Masons after they nominated William Wirt, some pragmatic National Republicans and Anti-Masons in Ohio, Pennsylvania, and New York did what they could to arrange a working relationship with each other, including forming joint electoral tickets.

The Jacksonians responded by tightening their party organization and surpassing their spectacular electioneering efforts of 1828. Doing so was not simple. In early summer a cholera epidemic ravaged the eastern cities, killing thousands, particularly in the poorer neighborhoods, and unnerving the country. (Among the dead was the radical leader of the New York Working Men, Thomas Skidmore.) Still, the Jacksonians mounted a spirited mass campaign. In late May, the party held its own national convention in Baltimore—a gathering envisioned by Jackson's operatives at least a year earlier—and at Jackson's insistence nominated Van Buren for the vice presidency. Then came the deluge of Jackson processions, hickory-pole raisings, and barbecues (one or two of the latter attended by the president himself), even more boisterous and passionate than four years earlier. Blair oversaw the printing and distribution around the country of huge runs of the *Globe*; Kendall, who managed the campaign, commanded the creation of local Hickory Clubs to augment the state parties' efforts.

Jackson's partisans flung themselves into celebrations of the Old Hero, as a fearless man of spotless honor and indomitable courage unlike the wily degenerate Clay. But the fight over the bank also gave the Jacksonians a popular issue more timely than the long-ago Battle of New Orleans, an issue made sharper because Clay was so closely identified with Biddle. In western New York and eastern Pennsylvania, the veto did, as Clay had hoped, put Jackson's supporters on the defensive, as did Clay's condemnation of the administration's Indian policies. But for the most part, the attack on the BUS captured the public's imagination as proof that Jackson was the intrepid defender of "the humble members of society"—a phrase Jackson's managers repeated endlessly—against the rich and privileged. Of the various issues agitated by the *Globe*, the BUS veto was by far the most popular with local Jacksonian editors, who took their cues from Blair's paper. "It is the final decision of the President," one set of state resolutions cried, "between the Aristocracy and the People—he stands by the People." A North Carolina Jacksonian put the matter squarely: "Who but General Jackson would have had the courage to veto the bill rechartering the Bank of the United States, and who but General Jackson could have withstood the overwhelming influence of that corrupt Aristocracy?"

The outcome was a personal vindication for Jackson and a crushing defeat for Clay. Although the total numbers of votes cast in 1832 rose by more than 100,000 over 1828—roughly 9 percent—Clay actually received 35,000 fewer votes than John Quincy Adams had four years earlier, a decline of nearly 7 percent. In the Electoral College, Jackson garnered 219 votes against 49 for Clay and broke the National Republicans' lock on New England by carrying Maine and New Hampshire. Few at the time doubted that the veto issue accounted for the lopsided totals. "The Veto is popular beyond my most sanguine expectations," Van Buren wrote. The veto message, the astute and cynical Thurlow Weed later observed, allowed the Jacksonians "to enlist the laboring classes against a 'monster bank' or 'moneyed aristocracy'"—winning "ten electors against the bank for everyone that Mr. Webster's arguments and eloquence secured in favor of it."

The elections also brought some disquieting news for Jackson's supporters. In the congressional races, Jackson had virtually no political coattails. The House of Representatives that convened in 1833 would still have a pro-Jackson majority of forty-six, although it was down from fifty-nine four years earlier. But in the Senate, a pro-Jackson majority of four votes had become a minority of eight. The bank veto, although popular overall, hurt the Jacksonians badly in certain key places, above all the BUS's home, Pennsylvania. Then there was the surprisingly strong showing by William Wirt and the Anti-Masons—less decisive than Clay had hoped it might be, but troublesome enough for northern Jacksonians. By winning nearly 8 percent of the popular vote, almost entirely in New England and the middle Atlantic states, Wirt ensured that Jackson's margin of victory in the popular vote (though not his popular vote total) actually declined marginally compared to 1828—the only such case in history for a president elected to a second term. Were the populist Anti-Masons ever to unite successfully with the National Republicans, the Jacksonian coalition would face a new and formidable threat in the North.

Of even greater immediate concern were the southern results, above all in South Carolina. Outside Maryland and Clay's home state of Kentucky, Jackson swept the South; in Georgia, Alabama, and Mississippi, the National Republicans did not even bother to mount a presidential campaign. But in South Carolina, antitariff nullifiers took charge of state politics and delivered the state's eleven electoral votes to their own breakaway presidential candidate, Virginia's extremist state-rights governor, John Floyd. In seven other southern states, Old Republican state-rights dissenters ran a ticket of electors pledged to the pro-Calhoun Virginian, Philip Barbour, instead of Van Buren, for the vice presidency. These defections were irrelevant to the outcome. Yet the nullifiers' schism and the echoes of sympathy outside South Carolina had enormous implications. In the aftermath of the

1832 election, they would lead to a showdown over the meaning of democracy even more dramatic than the early battles over the BUS.

"A SEPARATE GOVERNMENT": ORIGINS OF THE NULLIFICATION CRISIS

The South Carolina nullifers ostensibly rose to protest the administration-backed tariff of 1832, a mildly protectionist compromise measure passed at the end of the congressional session. The new tariff, prompted by the White House's concern about rising southern discontent, cut the average duties of the 1828 tariff by half. To the tariff-obsessed South Carolina slaveholders, however, this was grossly insufficient and cause enough to rally to Calhoun's nullification doctrines. Yet above and beyond the tariff, nullification was also a political reaction to numerous developments linked to slavery, including the Southampton uprising, the appearance of Garrison's *Liberator*, and the Virginia debates over suffrage and emancipation.

What more would it take, the nullifiers wondered, for the slaveholders en masse to understand the immediate dangers? First Denmark Vesey—at least Charleston knew how to handle its savages!—then David Walker, and then Nat Turner had incited the slaves to insurrection, each more successful in turn. In Boston, Walker's home, a crazed white man was publishing an incendiary abolitionist newspaper with impunity, spreading his hateful message everywhere. The oppressive tariff remained in place, while cotton prices languished at under ten cents a pound for the seventh consecutive year. And in the face of all this, Virginia's squirearchy had actually considered emancipation—proving, one nullifier claimed, that even the Old Dominion had become "infested" with "Yankee influence" and democratic misgivings about slavery. Threatened from without by abolitionists and high-tariff men and from within by the potential of a slave revolt provoked by the North, the slaveholders, Vice President

Calhoun said, might "in the end be forced to rebel, or submit." The burden fell on Old Carolina to lead the way and spare the entire South from a state of colonial submission—or utter annihilation.

Rich, snobbish, and arrogant, but anxious about the future, South Carolina's slaveholders had always produced the region's most forceful defenses of slavery's benevolence. And they had no use for the democratic dogma that seemed to be sweeping the rest of the nation. Hugh Swinton Legaré—lawyer, sometime state legislator, and the state's leading literary light—conveyed the tone as well as the thinking of his class: "The politics of the immortal Jefferson! Pish!" Not all of the slaveholding elite, to be sure, saw nullification as the best means to preserve the established order, least of all the old-line merchants and lawyers of Charleston, many of them die-hard Federalists who prized the bonds of Union. (Legaré was among those conservatives whose hearts were with the South but whose traditionalism rejected nullification.) When called on to resist some perceived external threat, as they were during the nullification campaign, South Carolina's antimajoritarian political leaders also proved enormously capable organizers of popular sentiment, among slaveholders and nonslaveholders alike. A peculiar temporary, top-down populism would emerge during the nullification crisis, mobilized by the nullifiers in defense of localist oligarchy against "enslavement" by the federal government.

Yet despite the divisions between pro- and anti-nullifers and despite the nullifiers' tub-thumping popular campaigns, South Carolina swerved outside the mainstream of southern politics. The spread of the cotton economy into its backcountry made South Carolina more uniformly reliant on slave labor—and more solidly dedicated to slavery's preservation—than any other state. Nowhere else were slaveholders so numerous across a wider portion of the state. Nowhere else did slaves comprise a larger portion of the total population, making South Carolina's whites singularly vulnerable to fears of slave insurrection. In no state were the structures of government (despite the wide suffrage for the legislature) less democratic than in South Carolina. And nowhere else did the defense of slavery and hostility to majoritarian democracy go hand in hand as they did among South Carolina's slaveholders. Some of the most fervent nullifiers would present themselves as American revolutionaries, to the point of appropriating carefully selected bits and pieces of Jefferson's writings in order to align their cause with the patriotic spirit of 1776. In fact, they were exactly the opposite—nabob counterrevolutionaries, increasingly at war with the democratic forces, identified with Andrew Jackson, that were coming to dominate American politics. They were, above all, the guardians of an idiosyncratic aristocratic-republican mixture, based on slavery, that they feared was about to be destroyed by Yankee exploiters, with the aid of spineless southerners.

Ironically, one of the South Carolinian nullifiers who was slow to rouse himself was the chief theorist, John C. Calhoun. Having completed his transition from nationalist to sectionalist, Calhoun was, nevertheless, oddly, a temperate force in state politics at the opening of the 1830s. Despite his break with Jackson, he was still trying to maneuver his way into the presidency in 1832—or, alternatively, build a political alliance between South and West, based on agreements over liberal land distribution policies, that might help in some later election. There were, Calhoun still believed, many southerners outside South Carolina who were restive over the protective tariff and who, united under his leadership, could take over the seemingly solid pro-Jackson South. The oppressed slaveholder minority might then be able to build a national majority, under his own command and not Jackson's, and defeat Yankee despotism. Precipitate advocacy of nullification—which Calhoun called in "every way imprudent"—might kill such hopes by isolating South Carolina from the other slaveholding states. A few of Calhoun's closest allies, including Senator Hayne and the young South Carolina editor and planter James H. Hammond, agreed with him, forming a distinct faction of what might be called moderate nullifiers, who fully approved of the nullification idea, yet were unpersuaded that its time had come. But other South Carolinians, including Calhoun's follower George McDuffie, thought this was all moonshine. Van Buren's triumph over Calhoun had proved the uselessness of trying to work from within, they believed—and the rest of the South would never rally around true state-rights principles unless compelled to do so.

Once again, as in the mid-1820s, Calhoun found himself out of step with the most vehement elements of South Carolina's ruling class. At first he appeared willing to let it be so by refusing either to renounce or support what he called "the ultra measures proposed by the Carolina Hotspurs." But under pressure from Governor James Hamilton Jr. and Hamilton's radical nullifier allies, Calhoun overcame the divisions in his own mind and composed at his plantation, in July 1831, what became known as the Fort Hill Letter—an open defense of nullification as a moderate, peaceful, and constitutional check on Yankee oppression.

"Happily," Calhoun wrote, the United States had been spared "artificial and separate classes of society." The disturbing divisions were geographical and required equipoise between the general government and the states. State interposition and removal of offensive federal laws could help preserve that stability and impede the conversion of "the General Government into a consolidated, irresponsible government," without endangering the Union—one of "the great instruments of preserving our liberty, & promoting the happiness of ourselves and our posterity." Although it stopped short of endorsing the radical nullifiers, and explicitly rejected "anarchical and revolutionary" intentions, the letter openly aligned Calhoun for the first time with the nullification idea—disclosing the secret that most political observers had long since guessed, and in effect announcing that he intended to remain South Carolina's premier voice in national politics. Now that his break with Jackson was complete and the nullifying movement seemed unstoppable, Calhoun would leave his lair to help give the movement direction.

Until Calhoun assumed a leading role, Governor Hamilton had been the nullifiers' chief agitator and organizer. He did an excellent job. Having already formed, with McDuffie, the State Rights and Free Trade Association, Hamilton redoubled his efforts over the winter of 1831–32, overseeing the creation of a formal political party, the staffing of public committees, the writing and printing of pamphlets, and the calling of two statewide antitariff conventions, one in Charleston, the other in the state capital, Columbia. There was significant opposition, strongest among upcountry planters and yeomen and Charleston merchants and lawyers. (One of these so-called Unionists, the former envoy to Mexico, Joel R. Poinsett, was in regular contact with a deeply concerned President Jackson, keeping him up-to-date about the nullifiers' latest moves.) But after the passage of the tariff bill in July 1832, Hamilton and the nullifiers, with Calhoun's support, sprang into action. Jackson had believed that by cutting the 1828 rates in half, the new tariff would prove his own free-trade bona fides and silence the extremist protests. "You may expect to hear from So Carolina a great noise . . . ," Jackson wrote to his old friend John Coffee, "but the good sense of the people will put it down." Yet Jackson had badly underestimated both the control that pro-Calhounite slaveholders could exert over South Carolina politics and how much popular support for nullification had grown in the state since 1828. It would have to be Jackson, and not the people of South Carolina, who put down nullification.

Over the summer and early fall of 1832, South Carolinians divided violently over politics: not over the bank veto, nor over Jackson and Clay, but over the state legislature elections, scheduled for October 8 and 9. In Charleston, scene of the worst battles, roving bands of armed Unionists and nullifiers confronted each other nightly. Nullifier rhetoric bristled with attacks on majority rule as oppressive, and with defenses of nullification as (in former U.S. Senator William Harper's words) the best means to "obtain all the good which has resulted from monarchies and aristocracies without any mixture of the evil." The nullifiers left little doubt that they believed the protective tariff was not simply an abstract political wrong but an attack by Yankee outsiders on the planters' prerogatives—and, finally, on slavery itself. In his famous, fanciful "forty bale" theory, McDuffie put the planters' interests foremost, charging that for every hundred cotton bales produced by the South, forty were lost to the tariff. The tariff, the Columbia State Rights and Free Trade Association declared, was but a means to effect "the abolition of slavery throughout the southern states."

The Unionists countered with a variety of appeals. In the yeoman-dominated northwestern parishes and among the artisans of Charleston, they attacked the undemocratic slaveholders and slavery itself as an evil. More often, they appealed to the voters' patriotism, insisting that South Carolina's interests were far more secure inside the Union than outside, and that nullification was a dangerous, unrepublican experiment. The Unionists nearly carried Charleston, and won handily in the northernmost, yeoman-dominated parishes. But the nullifiers' lopsided victory margins in the cotton-plantation districts gave them 61 percent of the total vote. Thanks to continued malapportionment of the state legislature, this was sufficient to gain the nullifiers the two-thirds' majority required to authorize the calling of a nullification convention, as laid out in the *South Carolina Exposition and Protest*. Governor Hamilton duly called for a special session of the legislature, which in turn passed a convention bill, setting a date in November for the election of delegates who would convene at Columbia five days later. The Unionists, dejected at their loss, had little fight left in them, and the nullifiers completely controlled the selection of delegates.

After five days of work, the convention, with Calhoun's blessing, approved several documents, the most important of which was the Ordinance of Nullification, written by William Harper. In six dry paragraphs, the Ordinance declared the tariffs of 1828 and 1832 unconstitutional; pronounced them null and void in South Carolina, effective February 1, 1833; and called for the legislature to pass all acts necessary to enforce that nullification. The demand for a nonprotective tariff was nonnegotiable. Should the federal government try to coerce South Carolina into denying the Ordinance, the people of South Carolina would secede from the Union and "forthwith proceed to organize a separate government." Governor Hamilton speedily asked the legislature to revise the state's militia laws and approve the raising of a twelve-thousand-man volunteer army.

Jackson, forewarned by Poinsett, took the precaution of ordering the federal forts in Charleston harbor to prepare for attacks, instructed federal customs officials to move from the city to Fort Moultrie offshore, ordered government revenue cutters to enforce the tariff before ships came close to the harbor, and sent a personal emissary to consult with the Unionist leaders. Jackson determined that if the crisis ever came down to shooting, South Carolina and not the federal government would be forced to be the aggressor. After the Ordinance passed, Jackson tried to isolate the South Carolinians by reinforcing his connections to southern leaders from other states and by offering a variety of concessions.

Firmly convinced that the tariff was constitutional, Jackson believed more than ever that its effects had become greatly exaggerated by protectionists and antitariff men alike. It was even less important, Jackson claimed, now that his policies had paid down the national debt nearly to the point of elimination. Accordingly, and with no great sacrifice on his own part, Jackson devoted a section of his annual message on December 4 to proposing an eventual reduction of tariffs to cover only what was necessary for federal revenue and national defense, in exchange for the exercise of "moderation and good sense" by all concerned. He appeared to have acceded to the Carolinians' low-tariff demands, even though he had acceded nothing that made much difference to him. He ended with an affirmation of traditional Jeffersonian state-rights doctrine—the true doctrine, Jackson implied, and not the disunionist folly of Calhoun and his friends. The annual message contained the president's carrot. Six days later, he pulled out his bludgeon.

"VAIN PROVISIONS! INEFFECTUAL RESTRICTIONS!": JACKSON AND NULLIFICATION

In meeting the nullification crisis, Jackson displayed his style of presidential leadership at its strongest. He had always called on his cabinet members and advisors for help in formulating specific proposals and doctrines. Van Buren and James K. Polk wrote the Maysville Road bill veto; Kendall was the chief author of the bank veto message; others chipped in on these and other major addresses. As the long buildup to the bank veto showed, Jackson was open to persuasion and sometimes wavered before making up his mind. But neither did anything go out under Jackson's name that did not meet with his full approval. The one person always involved was Jackson himself, leaning now toward his more state rights–oriented counselors, then toward those with a more nationalist bent, using them all to fashion what, finally, was his own democratic political philosophy, worked out on the job.

Late in 1832, Jackson turned to Edward Livingston to draft and redraft a stern official response to nullification, a follow-up to his conciliatory annual message. The sudden shift in tone led some of his critics, and has led some historians, to claim that the nullification paper was really Livingston's work, not Jackson's, and that it hopelessly contradicted the annual message. But the president probably labored harder on the nullification paper than on any other message of his presidency, sending Livingston memoranda, inserting his own prose into Livingston's drafts, and otherwise making certain that nothing appeared which did not exactly match his own thinking. (According to one account, Jackson worked so furiously, writing notes with a steel pen, that even when he had finished ten pages the ink on the first was still wet.) As ever, Jackson ran his presidency much as he had run his military and election campaigns, delegating authority, relying on the advice of others, but always in charge. The product was not the contradictory jumble that most observers complained about, containing what even a staunch supporter called "broad errors of doctrine." With the aid of his inner circle, Jackson created a volatile synthesis.

Jackson's declaration—officially titled, simply, "Proclamation"—was a triumph of political and constitutional argument. It opened with a calm but contemptuous restatement of the nullifiers' "strange position" and addressed the Ordinance of Nullification point by point. Then it cut to the heart of the issue: were the artifice of nullification countenanced, then "no federative government could exist" and the United States would simply dissolve. By the strictest reading of the U.S. Constitution, there could be no doubt that Article I, Section 8 granted Congress the power to lay and collect taxes, duties, imposts, and excises. Unlike the case of the BUS, there was no ambiguity about the tariff's constitutional correctness.

By what reasoning, then, did the nullifiers justify their claims that the tariffs of 1828 and 1832 abused the Constitution? They complained that the tariffs were unconstitutionally motivated by a desire to secure protection and not merely to raise revenue. Nonsense! Jackson replied that there was no such thing as unconstitutional motives, only unconstitutional acts. The nullifiers complained that the tariff operated unequally. So what? Jackson noted that a perfect equality in taxes was impossible. In any case, such inequality was no justification for declaring unconstitutional legislation that, unlike internal improvements, the Framers had expressly delegated to Congress. The nullifiers complained that the tariff was higher than necessary, its proceeds utilized to fund unconstitutional expenditures. Ridiculous! Jackson retorted that even though Congress might abuse its discretionary powers, the powers themselves were incontestably constitutional and subject to the popular will at elections. One by one, the nullifiers' alleged constitutional grievances collapsed.

But Jackson was not content to refute the nullifiers' reasoning on the tariff. He wanted to destroy the philosophical and political foundations of nullification itself. Once again he focused on the key issue: Calhoun's theories of the Union and undivided state sovereignty. Those theories, Jackson charged, were recent inventions, unanticipated by the Framers and ratifiers of the Constitution. Laws whose effects were far more controversial than the ones currently at issue—the whiskey excise law in the 1790s, Jefferson's embargo—had been deemed unconstitutional by a majority in one or more states, "but, fortunately, none of those States discovered that they had the right now claimed by South Carolina."

Calhoun's invention, Jackson proclaimed, was nothing more than a fraud wrapped inside an absurdity, produced by "[m]etaphysical subtlety, in pursuit of an impracticable theory." The nation, Jackson instructed, was not created by sovereign state governments when the several states approved the Constitution. In fact, the nation was *older* than both the Constitution and the states. Before 1776, "we were known in our aggregate character as the *United Colonies of America.*" The Declaration of Independence was promulgated by the nation before the state governments (save those of New Hampshire and Virginia) were even organized. Even the highly imperfect Articles of Confederation included a provision that "every State shall abide by the determinations of Congress on all questions which by that Confederation should be submitted to them." When framed and ratified "to form a more perfect union," the Constitution became a new framework for an already existing nation. "The Constitution of the United States . . . forms a *government*, not a league," Jackson concluded. Although the states retained all powers not delegated by the Constitution to the federal government, the federal government retained its complete sovereignty in those delegated areas. Any state's denial of that sovereignty—based on the underlying absurd supposition that "the United States are not a nation"—would injure the entire Union. Thus Jackson smashed the logic behind nullification. The politics of the great Calhoun? Hogwash.

Initial reactions to Jackson's proclamation blended puzzlement and shock. National Republicans applauded the document, but also expressed confusion about how Jackson could have approved it. "One short week," Henry Clay wrote to a political associate, "produced the [annual] message and the proclamation—the former ultra, on the side of State rights—and latter ultra, on the side of Consolodation." Jacksonians asked the same question, but in mortification at what they perceived as Jackson's abandonment of Jeffersonian fundamentals. Some contemporaries came up with explanations which boiled down to a suspicion that the president was now an incompetent old codger, easily manipulated by the nationalist advisers around him like Edward Livingston. And so later historians, equally baffled, have advanced their own explanations for the apparent inconsistencies, ranging from Jackson's alleged pathological rage at John C. Calhoun to the claim that Jackson compensated for his annual message by going too far in a nationalist direction and wound up doing "a poor job of defending the traditional states'-rights position."

Some of these interpretations were and are malicious; others merely misconstrue Jackson's purposes. (It was, for example, not Jackson's aim in the nullification proclamation to defend traditional state rights or a lowered tariff, although he did make clear he supported them.) Many share the inaccurate assumption that Jackson trapped himself in some large contradictions. In fact, Jackson, drawing on long-established beliefs, carved out a coherent and principled democratic nationalism on basic constitutional issues. In his mind, tariff rates and nullification were completely separate matters. The first, as he had said in his annual message, was always subject to negotiation, but the second was not.

Jackson had always objected to extending federal powers beyond what was set forth in the Constitution. He regarded programs like federal internal improvements with deep suspicion. Like Jefferson, he believed that the unchecked growth of federal authority would lead inevitably to new concentrations of power that would benefit the privileged few over the many. But Jackson's guardianship of state rights always allowed that the federal government had legitimate independent powers, in no wise at the whim of the state governments. Contrary to Calhoun's calm assertions, he contended, nullification would lead inexorably to secession and the undoing of all that was won in the Revolution. "There is nothing I shudder at more than the idea of the separation of the Union . . . ," he wrote to James Hamilton Jr. (not yet a nullifier firebrand) before the 1828 election. "It is the durability of the confederation upon which the general government is built, that must prolong our liberty, the moment it seperates, it is gone." Jackson had seen the ineradicable bonds of Union questioned before, by the blue-light New England Federalists of the Hartford Convention, who had squabbled and made disunionist noises while he was crushing the British at New Orleans. Now Calhoun and the nullifiers were questioning the bonds once again while he was trying to crush the Second BUS.

Jackson's position on nullification arose from his fundamental dedication to democracy and to the idea he expressed in his first message to Congress *"that the majority is to govern."* It was the very opposite of the neo-Federalist "ultranationalism" seen by so many critics, then and now, in the proclamation. Strict construction of federal power was necessary lest a minority try to advance its own narrow interests with only passing concern for the general welfare. Yet no single state—let alone, Jackson noted in the nullification proclamation, "a bare majority of the voters in any one state"—could be permitted to repudiate laws based on delegated powers and duly enacted by Congress and the president, the people's representatives. The *South Carolina Exposition and Protest* had explicitly rejected majoritarian democracy, claiming that "[c]onstitutional government, and the government of the majority, are utterly incompatible." Jackson denounced such astonishing propositions in the horrified cadences of an American seer: "Vain provisions! ineffectual restrictions! vile profanation of oaths! miserable mockery of legislation!"

Jackson's fury at the nullifiers did owe something to his detestation of John C. Calhoun, but Jackson's personal hatreds alone hardly determined his political reaction to nullification. Long before his break with Calhoun, let alone before the nullification crisis, he had been thinking along the lines spelled out in his proclamation. Those majoritarian nationalist ideas were not uniquely his, but in presenting them as forcefully as he did, and incurring huge political risks, Jackson showed how seriously he took them. "No my friend," Jackson told the characteristically squeamish Martin Van Buren, who had urged he refrain from issuing his proclamation, "the crisis must be now met with firmness, our citizens protected, and the modern doctrine of nullification and secession put down forever."

Ordinary Americans were not as flummoxed as some of the leading national politicians and party editors were by Jackson's hard-line stance. The legislatures of Pennsylvania, Indiana, and Illinois, followed by those of most of the other northern states (and Maryland) passed resolutions affirming the proclamation and condemning nullification as "heretical" and "anti-republican." Large and impassioned public meetings in cities from New York to New Orleans hailed Jackson's message. In Nashville, Governor William Carroll offered to lead a force of ten thousand men to South Carolina. Further east, in the mountainous, small-farmer region of the state, one old Jackson comrade, John Wyly, claimed that the "old chief" would be able to raise enough troops in two weeks' time that they could muster at the state border and "piss enough . . . to float the whole nullifying crew of South Carolina into the Atlantic."

In much of the South, the slaveholder-dominated legislatures responded differently. In Georgia, a powerful minority supported nullification, and although the legislators turned down a proclamation favoring it, they did call for a convention of southern states to discuss the issue. In Virginia, the Tidewater slaveholders were particularly supportive of nullification, but the state assembly, controlled by Jacksonians, refused to endorse South Carolina. The North Carolina legislature condemned South Carolina's "revolutionary" and "subversive" actions, but also denounced the protective tariff as unconstitutional and refrained from endorsing Jackson's proclamation. Alabama called for a federal convention to take up the issues raised by the crisis. But despite these qualms— and despite the quasi-nullifying stances taken by familiar extreme state-rights and antidemocratic leaders, ranging from George Troup in Georgia to Abel P. Upshur in Virginia—no southern legislature backed nullification. South Carolina stood alone. Jackson believed that even that result did not show fully how "the united voice of the yeomanry" despised the nullifiers' doctrines and supported him. South Carolina nullifiers, including Calhoun and James H. Hammond, thought that Georgia and Virginia would have joined their ranks but for the Jacksonians' power.

The president's proclamation was the turning point in the crisis. Jackson had already begun making preparations to aid a volunteer Unionist militia within South Carolina, organized by Poinsett in the northern countries. He ordered federal troops to Castle Pinckney and Sullivan's Island in Charleston harbor, and also sent General Winfield Scott to the city aboard a federal sloop, lest the nullifiers try to seize the customs houses. One week after releasing his proclamation, he ordered Secretary of War Lewis Cass to report on how quickly arms and troops (including three divisions of artillery) could be gathered to "crush the monster in its cradle." The South Carolina legislature, which had reconvened, reshuffled the state's leadership by accepting Governor Hamilton's resignation (he would head the state's new armed forces) and replacing him with Senator Hayne. A red-hot nullifier thus gave way to a more moderate nullifier. Hayne's Senate seat went to the now fully engaged John C. Calhoun, who resigned the vice presidency effective December 28. The legislature—the last in the nation empowered to name presidential electors—also officially handed South Carolina's presidential electoral votes to Virginia's governor John Floyd, who, recovering from his less than stalwart performance during his state's debates over slavery, condemned Jackson for his "warlike" preparations. Yet even as the nullifiers arranged for their showdown with Jackson and railed against federal usurpation, it became apparent that South Carolina was politically isolated. Cooler temperaments began asserting themselves on all sides.

The denouement lasted ten weeks into the new year. Governor Hayne, still hoping against hope to win support from other southern states, ordered the twenty-five thousand volunteers who had answered the call to train at home rather than in Charleston, lest South Carolina look like the aggressor menacing the federal forts in Charleston harbor. Jackson, who all along had wanted to force the nullifiers to back down without sending federal troops, modulated his tone and sent a special message to Congress with some very specific requests. These included permission to call up federal troops and state militia without warning the rebels to disperse, should the nullifiers forcibly confiscate federal property. It was largely a symbolic move—the military request would merely speed up the use of powers the president already possessed under laws passed in 1795 and 1807—and was nowhere near as belligerent as might have been expected. But it was severe enough for all concerned to call the proposal Jackson's Force Bill Message. Calhoun, now back in the Senate, ripped into the Force Bill as soon as it was read in Congress and would do so again in later debates, charging that the administration had issued an "imperial edict" and wished to impose a military despotism. Calhoun's speeches, mixing history and declamation, were brilliant, but they would turn out mainly to be bluster. The forces of compromise, chilled by the specter of civil war, were already at work—and Calhoun, in this crisis, finally, the moderate, was playing his part.

On January 21, with the Ordinance of Nullification due to take effect in ten days, the nullifiers held a mass meeting in Charleston and, in a tactical retreat, voted to postpone the implementation until Congress settled the tariff issue. Calhoun, sticking by nullification as an alternative to disunion, wrote the radical nullifier leaders to say that "we must not think of secession, but in the last extremity," and urged them to suspend the Ordinance for a year. Soon thereafter, an official commissioner from Virginia, the Tidewater grandee Benjamin Watkins Leigh, arrived in Columbia bearing a copy of the state's carefully crafted middle-of-the road resolutions, critical of both Jackson and nullification, and offered to mediate the dispute.

Clay, Webster, and Calhoun then began patching together an agreement. An administration tariff bill, forwarded by Van Buren's ally, the low-tariff New York Congressman Gulian Verplanck, impressed neither the nullifiers nor Clay's pro-tariff men. Clay and Calhoun set about devising an alternative to steal Jackson's thunder. The process was difficult, and not without rhetorical fireworks. First, Congress, cajoled by the master fixer Clay and with Calhoun's accord, hammered out a compromise tariff that lowered rates incrementally until 1842, when they would

drop sharply to the levels sought by the nullifiers. At every contested point in the bargaining, Calhoun gave way, assured by the
hard-dealer Clay and by Webster that northern protectionists
needed gradual adjustment and would go no further—thereby
perpetuating for a decade a decidedly protective tariff even as
cotton prices remained pathetically low. With the casus belli
removed—and with the nullifiers' supposedly nonnegotiable
demands negotiated away—the crisis might have appeared over.
But Jackson insisted on passing the Force Bill, just as Calhoun
insisted on putting on a show of resisting it. In the Senate debate,
Calhoun and Webster squared off and rose to their full oratorical
powers. Sounding, for once, something like Jackson, Webster
declared that "those who espouse the doctrines of nullification
reject . . . the first great principle of all republican liberty; that is,
that the majority must govern."

The Force Bill debate attracted enormous attention. (John
Randolph of Roanoke, who despised John C. Calhoun but
despised Daniel Webster even more, excitedly watched the proceedings from the Senate gallery and told a man seated in front
of him to remove his hat, which was blocking his view: "I want
to see Webster die, muscle by muscle," he said.) Yet the nullifiers, facing likely defeat in the Senate, quietly agreed to refrain
from obstructing the Force Bill's passage, probably in a prearranged deal. The measure carried in the Senate by a 32 to 1
vote, with many slaveholders, including Henry Clay, absenting
themselves. Then it passed the House, 149 to 48. Several hours
later, the Senate gave its final approval to the compromise tariff. Calhoun claimed the last word and delivered a learned,
irrelevant, and attention-getting speech denouncing the Force
Bill. He then departed Washington, riding night and day in an
open wagon through foul weather to Columbia to make sure
that the radical nullifiers stepped down. There was little chance
they would not, as what support they had received from the rest
of the South evaporated after the compromise tariff passed
Congress. A reconvened state convention rescinded the Ordinance of Nullification, but in a final defiant act, the insurgents

passed a new ordinance nullifying the Force Bill, salvaging shreds of honor.

Jackson had won a major victory—but a costly one. His losses came from within his own party, especially in the South. Although they spurned nullification, the southern slaveholders, generally, also spurned Jackson's proclamation as much too harsh and much too nationalist. Even staunch southern Jacksonians admitted that, though they thought nullification was madness, the nullifiers had a point. "You can rest assured," one pro-Jackson Mississippian wrote, "S.C. has our sympathies." In Virginia, the cradle of Jeffersonian doctrine, the crisis reopened the rift between the small-farmer, pro-Jackson West and the slaveholder-dominated Tidewater and Piedmont areas, where the nullifiers commanded great support. "I am no nullifier . . . ," one Louisiana planter wrote at the height of the crisis, "but my sympathies are with theirs; and as the nullifiers are contending against laws which are unconstitutional, unjust, oppressive, and ruinous to the South, I will never consent to see them put down by military force, and before I would take part in a crusade by the Yankees to put South Carolina to the sword, I would be hung for treason." In the congressional machinations leading to the compromise, southern Democrats peeled off from the administration and opened up the possibility of an ideologically promiscuous Clay-Calhoun alliance. Others stayed loyal to the party but would seek ways to square white men's democracy with a robust Calhounite idea of state rights. Some southerners who were Unionists in 1832—including a young up-country South Carolina editor, William Lowdnes Yancey—would become secessionists soon enough.

Adverse reactions were far less common in the North, where most of the state legislatures backed Jackson to the hilt on the matter of nullification. Yet many northern Jacksonians found the president's ferocious words and actions disturbing. In Van Buren's New York, orthodox views of state sovereignty and support for the compact theory of the Constitution prevented the Regency, which condemned nullification, from uniting in support of Jackson's proclamation. Van Buren himself opposed the

Force Bill. Viewed from a certain angle, this fallout, along with Jackson's fracturing of his southern following, can make it seem as if the nullifiers, and not Jackson, had won the battle. Add in the fact that the nullifiers succeeded in gaining a tariff reduction, albeit a very gradual one, along with the fact that South Carolina Unionism virtually collapsed after 1833, and John C. Calhoun might even look like a triumphant political thinker and strategist. Such, at least, was Calhoun's own assessment. More detached observers saw the long-term outcome as ominous. "Nullification has done its work," the Unionist James Petigru wrote. "It has prepared the minds of men for a separation of the states—and when the question is moved again it will be distinctly union or disunion."

Yet Jackson also was certain that he had won, and with good reason. "I have had a laborious task here," he wrote, "but nullification is dead; and its actors and exciters will only be remembered by the people to be execrated for their wicked designs." With a combination of coercive threats and well-timed moderation, Jackson had scotched the immediate threat. He had vindicated the Union with much of his popular following, if not his Washington following, still intact. Although he got no credit for the compromise tariff, he had helped maneuver events so that Calhoun and his Carolina allies settled for far less than they had demanded—and less than Jackson himself had seemed to offer in his annual message in December 1832. Of all the major figures in the controversy, only Jackson had backed the Force Bill and some sort of tariff reduction, a stand which affirmed his view that nullification and the tariff were completely separate issues. He got his way on both. More broadly, he had articulated a theory of American constitutional democracy that combined Jeffersonian strict construction and respect for state rights with a validation of the American Union. Above all, Jackson had vindicated the idea that had become the keystone of his politics: in the American republic, the majority governs. To uphold that principle, he called on the nation to reject the slaveholder aristocrats, who in their zeal would dismember the Union itself.

The struggle hardly turned the slaveholder Jackson's administration, let alone his intersectional party, into an antislavery force. Jackson did not even see the crisis in those terms. He always ascribed the nullifiers' motivations to sheer political ambition. Now that they had lost, Jackson predicted, they would seize on "the negro, or slavery question" as their "next pretext." The *Globe* agreed, charging that the impulse behind nullification was "a *politician's*, not a *planter's*." Yet the crisis did show that protecting slavery and slaveholders' rights did not lie at the core of Jackson's political philosophy. Democracy, not pro-slavery, was his animating principle, in the nullification crisis no less than when he vetoed the rechartering of the BUS. To defend democracy, he would fiercely attack the most vociferous pro-slavery bloc in the nation.

There was, to be sure, a great deal more to the nullification crisis than met the eye. As James Petigru sensed, the compromise of 1833 did not settle the deeper issues at stake any more than had the Missouri Compromises of 1820 and 1821. The battle between Jacksonian democratic nationalists, northern and southern, and nullifier sectionalists would resound through the politics of slavery and antislavery for decades to come. Jackson's victory, ironically, would help accelerate the emergence of southern pro-slavery as a coherent and articulate political force, which would help solidify northern antislavery opinion, inside as well as outside Jackson's party. Those developments would accelerate the emergence of two fundamentally incompatible democracies, one in the slave South, the other in the free North.

As Calhoun had suggested early on, the struggle involved not simply protective tariffs or state rights but the deeper alienation of the slaveholding South, whose "peculiar domestick institution" placed it in "opposite relation to the majority of the Union." Or, as a young, intransigent radical nullifier named Robert Barnwell Rhett proclaimed at the final gathering of the South Carolina nullification convention, not just the North but also "the whole world are in arms against your institutions: . . . Let Gentlemen be not deceived. It is not the Tariff—not Internal Improvement—

nor yet the Force Bill, which constitutes the great evil against which we are contending." The *Globe's* prediction, after the crisis had passed, that nullification would give way to an effort to arouse "the fear and jealousy of the South with regard to their slaves," and push for disunion would come to seem prescient, even if pro-slavery ideals and not merely ambition would lie behind that effort.

Yet however much Jackson and his supporters misunderstood the deeper motives and forces, they had presented a powerful and, for the moment, victorious case about the central political issue in the crisis, the legitimacy of nullification. In the final analysis, Jackson declared, devotion to the nation, democracy, and the will of the majority must take precedence over the nulli-fiers' allegiance to region, state, and locality—and to slavery. By stating his ideas as forcefully as he did, and threatening to take military action, Jackson offended many southern slaveholders, and even pro–state rights northerners. Yet he still managed to leave the nullifiers isolated and defeated. He also established a crucial democratic precedent. Over the decades to come, the southern slaveholders, pushed by Calhoun, his admirers, and his successors, would expand on the pro-slavery and disunionist arguments that underlay nullification. In time, the disunionists would force a secession crisis far graver than the confrontation over the tariff in 1833. But when that happened—and as Americans fixed their attention, once again, on Charleston harbor—another president, Abraham Lincoln, would turn to Jackson's doctrine for guidance.

"JACKSON CONQUERS EVERY THING"

Thirty-six hours after Congress put the final touches on the compromise that ended the nullification controversy, Jackson took the oath of office for his second presidential term. The ceremony, although surrounded by the usual festivities, was prudent and simple, with little of the exuberance of Jackson's first inaugural and none of the sublime wonder at what sort of president he would be. People now knew. Jackson's second inaugural message, almost exactly the same lean length as his first, noted, with understatement, the "many events" of the previous four years that had "called forth . . . my views of the principles and policy which ought to be pursued by the General Government." Jackson then delivered a concise summary of those views, blending respect for state rights with "the sacred duty of all to contribute to [the Union's] preservation by a liberal support of the General Government in the exercise of its just powers."

The previous four years had brought to a political head social and economic transformations already underway for decades. Jackson had initiated none of these, nor any of the political, social, and religious movements they spawned, including the Working Men, the evangelical moral reformers, the radical abolitionists, and the nullifiers. Toward some of those causes— above all, radical abolitionism and nullification—Jackson was deeply hostile, and would make his hostility even clearer over the years to come. Yet all created political disturbances fed by clashing ideas about democracy that, one way or another, shook the national government as well as the regions and localities where they had originated.

Jackson had entered the White House full of ideas about reforming government and ending the kind of insider corruption that he blamed for his defeat in 1824–25. For two years, scandals and schisms badly distracted his efforts. But on inauguration day in 1833, Jackson could look back with satisfaction at what he had achieved, on the bank veto, nullification, Indian removal, resisting Sabbatarianism—and crushing Henry Clay. In doing all that, Jackson had reshaped the political coalition that had elected him in 1828 to fit his own principles, complete with a chosen successor who would now be his vice president, Martin Van Buren. No longer an ad hoc alliance, his national political operation had begun to resemble a coherent party—what would soon become known simply as the Democracy. Jackson's supporters had rallied several democratic insurgencies—Workies from the eastern cities, western hard-money men and backcountry democrats, southern yeomen and Unionists—to the Democracy's banner. "General Jackson," wrote John Quincy Adams's son, Charles Francis, as much in awe and candor as in bitterness, "conquers every thing."

Jackson the conqueror still had many powerful enemies to face, though, not least in the Congress of the United States, one house of which now was firmly in the control of his opponents, led by Clay. The outcome of important campaigns, above all the struggle with the BUS, had yet to be settled. Although the nullifiers had been stopped, neither southern misgivings nor the northern antislavery movement that inflamed them would abate simply because of the compromise of 1833. "My opinion is," the defeated Anti-Mason William Wirt wrote after Jackson's reelection, "that he may be President for life if he chooses." The commotions that Jackson and the nation would face during his second term militated otherwise.

DEMOCRACY ASCENDANT

1. Andrew Jackson campaign
engraving, 1828

MAINE NOT TO BE COUPLED WITH THE
MISSOURI QUESTION.
✸✸✸✸

If the South will not yield, to the West be it known,
That Maine will declare for a *King* of her own;
And *three hundred thousand* of freemen demand
The justice bestow'd on each State in the land.
Free whites of the East are not blacks of the West,
And Republican souls on this principle rest,
That if no respect to their rights can be shown,
They know how to vindicate what are their own.
Their patriot zeal has been ever express'd ;
Their enterprize, Europe has often confess'd.—
They are founded on freedom, humanity's right,
Ordained by God against slavery to fight.
And Heaven born liberty sooner than yield,
The whites of Missouri shall dress their own field.
We are hardy and healthy, can till our own soil,
In labour delight ; make a pleasure of toil.
They spurn at our climate ; yet live in a bog :
We enjoy fair, cold weather ; they grope in a fog.
We fly in our sleighs ; they wallow in mire,
O'erwhelm'd with musquitoes ; we sing by our fire.
We have pork and potatoes, fish, mutton, and beef ;
Fill'd with agues, to physic, they fly for relief.
They too lazy to work, drive slaves, whom they fear ;
We school our own children, and brew our own beer.
We do a day's work and go fearless to bed ;
Tho' lock'd up, they dream of slaves, whom they dread.
We have learn'd too much wisdom to emigrate west,
As poor souls returning, too well can attest.
We this principle hold, as fixed, as fate,
Independent of them, *we will be a State.*—
While we sail in fine ships, they paddle a float,
The best of their navy a flat bottom'd boat.
A bushel of corn they often are glad
To exchange for a cod, or poor shotten shad :
And without their slaves, how long would it take
To shell corn enough to purchase one hake ?
We have coffee and salt and tea the year round ;
Six bushels of corn, they must pay for a pound.
By sea and by land never idle nor stingy,
Our houses are fill'd with the products of India.
And if a cold season, we all have a notion,
John Codline will bring us a fish from the ocean.
While we grant they can live on lean smok'd hams,
We fear not starvation on lobsters and clams.
Our bays are alive with geese, ducks, and widgeons,
And every scarce year our woods swarm with pigeons.
They may boast of fine pastures as much as they please,
But we stand unrival'd in butter and cheese.
They may boast of their blacks ; we boast of our plenty,
And swear to be free, eighteen-hundred and twenty.
South and West, now be honest, to MAINE give her due,
If you call her a child, she's an Hercules too.
A Sister in Union admit her, as free ;
To be coupled with slaves, she will never agree.

              TIMOTHY CLAIMRIGHT.

Brunswick, Jan. 1820.

2. Northern broadside attacking the
Missouri Compromise, 1820

3. Rufus King, 1819–20

4. Henry Clay, ca. 1818

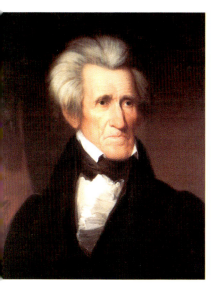

6. Sequoyah, ca. 1828

5. Andrew Jackson, 1835

7. Virginia Constitutional Convention, 1829–30

THE DOCTORS PUZZLED OR THE DESPERATE CASE OF MOTHER U.S BANK.

8. Antibank cartoon, ca. 1834–35. President Jackson at left, peeking through window; Henry Clay, Daniel Webster, and John C. Calhoun in the center; Nicholas Biddle on bed at right, holding the head of the symbolic monster bank

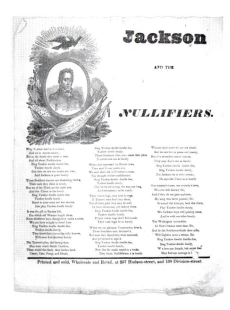

9. Antinullification broadside, 1832

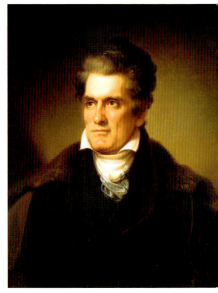

10. John C. Calhoun, ca. 1832

11. William Lloyd Garrison, 1833   12. James Forten, ca. 1818

13. Attack on abolitionist mailings, Charleston, South Carolina, 1835

14. Expunged censure of Andrew Jackson in the *Senate Journal*, 1837

15. Charles Grandison Finney, ca. 1850

16. Texan battle flag flown at the Battle of San Jacinto, 1836

Working Men, Attention!!

It is your imperious duty to drop your *Hammers and Sledges*! one and all, to your post repair, *THIS AFTERNOON*, at *FIVE* o'clock P. M. and attend the

GREAT MEETING

called by the papers of this morning, to be held at the CITY HALL, then and there to co-operate with such as have the GREAT GOOD OF ALL THEIR *FELLOW CITIZENS* at Heart. Your liberty! yea, your *LABOUR!!* is the subject of the call: who that values the services of HEROES of the *Revolution* whose blood achieved our Independence as a Nation, will for a moment doubt he owes a few hours this afternoon to his wife and children?

HANCOCK.

17. Labor broadside, 1837

18. Anti–Van Buren cartoon on the effects of the Panic, ca. 1838

19. Cartoon depicting Waddy Thompson intimidating John Quincy Adams over the gag rule, ca. 1839

20. William Leggett, ca. 1835

21. Whig campaign banner, 1840

22. Thurlow Weed, ca. 1861

23. Horace Greeley, between 1844 and 1860

8

BANKS, ABOLITIONISTS, AND THE EQUAL RIGHTS DEMOCRACY

On June 27, 1833, Harvard University granted President Jackson the honorary degree of doctor of laws. Jackson had embarked on a triumphant postelection tour of New York and New England, and Harvard's president, the aging patrician Josiah Quincy of the departed Boston Middling Interest, was persuaded that the nation's oldest university ought to honor Jackson, just as it had honored President Monroe when the latter visited Boston in 1817. John Quincy Adams, a Harvard overseer, boycotted the ceremony, appalled, he wrote, that his alma mater would entertain "a barbarian who could not write a sentence of grammar and hardly could spell his own name." But Josiah Quincy's son, Josiah Jr., the instigator of the degree, had found Jackson "a knightly personage," and the crowds that thronged his route across New England adored the president. "He is amazingly tickled with the Yankees," the humorist Seba Smith's fictional Major Jack Downing chuckled, "and the more he sees on 'em, the better he likes 'em. 'No nullification here,' says he."

Jackson, although delighted by the reception, was in physical agony for the entire trip, as one of his ancient dueling wounds caused bleeding in his lungs. In Concord, New Hampshire, he collapsed, and the tour abruptly ended. After regaining some strength in Washington, Jackson decided to continue his convalescence, accompanied by Francis Blair, at the Rip Raps, a man-made Virginia coastal island owned by the federal government. On the voyage down the Chesapeake, the chop knocked about the steamboat carrying the president's party, and one of the passengers became alarmed. "You are uneasy," Jackson said to him, "you never sailed with *me* before, I see."

Political disquiet was already leading to plots and innovations elsewhere along the eastern seaboard. In New York, divisions between Democrats for and against the Bank of the United States worsened. In Philadelphia as well as New York, trade unionists, picking up where the Working Men ended, launched a series of strikes and organized new citywide union organizations—a prelude to the formation of the National Trades' Union the following year. In December, William Lloyd Garrison and his allies gathered in Philadelphia to form the American Anti-Slavery Society, the first national immediatist organization. In South Carolina, John C. Calhoun, his mind fixed on Jackson's political destruction, interpreted the nullification debacle as a great success that had dealt the tariff system "its death wound blow" and had handed the slavocrats the balance of power in the new Congress.

Another storm was brewing a thousand miles to the southwest, in the northern Mexico state of Coahuila y Tejas, where independence-minded American settlers were squaring off against a new Mexican government headed by Antonio López de Santa Anna. But Tejas was light-years from the Rip Raps during Jackson's month-long stay. After nullification's demise, Jackson had turned his mind to completing the destruction of Biddle's bank. Most of his chief advisers expressed caution, but Jackson had supreme self-confidence. "[I]s it possible that your friends hesitate, and are overawed by the power of the Bank?" he wrote sardonically to Vice President Van Buren, one of the biggest doubters. "[I]t cannot overaw me. I trust in my God and the virtue of the people."

"TO HEAL . . . THE CONSTITUTION":
THE BANK WAR AND THE RISE OF THE WHIGS

When he was helping to compose the bank veto message in July 1832, Jackson suggested including some remarks about establishing a new national banking institution in place of the BUS. He wanted to calm the electorate's nerves as well as stand up for constitutional principle. "[N]o inconvenience can result from my veto," he wrote, noting that with four years of the bank's charter still left to run, there would be sufficient time to establish some version of "a national Bank or Banks" that would have the proper restrictions. Jackson's suggestion did not make it into the message's final draft. Nor, amid the distractions of the election and the nullification controversy, did the administration design an alternative to Biddle's bank. By the time Jackson returned to the issue in earnest in 1833, he had decided on a course of action that would cause considerable inconvenience—and lead to an all-out war over banks and banking policy.

Goaded by Amos Kendall and Francis Blair, Jackson began to consider removing the government's deposits from the BUS during the waning days of the 1832 campaign. Four years earlier, he had learned that certain branches of the BUS were secretly throwing their resources behind John Quincy Adams, but in 1832 the alliance between the bank and the National Republicans was overt—and, in some parts of the country, very effective. The bank, incensed by Jackson's reelection as well as the veto, might now be all the more dangerous to the country. Possessing the government deposits, the BUS could easily flood the country with bank notes, only to squeeze credit prior to the 1836 election and trigger a panic that would help elect pro-BUS men who would reverse Jackson's veto. "[T]he hydra of corruption is only *scotched, not dead*," the president wrote to his young Tennessee congressional loyalist James K. Polk, and its allies intended "to destroy the vote of the people lately given at the ballot boxes." Summarily stripping the bank of its government deposits would dramatically diminish the threat.

Jackson's annual message in December 1832 broached the subject of removal, questioning whether the bank was still a safe depository of the people's money. The Democratic-dominated House of Representatives replied the following March by emphatically rejecting a bill, proposed by Polk, to sell the government's shares in the bank. Convinced that the BUS had thoroughly corrupted Congress, Jackson told both his official cabinet and his Kitchen Cabinet that he was now inclined to remove the deposits on his own and redistribute them to various state banks. Most of Jackson's advisers, in and out of the cabinet, blanched at the prospect. "My first impression is," James Hamilton, no friend to the BUS, said in a brief note, "that the measure proposed was a very questionable one, and must lead to great disturbance in commercial affairs." Kendall, the outstanding exception, sent Jackson a memorandum on why removal was the best course for the country.

Kendall emphasized that the bank now posed a new political threat. Unless destroyed, Kendall charged, this "great enemy of republicanism" would resort to bribery, intimidation, and every other corrupt means to elect its own candidate to the White House in 1836 and regain its charter as soon as Jackson left office. Arousing Jackson's always sensitive manly honor, Kendall claimed that unless he moved decisively, his backers would decide he was "wanting either in the courage or in the good faith" to finish what he had started. Kendall also argued, frankly, that handing the government deposits over to sympathetic state banks would "raise up powerful friends" who would fulfill the bank's fiscal functions and provide a political counterweight to Biddle and the National Republicans.

Plainly, Kendall and Jackson regarded the transfer of the BUS deposits to the state banks with a cold political eye. There is a danger, however, in interpreting these politics too narrowly, as a brazen partisan gambit aimed chiefly at enlarging Jacksonian patronage. Among the chosen state bankers, idealism may well have taken a backseat to opportunism. (As Biddle, quoting Jonathan Swift, had observed, "Money is neither Whig nor Tory.")

But Jackson's latest attack on the bank arose from his long-standing objections to the BUS, mixed with his outrage at Biddle's political actions in 1832 and his fears that Biddle would eventually thwart the manifest will of the electorate. Distributing federal monies to selected state banks was hardly an innovation: Jackson was following the precedent set by the Madison administration in 1811. Seeing themselves in a death battle against unconstitutional forces—a "corrupt league," Kendall called it—Jackson and Kendall were not about to take the public funds out of Biddle's control only to place them in the hands of his allies.

More like the Jeffersonians than later generations of American politicians, Kendall and Jackson, reflecting the common party assumptions of the 1830s, still perceived themselves as protectors of the nation against a small, designing, illicit cabal, rallying what Kendall called "the friends of good and pure government"—including, in this case, competent and reliable state bankers. "I have no doubt of the Bank being rechartered unless by the removal of the deposits," Jackson wrote to Vice President Van Buren—a matter, he said, "in which I see the perpetuity of our republican Government involved." That the Jacksonians, like most of their contemporaries, were quick to detect conspiracies against public liberty hardly means that they were engaged in one of their own to fatten their supporters' coffers. The enrichment of loyal state banks was an effect, not a cause, of the Bank War.

Jackson dispatched Kendall to scout out possible recipients of the federal funds in lieu of the BUS. And in June, after a sudden reshuffling of the cabinet, Jackson named the leading son of Philadelphia's city democracy, the lawyer William John Duane, as secretary of the Treasury, a move he would later regret. Over the summer, the president plotted his removal plans with Kendall, Francis Blair, and Roger B. Taney. In August, he received additional support. A report from the government's directors on the BUS board affirmed that the bank had spent eighty thousand dollars on printing campaign materials hostile to Jackson in the 1832 election—and that Biddle himself had spent twenty thousand dollars, with no accounting records whatsoever. Armed with definitive proof of the bank's pollution of American democracy, Jackson presented to the new cabinet a paper, which he himself drafted and Taney redrafted, outlining the cessation of government deposits in the bank effective October 1. In both Jackson's and Taney's versions, the paper restated what, from the very start of the conflict, had been Jackson's central constitutional and political concerns: "The Bank of the United States," Jackson wrote, "is in itself a Government" whose power had only increased; and "the mass of the people" had much to fear from that illegitimate government, run by an "aristocracy" of "the wealthy and professional classes." Removal of the deposits was necessary to undo the aristocracy's insidious efforts at "preventing political institutions however well adjusted, from securing the freedom of the citizen." Secretary Duane's formal approval was all that was required for the removal plan to take effect.

Duane was eminently respectable from a business viewpoint, having worked for the Girard family banking interests in Philadelphia and having won outgoing Treasury Secretary McLane's personal endorsement. But Duane had also been a prominent and outspoken foe of the BUS for fifteen years, first in the Pennsylvania legislature and later as a member of the banking committee of the Philadelphia Working Men's Party. With his father and William Gouge, he had been one of the signers of the well-known Philadelphia report and memorial against the bank in 1829. Here was the perfect choice, a bank lawyer with links to the city democratic tradition. But Duane proved to be, to Jackson, less than his father's son. Conceiving his position as more beholden to Congress than to the president, and offended at Jackson's peremptory tone, the new secretary balked at removing the deposits and forced a showdown when he also refused to resign. "[H]e is either the weakest mortal, or the most strange composition I ever met with," the frustrated president wrote. On September 20, the *Globe* announced the plan to withdraw deposits in the BUS. Five days later, Jackson fired Duane and named the anti-BUS stalwart Taney as his replacement.

By the time the removal of the deposits occurred, its potential

effects on the bank had grown. In 1833, thanks to rising sur-
pluses in the federal budget, the government's monies in the
BUS had risen to nearly $10 million, about half of the bank's total
deposits. As Kendall warned the president, withdrawing those
funds precipitously would have a devastating impact on the BUS
and therefore on the entire country. By the same token, Biddle
could create enormous mischief if he were to meddle with the
politically friendly state-chartered banks where the federal funds
would now be deposited—soon to be known derisively as the "pet
banks." To succeed, Jackson and his men would have to find a
way to conduct removal slowly while warding off Biddle's
inevitable counterattacks.

Taney, placed in charge of the transit of funds, advanced with
care—and with one eye fixed warily on Nicholas Biddle. Three
days after the removal order took effect, Taney gave five of the
seven state-chartered "pets" a total of $2.3 million in Treasury
drafts on the federal deposits at the BUS. Should Biddle try to
launch a preemptive strike on any of the pets by suddenly presenting them with notes and demanding payment in specie, the
pets could use the drafts to remove federal deposits from the
BUS and preserve their own liquidity. But the precaution back-
fired when, only three days after Taney made his move, one of
the state banks presented drafts with a combined value of
$100,000 to the BUS, and then endorsed them to a third bank to
cover some unsuccessful speculation in stocks by the state bank's
director. Over the objections of some of his directors, Biddle
immediately reduced the BUS's loans by nearly $6 million. After
other state banks presented additional drafts on the federal
deposits amounting to $1 million, Biddle contracted credit even
further, ordering more than $9 million in reductions by January
1834.

Taney had badly miscalculated. But Biddle was hardly a
public-spirited national banker, reacting to events. Long before
the state banks began presenting their drafts, the BUS president
was planning to take action against an anticipated removal by
curtailing bank credit. At the end of July 1833, he warned the

New York branch of the BUS that the bank would soon move to "crush the Kitchen Cabinet." Two weeks later, Biddle ordered the branches to demand quicker payment of their bills of exchange. On October 1, when removal went into effect, the bank decided to begin tightening its credit. By January, Biddle's reductions exceeded pet bank withdrawals from the BUS by more than $4 million, and the contraction continued through the summer of 1834. Biddle never wavered in his belief that it was his sworn duty to strike back at Jackson—the sooner and the harder, the better. The timing allowed Biddle and his friends to blame the crisis entirely on what the New Yorker Philip Hone called Jackson's "supererogatory act of tyranny." But in private, Biddle admitted that he was trying to cause general hardship that would agitate state banks other than the pets and force Congress to step in on the BUS's behalf. To business associates, Biddle sounded cool and deliberate. "The ties of party allegiance can only be broken," he wrote one, "by the actual conviction of existing distress in the community." To others, he blustered. "My own course is decided," he wrote to one friendly congressman, "—all the other Banks and all the merchants may break, but the Bank of the United States shall not break." Later, when even sympathetic businessmen grew restive, Biddle snarled that the bank would not be "cajoled from its duty by any small driveling about relief to the country."

The crash resounded throughout the nation. Coupled with the credit crunch it placed on the state banks, the BUS's pressure on individual investors touched off business failures and unemployment that some feared would surpass the disaster of 1819. Businessmen, bankers, and National Republicans howled that the villain was Jackson—Jackson the demagogue, Jackson the spoilsman, Jackson the despot. Daniel Webster, who had been entertaining an entente with Jackson over the preservation of the Union, now led the denunciations with the familiar conservative charge that the Jacksonians were "arraying one class against another." More often, Jackson's opponents took the constitutional high ground, proclaiming the president a power-mad usurper who was using the partisan pet banks to help consolidate his rule. "We are in the midst of a revolution," Henry Clay told the Senate, "hitherto bloodless, but rapidly tending towards a total change of the pure republican character of the Government." Three months later, Justice Joseph Story thought the revolution had been completed: "[T]hough we live under the form of a republic," he wrote, "we are in fact under the absolute rule of a single man."

The firing of Duane and the removal of the deposits, followed by the crash, angered moderate and conservative Democrats nearly as much, just as Van Buren and Jackson's other cautious advisers had feared. Some of the perturbed Jacksonians deserted to the opposition; others stuck with the party but established themselves as so-called Bank Democrats—conservatives who, though they thoroughly approved of killing the BUS charter, thought the removal and deposit bank scheme a thoughtless and possibly unconstitutional act of executive aggression. Complaints from constituents about what seemed to be Jackson's blind vindictiveness weakened the president's position on Capitol Hill. "We cannot resist this tremendous pressure," one congressman cried to an appalled Amos Kendall; "we shall be obliged to yield." A New Hampshire senator remarked that although Jackson remained adamant, "many of his partisans are in much distress under the impression that his lawless and reckless conduct and his obstinacy will prostrate the party."

The threatened defections of antiremoval Democrats opened up fresh opportunities for John C. Calhoun. The bank's supporters might have expected Calhoun to defend the BUS, which had largely been his creation. But for Calhoun, though he would praise the bank's "indispensable" work, attacking Jackson and sustaining his own state-rights doctrine took precedence. In the current conflict, Calhoun claimed, the removal issue was but a pretext for a more fundamental struggle for supremacy between a tyrannical executive and a resistant legislature over who would control the nation's currency—a power, he asserted, that the Constitution expressly granted to Congress. Calhoun's stance was of a piece with nullification, he said. He and the other South Carolina nullifiers—"I am not afraid of the word"—were once again fighting a despotic executive, much as they had over the Force Bill. Just as important, although Calhoun would not say so openly, were the political rewards to be won by opposing removal. As Calhoun's editor Duff Green remarked, "every movement which throws off a fragment from the Jackson party promises to swell our numbers." Nullification was dead for now, but the Bank War might yet make Calhoun president.

Jackson's supporters did not flinch. If the credit and commerce of the country truly were reliant on the monster bank, one New York Jacksonian congressman exclaimed, "I, for one, say perish credit, perish commerce." Opposition claims that Jackson had become an autocrat sparked indignant replies that the bank's backers were trying to divert the voters from the real issue at hand—pretending to be champions of the Constitution and foes of partisan favoritism when they were merely champions of the bank. "It is [Jackson's] measures against the United States Bank, which have excited them to such ferocious political war against him," the contentious pro-Jackson New York editor William Leggett charged.

Jackson himself was immovable, bombastic, and cunning. When groups of concerned businessmen and merchants paid calls on the White House, beseeching him to change course, the president rudely interrupted and dressed them down. "Go to Nicholas Biddle," he told one New York deputation. "We have no money here, gentlemen, Biddle has all the money. He has millions of specie in his vaults, at this moment, lying idle, and yet you come to *me* to save you from breaking. I tell you, gentlemen, it's all politics." The warfare was as much psychological as ideological, and Jackson deployed his vehemence shrewdly. (Once the New York businessmen were safely out of earshot, Jackson was found chortling, "Didn't I manage them well?") The ploy worked, at least in convincing some distinguished men that Jackson was not bluffing and that civilization itself was on the brink of ruin. "The present contest," the Brahmin notable Edward

Everett told an English banker, "is nothing less than a war of Numbers against Property."

The retaliation against Jackson peaked during the winter congressional session, thereafter known as "the Panic session." According to the bank's charter, removal of the federal deposits required congressional agreement that the deposits were no longer safe, and Taney duly submitted to the House a report to that effect, blaming Biddle's curtailments. Thanks to the steady work of Congressman Polk, four resolutions passed the House backing Jackson's policies. But in the Senate, Henry Clay, enjoying a commanding National Republican majority as well as the support of John C. Calhoun, won a repudiation of Taney's report. More important, Clay introduced, early in the session, a motion condemning both the removal of Duane and the removal of the deposits, and censuring Jackson for assuming unconstitutional powers "dangerous to the liberties of the people." Thomas Hart Benton attacked the censure move as usurpation by the Senate majority of the House's impeachment power, but Clay and his supporters meant to have their way. For three months, they allowed the resolution to lie open, giving National Republicans repeated chances to denounce Jackson, right under the nose of the president of the Senate, Vice President Van Buren. As the session wore on—one of the most "extraordinary" in memory, Churchill Cambreleng wrote—it became clear that the censure could not be stopped. Finally, at the end of March, the Senate dramatically (if predictably) approved Clay's resolution.

Jackson's lengthy and solemn protest of the censure dwelled on the irregularities of the Senate condemning the executive for committing high crimes and misdemeanors against the state. According to Article II, Section 4 of the Constitution, consideration of such offenses must begin with the House of Representatives, which had the sole power of impeachment. Now, however, the Senate majority had stopped short of impeachment but declared the president had committed impeachable offenses while bypassing the Democratic-dominated House altogether—a process, Jackson declared, that "reverses the whole scheme of this part of the Constitution." Jackson also placed the censure in the larger political context of the Bank War, pointing out that the state legislatures of four pro-censure senators had expressly approved both the recharter veto and the removal of the deposits. Above all, the president used the message to flesh out his conception of democracy and a democratic presidency. Regarding the dismissal of Duane, Jackson insisted that the Senate had the power of advice and consent over cabinet nominations, but no more. Once approved, cabinet secretaries served entirely at the president's pleasure; always the president was in full command of the executive branch. "The President," Jackson intoned, "is the direct representative of the American people"—the only such elected official (apart from the vice president) in the entire government. The Senate's censure attacked democracy by trying to give to Congress—"a body not directly amenable to the people"—a degree of influence and authority that undermined executive power and endangered public liberties. It thereby advanced the consolidation of "a splendid government supported by powerful monopolies and aristocratical establishments."

Senator Poindexter of Mississippi told his colleagues that since Jackson's protest had not been delivered on any official occasion, it was only "a paper with the signature of Andrew Jackson" and should not even be received. But debate continued, in and out of the Capitol, as Jackson's critics compared his response to the edicts of Napoleon, and bid Clay and his friends to go all out and "*impeach* the old *scamp*." Insofar as traditional republican thinking vaunted legislatures over executives as more directly beholden to the voters, Jackson's assertions did mark a great departure. Yet Jackson's protest reflected the changed political realities of the 1830s, whereby in most states the voters and not the legislatures chose presidential electors. If Jackson's original message went too far in claiming executive power over public monies (requiring a quick corrective postscript message), his aim was not to establish a new executive despotism, or what later generations would call an "imperial presidency." He wanted, instead, to head off Clay's pretensions to establishing an imperial

Congress, with the president's powers diluted by some fancied responsibility to the Senate and by the threat of repeated harassment through censure. Jackson sought to sustain and enlarge the American presidency as an independent instrument of the popular will, and ward off the rise of a rough equivalent of a prime ministership at the other end of Pennsylvania Avenue. The argument impressed Clay and the Senate not at all. After two weeks of excoriating rhetoric, the censure motion passed again, by an even wider margin than before, and the Senate refused to place Jackson's protest in its official journal.

It was now almost the middle of May 1834. Clay was in his full glory—or so it seemed to Henry Clay. In fact, on the issue underlying everything, the tide had turned against Nicholas Biddle and the bank's defenders. Disgusted by the continuing recession, business leaders in Boston and New York had shifted their ire away from Jackson and toward the BUS, which, they were now persuaded, was hurting them in order to satisfy Biddle's hatred of Jackson. By the end of 1833, the *Journal of Commerce*, the leading anti-Jackson business paper in the country, was criticizing Biddle's contraction. In March, a concerned Biddle hastened to New York to consult with prominent New York merchants and financiers, led by the venerable Albert Gallatin. With the backing of their friends in Boston, the New Yorkers laid it on the line to Biddle: either relax the bank's policies or face exposure and repudiation.

Biddle played along for a while, but in May resumed the reductions more aggressively than ever. Fed up, the eminent Bostonian manufacturer, businessman, and former opposition congressman Nathan Appleton wrote a long letter to the directors of the Boston BUS branch to be forwarded to Biddle, blaming the bank's arbitrary and "regular system of contraction" for the continuing paralysis of business. Appleton warned Biddle that the direst of consequences would befall him and the country without an immediate change in policy. Biddle hemmed and hawed; Appleton wrote a second and even sterner letter, filled with evidence from the bank's own statements that contraction was neither necessary nor desirable. Finally, in mid-September, Biddle relented, eventually restoring the bank's loans to the same level as when the contraction began, and placing even more notes into circulation than before. Biddle's counteroffensive was crushed. The panic was over.

The clampdown's economic impact turned out to be milder than had been originally feared. Few banks suffered disastrous runs. State bank emissions of paper currency kept the overall money supply stable. Wholesale prices dipped but did not collapse. Interest rates and the price of commercial paper rose sharply, but the increases, coupled with a rising surplus of American imports over exports, further stimulated foreign investment in American internal-improvements projects, which restocked both the BUS and the state banks with millions of dollars in needed precious metal. There were numerous accounts, especially in the more commercially developed parts of the country, that the suffering was, as one Democrat observed, "as great as any community can bear." But "Biddle's panic" did more damage to Americans' nerves than it did to their economy.

The Bank War's political impact was much more severe and lasting. Losing the struggle with Jackson plunged Nicholas Biddle into a furious and unsteady gyre. Biddle could never understand the democratic principles behind the attack against him and his beloved bank. With undisguised contempt, he refused to cooperate with a House committee charged with investigating his management of the BUS, thereby deepening the impression that he believed he and his bank were above the law. By the autumn of 1835, Biddle was reduced to delivering a delusional speech to his fellow Nassau Hall alumni, predicting with confidence that the Democratic "banditti" would yet "be scourged back to their caverns," and finally be remembered only because of "the energy with which you resisted and defeated them." A year later, when its federal charter finally ran out, the bank was rechartered as the Bank of the United States of Pennsylvania, a state institution with considerable weight but bereft of its former influence and power.

For Clay and the National Republicans, the Bank War brought a different kind of turning point. The crises of Jackson's first term had stripped away elements of his original coalition but created little basis for the rise of a coherent opposition. On nullification and the Union, Daniel Webster, among many other National Republicans, was more in tune with Jackson than some Jacksonians were. On the tariff, anti-Jackson nullifiers and anti-Jackson friends of the American System were at polar opposites. Clay's refusal to renounce his membership in the Masonic order instantly dashed any hopes of an alliance between the National Republicans and the Anti-Masons.

The Bank War gave these oppositional elements common ground—not in defense of Biddle's bank (which, by the end of 1834, was a lost cause) but against Jackson's assertions of executive power and his creation of pet banks as yet another fountain of partisan corruption. To many later historians, this shared grievance has sometimes seemed, at best, meager and, at worst, an exercise in bad faith, covering deeper political and economic motives—the view expressed by pro-Jackson contemporaries like William Leggett. To be sure, Clay and the National Republicans, the most powerful segment of the opposition, were uniformly favorable to Biddle's bank. Switching from defending the bank to defending the Constitution was in part a calculated tactical move, taken in view of Biddle's tarnished reputation. (Clay told the excitable banker that it was now imperative to keep the question of rechartering the bank "in the rear" and that of executive tyranny "in the front.") But dismissing the attacks on Jackson as diversions from the authentic issues misperceives the opposition's outlook no less than ascribing the Jacksonians' Bank War to narrow economic interests or crass partisan motives.

A belief in the primacy of political structures and institutions had always driven Jackson and his followers in their efforts, as Jackson's protest of the Senate's censure put it, "to heal the wounds of the Constitution and preserve it from further violation." The attacks on Jackson's alleged executive tyranny flowed from the same presumptions. To conservative National Republicans, Jackson's claims were identical to those of the classical Caesars, who had usurped all power by whipping up the mob and handing governance to their corrupt minions. To humanitarian reformers drawn to the opposition, Jackson was a despot who had conspired with southern slaveholders and forced the removal of peaceful American Indians to the West. To nullifiers and their sympathizers, Jackson was the embodiment of the centralizing forces that threatened the slaveholders' liberties. To Anti-Masons, Jackson was an arrogant politician (and a Mason to boot) who had set himself above the rule of law. To a broader troubled populace, including some who had backed Jackson in the past, the events of 1833 and 1834 showed that Jackson had been overcome by what one New Yorker called "an unbridled lust of power, that attacked the very foundation of our free institutions." Whatever the multifarious economic, sectional, or partisan interests beneath them, these were sincere, principled, and potent concerns, strong enough to bind together a powerful anti-Jacksonian coalition.

At every stage of the battle over the deposits, that coalition gained greater coherence, at least in Washington. Henry Clay initiated the process with a series of private dinners over the winter of 1833–34, assembling nullifiers, his own National Republicans, and Anti-Masons (including a recent Anti-Mason convert, John Quincy Adams) to discuss strategy for the presidential contest in 1836. The harmonization became increasingly evident in Congress, as divisions over various issues, including censure, deepened into what looked like unified party blocs. By the spring of 1834, when the emerging opposition won surprising victories in New York City's rough-and-tumble local elections, the new coalition even had a name—the Whig Party, presented as the spiritual progeny of the glorious opponents of King George III, now battling Andrew I's Tory conspiracy against the people's liberties. Under "[t]he happy cognomen of Whigs," a North Carolina anti-Jackson paper exulted soon thereafter, "all the parties opposed to Executive usurpation" could now "rally in defense of LIBERTY against POWER."

It all sounded very different from John Quincy Adams's declaration, in 1825, that liberty *is* power. Some Whigs, like the editors of the Washington *National Intelligencer*, went even further and proclaimed themselves, and not the Tory Jacksonians, "the true Democracy of the Country." In time, other ideological and intellectual currents, above all the anxious, self-improving evangelical fervor of the Presbygational revivals, would reinforce these claims. Whiggery would become a variant of democratic politics just as compelling to its adherents as Jacksonianism had become to Democrats. But that evolution occurred alongside other dramatic developments in the mid-1830s involving radical movements well removed from mainstream party politics. These movements were themselves signs of intensifying social turmoil. Looking back on the upheavals from 1840, the British émigré Thomas Brothers—a one-time Philadelphia labor agitator who turned conservative during these six years—published a book, *The United States of North America as They Are; Not as They Are Generally Described: Being a Cure for Radicalism*. One appendix listed "Miscellaneous Murders, Riots, and Other Outrages, in 1834, 1835, 1836, 1837, and 1838." Several others included the details of additional mob attacks. The bulk of Brothers's citations concerned violence occasioned, first, by the spread of radical abolitionism and, second, by renewed labor unrest.

"THE ONLY *REAL* DEMOCRACY IN OUR REPUBLIC": ABOLITIONISM AND REACTION

On July 26, 1833, the House of Commons approved the compensated abolition of slavery throughout the British Empire. Nearly half a century of agitation, in and out of Parliament, was finally triumphing—and three days later, Britain's greatest abolitionist leader, William Wilberforce, died, one month short of age seventy-four. William Lloyd Garrison, on a British sojourn visiting abolitionist leaders, had met the ailing Wilberforce and received his blessing weeks earlier, enlarging his own reputation as American abolitionism's great man. Now Garrison joined his British friend, the antislavery campaigner George Thompson, in the bittersweet funeral procession to Westminster Abbey. Garrison obtained commitments from Thompson and others that they would put themselves and their financial resources at the disposal of the American immediatists. In October, an invigorated Garrison sailed back across the Atlantic to Manhattan, where he was scheduled to give a lecture to the Tappan brothers' New York City Anti-Slavery Society. But a raucous mob, fifteen hundred strong, prevented the lecture and forced Garrison to flee for home in Boston. "This young gentleman . . . ," the New York *Commercial Advertiser* sneered, "will act wisely in never to attempt addressing a public meeting in *this* country again."

Garrison's odyssey foretold the travails of the radical abolitionist movement in the mid-1830s. Supported financially by a few wealthy evangelical businessmen, and propelled by fresh and enthusiastic converts and organizers, abolitionism became a genuine popular movement. At its peak in 1838, membership in the American Anti-Slavery Society (AA-SS) rose to three hundred thousand men and women, enlisted in approximately two thousand loosely affiliated local chapters. In its most ambitious campaigns, the movement flooded Congress with more than four hundred thousand separate petitions calling for radical reforms ranging from the abolition of slavery in the District of Columbia to the repeal of the Constitution's three-fifths clause. Yet despite its rapid growth and impressive organizational skills, abolitionism engendered far more hostility than sympathy in the northern states, quite apart from the hatred it engendered in the South. By attacking not merely southern slavery but all forms of racial inequality, the abolitionists appeared to the vast majority of white Americans like fanatics, at war with all social order and decency. For every convert to the cause, there were hundreds of northerners who were repulsed by what the New Hampshire anti-abolitionist writer Thomas Russell Sullivan called the movement's "false zeal and political aggression." Although the abolitionists successfully reawakened moral concern over slavery, they paid for it by becoming repeated targets for mob violence and official repression.

The organizing assembly of the AA-SS in Philadelphia in December 1833 gave a good indication of how the movement had spread beyond its origins among urban free blacks. Garrison was the preeminent participant. In 1832, partly at the behest of his black supporters, he had published a long but widely read pastiche, *Thoughts on African Colonization*, which exposed the racism of the American Colonization Society and reprinted various black abolitionist speeches and resolutions condemning the society. As Garrison hoped it would, *Thoughts* swayed gradualist antislavery sympathizers into the immediatist camp. Garrison wrote the new association's immediatist Declaration of Principles at the home of the Philadelphia black abolitionist James McCrummell, where he was staying as a house guest. The declaration firmly endorsed nonviolence and the use of moral suasion to eradicate the sin of slavery, while also demanding for blacks "all the rights and privileges that belong to them as men and as Americans."

The other sixty-two official participants and the interested onlookers who attended the meetings represented diverse backgrounds and faiths. Arthur and Lewis Tappan appeared along with other benevolent evangelical businessmen and professionals who had moved from Sabbatarianism and other reform projects into abolitionism. (Arthur was selected as the group's president.) A number of New England Unitarians, including Garrison's Boston associate Samuel May, were present. One-third of the participants were Quakers, among them John Greenleaf Whittier. Black attendance was relatively small, a portent of the AA-SS's future as a largely white-led organization, but a trio of important black leaders—McCrummell and Robert Purvis of Philadelphia, and James Barbadoes of Boston—took an active role. More remarkable was the energetic involvement of a small group of Quaker women, including the outspoken lay preacher Lucretia Mott—a degree of integration in politics across the sex line unheard of in the 1830s outside of Frances

Wright's radical platoons, and another portent of where the AA-SS was headed.

Garrison returned to his post at the *Liberator*, and the Tappan brothers and their friends took charge of managing the AA-SS. Right away, they established its headquarters in New York, already the capital of the budding evangelical empire of moral reform. On the model of the temperance and Sunday-law crusades, the Tappans flung together a network for converting the benighted, complete with a newspaper, the *Emancipator* (edited by Elizur Wright on behalf of the New York City abolitionist society, established by the Tappans in 1831), as well as a string of local AA-SS chapters and a company of field agents and itinerant lecturers. AA-SS chapters began sponsoring bazaars, sewing bees, picnics, and other social events to raise money and boost morale. At the movement's height, members could purchase abolitionist newspaper subscriptions, antislavery almanacs, music books, stationery, and pieces of ephemera, including portraits of Garrison priced at one dollar apiece. On the political front, building on the example of the Sabbatarian and anti-Indian removal movements, the abolitionists started their mass petition drives.

Abolitionism's first breakthrough came in Cincinnati, thanks to Arthur Tappan's sponsorship there of the new evangelical Lane Seminary, which he and his brother hoped to turn into a training ground for AA-SS agents. For years, Cincinnati, across the Ohio River from slavery, had been racked by violent racial turmoil and attacks on antislavery advocates, including a rising young editor and ex-slaveholder from bordering Kentucky, James G. Birney—unrest that redoubled the Tappans' determination to make the city an abolitionist center. These efforts began in earnest after the arrival at Lane of a young seminarian, Theodore Dwight Weld. A disciple of Charles Finney's, Weld had graduated from Hamilton College in 1825, already a convert to what he later called "radical abolitionism." He then studied for the ministry and advanced to become a preceptor at the Oneida Institute, an evangelical hotbed in upstate New York supported financially by Lewis Tappan. Weld and Tappan befriended each other, and in

1834, the Tappans sent Weld to Lane, where Lyman Beecher had taken up the presidency two years earlier. Weld brought with him some promising Oneida students, including one Henry B. Stanton, and began holding public meetings and prayer sessions to promote immediatism. Less than three weeks later, to great public notice, Lane's students and faculty endorsed the abolitionist crusade, organized their own antislavery society, and made plans to provide reading and religious instruction to the black residents of Cincinnati.

Leading Cincinnati businessmen pressured the seminary's trustees into ordering the rebels to disband their antislavery society. President Beecher, proclaiming his devotion to free speech and discussion, tried to mediate, but to no avail. "Shall those who are soon to be ambassadors for Christ . . . ," Weld declaimed, "shall *they* refuse to think, and feel, and speak, when that accursed thing . . . wags its impious head, and shakes its blood-red hands at heaven?" Although the abolitionist efforts received wide publicity, the trustees were adamant, and the antislavery seminarians eventually decamped to a new home in the small town of Oberlin, in northern Ohio, where the Tappans founded yet another college and persuaded the charismatic Finney to join the faculty. (Weld turned down a similar offer and became a full-time traveling antislavery lecturer.) The new college became the first American institution of higher learning to open its doors to men and women, blacks and whites—and soon became what Lane was supposed to have become, the nerve center of abolitionism in the Old Northwest.

The uprising at Lane and subsequent abolitionist disturbances marked the emergence of a new kind of American political community. Joining the abolitionists was no rote profession of faith: it was an act of defiance of widely and deeply held social conventions, placing oneself in a position that courted disapproval, ostracism, and even physical attack. Those impelled to do so regarded one another as brothers and sisters in righteousness and sacrifice who had devoted their lives to eradicating slavery—a kind of commitment and identification previously found in religious sects, but now secularized and shifted into radical politics. Like later generations of American radicals, the abolitionists of the 1830s regarded their personal rededication as a life-transforming event, and their participation in the movement as an exhilarating experience of what later generations of dissenters would call "the beloved community." Looking back half a century later, the abolitionist writer Lydia Maria Child remarked that "mortals were never more sublimely forgetful of self than were the abolitionists of those early days"—a nostalgic exaggeration, certainly, but one that captured the movement's animating spirit, setting itself apart from sinful complicity with slavery and racism, and creating a new humane model of equality, freedom, and love.

Two years after the AA-SS's founding, the antislavery radicals had reasons to be encouraged. In the revival-soaked arc of settlement that defined greater New England, from the Erie Canal towns and rural hinterland to Ohio's Western Reserve, support for abolitionism grew steadily. Even in major northeastern cities that were more hostile to the evangelicals, the abolitionist cause made headway among ordinary workingmen and radicals. Paineite urban democrats, beginning with Thomas Paine himself, had always been antislavery: Thomas Skidmore and Frances Wright were outspoken abolitionists, and in 1831, George Henry Evans was the only editor in New York City publicly to defend Nat Turner's rebellion. Some conservatives condemned abolitionism as impious working-class dogma. ("Every one knows," wrote one New York editor, "that [abolition] was one of the original doctrines of the Fanny Wright, no-monopoly, no-property, and no-marriage party.") Abolitionists replied that they did, indeed, represent, in William Goodell's words, "the laboring people of the North," who "alone have constituted the only *real* democracy in our republic."

The abolitionists were not merely posing. True, there were some missed connections between the radical abolitionists and the evolving labor movement. In 1831, Garrison, reflecting his National Republican background, attacked the Working Men for inflaming class resentments in a land where, slavery aside, the path to prosperity was open to all. There was a spiritual and political gulf between the evangelical immediatists and the "Fanny Wright" radicals and pro-Jackson workingmen. Some trade union leaders denounced the abolitionists, while others simply held their tongues, not wanting to disrupt the Democracy. The mainstay of abolitionism's white constituency always consisted of modest farmers, small shopkeepers and businessmen, and their wives and daughters, living in and around the smaller cities and towns—not, as some of its critics claimed, a movement of displaced Federalist elites or upper-class monied capitalists, but also not, primarily, a movement of urban wage earners.

It is important, however, not to exaggerate the mutual disdain between white urban labor and the abolitionists in the 1830s, or to minimize labor's involvement as activists and supporters. Although the preponderance of workers (like the preponderance of white northerners) were hostile or indifferent, urban wage-earners and petty proprietors formed a substantial bloc within the abolitionist constituency. In New York, artisans and small shopkeepers signed abolitionist petitions in rising numbers between 1834 and 1837, their ranks including a mixture of well-known evangelical moral reformers and secularist radicals and trade unionists, among them several former Owenite deist veterans of the Working Men's Party. Lynn, Massachusetts, the outwork shoemaking capital, was an abolitionist stronghold, its membership dominated by skilled workers, including officers of the journeymen shoemakers' trade union. Lowell and other New England factory towns had their abolitionist society chapters, which included artisans and mill hands, women as well as men. The abolitionists, for their part, increasingly expressed sympathy for workers and their difficulties. Garrison, challenged over his anti-Workie stand, quickly changed his mind and praised the New England Association of Farmers, Mechanics, and Other Workingmen. Other abolitionists denounced greedy employers and declared that their movement defended "the life, liberty, and happiness of all the lower orders of society in the land, especially at the North."

Black abolitionists, regardless of their wealth, also remained stalwart activists. The AA-SS's original board of managers included half a dozen black leaders, and several others helped establish state affiliates and ladies' auxiliaries. The formidable Forten and Purvis merchant families of Philadelphia were especially prominent, providing leadership to both the AA-SS and the Female Anti-Slavery Society, which was organized soon after the AA-SS. Yet relations between blacks and whites in the movement were strained. Abolitionist polemics about the degraded state of America's people of color, although well intended, rankled their black allies, many of whom had managed to win at least a toehold, and sometimes more, of respectable prosperity. No matter how idealistic they were, few white abolitionists (Garrison being the great exception) could escape sounding patronizing to black abolitionists. Writing to the southern white abolitionist Angelina Grimké, Sarah Forten complained candidly that "even our professed friends have not yet rid themselves" of racial prejudice— although, she added, "when we recollect what great sacrifices to public sentiment they are called upon to make, we cannot wholly blame them." Partly in response to these misgivings, black activists organized their own independent efforts, ranging from groups to promote moral uplift, to the vigilance committees (the most famous of them headed by New York bookseller and printer David Ruggles) that searched out slaves being held in the seaports illegally by their southern masters.

As the abolitionist movement grew larger, more diversified, and more determined, the reactions against it grew fiercer. The mob violence that greeted Garrison in New York, along with an earlier riot in the small town of Canterbury, Connecticut, that destroyed a Garrisonian interracial school, were only the beginnings of a vicious backlash that escalated in 1834 and 1835. Over an eight-day period in early July 1834, New York crowds stormed abolitionist meeting halls, sacked Arthur Tappan's store and Lewis Tappan's house, and besieged black homes and churches. A month later, a briefer but even more destructive series of riots in Philadelphia targeted the homes of forty black families, including the Purvises', and killed at least one black resident. In October 1835, a Boston mob, screaming racist insults, nearly lynched Garrison. (A few weeks earlier, persons unknown, under cover of night, had erected a chilling mock gallows on Garrison's doorstep.) In Hartford, Utica, Washington, Pittsburgh, and Cincinnati, angry whites disrupted abolitionist meetings, wrecked abolitionist press offices, and terrified black neighborhoods. A shower of bricks and exploding firecrackers broke up an appearance by Samuel May in Haverhill, Massachusetts; Theodore Weld, John Greenleaf Whittier, Lydia Maria Child, and other abolitionist lecturers endured volleys of rocks and rotten eggs. One Charleston, South Carolina, newspaper reported cheerfully that a purse of twenty thousand dollars had been set aside in New Orleans for anyone who would kidnap Arthur Tappan and deliver him on the city's levee.

A variety of fears and prejudices, stoked by local political leaders, inflamed the northern mobs. Powerful racist myths and fears—not least the myths of innate black male sexual prowess and depravity, and fears of what some demagogues called the impending "mullatoization" of America—provoked a blind hatred of radical reformers. The great wealth of a few of the movement's most prominent financial backers, including the Tappans, and the antagonism they sometimes expressed toward organized labor, became a pretext for labeling the abolitionists as capitalist snobs who would raise lazy, inferior blacks to the same social level as the hard-working whites—the "limousine liberals" of their day.* The evangelical background of so many abolitionist leaders only deepened their image, among anti-abolitionists, as meddlesome fanatics out to impose their strange views on society

---

* Since 1827, the Tappans had been the publishers of the country's leading mercantile newspaper, the pious and adamantly antilabor *Journal of Commerce*. Lewis Tappan would go on, in 1841, to found the successful Mercantile Agency, which would later become the firm of Dun and Bradstreet. More than any other individuals, the Tappans came to symbolize the misleading conception of evangelical reform, and abolitionism in particular, as upper-class efforts.

at large. Abolitionism's British connections led some to call the movement an Anglo-American aristocratic plot. The acceptance of women as active participants persuaded opponents that the abolitionists were hell-bent on overturning all decorum. "Nothing . . . ," one New England anti-abolitionist pamphleteer wrote of antislavery women, "out-measures the evil that might follow from her political interference in times which try men's souls, when fear of change perplexes the wise."

For all its populist pretensions, however, anti-abolitionism was stoked chiefly by prosperous conservatives of both major political parties who enlisted a slice of the more socially insecure elements of the lower-middle and working classes in their activities. Most of the urban mobs were led not by lower-class rowdies but by local notables—described mordantly by their targets as "gentlemen of property and standing"—who abhorred the abolitionists' challenge to their own social authority. In Cincinnati, the scene of particularly severe rioting, Whig merchants and professionals were represented more heavily in the mobs that broke up abolitionist meetings than they were in the abolitionist constituency. In New York, where the assailants were more likely to be petty tradesmen, artisans, and laborers, the most inflammatory racist verbal attacks on abolitionists (and on "the blubber lips and sooty blood of negroes") appeared in the anti-Jackson, Whig-tinged, so-called Independent Democratic newspapers of James Watson Webb and Mordecai Manuel Noah. Whig prints assailed abolitionism and blamed it on the Jacksonians' hatred of "the rich and intelligent," and their flattering of the ignorant masses with dangerous democratic nostrums. As early as 1831, in the aftermath of the Southampton insurrection, the leading anti-Jacksonian (and later Whig) paper in the country, the *National Intelligencer*, began calling for the suppression of the abolitionist press, a demand it repeated amid the anti-abolitionist upsurge of mid-decade.

The Jacksonian leadership, for its own part, regarded the antislavery agitation as a distraction from the really important issues of banking and the currency, and as a grievous attack on sectional harmony that menaced the Missouri Compromise. Democratic spokesmen accordingly, and fancifully, denounced the abolitionists as democracy's latest enemies. In league with the pro-bank Whigs, supposedly, the movement wanted to stir up what one editorial in Blair's *Globe* called "the SLAVE EXCITEMENT" and divide section against section, to the prepare the way for the dissolution of the Democratic Party and the restoration of plutocracy. Some Democratic editors even thought they detected the malefic influence of John C. Calhoun and Duff Green, now trying to achieve with the slavery issue what they had failed to achieve battling the tariff. "Who agitate the slave question?" one editorial asked. "Who seek to produce sectional parties, founded on local jealousies, to obliterate the great landmarks of party founded on principles?" Who but the nullifiers, along with "[t]he Northern Bank Aristocrats," who saw disrupting the Democratic Party as "their only hope."

President Jackson tried to contain the abolitionists without either endorsing their attackers or abdicating federal authority. Developments in Charleston, South Carolina, soon tested his resolve. In 1835, the AA-SS, having already begun its mass petition drives to Congress, undertook a new campaign, using the federal postal service, to flood the South with immediatist tracts—an effort to circumvent the southern restrictions on the distribution of antislavery literature that had tightened since the David Walker affair. When the AA-SS materials started turning up in Charleston at the end of July, Alfred Huger, the city's postmaster, wrote to the newly named but as yet unconfirmed postmaster general, Amos Kendall, pleading with him to banish the offensive publications and asking him for instructions on how to proceed. Huger was caught in a bind: he had a sworn public obligation to deliver the mail, but the abolitionist materials also fell under South Carolina's ban on "incendiary" publications, and he personally found them intolerable. While awaiting Kendall's reply, Huger—a planter but also a Unionist during the nullification struggle, and thus suspect among pro-slavery extremists—tried to placate state authorities by agreeing to detain all future abolitionist mailings. He duly gathered together the new batches of AA-SS materials, put them in a separate sack, and locked them away. Word of the latest mailings, however, spread quickly, and a small band of prominent Charlestonians—known informally as the Lynch Men—broke into Huger's office, stole the pamphlets, and staged a raucous public burning of them at the Charleston parade grounds. Plainly, the seizure was a deliberate violation of federal law—but South Carolina officials defended it as a sensible effort to keep the inflammatory material from reaching the ken of ignorant slaves.

Amos Kendall, himself a slaveholder, understood the sensitive political issues in play and sympathized with the Charleston authorities. In an open letter to Huger, he said that he could neither sanction nor condemn what had happened, but affirmed that there were occasional extraordinary circumstances in which one's obligations to federal law might be superseded by loyalty to one's community. Kendall ordered the Washington, D.C., postmaster not to deliver the abolitionist tracts, told Jackson that he wanted to halt the abolitionists' campaign with as little commotion as possible, and asked the president for directions. Jackson had not the slightest doubt that the abolitionists were "guilty of the attempt to stir up amongst the South the horrors of a servile war." But the president also detested the anti-abolitionist mobs (and, perhaps especially, the upper-class mob of nullifying Charleston): "This spirit of mob-law is becoming too common and must be checked," he told Kendall, "or ere long it will become as great an evil as a servile war."

As a stopgap measure until Congress reconvened in December, Jackson advised delivering the AA-SS materials only to those who had actually subscribed to them—which would have been few persons, if any, in Charleston—and then to publish the names of any subscribers in the newspapers so that they might be shunned and humiliated. Kendall, however, went his own way, and after scores of southern towns passed resolutions proscribing the abolitionist material, he established a policy of obeying state laws on circulating incendiary publications. Jackson disapproved but did nothing, preferring to allow the situation to cool down until he requested of Congress, in his annual message, a new law banning from the southern mails "incendiary publications intended to instigate the slaves to insurrection."

Jackson's proposal, if enacted, would have amounted to a federal law censoring the mails—another blot on his presidency. Yet even that was insufficient for more obdurate southerners, friend and foe alike. Secretary of State John Forsyth, a Georgian, complained that the administration was coddling the abolitionists and suggested to Vice President Van Buren, more anxious than ever to placate slaveholder Democrats, that he arrange for a little more "mob discipline" up North. (How directly involved Van Buren became is unclear, but New York Democrats did take the lead in organizing fierce anti-abolitionist demonstrations that sometimes degenerated into violence and that pleased Kendall and Huger.) John C. Calhoun and the other congressional nullifiers objected to Jackson's message and demanded a federal law prohibiting the distribution of abolitionist materials wherever state or territorial laws forbade it. Imposing this degree of state rights over a federal department was, to Jackson, ridiculous, and once again he and Calhoun were at loggerheads.

Finally, in July 1836, through a bipartisan backroom effort led by northern Whigs and Democrats, Congress passed its new postal law. Aimed at correcting the abuses of Postmaster General Barry's corrupt tenure, the law upheld the government's traditional commitment to the inviolability of the mails. A rejection of both the Jacksonian and the Calhounite positions, this portion of the law marked a formal victory for, if anybody, the abolitionists. Yet throughout the South, it went unenforced, and postmasters did as they pleased, with the tacit assumption that federal authority over the mails ended at the post office door. Jackson disapproved of the latest passive resistance to federal authority—but mistrustful of the federal courts, not wanting to stir up further trouble so late in his presidency, and satisfied that he had at least enunciated the principle of federal supremacy, he turned a blind eye. In effect, Kendall's policy prevailed, as it would continue to do until after the Civil War, creating an informal bar that blocked abolitionist writings from the South.

This show of Jacksonian prudence, shaped by hostility to the abolitionists, political expediency, and indifference to civil rights, amounted to a failure of leadership. Jackson's views about the abolitionists and their materials were not the central problem. Those views were commonplace outside the most radical abolitionist circles. John Quincy Adams thought the AA-SS mailings were "inflammatory" and might "kindle the flame of insurrection" among the slaves. Influential Whig editors advocated censorship of the abolitionist literature well before any important Jacksonian paper or spokesman did. Nor was Jackson's position particularly extremist or pro-slavery. Unlike Democrats and Whigs who defended and even sparked anti-abolitionist violence, Jackson specifically denounced it. Caught in his own bind, he was careful to attack what he called particular efforts to foment rebellion, and not the abolitionists per se—overt acts, and not ideas. Unlike Kendall, he never endorsed nonenforcement of federal laws; unlike Calhoun, he would not formally subordinate a federal department, accountable to Congress, to laws and regulations established by the states. Yet by allowing the situation to get out of hand before Congress met, and then by failing to enforce in full the 1836 Post Office Law, Jackson overlooked basic principles about the rule of law that he claimed to be upholding, and left suspended a basic question of jurisdiction between the national and the state governments.

In trying to quiet the problem with a minimum of controversy, Jackson and his administration made the situation worse—and mired the Jackson Democracy in contradictions that would one day prove its undoing. Some northern Democrats viewed both the mob violence and Kendall's actions over the abolitionist mailings as unconstitutional and immoral. "We cannot trample on the charter of our national freedom," New York's *Evening Post* asserted, "to assist the slave-holder in his warfare with fanaticism." Just as ominously, an upstate Jacksonian editor later complained, "the enforcement of '*prudential restrictions*' against the abolitionists" became for some Democratic leaders a measure of party loyalty. With the anti-abolitionist outbursts and the mails controversy appeared the first divisions within the northern Democracy over the compatibility of slavery and Jacksonian equality.

By arousing northern opinion over constitutional rights, the attacks also left the "SLAVE EXCITEMENT" open to continuous agitation in the years to come. During the year that the postal controversy unfolded, the numbers of abolitionist societies more than doubled, in part because of northern outrage at the repression. By seizing on and expanding the democratic techniques of petitioning public officials and mass mailings to the public, the abolitionists forced a crisis that brought them even more attention and support. "Our opposers," said the AA-SS's publishing agent, R. G. Williams, "took the wrong course to accomplish their purpose. Instead of putting us down, they put us and our principles up before the world—just where we wanted to be."

WORKIES, UNIONISTS, AND LOCO FOCOS

While Congress considered the abolitionist mails question, a thin, nervous New York congressman named Ely Moore rose from a sickbed and addressed the House to defend northern labor against southern pro-slavery insults. The rebarbative South Carolina congressman, Waddy Thompson, had described northern workers as overpaid improvident thieves who would raise their wages "by lawless insurrection, or by the equally terrible process of the ballot-box." Moore, the past president of both the New York General Trades' Union (GTU) and the National Trades' Union (NTU), seized on Thompson's slur and composed an ornate but harsh reply. "[I]f it shall be the last act of my life," Moore began, "I will attempt to hurl back the imputations."

It nearly turned out to be Moore's last act. His voice rising with a tremulous rage, he upheld organized labor as honorable and denounced the entire history of aristocracy, especially "mon-eyed aristocracy," as one "of aggression, of perfidy, sedition, debauchery, and of moral and political prostitution." Moore built toward his closing; one southern congressman muttered to another, "Why, this is the high-priest of revolution singing his war song." When Moore reached his peroration, an attack on Nicholas Biddle, a frightening pallor covered his face: "And let it be remembered, sir, that this enemy of equal rights, this contem-ner and libeler of the people, is the chief priest, nay, the very Moloch, of the bank-whig aristocracy. No prince better deserves the homage of his subjects; none so well qualified to direct the councils of that political Tartarus, which he has obtained the empire of, and delights to reign over!" Suddenly, Moore stopped and, eyes closed, clutched at the air, pitched forward, and fell to the podium, as his wife, in the gallery, shrieked with horror. Moore later recovered and returned to politics, but this was his finest hour. Northern printers issued special editions of "Moore's Reply to Thompson," by the thousands, and it became a mani-festo of the reawakened labor movement.

Labor's revival had begun in New York in 1833, amid the rapid inflation that, apart from the brief downturn caused by Biddle's panic, sent commodity prices soaring far beyond journeymen's wage rates. Following a bitter carpenters' strike in late spring, representatives from nine trades formed the New York GTU, the city's first organization of employees from different crafts. Over the next four years, the GTU led an upsurge that saw New York wage-earners organize more than forty trade unions and conduct nearly as many strikes. A similar citywide federation appeared in Philadelphia in December 1833; then the movement rapidly spread along the seaboard from Boston to Washington and as far west as St. Louis. Delegates from six of the eastern city central unions formed the NTU in 1834; journeymen in individual trades, including the printers and house carpenters, founded their own national organizations; in time, handloom weavers, female factory operatives (including the young women of Low-ell), coal heavers, dock hands, day laborers, and other workers outside the artisan trades formed unions and organized strikes in numerous locales. Although exact numbers are impossible to determine, the outbreak certainly led to the organizing of more workers than ever before in American history. "'Tis the only palladium that can protect," Ely Moore proclaimed after his inauguration as NTU president, "'tis the only *Sacred Mount* to which you or your posterity can flee for refuge."

Although not always initially aimed at conducting strikes— "strikes," one New York unionist claimed in 1834, "are scarcely considered by the projectors of Trades' Unions as essential to their purpose"—the unionists' militancy grew as inflation worsened. Most walkouts concerned demands for higher wages or resistance to wage cuts. Shoemakers in Geneva and Hudson, New York, and bricklayers in Pittsburgh struck to establish union-only (or "closed") shops, and Boston's printers union struck to protest the hiring of young women as compositors at cut-rate wages. Otherwise, unions focused on gaining the ten-hour workday. The limitation was already a general rule among private employers in New York, and demanding it became a crusade in Philadelphia and other cities, bringing masses of working-men into the streets for rallies and torch-light processions as impressive as those mounted by the political parties. "Humanity," one Philadelphia newspaper proclaimed, "requires us not to abuse the brute creation by over-labour, and surely our fellow-man is entitled to as much consideration." Buttressed by claims that excessive work encouraged intemperance and dissipation, the ten-hour movement won repeated victories.

The unions formed their own political community, not only with roots in the evolving city democracy but also with some crucial innovations. A new labor press quickly emerged, to spread the word about union activities and strikes, reprint speeches, and allow rank-and-file union members to have their say on public events. The NTU had its own official organ, the *National Trades' Union*, published weekly under the formal direction of Ely Moore. Local citywide union papers appeared in Boston, New York, Philadelphia, and Washington. Friendly nonunion editors also publicized the cause, above all George Henry Evans's *Man* (published as a union-oriented weekly alongside Evans's continuing *Working Man's Advocate*). Regular union meetings, run according to open democratic guidelines, elected officers to the city-central unions and deliberated over strikes and protests. Processions and festivals enlivened the unionists' efforts, proclaiming to all their public identity and social ideals with banners like the New York GTU's standard of Archimedes lifting a mountain with a lever. "Can you," Moore asked the crowd in a speech following the GTU's first march, "as mechanics and artists, look upon that banner without being reminded of your united strength?"

The personnel as well as the ideas of the union movement had some obvious links to the Working Men's upsurge of the late 1820s and early 1830s. William Heighton's Mechanics' Union of Trade Associations (MUTA) in Philadelphia, the parent organization of the city's Working Men's Party, had been a forerunner of the new city unions. Several MUTA leaders, including William English and John Ferrall, turned up again as union leaders after 1833. In New York, the chairmaker John Commerford, Moore's successor as president of the GTU and the editor of the New York labor paper, *Union*, had been an active member of the Owenite faction of New York Workies; two of the Working Men's candidates from 1829, the victorious assemblyman-carpenter Ebenezer Ford and the chairmaker Joseph Parsons, represented their respective trades in the GTU; and the printers' leader, John Windt, had proofread Frances Wright's essays and worked closely with George Henry Evans at the *Working Man's Advocate* in 1829 and 1830. From time to time, reprises of the freethinkers' old campaigns glimmered in the unionists' broadsides, like the demand by one group of striking carpenters to end tax exemptions on clerical property. Always the unionists repeated the by-now familiar Workie denunciations of monopoly and the manipulators of "fictitious capital"—those whom Commerford called the political promoters of "the paper or Hamiltonian scheme."

The union movement, however, was deeper and narrower than the Working Men's had been. Most important, it was specifically a movement of journeymen and wage earners based on a consciousness of class within the various trades and industries that had hardened since the Working Men's demise. Increasingly, the New York unionist John Finch explained, it had seemed that "the *employer* was rapidly running the road to wealth [while] the *employed* was too often the victim of poverty and oppression, bound to the vassalage of inadequate reward for his labor." Without forgetting about bankers, speculators, and monopolists from outside of the trades, the unionists focused on employers as a class, who with "deep and matured design," John Commerford wrote, made their profits by filching from labor. Neither employers nor the blind, abstract market had the right to establish wage rates—"a usurpation of authority," one journeyman shoemakers' group declared.

Some urban democrats objected to this proletarian dividing line and argued, to no avail, that small employers and other sympathizers ought to be included in the journeymen's organizations. Greater problems arose over where to draw lines among different kinds of wage earners—or whether to draw any lines at all. Although women workers organized their own unions, many union men were skeptical of them. The very existence of female wage-labor struck some male journeymen as both a social affront and an economic threat. A woman's "physical organization, natural responsibilities, and moral sensibilities," one unionist argued, "prove conclusively that her labors could only be of a domestic nature." Worse, in a growing number of trades and industries, the employment of low-paid women workers had become a means to cut men's earnings, or dismiss men completely. Unskilled day laborers were similarly problematic, normally kept at arm's length by unionists in the proud skilled artisan trades. This prejudice against the dependent unskilled carried over into racial distinctions. The depressed economic conditions of the vast majority of urban blacks, and the constraints that left the relatively small numbers of upwardly mobile blacks to petty retailing and to service trades such as barbering, put most black workers outside the purview of the trades' unions. Although none of the major unions barred blacks from membership, neither did any black worker assume a position of even minor importance within them.

In time, however, some of the divisions within organized labor softened, and sometimes they disappeared completely. The NTU urged the journeymen in all trades affected by female labor to organize ladies' auxiliaries to their unions. The operatives in the cotton-mill factories of Manayunk, along the Schuylkill River on the outskirts of Philadelphia, went further, organizing a strike over wages in which wives and daughters picketed alongside the men, and in which the committee overseeing management of the strike consisted of three men and two women. Connections between skilled and unskilled workers strengthened most dramatically in the seaboard cities. The New York GTU sponsored a joint meeting of mechanics and laborers in 1836, and its president, John Commerford, called on the unions to support a strike by local stevedores, who had "as good and just" a right to ask what they pleased for their labor as any mechanic or merchant did. Even more remarkably, a coal heavers' strike for the ten-hour day in Philadelphia later in the year prompted journeymen from numerous trades to walk off their jobs in a virtual general strike, and to march alongside the laborers, chanting, "We are all day laborers." The prospect loomed of a more comprehensive movement throughout the country, embracing what Commerford called "the family of labor," "the working classes."

Employers' counterattacks on the movement became a concerted crackdown. In virtually every trade and in every city where labor had organized, employer associations arose as well, denouncing the unions (as the Philadelphia makers of women's shoes put it) for "fostering oppression, tyranny and misrule, and thus obstructing the free course of trade." Blacklists circulated, but these had little impact on the well-organized and, thanks to members' dues, well-funded unions. More effective was the employers' use of the courts to try to break the unions as illegal combinations, either at common law or (in New York) under recently passed legislation that banned associations "injurious to public morals or trade or commerce." Five major prosecutions took place between 1833 and 1836. In three decided by juries—involving carpet-weavers in Enfield, Connecticut, shoemakers in Hudson, New York, and plasterers in Philadelphia—the defendants were acquitted. But a conspiracy case brought against the union shoemakers in Geneva, New York, wound up going all the way to the state supreme court in 1836, where Chief Justice Edward Savage virtually declared trade unions illegal. Armed with the Geneva ruling, Manhattan's employing tailors brought twenty journeymen union strikers up on similar charges. In his charge to the jury, the presiding judge, Ogden Edwards, essentially directed a verdict of guilty, which the jury duly returned.

Within days of the conviction, copies of an ominous handbill, headed by a coffin, appeared all around the city:

> The Rich against the Poor! Judge Edwards, the tool of the Aristocracy, against the People! Mechanics and workingmen! A deadly blow has been struck at your Liberty! The prize for which your fathers fought has been robbed from you! The Freemen of the North are now on a level with the slaves of the South! with no other privileges than laboring that drones may fatten on your life-blood!

Bid by the so-called coffin handbill, a large crowd turned out to hear Edwards pronounce his sentence and began taking up a collection to pay off the convicted unionists' fines. One week later, an evening rally of mechanics and workingmen, estimated at thirty thousand, converged on City Hall Park to hear speakers—"chiefly radicals," the press reported—denounce Edwards, bankers, merchants, employers, and the two major political parties for being "at variance with the spirit and genius of Republican government." After a final cheer, the crowd headed peaceably home, its path lit by the flaming effigies of Justice Savage and Judge Edwards hung from the main gates of the park. Two days after the demonstration, news came from Hudson that a jury had acquitted the shoemakers indicted there, giving the unionists hope.

The giant New York demonstration remained peaceful, but the

strikes and protests of the mid-1830s did degenerate into violence. The largest incident involved striking construction workers and diggers along the Chesapeake & Ohio Canal, whose attacks on strikebreakers and local authorities prompted Maryland's governor to call for federal military intervention in 1834. The brutish conditions in the canal-diggers' camps helped explain the violence, but disorder and bloodshed were all too common in the cities as well. In New York alone, violence and the threat of violence arose repeatedly, most notoriously in an affray pitting striking stonecutters against "blacklegs" (or "scabs") in 1834 but also in strikes involving cabinetmakers, piano makers, dockworkers, coal heavers, and tailors. Not surprisingly, the conservative press loudly condemned these incidents as the essence of trade unionism. Yet the remarkable thing was not the use of physical force but that there was not more of it, given the numerous provocations by employers, local marshals, and the courts. The unions tried to play a disciplining role by restraining their members from self-defeating riotous behavior, and by officially repudiating workers who (in the words of the New York GTU) did not act "with that propriety becoming good citizens."

The unions' quest for orderly organization in the economic field still left open, however, the question of whether to organize in elections as well. Questions over participating in politics had bothered the new labor movement from its inception. The examples of the Working Men's parties were discouraging, as was the takeover of local and national politics by insider professionals—those "wire pullers who move the juggling machines of 'the party,'" as the *Union* called them. At the first convention of the NTU, one New England labor leader declared the common view that the workingmen "belonged to no party; they were neither disciples of Jacksonism nor Clayism, Van Burenism nor Websterism, nor any other *ism* but *workeyism*." Yet organized labor never opted out of politics. Although never "intended to interfere in party politics," the *National Trades' Union* observed, the unions granted that "many of the evils under which the workingmen are suffering are of a political origin and can only be reached in that

way." On numerous specific issues, ranging from the employment of prison labor to factory work conditions for women and
children, unions issued investigative reports and demanded legislative reforms. Some union leaders, most famously Ely Moore,
also became deeply involved in electoral politics independently
of their unions, most as Jacksonian Democrats. A host of others
played important political roles in different party factions that, by
1836, emerged as the northern pro-labor left-wing bloc of the
Jackson Democracy.

The first sparks of this more politicized labor Jacksonianism
appeared in New England, thrown off by the sputtering embers
of the Working Men's movement. In September 1832, the New
England Association of Farmers, Mechanics, and Other Workingmen, founded a year earlier by Workies and Workie sympathizers, held its first formal convention in Boston. The presiding
officer, Charles Douglas, was the editor of a weekly Rhode Island
labor paper, the *New England Artisan*, and among those present
was Douglas's "traveling agent," a flamboyant, vociferous organizer named Seth Luther. With Luther supplying lung power, peripatetic energy, and caustic wit, and with Douglas providing the
guiding ideas, the *Artisan* and the association stoked existing discontent in the mills of Pawtucket and points north, as well as
among hard-pressed small farmers in western Massachusetts. Yet
they offered little in terms of practical reform remedies. Douglas,
in particular, had a visceral distaste for party politics, which he
thought had been thoroughly corrupted by "aristocrats" like the
Jacksonian boss and banker David Henshaw.

In 1833, new recruits to the association began to consider
mounting an independent challenge against both Henshaw and
the dominant National Republican (and later Whig) coalition.
Samuel Clesson Allen, a sixty-year-old former congressman, was
the least likely convert to the cause. A high-toned Federalist early
in his career, Allen had served as a delegate to the Hartford Convention in 1814, then won election to six terms in Congress, leaving office in 1829 disgusted at the ascension of Andrew Jackson,
"a man covered with crimes." Yet when he returned to his country

home in Northfield, Allen could see that the old rural idyll of his conservative reveries had passed away, transformed from a land of sturdy yeoman into one of dependent tenant farmers, household-bound pieceworkers, and factory hands. At the root of the problem, he gradually concluded, was the monied class, men who "though they produced none of the objects of wealth, of themselves . . . became mighty instruments of accumulation." By 1833, Allen's musings had carried him all the way into Workey-ism, and to supporting Jackson's war on the Second Bank of the United States. With the New England Association's endorse-ment, a committee of Charlestown Working Men persuaded him to be their protest candidate for governor, and did so again in 1834, on a ticket that included another rural Federalist turned Workie, Theodore Sedgwick Jr., the son of the former U.S. Speaker of the House. Neither nominee fared well, but their can-didacies commenced a challenge to the state's conservative Democratic leadership.

Another unexpected figure from western Massachusetts joined the Workie crusade during Allen's first campaign in 1833. The greatest American historian of his generation, George Bancroft, a Harvard graduate and failed progressive schoolteacher, had been a literary star since the mid-1820s, best known for his contributions to the eminent *North American Review*. Like all New Englanders of taste and intelligence, Bancroft intensely distrusted Andrew Jackson, yet he was also given to making romantic, liberal demo-cratic public utterances that unsettled his friends and readers. Bancroft's liberalism finally won out over his breeding, and in 1834, the same year he published the first volume of his monu-mental *History of the United States*, he threw his support to the Working Men and the newly formed Boston Trades' Union, charg-ing that "[t]here is more danger from monopolies than from com-binations of workingmen." A year later, he attacked the Whigs as an American Tory party that merged three classes of aristocratic oppressors: commercial monopolists, manufacturing corpora-tions, and southern slaveholders, "the most selfish, the most united, and the most overbearing of all."

Joined by a phalanx of other writers and politicians, including the anticapitalist polemicist Theophilus Fisk, the pro-labor Democratic state legislator Frederick Robinson, and the state supreme court justice and perennial Democratic gubernatorial candidate Marcus Morton, the renegade Bancroft helped push the Workies into a renewed war against the Henshaw Democrats—but this time from within the Democratic fold. Since the inception of the New England Association, radical, hard-money Jacksonians had appealed to the group's members to join the president's crusade against privilege. Shortly after the 1832 election, New England native Amos Kendall spoke in Boston on the brutal effects of the manufacturing monopoly. The following year, the New England Association and its gubernational candidate, Samuel Clesson Allen, endorsed Jackson's war on the BUS and "*the power of associated wealth.*" All but the most stubborn antipolitical Workies switched to the Democrats, determined to displace the Henshaw machine with one of their own. In 1836, Henshaw, gout-ridden and exhausted, offered to resign the Boston collectorship—and the Democrats stocked their election tickets with Workie leaders and sympathizers, including Bancroft, Allen, and Sedgwick, all of whom ran for Congress. Although the Whigs carried the state, the Democrats for once ran respectably. Having made the Working Men's measures, as one newspaper remarked, "part and parcel of their cause," the Massachusetts Democrats, once a reviled minority, were legitimate contenders for power. Within two years, the new collector of Boston and chief of the Massachusetts Democracy was George Bancroft.

Across the Northeast, a similar dynamic unfolded, pitting moderate and conservative Bank Democrats against more radical Democrats who were partial to the labor movement and supported Jackson's Bank War. In Connecticut, the radical Democrats rallied behind the former Jeffersonian Republican and founding editor of the *Hartford Times*, John Milton Niles, and elevated him to the U.S. Senate in 1835. In Pennsylvania, Thomas Brothers, the English émigré who would later sour on the movement, succeeded William Heighton as Philadelphia's chief labor editor with his newspaper the *Radical Reformer and Working Man's Advocate*. In 1835, an uprising within the Pennsylvania Democracy led to the nomination of Congressman Henry Muhlenberg on a Democratic ticket that also included the veteran Workie and union leader, William English. Although the split handed the gubernatorial election to the Anti-Masonic candidate, himself an ex-Democrat, it served abrupt notice on the state's Bank Democrats that the radicals had arrived.

The most spectacular uprising occurred in New York City. In the autumn of 1834, Tammany Hall announced its opposition to all banks and monopolies in order to flatter the ex–Working Men in its ranks, promote party unity, and help reelect the Van Burenite governor William Marcy. Tammany also nominated four antibank sympathizers for the state legislature and, in his first election, Ely Moore for Congress. Yet in January, as soon as the new Democratic-controlled legislature met in Albany, the members began approving new bank charters to party insiders and their friends, calling it a "judicious" form of attacking monopoly. Antimonopoly newspapers lashed out; the state Democratic committee replied with slurs; and over the ensuing months, the radical Democrats plotted a revolt. In early autumn, the antimonopoly men sponsored a dinner honoring Richard Mentor Johnson, already the national Democrats' designated vice presidential nominee. Congressman Churchill Cambreleng spoke, as did the visiting Boston radical Theophilus Fisk and the printers' union leader John Windt. The event led to a string of crowded meetings of the newly dubbed Equal Rights Democracy.

After sundown on October 29, Democratic officials assembled at Tammany Hall's headquarters, the Wigwam, across from City Hall, for the anticlimactic business of receiving pro-forma approval from the Democratic rank and file for a prearranged slate of candidates. The leadership, with a list of conservative nominees, crept up the backstairs to the spacious meeting room, while outside a dense crowd crammed the front hall staircase and spilled out into Frankfort Street. At seven, the crowd poured in and called Joel

Curtis, a veteran Working Man, front and center. A banner was unfurled proclaiming *"Joel Curtis, the Anti-Monopolist chairman."* Then another banner appeared, denouncing the regular party slate, and then several others, while the crowd booed the Tammany regulars and struggled to keep them seated at the podium and prevent an adjournment. The Equal Rights man Alexander Ming Jr.—son of a close associate of Thomas Skidmore's and himself the printer of *Rights of Man to Property!*—clambered atop a table and motioned for silence, when suddenly the room went dark. One of the regular Democrats had escaped and switched off the gaslights, a time-honored Tammany method of stifling rebellion. But the Equal Rights insurgents had come prepared with primitive friction matches, popularly known as "Lucifers" or "loco focos." Holding aloft fifty lit candles and now in total control of the room, they nominated their own ticket.

The conservative Bank Democrats were not to be deterred, and in November their candidate for mayor, the leather manufacturer Gideon Lee, won handily, almost certainly with Whig support. But the Equal Rights Democrats—now mocked as the Loco Focos—won over thirty-five hundred votes, about 15 percent of the total, and established themselves as a viable independent force. Over the next two years, working out of a small, smoky chamber on the second floor of the down-at-heels Military and Civic Hotel on the Bowery, the Loco Focos enlarged their following. Former Workies joined with union men including John Commerford and the journeymen locksmiths' leader Levi Slamm, as well as with radical thinkers such as the currency reformer Clinton Roosevelt, in the hopes of redeeming the Democracy from the bank men and the wire pullers. In the spring of 1836, the Loco Focos ran Ming for mayor and founded their own newspaper, the *Democrat*, edited by Windt and Roosevelt. Following the massive demonstration in support of the convicted journeymen tailors, they called for a new state party convention and sent several delegates to the gathering that eventually met in Utica to nominate yet another Working Men's Party veteran, Isaac Smith, as governor. In the autumn city elections, they struck a marriage

of convenience with the Whigs by co-nominating several legislative candidates while also backing the Democrats Cambreleng
and Moore—the only two Democrats to win reelection. The
Equal Rights Democrats now held the balance of power in New
York City politics.

Reporting on the Loco Focos, and inspiring them as well, was
the journalist and self-educated intellectual William Leggett. After
a knock-about youth that ended with his being cashiered from the
navy for insulting an officer, Leggett had washed up in Manhattan,
where in the late 1820s he wrote short stories and theater reviews.
In 1829, the editor of the Evening Post, poet and Jacksonian sympathizer William Cullen Bryant hired him as his assistant, and over
the ensuing decade Leggett emerged as the most vehement and
most thoughtful of the city's antimonopolist Democratic editors
and essayists. Leggett's pugnacious side, and his talent for winning
attention, turned up in his slashing verbal assaults on his political
and journalistic opponents, as it did in a celebrated brawl with
James Watson Webb on Wall Street in 1833. But he was also a
serious writer of democratic political theory.

An apostle of Jeffersonian economics, hostile to combinations
of government and private enterprise, Leggett turned the free
market dogma of propertied conservatives inside out. Proclaiming the cause of labor against capitalist special interests and the
paper-money system, Leggett also defended the unions as voluntary and necessary associations of embattled workers. "[L]et us
ask," he wrote, "what and where is the danger of a combination of
the labouring classes in vindication of their political principles, or
in defence of their menaced rights?" Leggett's radicalism went
further than that of most, even within the Loco Focos' ranks,
notably on slavery and race. Enraged by the mob attacks on the
immediatists, and by Amos Kendall's handling of the mails controversy, Leggett converted to abolitionism and the cause of racial
equality—leading to the withholding of what looked like a sure
nomination to Congress and to what he later called his "excommunication" by the national party. Yet even those radical Democrats who did not share Leggett's views on slavery and the
abolitionists never wavered in their affection and admiration for

the man; indeed, Leggett's removal from the party helped to trigger the Equal Rights revolt. One of the mutineers' banners displayed the night New York's Loco Focos earned their nickname contrasted a despised Democratic paper with Leggett's: "*The Times must change ere we desert our Post.*"

The labor movement and the radical Democrats would have their greatest influence on the national scene in the realm of political ideas. President Jackson briefly felt the movement's impact in 1834 when, at the request of Maryland authorities, he dispatched federal troops to suppress the violent strike of Irish day laborers along the Chesapeake & Ohio Canal, and, more positively, in 1836, when he approved a federal order to adopt the ten-hour workday at the government shipyard in Philadelphia. Jackson would not tolerate civil disorder, whatever its origin. But his administration's basic sympathies with the labor movement (in contrast with its enmity toward the abolitionists) came across clearly, most explicitly in the *Globe*, which bid "All Democrats or Working Men" to tolerate no proposals that gave "*legal* advantages to *capital*, over *labor*" or otherwise helped harden society into "two distinct classes: namely—masters and slaves." On both practical and ideological grounds, the administration and the more radical wing of the Albany Regency regarded the divisions in the northern Democracy over banking issues with alarm—and viewed the stubbornness of the conservatives, especially in New York, with dismay. It would take a few more years to complete, but an alliance between the Loco Foco Democracy and the Democratic Party's national leadership was already in the making.

JACKSONIAN CONTRADICTIONS

The affinities between the Jackson administration and what John Commerford called the "family of labor" underscored the peculiarities of Jacksonian Democracy as it evolved in the mid-1830s. The removal of the government deposits and Jackson's victory over Nicholas Biddle were completely in line with what the city democrats, now Jackson Democrats, had been demanding about banks and currency for years. In their political efforts, labor leaders naturally gravitated to the Jacksonians. Yet once they did so, they found pro-Jackson politicians who were either offended by the Bank War and not at all friendly to their views or who (like the Tammany "antimonopolists") paid mere lip service to their cause. Radical Democrats were pitted against Bank Democrats. The future of both democracy and Jackson's Democracy would depend on which of these two wings of the party would gain ascendancy in the North.

The politics of antislavery exposed another side of Jackson's coalition. Jackson and his party were decidedly hostile to the antislavery radicals. Without endorsing Calhounite pro-slavery positions, the unapologetic slaveholder Jackson, especially in the postal controversy, tried to silence the immediatist agitators, even if it took a federal censorship law to do so. Those efforts only reinforced the radical abolitionists' conviction that Jackson himself, as well as his party, was no better than any of the other slavocrats, and that their professions to democracy and equality were vitiated by their racism and self-interest. The suppression also alienated some northern Jacksonians as well as Whigs who had had little or nothing to do with the abolitionists.

These contradictory sides of Jacksonianism could not coexist forever. Although still on the defensive—and risking, like William Leggett, political excommunication—some northern Jacksonians were growing uncomfortable at the party's deference to the southern slaveholders, just as larger numbers of Democrats (including Leggett) were pressing for even more dramatic changes in the banking and currency systems. On the latter issues, the radical Democrats were winning the initiative. But on slavery and antislavery, Jacksonians like Leggett remained the exception through the mid-1830s, their influence hampered not simply by the party's fears about abolitionist disruption but by continuing events in the South and Southwest during the final years of Jackson's presidency. Those events would deepen the Jacksonians' contradictions—and hasten the end of one phase of American democracy's rise and the beginning of another.

9

"THE REPUBLIC HAS DEGENERATED INTO A DEMOCRACY"

The tumults of the mid-1830s had many causes, but to conservative Whigs, they all boiled down to one—the rise of Andrew Jackson and his demagogic Democratic Party. "They have classified the rich and intelligent and denounced them as aristocrats," the *Richmond Whig* declared, "they have caressed, soothed, and flattered the heavy class of the poor and ignorant, because *they* held the power which they wanted." In pursuit of their selfish ends, the Jacksonians had destroyed the political system designed by the Framers: "*The Republic*," the Richmond paper cried, "*has degenerated into a Democracy.*" Yet to the Jacksonians, for whom democracy was the fulfillment of republicanism, the transition was far from complete, and the continuing political challenges of Jackson's second term raised difficult questions about how it might be done.

The concept of state rights and its connections to southern politics were especially vexing. When linked to the tariff and nullification, state rights had led Jackson to renounce nullifier extremism in favor of his own democratic nationalism, and fracture his original coalition. But when linked to Indian removal, state-rights claims had helped bind Jacksonians' loyalties to Jackson, especially in the Deep South and Southwest. After the passage of the Indian Removal Bill in 1830, Jackson resettled nearly forty-six thousand Indians west of the Mississippi and cleared the way for moving a like number in the future. In the process, he obtained over a hundred million acres of Indian land for white settlement, preeminently in the nascent cotton kingdoms of Alabama and Mississippi. While he battled the aristocratic slaveholders of South Carolina, Jackson opened up grand new vistas to the West for slaveholders as well as yeoman farmers.

During his last two years in office, Jackson commenced the final removal of the southeastern Indians, ignoring the objections of northern humanitarians and John Marshall's Supreme Court. Southern and sectional politics on other issues remained troublesome for the administration. For years, Anglo-American settlers, a large number of them slaveholders, had been streaming into the Tejas region of Mexico with the encouragement of the newly independent Mexican government. Although exempted from Mexico's abolition of slavery in 1829, the settlers were beginning to chafe at Mexican rule, particularly at a prohibition on further immigration in 1830. By 1835, having drafted their own Texas state constitution two years earlier, the Texans were on the edge of armed revolt, which the Jacksonians fervently supported. But the Texas Revolution also opened up fresh sectional rifts that needed to be handled with care—especially given the rising vociferousness of the northern abolitionists. And while the slaveholders affirmed their control of the region's political system, partisan divisions within the South, chiefly over banking policy, generated a growing and coherent southern anti-Jackson opposition.

Jackson's struggles over economic policy proved just as fractious in the North, and with the approach of the presidential contest of 1836, they continued to dominate national affairs. By all but killing the Second Bank of the United States, Jackson left open how the nation's finances would now operate, which provoked additional divisions inside his own party. The problem became acute when, after the downturn caused by the panic in 1834, the economy entered a period of fevered speculation as bad as any Jackson and his allies had blamed on the BUS. In addition to defections from Democratic ranks, the White House faced resistance from an enlarged and better-organized Whig opposition in Congress, working in concert with John C. Calhoun, who was now consumed by his pro-slavery sectionalism and hatred of Jackson. Yet Jackson, implacable as ever, responded by endorsing new, sometimes drastic experiments in banking policy while implementing a hard-money currency program more radical than any yet proposed.

INDIAN REMOVAL, SOUTHERN POLITICS, AND THE TEXAS REVOLUTION

After 1830, some of the administration's bloodiest encounters with the Indians occurred, paradoxically, outside the areas in the South and Southwest where the removals were heaviest. In 1832, Chief Black Hawk led members of the northwestern Sac and Fox tribes eastward across the Mississippi to reoccupy lands from which they had already been removed. Jackson sent federal troops, which, along with Illinois militia, drove Black Hawk into Wisconsin, where he suddenly halted, turned, and drove off his pursuers. The Black Hawk War, three months in duration, ended in August, when Black Hawk surrendered at Prairie du Chien. Three years later, hostilities broke out with the Seminoles of Florida under Osceola, inaugurating a vicious guerrilla conflict that lasted seven years, at a heavy cost in lives to both sides, before the majority of the surviving Seminoles were removed.

The largest removals involved the Choctaws, Creeks, Chickasaws, and Cherokees. In the summer of 1830, the Choctaws of Mississippi riled Jackson by failing to send representatives to an agreed meeting in Tennessee. Thereafter, Jackson proclaimed the federal government powerless to contravene state law over Indian settlements, and he arranged for an allotment treaty that ultimately sent the majority of the Choctaws, roughly fourteen thousand out of nineteen thousand, to the West, amid horrifying scenes of hardship and death from cholera and malnutrition. The

Creeks, living in Alabama, signed an allotment treaty in 1832, only to have speculators move in, buy up their land at a pittance, and push them out. Some displaced Creeks turned to theft and even murder, prompting the War Department to send troops, which forced fifteen thousand Creeks to emigrate west before Jackson left office. The Chickasaws in Mississippi waited two years for western land to be found, then signed an allotment treaty in 1832. Five years later, five thousand were relocated across the Mississippi.

The Cherokees, with the aid of their evangelical allies, put up a stiffer resistance through the courts. As soon as Jackson's removal act went into effect, the Georgia legislature declared all Cherokee laws null and void. The Cherokees hired William Wirt and the prominent ex-congressman John Sergeant, who filed an injunction with the Supreme Court to block the Georgians from executing their laws in Cherokee territory. The case of *Cherokee Nation v. State of Georgia* ended in an apparent defeat for the Indians in 1831 when Chief Justice John Marshall declared in a majority opinion that because the Cherokees were a "domestic dependent nation," they lacked standing to sue. Administration Democrats were elated and claimed that their old nemesis Marshall had affirmed the Cherokees' case was, as Martin Van Buren put it, both "fictitious, not to say factious, and designed for political effect." But the fight over the Cherokees—and by them— was not yet over.

A second Supreme Court ruling a year later, in the *Worcester v. Georgia* case, moved in the opposite direction—and reconnected Indian removal to state rights. A new Georgia law required all white persons to obtain a state license if they wished to live in Cherokee territory. Samuel A. Worcester and Elizur Butler, missionaries from the American Board of Commissioners for Foreign Missions, refused to comply, were sentenced to four years at hard labor, and, with the help of Wirt and Sergeant, appealed their case to the Supreme Court. Interest in the case was high—by this time, Wirt was the Anti-Mason's presidential nominee, while Sergeant was Henry Clay's National Republican running mate—

and more than fifty congressmen dropped their business to hear the arguments before the Court. Marshall's decision overturned the Georgia state supreme court, declared Georgia's licensing laws unconstitutional, and directed the state to heed the Court's ruling. The Cherokee Nation, the chief justice declared, was "a distinct community, occupying its own territory," in which the state of Georgia had no jurisdiction and with whom intercourse was vested solely in the federal government. Georgians immediately complained that the Court had violated their state's sovereign rights.

The outcome created a dilemma for President Jackson. Marshall's court would be out of session until January 1833, which gave Georgia authorities ten months to reply to the Court's mandate. As the deadline approached, however, Jackson's struggle with the South Carolina nullifiers escalated. He did not want to do anything to relieve the pressure on the Cherokees to relocate, and did not want to provoke the Georgians to join the South Carolinians in a state-rights frenzy. Neither, however, did he want to appear as if he were knuckling under to the Georgians—or allowing the missionaries to become anti-administration martyrs. The White House persuaded Georgia Governor Wilson Lumpkin to release the two prisoners, and got the now-defeated presidential candidate Wirt to agree that he would file no further motions when the Supreme Court reconvened. The missionaries Worcester and Butler walked free, and the immediate crisis ended.

The Cherokees' battle against removal continued for another five years. Although Secretary of War Lewis Cass negotiated a removal treaty in the spring of 1834, the majority of the Cherokee chiefs and their followers opposed it. Leading the opposition was John Ross, one-eighth Cherokee by birth. A former army lieutenant who had fought side by side with Jackson during the Creek War in 1814, but who had turned against him over Indian removal, Ross had been elected the Cherokees' principal chief in 1828. Now, as head of the antitreaty National Party, Ross staved off the administration with delay, subterfuge, and, in 1835, an election in which the Cherokees overwhelmingly rejected the proposed treaty. Finally, Governor Lumpkin mobilized the Georgia militia, which rousted and terrorized the antitreaty Indians and temporarily imprisoned Ross. When Ross, upon his release, traveled to Washington to plead for better terms, the pro-treaty party called a rump session and approved a new removal treaty at New Echota that passed the Senate by a single vote in May 1836. Although given two years to prepare for their departure, the Cherokees soon found themselves in need of federal protection. Two antitreaty counselors who had grudgingly signed the new agreement, Major Ridge and his son, John, advised Jackson in 1836 that "[t]he lowest classes of the white people" had begun "flogging the Cherokees with cow hides, hickories, and clubs" to drive them off their allotments. Jackson did nothing.

As ever, Jackson asserted that removal was the best possible solution for the Indians themselves. That position may have had merits, but it lacked the crucial one of having the Indians' assent. On the matter of majorities and minorities, the linchpin of Jackson's politics, the majority within the Indians' camp counted for nothing, whereas the white majorities in the specific states counted for everything. Jackson had accomplished his great goal of removing the Indians to what he considered a safe haven—and, in the process, spared them the annihilation that had befallen Indians in the Northeast. But to save the Indians, Jackson's policy also destroyed thousands of them.

Less cruel paradoxes in the Indian removal struggle lay in the area of southern politics. Among those leading the fight against the New Echota treaty (joining Clay, Webster, and a mixture of New England and middle-state Whigs) were three prominent southerners: the veteran Virginia Tidewater conservative Benjamin Watkins Leigh; Alexander Porter, a lawyer and sugar planter from Louisiana; and John C. Calhoun. None was known as an outspoken defender of the Cherokee, although Calhoun had earlier supported "civilizing" missions instead of removal. (Porter opposed Indian removal because he wanted to keep the displaced Indians from crossing through the Southwest.) None had common agendas on other government policies, least of all the protectionist sugar grower Porter and the nullifier Calhoun. All three, however, were devoted pro-slavery men whose devotion was deepening amid the assaults from the abolitionists. And they were passionate opponents of Andrew Jackson and all his works—including, now, the treaty with the Cherokees. Under Calhoun's leadership, this strain of conservative pro-slavery southern politics would, through the mid-1830s, begin to consolidate an anti-Jackson opposition in what, less than a decade earlier, had been a solid Jacksonian South.

Calhoun opposed Jackson at every turn. After trying, and failing, to get the Senate to repeal the Force Bill, Calhoun ripped into the president's protest of the Senate censure with a sharp personal attack: "Infatuated man! Blinded by ambition—intoxicated by flattery and vanity!" On the abolitionist mails controversy, Indian removal, corruption in the post office, and the abuse of executive patronage (about which he prepared an entire report), Calhoun was a single-minded foe. He had ample reason to bear an enormous grudge against Jackson, but he was not a petty man, and his monomania was more philosophical and political than it was personal. Still, in the taut coils of Calhoun's deductive mind, everything Jackson and his supporters did, no matter how innocuous, turned into additional evidence of the president's cancerous ambition and the imminent death of public liberty.

Slavery became Calhoun's other fixation. Prior to the 1830s, even amid the battle over the tariff, Calhoun rarely mentioned slavery, except in direct connection with running his Fort Hill plantation. Early in his congressional career, he registered his shame at witnessing South Carolina oppose the prohibition of the transatlantic slave trade in 1807, perhaps betraying some Yankee influence from his years at Yale and at Tapping Reeve's academy. Slavery was, to be sure, at the bottom of what, during the nullification crisis, Calhoun had called the "opposite relations" between North and South. Yet only when nullification collapsed and the abolitionists began winning a large following did Calhoun begin defending slavery explicitly as a necessary, even preferred way of life. The Calhounite *United States Telegraph* signaled the shift in 1833, crying that it was high time to renounce the "cant" about the evils of slavery. A year later, Calhoun accosted a Philadelphia Whig congressman outside the Capitol and delivered a two-hour tirade about slavery's great advantages, and about how the degraded working masses of the North were bound to use the suffrage to despoil the wealthy. Slavery, Calhoun said, solved this problem "by the denial of all political rights" to the toilers, allowing the whites "to pursue without apprehension the means they think best to elevate their own condition." Slavery, Calhoun concluded, was "indispensable to republican government," a judgment he was soon proclaiming on the floor of the Senate while ridiculing the claims of the abolitionists. "Will our friends of the South," he asked sarcastically after quoting one of the abolitionists' petitions, "agree that they keep shambles and deal in human flesh? . . . Strange language! Piracy and butchery? We must not permit those we represent to be thus insulted on that floor."

Always protective of his political independence, Calhoun did not formally join the Whig Party, keeping his distance by proposing policies of his own on key issues like banking. His chief aims were to sustain the southern nullifier position and, as best he could, his own political ambitions. Other southerners whom Jackson had alienated—state-rights men, up-country improvers, pro-BUS planters, and conservative nationalists—joined the Whig opposition. In Virginia, western pro-improvement men who had supported Clay in 1832 allied with the much larger numbers of state-rights advocates and National Republicans from the Tidewater and Piedmont in angry reaction to Jackson's removal of the deposits. Calling themselves Whigs, engaged in "a struggle between liberty and power," the Virginians forced the Jacksonian William C. Rives to resign from the Senate and replaced him with Benjamin Watkins Leigh, while they also elected a governor and gained control of the state legislature. In North Carolina, nullifiers and the popular state-rights senator Willie P. Mangum struck an alliance with the state's pro-BUS Democrats and its small numbers of National Republicans. In Georgia, Jackson's former attorney general, the Savannah lawyer and attorney for the BUS John M. Berrien, led the new State Rights Party, dominated by men formerly associated with George Troup. Mississippi's state righters, offended by Jackson's actions during the nullification crisis, formed their own association in the spring of 1834 and were almost immediately courted by the state's business-minded former National Republicans to join in a common electoral front.

The rise of a powerful southern Whig opposition to Jackson sharpened some of the class and subregional divisions within southern politics. Southern Whiggery was preeminently a party of commercial development—friendly to the expansion of commercial banking facilities (and offended by Jackson's war on the BUS), partial to internal improvements, and (especially in the hemp-growing areas of the upper South and in the sugar parishes of Louisiana) pro-tariff. The largest planters, ranging from sugar growers in Louisiana to state-rights men in the eastern states, gravitated to the Whigs, taking with them districts where slaveholding was most thickly concentrated. Whigs also drew support, and a good deal of its leadership, from the business and professional classes as well as skilled workers of the coastal and river cities. Rather paradoxically, some of the more remote mountain areas such as western Virginia and East Tennessee also favored the Whigs, drawn to the national party's touting of internal improvements as a means to expand national prosperity. In the rest of the South, especially the Deep South, the Democrats came to depend largely on yeoman farmers in the less developed areas—northern Alabama, eastern Mississippi—who were distrustful of the planters' power, fearful of commercial banks and other monied institutions, and who saw politics, one southern Democrat wrote, as a contest between "*Aristocracy* . . . with the Money Power, Against Democracy or the Will of the People."

Although divided by party, the slaveholders retained their collective domination of the region's political system. Sometimes they did so with carefully calibrated structural reforms that offered minor concessions to nonslaveholders in order to solidify support for slavery—and deflect any hint of antislavery politics. Two sets of state constitutional revisions moved voting requirements and restrictions closer to the Master Race democratic model adopted in the new Deep South states after 1815. In 1835, the North Carolinians extended popular voting for governor to include all male taxpayers over age twenty-one, but sustained the freehold property requirement in voting for members of the state senate and totally eliminated suffrage rights for the state's small numbers of free blacks. A year earlier, a Tennessee state convention completely rewrote the state's constitution. A few delegates from the mountainous eastern portion of the state, where religious antislavery societies had arisen earlier in the century, advanced gradualist abolitionist proposals, claiming that bondage was hampering the state's economic development. But these were bottled up in committee and then voted down. Instead, the convention dropped the symbolic freehold requirement for white male voting (an alternative, minor residency requirement had been in effect since 1796), while closing the suffrage to free blacks except for those men of color who were now "competent witness[es] in a court of justice against a white man."

In less formal ways, slaveholders regardless of party did their utmost to secure the loyalty of the nonslaveholding majority to slavery. As South Carolina's Arthur P. Hayne explained in a paper he sent to Jackson, "a restless feeling" plagued "the South, and not without just cause, in relation to the Question of Property at the South, and unless this feeling be put at rest, who would desire to live in such a community?" One way to keep the lid on was to curtail antislavery talk, with what Hayne called its dangerous "abstract love for liberty." Another—the carrot instead of the stick—was to celebrate the sovereignty of the people, denounce the Yankees, and turn election contests into endless debates over which party or faction was the more loyal to the South—thereby, supposedly, protecting the status and well-being of all southern white men and their households. Southern Jackson Democrats could point to their party's crackdown against the abolitionist menace; Whigs proclaimed that their fights against federal executive tyranny made southern rights more secure than ever, in contrast with the untrustworthy Jacksonians. "Our domestic institutions are threatened with annihilation," one Georgia Whig paper declared.

A third method was to co-opt talented nonslaveholder politicians who looked as if they might pose a political threat to the slavocracy. The case of Franklin Plummer of Mississippi, the most radical southern country democrat of the Jacksonian era, is illustrative. A New Englander who had moved to Mississippi as a young man, Plummer was the political favorite of the impoverished so-called Piney Woods semisubsistence counties in the south-central part of the state. A scabrous, leather-lunged stump-speaker and campaigner—especially effective when he cast his opponents as effete, river-county planter snobs—Plummer won election to the state legislature and then, in 1830, to Congress, over the objections of the local Jackson organization. In Washington, he made his mark as an antibank Jacksonian every bit as radical as any northern Workie or Loco Foco, claiming to stand unterrified for the only principles that could "save our bleeding constitution from destruction." So he remained—until after he left Congress and the bankers and planters of Natchez got hold of him, inviting him to their lavish dinners, fronting him a twenty-five-thousand-dollar loan, and encouraging him to run for the Senate. Plummer, bewitched, bought a fancy carriage, hired liveried servants, and campaigned hard, only to be crushed by fellow Jacksonian Robert J. Walker—a more conventional Democrat, but who could not be accused of betrayal by the yeoman of the Piney Woods. Plummer, his political career over, careened about over the next ten years, finally dying a forgotten drunk in Jackson in 1847. Unimaginable in Calhoun's South Carolina, his meteoric career proved that even in the rough-and-tumble Southwest, plebeian democratic politics would be allowed to rise only so far before being neutered.

Another southern rural democrat seduced by moneyed politicians—but who wound up wrapped in glory—was the Tennessean Colonel David Crockett. Born in 1786 at the confluence of Limestone Creek and the Nolichucky River in what is now northeastern Tennessee, Crockett's renown as a rifleman and Indian fighter under Jackson during the Creek War helped win him election to the Tennessee state legislature in 1821 (where he supported the regime of Governor William Carroll). In 1827, he advanced to Congress as a Jacksonian. "I'm David Crockett, fresh from the backwoods . . . ," he supposedly bragged upon his arrival in the capital, "I can wade in the Mississippi, leap the Ohio, ride a streak of lightning, slip without a scratch down a honey locust, whip my weight in wildcats, hug a bear too close for comfort, and eat any man opposed to Jackson!" Reelected twice more, he had a falling out with the president over some land legislation in 1831 and was eagerly snatched up by the emerging Whigs, who were eager to prove their populist credentials with the electorate. After inventing an entire life of embellished Crockett folklore and publishing it in numerous forms—including a popular biography written by a good friend of Nicholas Biddle's—the Whigs sent him on a tour of the Northeast in 1834, where he praised the BUS, blamed Biddle's panic on Jackson, and performed his disarming king-of-the-frontier act. Eventually, Crockett's political enthusiasm diminished. Defeated for reelection in 1834, and embittered at what he imagined was Martin Van Buren's imminent rise to the White House, he decided to light out, he told a friend, "for the wildes of Texas," where the long-brewing fight between Anglo settlers and the Mexican government had finally become open rebellion.

By the time Crockett crossed the Red River and headed for Nacogdoches, the Texas Revolution had been underway for nearly three months. In November, following a battle between Mexican troops and settlers in Gonzales, a provisional Texan government formed in San Felipe de Austin. Stephen Austin, the great Anglo colonist and landholder (or *empresario*), having been jailed by the new Mexican military government, gave the movement his wholehearted support. On March 2, 1836, fifty-eight delegates, including President Jackson's close friend, the former Tennessee governor and Indian trader Sam Houston, signed a formal declaration of independence in Washington-on-Brazos. The insurgents then fell into squabbling about how to repel the Mexican Army, which was marching northward to crush the rebellion, under the personal command of Mexico's ruler, Antonio López de Santa Anna. One rebel force of about three hundred gathered at Goliad, the gateway to east Tejas, under Colonel James Fannin, while another smaller group, numbering just under two hundred men, held on in San Antonio. On February 23, Santa Anna and his army, eventually reinforced to twenty-five hundred men, laid siege to San Antonio, where the insurgents— commanded by the South Carolina–born William Travis and James Bowie, a frontier drifter, knife designer, and Mexican citizen—holed up in a Spanish mission popularly known as the Alamo. Among them was Crockett.

Rarely has such an overwhelming show of force won so little military advantage. Goliad, not the Alamo, was the real prize. Had the Mexicans simply waited until the arrival of their full artillery, they could have reduced the old mission to rubble with comparatively little sacrifice on both sides. But Santa Anna, humiliated by an earlier defeat suffered by his brother-in-law, General Martín Perfecto de Cos, was inclined to wipe out the San Antonio garrison, and the Texans' stubborn, suicidal resistance only deepened his resolve. "Our commander became more furious," a Mexican lieutenant colonel recalled, "when he saw that the enemy resisted the idea of surrender. He believed as others did that the fame and honor of the army were compromised the longer the enemy lived." Before sunup on March 6, Santa Anna ordered a full assault on the now encircled fortification, his soldiers raising ladders to climb over the mission's old adobe walls. Ninety minutes later, it was over. All but a handful of the rebels were dead, as were approximately six hundred Mexican soldiers, about one-third of the army's assault force. Although Santa Anna spared the insurgents' wives, children, and slaves, he ordered the surviving rebels, including Crockett, bayoneted and shot as "pirates," to serve as an example of the uselessness of the Texans' struggle.

An even worse atrocity was to befall the insurgents near Goliad, who, after surrendering in mid-March to an overwhelming force under General José de Urrea, were imprisoned but then summarily slaughtered on direct orders from Santa Anna. With the Mexican victory at the third major rebel redoubt at San Patricio in early March, the revolution seemed doomed. But in trying to mop up what was left of the Texan rebels—about nine hundred men under Houston's command—Santa Anna divided his armies and left his main force dangerously exposed. On the afternoon of April 21, as screams of "Remember the Alamo" and "Remember Goliad" filled the air, Houston surprised and overran Santa Anna near Lynch's Ferry on the San Jacinto River. After less than half an hour's heavy fighting, followed by an hour or more of vengeful bloodletting by the Texans, Santa Anna's army had been destroyed, and the next day, Santa Anna himself was captured trying to flee, dressed in a common soldier's uniform. At Houston's insistence, the Mexican commander ordered all Mexican forces to depart from Tejas. With the signing of the Treaty of Velasco in mid-May, the Republic of Texas was effectively free and independent—open for recognition and, many Texans hoped, annexation by the United States.

Not since Jackson's victory at New Orleans had Americans been stirred as they were at the news of Houston's startling triumph. "We have barely room to congratulate every man who has Anglo-Saxon blood in his veins," the *Globe* crowed, "on the redemption of our brethren in Texas from Spanish power." The mingling of racial and nationalist themes was no coincidence. To jubilant Americans, the Texans represented Anglo-American freedom and enlightenment, in a war against an inferior political offspring of the rotten, obscurantist Spanish Crown. Although an independent republic, Mexico, under its military chieftain, was at odds with its own liberal democrats (whom, the celebrating Americans usually failed to note, despised the American invaders even more than they did Santa Anna). It was also, supposedly, a clear and present danger to national security, against which the new Texas Republic offered a buffer.

President Jackson, for his part, had long regarded annexing Tejas to the United States—or more properly, he thought, reacquiring it—as an essential element of American expansion. He held the fanciful but sincere view that Tejas rightfully belonged to the United States as part of the Louisiana Purchase, and had been wrongly bargained away by Secretary of State John Quincy Adams in the Adams-Onís Transcontinental Treaty of 1819. By the middle of 1836, however, various considerations forced Jackson to move cautiously on the Texas question. Already suspected of having had a hand in the Texan uprising, Jackson could not afford to act precipitously without making some effort to negotiate with Santa Anna. On the domestic front, noisy abolitionists were beginning the charge that the Tejas uprising was part of a plot to grab a huge new area for the creation of many slave states. The veteran antislavery activist Benjamin Lundy, who had spent considerable time in north Mexico trying to resettle freed American slaves, led the attack, charging that the rebels' rhetoric about "the sacred principles of Liberty, and the natural, inalienable Rights of Man" was utterly bogus, and that they were actually engaged in a "*settled design*" to steal Tejas from Mexico and "*open a vast and profitable* SLAVEMARKET *therein.*" Normally, Jackson might dismiss Lundy and the other abolitionists as fanatics, but a presidential election was approaching, and Lundy had linked up with more prominent sympathizers including John Quincy Adams, who had returned to Congress in 1831. Care had to be given not to allow sectional suspicions from interfering with the victory of Jackson's chosen successor, Martin Van Buren.

The difficulties surrounding Tejas exemplified the paradoxical sectional stresses afflicting the Jacksonian Democrats. Although Jackson secured formal recognition of the Texas Republic, he only did so well after the 1836 presidential election had been decided, and after a personal visit to Washington by Santa Anna. Even then, the Texas question was far from closed, particularly over whether the new republic should be annexed to the United

States. And the prolonged battle over annexation would be shaped by both the effects of Jackson's policies and the evolving trends within southern politics. Indian removal had made possible the great expansion of the cotton slave kingdom. The success of the Texas Revolution, and the strong possibility of annexation, opened up even larger possibilities for slavery's spread. And so, Jackson further alienated (if it were possible to do so) antislavery northerners. Simultaneously, however, Jackson's policies on the BUS and nullification had generated a viable southern opposition to his Democracy, from the very planter elite whom the abolitionists accused him of coddling.

The burdens of these cross-pressures would be borne most heavily by Martin Van Buren, first in his presidential campaign in 1836 and then for the rest of his political career. Their full weight would only be felt, however, once the southern and northern anti-Jacksonian forces coalesced—an elusive goal for even the most-determined opposition organizers. Those efforts would unfold amid the last battles between Jackson and his congressional foes over banking and the currency.

"EITHER THE STATE IS SOVEREIGN, OR THE BANKS ARE"

On January 30, 1835, a misty cold morning in Washington, President Jackson attended the funeral services in the House of Representatives chamber for a nullifier congressman from South Carolina. Jackson looked careworn and frail, "scarcely able to go through with the ceremonial," the British traveler and writer Harriet Martineau observed from the gallery. At the end of the funeral, he followed the procession of official mourners onto the East Portico of the Capitol, where a young, thickly bearded man vaulted out of nowhere, aimed a pistol from point-blank range at Jackson's heart, and squeezed the trigger. The pistol cap exploded but failed to ignite the fine powder in the barrel, probably because of the wet weather. Jackson, instead of ducking, cocked

his walking cane like a club and charged his assailant, who produced a second pistol, which also misfired. With Jackson still
advancing and flailing away, the crowd subdued the would-be
assassin and carried him off.

The prisoner turned out to be an unemployed housepainter
named Richard Lawrence. When asked, under medical examination, whom he preferred as president, Lawrence replied, "Mr.
Clay, Mr. Webster, Mr. Calhoun," but he also claimed that he
was the legitimate heir to the British throne and that Jackson had
personally prevented his accession by killing his father three
years earlier. (The father, it turned out, had been dead for over a
decade.) Judged insane, Lawrence was cleared of criminal
charges and committed to an asylum. Jackson—who but for the
moistness of the morning air almost certainly would have been
killed—harbored his conviction that Providence had spared him
from a well-laid conspiracy by one of his powerful enemies. Others claimed that the violent mood of the riot-torn nation, and the
intense animus that Jackson provoked, helped push the gunman
over the edge and into the first attempted presidential assassination in American history. "A sign of the times," Bryant and
Leggett's *Evening Post* observed.

The months during and after the congressional Panic session
in 1834 had brought Jackson a stressful mixture of gloom and
elation. The Senate had censured him for removing the deposits
from the BUS and refused to recognize his protest. In the House,
the Whigs had bottled up a White House bill for the regulation of
the deposits and, at the session's close, combined with Bank
Democrats and anti–Van Buren southerners to elect John Bell of
Tennessee as Speaker over Jackson's loyalist James K. Polk. In
poor health once more, the president enjoyed a short rest at the
Hermitage during Congress's summer recess, only to learn after
his return to Washington that his estate house had burned nearly
to the ground after his departure. And still: the House had
approved, during the Panic session, resolutions supporting the
BUS veto and backing Jackson's decision to place the removed
deposits in a number of friendly state banks. With bipartisan sup-

port, the administration won passage of the Coinage Act, which revalued gold upward and led to the minting of vast quantities of gold coins (known as "Jackson eagles" or "Benton gold lozenges") as currency for small transactions. In foreign affairs, tortuous negotiations with France over American spoliation claims left over from the Napoleonic wars had led to a break in relations and the near outbreak of a new war late in 1834. But in February word came that upon receiving a moderately apologetic message from Jackson, the French Chamber of Deputies had backed down, and the crisis was over.

The happiest news for Jackson was the Treasury Department's announcement that, as of January 1, 1835, the federal debt would be completely extinguished. Having peaked at $127 million after the War of 1812, the debt still stood at $58.4 million when Jackson took office. Now, thanks to continuing receipts from the tariff and Jackson's insistence on applying the funds to debt reduction, it was gone. Roger Taney reckoned that it was the first time any major nation had ever succeeded in paying off its debt, which was true then and remains true today. Jackson, whose detestation of financial debt in any form had been born of personal experience as well as Jeffersonian dogma, hailed the impending achievement in his sixth annual message, crediting "the industry and enterprise of our population." The acclaim was nearly universal. To mark the coincidence of the twentieth anniversary of the Battle of New Orleans and the removal of the debt, Jackson's supporters held a gigantic, sparkling celebration in Washington. The *Globe* exulted over its hero's two great victories, "the first of which paid off our scores to *our enemies*, whilst the latter paid off the last cent to *our friends*."

The celebrations masked the appearance of a fresh set of political problems about what should be done with the new federal surplus, which by the end of 1835 would reach an astounding $17 million. That question was, in turn, entangled with the larger issue of what the administration would do about banking and currency policy now that the Second Bank of the United States was all but dead. Although Jackson had committed himself to giv-

ing a "full & fair" trial to his "experiment" in state deposit banking, there was still a chance he would support a moderate, constitutional version of a new national bank if the experiment proved
in any way deficient. Several plans appeared. The one that got
the most attention, formulated by Attorney General Benjamin
Butler's brother, Charles, was for a limited deposit and exchange
public bank, headquartered in Washington, that would also curtail the issue of bank notes of small denominations and substitute a metallic currency for most transactions. The last element
was the most salient, for Jackson had decided that shifting from
paper to coin was the best way to ensure that the nation's currency was well regulated. Butler's plan got nowhere, but the idea
of gradually prohibiting bank notes up to twenty dollars became
the latest object of Jackson's exertions.

Apart from Jackson's Indian policy, nothing in his presidency
has attracted more sustained criticism in recent decades than his
expansion of the so-called pet bank system and his push for a
specie currency after 1834. At worst, historians have ascribed the
continuation of the Bank War to Jackson's ignorant antibank rage
and his abiding hatred of Biddle, which ambitious state bankers
exploited to enrich themselves and create a gigantic speculative
bubble in 1835 and 1836. Even some of his most sympathetic
biographers and interpreters have conceded that Jackson's understanding of banking and currency was "naive" and even "a little
foolish," and that by sponsoring the pet state banks, he removed
"a valuable brake on credit expansion" and "accelerated the tendencies toward inflation." Others cite the policies as examples of
the rigid laissez-faire ideology—"to liberate business" from government—that supposedly guided the Jacksonians' every move.

There was, without question, a dominant antistatist cast, both
symbolic and substantive, to Jacksonian economic politics. The
neo-Jeffersonian motto of Blair's Washington *Globe*, later picked
up by John O'Sullivan's *Democratic Review*—"That government is
best, which governs least"—powerfully expressed the antigovernment creed. Yet as Jackson himself always made clear, the Jacksonians opposed large government not because it burdened

business but because they believed it was a creature of the monied and privileged few, constructed in defiance of popular sovereignty, that corrupted democracy. "Experience will show," the New York *Evening Post* said, "that this power has always been exercised under the influence and for the exclusive benefit of wealth." Too rarely have historians understood or even taken seriously the Jacksonians' repeated claims, after as well as during the BUS veto battle, that they aimed not to liberate private business interests from a corrupt government, but to liberate democratic government from the corrupting power of exclusive private business interests. Too rarely have historians appreciated the Democrats' willingness to wield federal power forcefully, over economic issues no less than over nullification, when they thought doing so was necessary to protect the democratic republic.

The administration designed its evolving economic and fiscal policies, including creating a specie currency, as new, fully constitutional means to perform Nicholas Biddle's old job. Those policies, although developed in a piecemeal, halting fashion, originated not in rage or ignorance but in reasoned theories of finance and economic development, as well as in readings of the Constitution in line with Jackson's own. Known, by now, under the general rubric of "hard money," these democratic theories had a long history, from the critiques of the Hamiltonian paper-money system in the 1790s to the writings, forty years later, of the antimonopolist Working Men and western money radicals like Thomas Hart Benton and Amos Kendall. They began to crystallize as a coherent intellectual force in national politics in 1833, with the emergence of what might be called a hard-money intelligentsia, later to be identified with the Loco Focos. Only then did the Jacksonians seize on these theories as a positive justification for their own banking ideas and policies.

The most successful statement was a treatise with an unpromising dry title, *A Short History of Paper Money and Banking in the United States*. Its author, the self-taught printer and journalist William M. Gouge, had been one of the signatories (and probably chief author) of the important Philadelphia Workie memorial against the BUS in 1829. Now, his limpid, massively documented explication became a runaway best-seller, both in its first edition published in 1833 and in a cheap popular edition printed two years later. The *Evening Post*, Blair's Washington *Globe*, and many other newspapers either serialized it or reprinted large excerpts from it. Theophilus Fisk, William Leggett, and other radical Democrats devoured the book, sang Gouge's praises, and became hard-money publicists themselves. Francis Blair made certain that the Kitchen Cabinet members read it, and early in 1835, the Treasury Department, under its new secretary, Levi Woodbury, hired Gouge as an in-house adviser, writing notes and memoranda that would help shape government policy long after Jackson's presidency.

The hard-money men's economic arguments were geared to minimizing the speculative boom-and-bust cycle that plagued all developing commercial economies. Banks, they charged, have a propensity to overissue notes, leading to inflated prices and, in time, to speculative mania. That mania feeds on itself, leading to further expansion of credit and overtrading, a depreciation in the value of currency, and a drain on precious metals. That shortage of metal, in turn, forces banks to contract their credit to borrowers and their emission of bank notes, which has a domino effect on the entire banking and business system, leading to panic and, finally, economic collapse. Thereafter, a few surviving speculators snatch up the property of the prostrate many—and the vicious cycle commences again. To bankers like Nicholas Biddle, the material gains, the transforming improvements, and the sheer adventure of this bold new sort of capitalist commerce were worth the risk of occasional setbacks and even depression. But to Americans with lesser resources, the "humble classes" for whom Jackson presumed to speak, the chronic insecurity was both baffling and hurtful, especially since the lion's share of profits in good times went to others, whereas in hard times they were the ones to suffer most. The surest corrective, the hard-money intellectuals contended, was to remove, as far as possible, bank-issued paper from the day-to-day transactions of the laboring many and replace it with reliable specie—"*real* money," Leggett called it—which would help in "the great work of redeeming this country from the curse of our bad banking system." Suppression of small notes, Roger Taney contended, would end the "fluctuations and disasters" inherent in a paper-based system. With a hard-money currency, the *Globe* agreed, workingmen "would be effectually protected against all the casualties and frauds of paper money."

Hard-money doctrines were not merely economic, nor were they dogmatically laissez-faire. Like Jackson's original justifications for attacking the BUS, they were essentially political and democratic, and they augured, in some respects, increased government authority over the economy, not less. Hard-money men insisted that no institutions independent of the sovereign people ought to be tolerated within the American government. Banks' involvement in extending credit to large borrowers was, by that standard, perfectly legitimate—a purely commercial task that did not encroach on the constitutional powers of the duly elected federal government. To give commercial banks power over the currency itself, however, was a plain encroachment, extending "too great a power," in Benton's words, "to be trusted to any banking company whatsoever." The only remedy was to exclude the banks from control of the currency and reassert the government's responsibilities and oversight—extending "the prerogatives of the Government to the very limits of the Constitution," as Francis Blair's *Globe* put it. Theophilus Fisk stated the matter even more bluntly: "Either the State is Sovereign, or the Banks are."

The implications of these arguments and the policies that they inspired cannot be minimized. The hard-money men explicitly rejected the idea of a commercial system run wholly by and foremost for capitalists. Instead, they favored a different, more modulated commercial system partially regulated by a democratically elected federal government—what might be called "democratic commerce." Sharp periods of rapid growth and intense speculation would be reduced in a hard-money America, but so would sharp bust periods of mass misery. Government would exert, in

some important spheres, more power than before to curb speculative frenzies, supplanting what one state Democratic convention called "a great irresponsible monied power . . . permanently
fastened upon the country," with a system that was directly
accountable to the people.

Although primitive by modern standards, this reasoning was
the furthest thing from the kinds of cure-all panaceas churned
out by later generations of marginal American money cranks. If
anything, the treatises of Gouge and his followers surpassed, in
technical rigor and thoroughness, those written by their opponents—including formal political economists like John
McVickar, publicists like Willard Phillips and the Reverend
Alonzo Potter, and political leaders like Henry Clay and Daniel
Webster. Nor, as many historians have charged, were the hard-
money men's arguments nostalgic, aimed at turning back the
clock to a bygone time of precommercial rustic virtue. Although
they often spoke of restoring the values of "plain republicanism"
and of curbing the moral corruptions of speculation, the hard-
money men did not agitate for a return to a fanciful America of
the past. They offered an alternative road to the future, one very
different from that proposed by bankers like Nicholas Biddle or
political leaders like Henry Clay—a future that was commercial
and expansive, but also more democratic, less prone to sharp
reversals of individual and collective fortune, and intended to
protect the acquisitive interests and prosperity of the industrious
many against the political abuses of the privileged few. And, most
remarkably, the chief hard-money advocate in America was also
the president of the United States—poised yet again, in 1835, to
reform the nation.

Jackson and his lieutenants went to work amid rising alarm
over the speculation and rising prices that had resumed after the
reversal of Biddle's panic in 1834. Several developments contributed to the mania. Jackson's removal of the deposits to the pet
banks (whose number would rise to twenty-nine by the end of
1835) inevitably encouraged some irresponsible lending, now
that the check once provided by the BUS had been largely

removed. But those effects have been exaggerated. Secretary of the Treasury Levi Woodbury—appointed by Jackson after the Senate rejected the anti-BUS man Roger Taney's appointment during the Panic session in 1834—acted to turn his department into what he later called "a central Banking institution," exerting a strong hand over the pet banks, especially in New York, by making new federal deposits contingent on the banks' holding sufficient specie reserves and not overissuing notes.

More decisive were the shocks caused by the skyrocketing federal surplus, a fortuitous (and, for the hard-money advocates, cruelly unlucky) glut in silver caused by international bullion flows, and a speculation boom in the buying of federal lands in the West, encouraged by the silver glut and the rising price of cotton. With the government still accepting paper notes for land-office purchases, the flow of paper westward became a torrent, and eventually filled the treasury's deposits with almost worthless currency. And as long as the circulation of small paper notes nationwide was not actively suppressed, currency values continued to plunge, despite the flood of Jackson eagles into the American market. "[T]his state of things cannot last . . . ," the *Globe* remarked in late spring 1835, reflecting a disquiet felt by hard-money men everywhere. "A reaction is certain to take place as the sun is to continue in its diurnal course."

The administration had already undertaken major efforts to curtail small-denomination paper and to assume the responsibilities formerly met by Biddle and the BUS, most successfully with the Coinage Act and Secretary Woodbury's regulation of the pets. In the face of the speculative boom and accompanying inflation, it continued its incremental reforms. In February 1835, James K. Polk reintroduced a regulatory bill, stifled by the Senate during the Panic session, that would have required deposit banks to hold in precious metal one-quarter the value of notes they had in circulation, and would have banned U.S. receivers from accepting the notes of any bank that issued notes under five dollars. A month later, Woodbury ordered the deposit banks not to issue notes under five dollars or to accept such notes in payment of debts owed the government. The suppression of small bills would continue over the following year until Congress, in April 1836, enacted a ban on notes under twenty dollars effective in March 1837 and required instant convertibility to specie of all notes. Woodbury, in an effort to end "all mystery" in banking, further ordered that the deposit banks issue regular weekly statements, open to public examination. The Treasury Department also expanded the number of state deposit banks to thirty-three, including institutions in North Carolina, South Carolina, Mississippi, and Michigan that were tied to the Whigs. Secretary Woodbury maintained that the primary criteria for selection of deposit banks was a record of sound management. Although political considerations always played a part, they could no longer always govern an expanding system.

Time and politics ran against the administration's reforms. Although several states joined with the federal government in suppressing small bills, the temptations of speculation inspired by the land boom had grown too intense to be denied. Biddle's supposedly responsible Second BUS—which originally touched off the inflationary spiral with its breakneck expansion before Biddle's panic—moved from capricious contraction back to rapid expansion and increased its loans by $15 million during the first six months of 1835; smaller banks followed suit. In 1835, with more than $22 million in federal funds sitting in the state banks, the amount of paper money in circulation rose by nearly one-third to $108 million. A year later, Secretary Woodbury's annual report predicted that there would be "much distress, embarrassment, and ruin" before the hard-money system's moderating effects could be felt. Thomas Hart Benton, speaking in the Senate, foresaw economic collapse: "The revulsion will come, as surely as it did in 1819–'20."

In Congress, the administration faced new resistance within Democratic ranks as well as from the emerging Whigs. If some Democrats had been put off by the removal of the deposits from the BUS, Jackson's hard-money plans sent a shudder of fear and disgust through the ranks. The Tennessean Hugh Lawson White, once a trusted friend of Jackson's, had already defected, less over finance policy than over the president's closeness to Van Buren, whom White despised. At the end of 1834, the Tennessee congressional delegation had caucused and nominated Judge White for the presidency, a shock and surprise for Jackson. So-called paper or Conservative Democrats, led by Senator Nathaniel P. Tallmadge of New York, who had backed Jackson's war on the Second BUS and resisted Clay's censure motion, now balked at Jackson's experiment in hard-money politics and financial regulation, seeking instead to advance the power of the state banks. Later mocked by Jackson as "*all Bankites in desguise*" and "the no party party," Tallmadge and the Conservative Democrats would eagerly pursue the expansion of paper currency. Some would even edge toward supporting a reformed national bank along the lines of Biddle's, assured that national prosperity required, in the words of the Conservative Gideon Lee, "a great moneyed power."

The Whigs, whom the Conservative Democrats increasingly resembled, resisted hard-money policies by reviving an old proposal of Clay's on land policy. As early as 1829, Clay and his followers had proposed a system of distributing a portion of federal monies made from land sales as an alternative to cheap land policies advanced by western Jacksonians—a system that would serve as a roundabout way for state governments to receive federal assistance for new internal-improvement projects. As long as the federal debt remained, the prospects for distribution were dim, but in 1835, with the debt erased, the plan attracted new attention. Clay devised a new version that would offer 15 percent of federal land sale proceeds to the states in which the sales had occurred, with the rest to be divided equally among the remaining states. Ignoring Secretary Woodbury's warnings that the surplus be set aside for federal construction programs and not left open to the states "for reloaning and private gain," congressional Whigs rallied to the plan. After Clay introduced his measure to the Senate, John C. Calhoun introduced a bill of his own on regulating the deposit banks. Over the next several months, the Senate Banking Committee, controlled by Whigs and Conservative

Democrats, knit the two proposals together, producing what was called the Deposit Bill—a measure that increased regulation of the state banks and further curtailed the issuance of small bank notes, but that included Clay's distribution plan, obnoxious to the Jacksonians, and more than doubled the number of deposit banks to eighty-one, to include even more banks friendly to the Whigs. Outmaneuvered, the hard-money Democrats tried weakly to separate the regulation and distribution portions of the proposal, but the Whig-Conservative bill passed both houses of Congress in June 1836.

Jackson and his allies were certain that their adversaries were out to destroy the hard-money experiment. Not only had the opposition saddled the administration with a distribution bill it did not like, the addition of forty-eight new deposit banks made Secretary Woodbury's job of restraining speculation much more difficult. Woodbury reported to Congress that the new bill placed enormous pressures on state banks. The *Globe* accused the congressional Whigs of deliberately trying to engineer another financial panic. Jackson had Taney draft a veto message but finally decided against delivering it rather than risk charges that he and his hard-money supporters were playing patronage politics by investing the huge federal surplus entirely in the existing, mostly-friendly deposit banks. Though repelled by the Deposit Bill, Jackson signed it. The land boom, predictably, continued, swelling federal deposits by 50 percent between February and November 1836. The federal land office turned into a gigantic government-sponsored confidence scheme, whereby speculators borrowed large amounts of paper money, used it to buy federal land, then used the land as collateral on further loans—all of which ensnared the federal government, as Benton observed, in "the ups and downs of the whole paper system."

As soon as Congress adjourned, Jackson unilaterally struck down the con game by having Woodbury issue a Treasury Department order (heavily influenced by Benton, and soon known as the Specie Circular) requiring gold or silver coin payments for the purchase of all federal lands—a "tremendous bomb thrown without warning," a contemporary later recalled. The circular's impact was almost immediate, as millions of dollars' worth of paper money was turned away. The Whigs hit the roof at Jackson's latest display of executive tyranny, and the Conservative Democrats joined them. When Congress reconvened in December 1836, the Whigs and Conservatives proposed a bill rescinding the circular and reopening land purchases to paper money. Only five senators, including Wright and Benton, supported the hard-money position. The House added its assent, and the bill reached Jackson's desk the day before the brief session's adjournment. Jackson, who in his last annual message had boasted about the circular and its great advantages to (once again) "the laboring classes," quietly killed the bill with a pocket veto, the final important act of his presidency.

Jackson's Specie Circular, by slamming the brakes on the western land mania and halting the shift of specie from eastern banks to the West, has traditionally received the blame for causing economic disaster. That interpretation now appears simplistic at best. The circular did not halt the land boom as much as had been previously assumed—or as Jackson hoped it would. Continued land sales, now paid for in metallic currency, ended up requiring large transfers of specie from the East, especially the New York City banks, over the winter of 1836–37. (Realizing this, Secretary Woodbury tried frantically to redirect specie eastward late in the autumn of 1836.) More important, supplementary interregional transfers of government funds by the Treasury Department, undertaken in anticipation of the redistribution that the Whigs' and Calhounites' Deposit Act stipulated would begin in 1837, were enormous. The largest New York City banks lost more than $10 million in federal deposits between August 1836 and July 1837. They saw their specie reserves drop from $5.9 million in August 1835 to $3.8 million at the end of 1836 (just before distribution began), and then drop again to $1.5 million by May 1837. Factors outside of American control, based on bullion flows and international trade patterns, also caused British banks to defend their own specie reserves and precipitously raise their interest rates. British demands for payments in metal from depleted New York banks, accompanied by northern crop failures and a sudden drop in cotton prices due to a glut on the world market, sparked the bank failures of early 1837 that were the harbingers of doom. But some sort of blowup had been foreseen by the hard-money advocates, alarmed by the western land speculation, long before the Specie Circular went into effect. The hard-money policies put into place to forestall disaster and change the entire basis of the currency were not so much the triggers for the subsequent distress as they were reforms that came into existence too late—and, thanks in part to the mitigating efforts of the Whigs, western land speculators, and soft-money men, too unevenly—to have much effect. Benton had been correct. In 1837, the crash came.

Jackson realized that his banking experiment had been thwarted, and that the economy had fallen into precisely the kind of speculative boom he had hoped to banish. In the later months of 1836, thoroughly disillusioned with what he now regarded as the irresponsible, unpatriotic state banks, he began thinking about what options remained open to him. He presented Kendall with the outline for a "Third" national bank of exchange and deposit, which would operate out of Washington, report regularly to Congress, and have the power to issue bills worth over twenty dollars. While passing muster, in Jackson's eyes, as a constitutional and democratic institution, the proposed bank could, he believed, provide a "model" to the runaway state banks and "check the paper system and gambling mania that pervades our land." But time had run out: Jackson's presidency was nearly over; the campaign to elect his successor was well underway; and any proposal for a new bank was bound to batter an already weakened Democratic coalition at, politically, the worst possible moment. Although just as worried as Benton and Woodbury were by the inflationary spiral, Jackson kept his proposal confidential, and the economy continued to gallop toward a breakdown.

To critics who blamed the situation on his hard-money policies and the Specie Circular, Jackson could reply that his political opponents, Biddle and Clay, with their obstructions to implementing his experiment in full, were actually the responsible parties. Yet the political impact of Jackson's policies proved greater, in 1836, than their economic and fiscal impact. The fallout from the Bank War and its aftermath united, as never before, the radical antibanking, antimonopoly elements of the Democracy, especially in the Northeast, with the administration. Apart from the singular case of New York City—where the Loco Focos harbored a distrust of Vice President Van Buren as an evasive trimmer on currency and banking issues—the pro-labor, anti-BUS radicals were now fully in the national Democracy's camp, and could be counted on to support it wholeheartedly in 1836. At the same time, the intense divisions between hard-money and Conservative Democrats encouraged the Whigs to believe that Jackson's policies—what Clay called his "ill-advised, illegal, and pernicious" experiment—had proved a political disaster.

In later years, the Whigs would take full advantage of the economic tribulations of Jackson's second term. Yet in 1835 and 1836, as both major parties prepared for the upcoming presidential election, economic disaster lay in the future and the continuing boom times drowned out any complaints about the Jacksonians' handling of the economy. At the state level, Whig candidates fared poorly in the 1835 elections for governorships and state legislatures as well as for federal offices. ("Politically, I am sick at heart," wrote the former Anti-Mason, now a Whig, Thurlow Weed, after he watched the Jacksonians sweep to victory in, of all places, Connecticut. "All looks fearfully, hopelessly black.") John C. Calhoun could be counted on for political mischief but little else, while the southern planters who had bolted from the Jacksonians had only begun to forge a working alliance with northern Whigs. Jackson's opponents had yet to prove themselves capable of doing more than mobilizing against him personally—and he would not be a candidate in 1836. As yet unable to mount a national strategy, they would conduct regional favorite-son campaigns. To fortify themselves and build public appeal, they also would viciously attack the imperial brute Jackson's chosen political heir, Martin Van Buren.

THE DILEMMAS OF MARTIN VAN BUREN: SLAVERY, HARD MONEY, AND A FRACTURED ELECTION

By the time Van Buren was formally named the Democracy's presidential candidate in May 1835, he had been hearing stories about how he would win the nomination for nearly six years. The nation, and its politics, had changed enormously—and in his appearance, if not in his politics, Van Buren had changed nearly as much. His auburn-blond hair had whitened and thinned, making him look less like the dashing pol of his early years than like a dignified, if a bit overripe, statesman. He had toned down his wardrobe, replacing the rakish orange cravats and white duck trousers he once preferred with more somber attire. He was as affable and engaging as ever—"l'ami de tout le monde," John Quincy Adams wrote—although decades of diplomatic dinners and formal receptions had thickened his waistline into a bourgeois gentleman's settled paunch. His prominent forehead, now completely bald, and his broadened features, framed by ample mutton-chop whiskers, had none of Jackson's tortured grimness, and could easily be construed as a visage of pliable complacency. But his deep-set, arresting blue eyes—twinkling at a clever remark, penetrating in discussion—showed that he remained a formidable political presence.

Since returning from his ill-fated brief journey to London as Jackson's designated minister, Van Buren had trod cautiously, always loyal to the administration but trying his utmost to avoid offending important constituencies. The original broker of the Jacksonian coalition—a product of ingenuity, shrewdness, and prudence—Van Buren had tried to contain the coalition through the mid-1830s, out of concern in part for the administration and the nation and in part for his own political future. His break with Calhoun had initiated his rise to becoming Jackson's anointed successor, yet the break and the ensuing battles over the tariff and nullification also caused Van Buren great difficulty because of his close personal and political ties to many South Carolinians, some of whom became nullifiers. He privately disliked Jackson's nullification proclamation because of what he called its "heresies [to the] republican faith," and he counseled the president to show greater forbearance. ("You will say I am on my old track—caution—caution," Van Buren wrote to Jackson, in a tone more loyal than critical.) Initially opposed to the removal of the government deposits from the BUS, Van Buren moved from artful ambiguity to support of the president. In the hard-money controversies that followed, Van Buren did his best to carve out a compromise position within the Albany Regency, which had split into a radical wing and a soft-money wing. In his official duties as vice president, Van Buren performed well, appearing, a friend of Webster's observed, "unruffled in the midst of excitement."

As he geared up for claiming the presidential nomination, Van Buren faced immediate problems in the South, especially in Virginia, where the Bank War and Jackson's resolute stand against nullification had caused massive defections from the Democracy. After the Southampton uprising, the suffrage and slavery debates, and the rise of radical abolitionism, Tidewater Virginians were skeptical of Van Buren for no other reason than that he was a northerner. It was said that he had opposed the War of 1812 (which was untrue) and that he had opposed the spread of slavery into Missouri (when he in fact had supported the Missouri Compromise). Because, in earlier times, he had been on friendly terms with Lewis Tappan, there were even charges that he was a closet abolitionist radical—"an avowed abolitionist in principle," the *Charleston Mercury* asserted. "God knows I have suffered enough for my Southern partialities," Van Buren complained in a rare show of frustration. "Since I was a boy I have been stigmatized as the apologist of Southern institutions, & now forsooth you good people will have it that I am an abolitionist."

Southern misgivings deepened when Van Buren began dealing with the one major obstacle to his nomination—the preference in some western and radical northern circles, including the New York Loco Focos, for Richard Mentor Johnson of Kentucky. Still beloved for his forthright attack on the Sabbatarians and his leadership on abolishing imprisonment for debt, Johnson had been touted for president by George Henry Evans and the *Working Man's Advocate* as early as 1833. Before long, an official campaign biography and pro-Johnson ballad were in mass circulation. A popular play, lionizing Johnson for his supposed slaying of Tecumseh at the Battle of the Thames in 1814, attracted enthusiastic audiences in Baltimore and then in Washington. Struck by Johnson's vigor—along with his ability as a western candidate, Indian-killing war hero, and Kentucky slaveholder to balance the ticket—Van Buren's managers decided to win him over by offering him the vice presidency. Johnson accepted, and his backers' battle cry—"Rumpsey, dumpsey, Colonel Johnson killed Tecumseh"—became attached to the Van Buren campaign.

Johnson's selection caused intense dismay in the South. Some planters regarded him as a coarse braggart who had exaggerated his claims to military fame. More worrisome were his domestic arrangements. Johnson had two daughters, Imogene and Adeline, by his housekeeper, a mulatto ex-slave named Julia Chinn. After Chinn died in 1833, Johnson took up with another woman of partial African descent, and in Washington he accompanied his out-of-wedlock daughters (whom he had provided with excellent private educations) to public functions and festivities, sometimes in the company of their respective white husbands. Johnson's flaunting of his sexual practice was a scandal, far worse than anything charged against John and Margaret Eaton. Johnson, one powerful Tennessee official wrote, was "not only positively unpopular . . . but affirmatively odious." When the Democrats finally convened in Baltimore in May 1835, with Van Buren's nomination a foregone conclusion, the Virginians offered William C. Rives as an alternative to Johnson. Van Buren's men barely assembled the required two-thirds' majority for Johnson, and the Virginia delegation hissed the outcome. In the autumn elections, the Virginia Democracy defiantly substituted Rives's name for Johnson's on the Democratic ticket.

The Whigs' dilemmas were even graver than the Democrats'. Although politically unified as never before, none of the nationally prominent opposition leaders could possibly win, as the ever-astute Thurlow Weed explained: "With Clay, Webster, or Calhoun, or indeed any man identified with the war against Jackson and in favor of the Bank or the Bank's Shadow, the game is up." Although drawn together against Jackson, the Whigs did not yet resemble a national party as much as a coalition of convenience. So heterogeneous was the opposition that there was little point in calling a national convention or even regional conventions. Instead, local editorialists and legislators came up with their own nominees. At best, such a fragmented, multicandidate effort might throw the election into the House; at the very least, it would help oppositionists mount strong fights for state and local offices.

In the South and Southwest, the quondam Jacksonian senator Hugh Lawson White of Tennessee recommended himself to oppositionists wary of the National Republicans with his standing as an "original" Democrat who had backed the bank veto. More important, White's supporters presented him as the only southern candidate in the field, a man of eminence who would stand up to the unsafe Yankee Van Buren and the abolitionist menace. In the North, a combination of midwesterners and mid-Atlantic Anti-Masons advanced the candidacy of William Henry Harrison, the undisputed hero of the Battle of Tippecanoe as well as, Harrison charged, the real hero of the Battle of the Thames. Currently living in obscurity as a court clerk in Cincinnati, Harrison had, in a successful run for a seat in the Ohio state senate in 1819, proclaimed himself a sworn enemy of all banks, above all the BUS, even though he was a director of the local branch of the BUS—a confusing and possibly disabling past that his managers did their best to bury, while Harrison claimed he was "not committed to any course" on the banking issue. But aside from his military glory, albeit somewhat faded, Harrison was a one-man balanced ticket, having been born in Virginia but relocated to Ohio. He was also a man, conveniently, with no recent political record whatsoever other than having been dismissed by Jackson for incompetence as minister to Colombia in

1829—which made him sufficiently anti-Jackson for his supporters' satisfaction. In New England, Daniel Webster refused to step aside in favor of the nonentity Harrison and had his friends continue efforts on his behalf, although finally he would stand as the main Whig standard-bearer only in Massachusetts. In the Southeast, Calhoun, although he would not jump completely into the Whig camp, could be counted on to dampen any remaining enthusiasm for Van Buren.

The Whig campaigners, at their most high-minded, repeated the charge that Jackson's executive tyranny endangered public liberty, and claimed that Van Buren had played a major role in creating that tyranny. The more perspicuous Whigs, including the state party of New York, also proclaimed themselves democrats, declaring that Van Buren and the Democrats were the designers of "a conspiracy, which seeks to promote the interests of the few at the expense of the many" and despoil the "money of the people," and that would eventually destroy all free institutions. Whom the Whigs were referring to as "the few"—political spoilsmen? pet bank stockholders?—was left to the eye of the beholder; the "many," however, were obviously the great honest mass of Americans, including whomever the beholder happened to be. Gradually, but steadily, the Whigs, at least in the North, were learning to befriend His Majesty the People and to cast the Democrats as the People's lethal enemy.

More often, the Whigs indulged in scurrilous personal attacks on Van Buren and his running mate that evoked the broader Whig imagery of the Democrats as parasitic partisans. Whig speakers and editorialists portrayed Van Buren as a cunning and unprincipled politician, out simply to enlarge his own power—"a crawling reptile," the former Anti-Mason William Henry Seward proclaimed, "whose only claim was that he had inveigled the confidence of a credulous, blind, dotard, old man." One slanderous biography of Van Buren, purportedly written by David Crockett before he lit out for Texas, described the vice president as "secret, sly, selfish, cold, calculating, distrustful, treacherous"—the perfect model of a slippery party politician. More elevated in prose but just as damning was a dystopia, *The Partisan Leader*, written by the southern novelist Beverley Tucker and published secretly by Calhoun's ally Duff Green. It depicted a shattered nation in 1849, suffering through the fourth term of Van Buren's presidency, with Virginia trying to decide whether to join the rest of the southern states and secede from the Union. Tucker, like other Whig caricaturists, also smeared Van Buren as an effeminate dandy, with hands "fair, delicate, small, and richly jeweled." Colonel Johnson found himself denounced in the North as a cruel slaveowner and in the South as a mongrelizer of the white race.

The Democrats countered with testimonials to Van Buren's "cool judgment," "practical wisdom," and "democratic principles." They also placed their candidate within the great democratic tradition, as a loyal Jeffersonian who, like Andrew Jackson, had been born to humble circumstances and had risen by his own merit and not by dint of privilege. Above all, the Democrats proclaimed, Van Buren had stuck by Old Hickory through thick and thin. Yet these encomia betrayed a nervous defensiveness on the Democrats' part, a fear that the Whigs' attacks on Van Buren's character were hitting their mark. As popular heroes went, the unfascinating Martin Van Buren was nothing compared to Andrew Jackson. Many of the virtues that Van Buren embodied and respected—loyalty to party, the ability to compromise, political cunning applied with supreme tact—were easily twisted into the vices of spoilsmanship, flaccidity, and false politesse. Above all, the political strains of the previous eight years caused Van Buren and his managers to worry whether their electoral base was truly secure.

One unexpected issue in the campaign, nativism, had only just begun to surface as a political distemper in the northeastern states. In the 1830s, the numbers of Irish Catholic immigrants to the United States had grown sharply, thanks largely to the falling prices of transatlantic steerage voyages. Protestant native Americans and British immigrants, intensely distrustful of the Papists as a political as well as a cultural threat to the nation's liberties, grew increasingly distressed, and at times, violence broke out. In

1834, a nativist mob stormed and destroyed an Ursuline convent in Charlestown, Massachusetts, stirred by lurid rumors of immoral acts by the nuns. A year later, the celebrated artist and inventor Samuel Finley Breese Morse, a virulent anti-Catholic and sometime Jacksonian, ran for mayor in New York City, and a largely Whig middle-class group, the New York Protestant Association, fell into street battles with Irish mobs. Van Buren ran afoul of nativist opinion when someone unearthed a fairly mild letter he wrote in 1829, as secretary of state, informing the Vatican that Roman Catholics enjoyed the freedom to worship in the United States. Questioned by nativist Whigs about his involvement in a "*popish plot*," Van Buren demurred and pointed out that he was not, himself, a Roman Catholic—trying his best to evade and defuse the issue without offending Irish-born voters.

Genuinely worried about Hugh Lawson White's candidacy in the South, Van Buren took a firm stand against the abolitionists while eschewing Calhounite pro-slavery. Having already been grilled by the Virginians about his alleged antislavery sympathies, Van Buren faced repeated allegations and innuendo that he was soft on abolitionism. The book with Crockett's byline noted Van Buren's past associations with the antislavery "fanatic" Rufus King, and charged that the two "thought, or pretended to think, alike on the Missouri question." Rumors persisted through the South that Van Buren was a radical Yankee who planned to free the slaves by act of Congress as soon as he gained the White House. (Overheard and then repeated, the rumors reached slaves' quarters and raised false hopes of imminent emancipation.)

Van Buren denied all of this utterly, as much to reassure the anti-abolitionist majority in the North as to mollify the South. Slaveholders, he wrote to one associate, were "sincere friends to mankind," whereas abolitionists were crypto-Federalists out to undermine the Democracy. When the postal controversy broke out, Van Buren made sure that New York authorities firmly sided with Amos Kendall and pledged that they would no longer forward any objectionable material to the South. In Utica, one

Democratic newspaper supported both Van Buren and the abolitionists; but when New York's abolitionists convened in Utica in the autumn of 1835, Jacksonian congressman Samuel Beardsley led a mob that broke up the meeting and destroyed the newspaper's offices, an event then publicized by Van Buren's men as proof positive that their leader had no use for the immediatists. Francis Blair's *Globe* pitched in by reminding readers of the obvious political realities surrounding the slavery issue. "Neither the Whigs nor the Democrats are exclusively confined to the slaveholding or free States," the paper pointed out. "How then can it be the exclusive work of either party?" Tolerating agitation over slavery would destroy the nation's political fabric—and both parties knew it.

Van Buren's most consequential demonstration of his antiabolitionism—and of his political clout—occurred behind the scenes on Capitol Hill. In 1835, as the mails controversy raged, the American Anti-Slavery Society stepped up its campaign, conducted since 1833, to petition the House of Representatives over a variety of issues related to federal support for slavery. Hundreds of thousands of fresh petitions bombarded Congress, now demanding an end to slavery in Washington, D.C. One of Calhoun's friends, the slaveholder freshman congressman James H. Hammond, saw in the petitions an issue even more incendiary and divisive than the mailings, and in December he proposed a House resolution that would instantly bar the abolitionist entreaties from consideration. Van Buren, seeking to defuse the abolitionist campaign without capitulating to the southern hardliners, supported a compromise version of the proposal that would refer the petitions to a House committee and keep them off the floor for debate. Such a policy, he said, would give "the abolition question . . . its quietus," and preserve "the harmony of our happy Union."

Luckily for Van Buren, a South Carolina nullifier, Henry L. Pinckney, agreed to propose the milder plan in the House. Although branded a traitor by the most vociferous anti-Jackson southerners, Pinckney stood by his resolution, and Van Buren rallied northern Democrats to support it. On May 26, 1836, a slightly toughened version of Pinckney's plan—which would soon become known as the "gag rule"—was overwhelmingly adopted as a standing rule of the House, over the stifled objections of John Quincy Adams, who declared the proposal unconstitutional, and the loud complaints of southern editors, who considered it a sellout. The outcome reflected the political realities the *Globe* had talked about. Roughly half of the Whigs and other anti-administration congressman simply abstained, while the rest split on sharply sectional lines, with the vast majority of northerners voting against it—some out of antislavery conviction, others knowing the affair might embarrass Van Buren in northern districts. Nearly four out of five northern Democrats backed the resolution, as a political compromise between the extremes of abolitionism and pro-slavery. Notably, the overwhelming majority of Democrats from Van Buren's New York, ranging from the Radical Churchill C. Cambreleng to the Conservative Gideon Lee, voted aye. The Calhounites and other state-rights extremists, having been outmaneuvered, either cast negative protest votes or, like the Whig Waddy Thompson of South Carolina, abstained.

While simultaneously gagging the abolitionists and isolating the hard-liners, Van Buren also sharpened his position on banking and the currency. In part, he hoped to counter the Whigs (and especially the southerner White) by charging that they were trying to throw the election to the House of Representatives to clear the way for Nicholas Biddle to step in, purchase the presidency, put the government, as one supporter exclaimed, "under the dominion of the Bank," and saddle the country with "a regularly organized Aristocracy." But Van Buren also had to patch up relations with the Democracy's northern hard-money wing. Although he had backed the Bank War and supported the use of coin in place of paper in minor transactions, Van Buren had angered New York's Loco Foco radicals by ignoring the proposals of William Leggett and others in favor of a so-called free banking system. The Loco Foco plan would have enacted a general incorporation law permitting any group to obtain a banking charter, but coupled with stringent state regulation of all banks. Van Buren's half-heartedness, along with his political alliances with the Tammany pols, whom the radicals despised, prompted the New Yorkers to withhold their endorsement. After attempting to straddle the issue, Van Buren finally decided, late in the campaign, to issue a ringing statement supporting the Specie Circular and to write a private letter (meant to be publicized) backing the deposit banks provided they were strictly regulated. Although he could not bring himself finally to support the Loco Focos outright (nor they him), his views were sufficiently radical to win the strong support of, among others, George Bancroft, Samuel Clesson Allen, William Leggett, and—in her return to radical politicking—Frances Wright. An old associate of Wright's and former contributor to the *Free Enquirer*, William Holland, ended up writing Van Buren's semiofficial campaign biography, hailing his subject as a proponent of "the most ultra democratic doctrines."

Viewed from a certain angle, there was merit in Holland's claim. In 1836, the Democratic ticket included a presidential candidate who had endorsed some of the most radical economic doctrines of his day, and a vice presidential candidate who had endorsed those same doctrines while defending the separation of church and state—and also flaunted the nation's most fearsome racist taboos. Change the angle, however, and the Van Buren–Johnson ticket looked very different—the coupling of a cautious party man eager to mollify southern slaveholders and silence the abolitionists, with an actual slaveholder whose major claim to national fame was his dubious celebrity as the supposed killer of a feared and despised Indian. Both images contained part of the truth, which is precisely how the Democratic managers hoped their ticket would appear—persuading just enough voters to see just enough of what they wanted to see in Van Buren and Johnson, and then vote Democratic.

They succeeded, although not without some troubling political developments. In the popular vote, Van Buren outdistanced the combined total for his opponents, but only barely, by about twenty-five thousand votes out of 1.5 million cast. Van Buren's margin of victory in the Electoral College was much healthier, and the Democrats generally ran strong in state and local races, but there were disappointments. A close look at the state-by-state returns nationwide shows that the great majority of new voters who had joined the electorate since 1832 voted Whig. The Democracy had not lost its hold on its older supporters, but was having a very difficult time attracting younger ones and voters who had previously abstained. Although Webster won only in Massachusetts, the cipher Harrison carried seven states, including at least one from every major region outside the South. Although Van Buren won most of the South and ran surprisingly well in Virginia, his margins in Mississippi and Louisiana were razor thin. Worse, he lost both Georgia and (to Jackson's disgust) Tennessee to Hugh Lawson White's "true Jacksonian" campaign. Even where he won, Van Buren's southern totals were feeble compared to Jackson's in 1828 and 1832. (The oligarchy of South Carolina, the last state whose legislature still picked presidential electors, cast its eleven votes in protest on behalf of the pro-nullifier North Carolinian, Willie P. Mangum.)

And still the Jacksonian majority held, retaining both houses of Congress (including a nine-seat pickup in the Senate) and sending the evolving coalition and its experiment in economic policy into another term in the White House. On March 4, 1837, the outgoing president, looking sallow but serene, rode to the inauguration ceremonies at the Capitol alongside his handpicked successor. Jackson had a new reason to feel vindicated. In the 1834 elections, his supporters had won a bare majority in the Senate, and after a long struggle, Democrats led by Thomas Hart Benton finally succeeded, in January 1837, in having Jackson's censure officially expunged in bold black lettering from the Senate's official journal. With satisfaction, Jackson watched another of his handpicked men—Chief Justice Roger B. Taney, his replacement for the old Federalist, John Marshall, who died in 1835—administer the oath of office to the new president. Van Buren, in his inauguration speech, promised he would uphold the spirit of his predecessor and keep slavery out of national politics—and included a pledge to veto any bill authorizing abolition in the District of Columbia.

The ceremony done, Jackson descended to his carriage, to an immense cheer from the throngs. If the nation was in greater turmoil than it had been eight years earlier, the transit of power was far more surefooted and self-assured than the inaugural melee of 1829. The displays that Washington insiders had found pitiable had been replaced by something more tested, more majestic. "I had seen the inauguration of many presidents," Senator Benton recalled, all of which "appeared to be as pageants, empty and soulless." Van Buren's installation, by contrast, "seemed to be a reality—a real scene."

JACKSON'S FAREWELL

Early on inauguration day, Jackson issued his farewell message, an address brimming with gratitude and a sense of fulfillment at what his administration had achieved. Yet Jackson's valedictory, like George Washington's forty years earlier, also included words of foreboding. The war against the banking aristocracy begun with the destruction of the Second BUS was not over, Jackson warned. "The paper-money system and its natural associations— monopoly and exclusive privileges—have already struck their roots too deep in the soil," he said, "and it will require all your efforts to check its further growth and to eradicate the evil." Then there were the sectional battles, instigated by those who would "sow the seeds of discord between different parts of the United States . . . to excite the *South* against the *North* and the *North* against the *South*, and to force into the controversy the most delicate and exciting topics—topics upon which it is impossible that a large portion of the Union can ever speak without strong emotion."

Having entered the presidency proclaiming the democratic idea that *the majority is to govern*," Jackson left it having witnessed how that idea brought not peace but further conflict, not the settling of arguments but their continuation alongside new arguments and rediscovered old ones. For Jackson, legislating the people's will and preserving the Constitution had come to mean advancing the battle against concentrated monied power while quieting the growing tumults over slavery. President Van Buren would follow his lead, only to discover that even Jackson's creative destruction and majoritarian reforms could neither fully describe, nor contain, the people's will.

10

THE POLITICS OF
HARD TIMES

Five weeks after Martin Van Buren's inauguration, the long-feared financial crash finally came. Commodity prices had skyrocketed over the winter of 1836–37, an inflationary boom fueled by foreign investment and worsened by two successive years of wheat crop failures. In Manhattan, a public meeting called by the Loco Focos in February to protest the runaway prices turned into a riot, as hungry workers plundered private storerooms filled with sacks of hoarded flour. While farmers failed to pay their bank debts, placing new pressures on overextended bankers, the decline of agricultural exports abroad threw the balance of trade against the United States. The imbalance, coupled with falling cotton prices, led British banks and creditors to demand repayment in hard currency from American borrowers.

On May 10, 1837, New York City's banks, having been stripped of much of their specie reserves in anticipation of the Whig-Calhounites' Deposit Act coming into effect, suspended the redemption of paper in gold or silver. Soon thereafter, nearly every bank in the country followed suit, causing prices and property values to tumble. In some places, bank failures and rising unemployment seemed to level the economy. "At no period of its history," one radical Democratic paper said of New York at month's end, "has there been as great a degree of general distress as there is at this day." The panic proved a prelude to more severe and widespread suffering. After a fifteen-month recovery beginning in 1838, the economy crashed again, causing a national depression that lasted three more years.

The Panic of 1837 and ensuing depression, and how to deal with them, were the outstanding political quandaries of Van Buren's presidency. Yet the struggle over economic issues did not distract from fights on other fronts, above all over slavery. Amid rising sectional discord, Van Buren continued to try placating the South without giving in to the most militant pro-slavery forces. Following the panic, Van Buren turned more and more to hard-money economic policies, but he governed as if radicalism on economics required conservatism on slavery, in order to keep Jacksonian slaveholders in line and the Democrats in power. The political results were devastating for Jacksonian loyalists. Hamstrung over slavery issues and divided over economics, Van Buren's party found itself upholding an increasingly unstable conception of democracy. By 1840, opposed by a fully evolved Whig Party, it faced repudiation at the polls.

LOCO FOCOISM IN THE WHITE HOUSE

Jackson's Specie Circular, and his administration's larger hard-money experiment, became the immediate scapegoats for the economic disasters of 1837 and after, but Jackson's opponents were up in arms even before the panic struck. Immediately after Van Buren's installation, Senate Whigs offered new legislation to repeal the circular. Conservative Democrats, led by Nathaniel Tallmadge and William C. Rives (who had returned to the Senate in 1836), tried to persuade the new president to abandon his loyalties to Jackson. After the panic, businessmen remonstrated with Van Buren and swore to resist the circular, peaceably if possible, forcibly if necessary. Nicholas Biddle, more convinced than ever of his own greatness, added a suggestion that his Pennsylvania Bank of the United States be made a government bank of deposit, so that the wounds inflicted by Jackson might be healed. ("If *I* can forgive them," he said, "they may forgive me.") Yet as spring turned into summer, Van Buren buckled but did not break.

Van Buren had three choices. He could renounce Jacksonian policy, rescind the Specie Circular, and propose the creation of a Third Bank of the United States—capitulating to the Whigs and restoring, institutionally, the status quo. He could rescind or modify the circular and sustain the deposit-bank system as it had existed, thereby moving closer to Tallmadge, Rives, and the Conservative Democrats—salvaging his Jacksonian label but rejecting Jackson's hard-money experiment. Or he could attempt the unprecedented by fighting for the divorce of the government's fiscal affairs from all private banks—what some radical Democrats and their supporters had begun demanding as "the absolute and unconditional SEPARATION OF BANK AND STATE." The majority of politicians, Democrats and Whigs, as well as virtually the entirety of large American business, would have preferred Van Buren to select either of the first two options. But as president, Van Buren mixed political pragmatism with a quiet but growing affinity for hard-money writers and radicals.

William Gouge had broached the idea of an independent treasury or "sub-treasury" plan in his *History of Banking and Paper Money* in 1833. By cutting all connections with private banks and collecting and paying out its revenues in specie, he argued, the federal government could end its corrupting collaboration with private capital, rein in credit expansion by locking up most of the nation's specie, and thereby modulate the boom-and-bust cycle. Reformulated by Gouge's Philadelphia friend, the free-trade theorist Condy Raguet, the concept caught on briefly in 1835 with southern anti-BUS state-rights men, but the time was not ripe. The union leader John Windt and other former New York Working Men picked up the idea, and in July 1836, at the outset of the Specie Circular struggle, the *Evening Post* vigorously endorsed it.

Thomas Hart Benton, who had first heard a rough version of the plan from John Randolph, outlined a two-stage process to the Senate in April 1836, involving removing the deposits from all banks and eventually excluding all paper money from government transactions. "The state of the paper system," Benton declared, had become "hideous and appalling, and those who [do] not mean to suffer by its catastrophe should fly from its embraces."

The failures of 1837 turned the independent treasury idea into a politically practical proposal, as a substitute for the pet bank system. Gouge's energetic memoranda and pamphlets from inside the Treasury Department tried to persuade Van Buren that the national welfare would be ruined unless the government's fiscal operations were affected "as little as possible by the doings of banks and speculators." Hard-money friends of Van Buren's, including the Loco Focos' ally Churchill Cambreleng and, from his deathbed, the venerable Old Republican Nathaniel Macon, wrote strong letters urging the president to stay the course. A freshet of polemics by Frances Wright, William Leggett, Theodore Sedgwick Jr., Theophilus Fisk, and other radicals pushed the subtreasury idea, as did public meetings in towns and cities across the country. One demonstration in Philadelphia— "projected and carried on entirely by the working classes," Henry Gilpin told Van Buren—drew an orderly but agitated crowd of twenty thousand, purportedly the largest the city had ever seen. Trade union leaders denounced the paper system, and a committee of Philadelphians soon produced a report that called for the government to cut its financial relations with the banks.

Van Buren—a self-styled Jeffersonian but no radical, and protective as always of party unity—took the advice of his sober political friends more seriously than he did any Loco Foco rumblings. Only after the moderate John Brockenbrough, president of the Bank of Virginia, endorsed a watered-down version of the independent treasury as a means to liberate state banks from government regulation did Van Buren begin to rally his forces behind the idea. As it happened, Treasury Secretary Levi Woodbury had already placed a considerable portion of the federal surplus in government vaults immediately after the crisis in May. (Woodbury was acting in compliance with the Deposit Act of 1836, which forbade depositing public money in banks that had suspended specie payments.) The effect was to take some of the exotic edge off the subtreasury plan. And when Van Buren prepared his version of the plan for delivery in September, he made sure to add features that pleased state bankers and might attract Conservative Democrats, including a proposal to issue new paper money in the form of federal Treasury bills. He also claimed he wanted to disentangle the economic crisis from "the passions and conflicts of party." Van Buren seemed to be on his old track, caution.

To emphasize Van Buren's restraint, however, slights his growing conviction that some sort of hard-money program was required to salvage both his Jacksonian bona fides and the nation itself. Like the rest of his party, the president blamed the failures of Jackson's deposit bank policies on the irresponsible banks themselves, as well as on the obstructionist Whigs. After the panic, only a divorce of the federal treasury and the banks would suffice. Although some of his advisers counseled otherwise, Van Buren paid very close attention to Gouge, the author of the radicals' primer, as well as to close friends like Cambreleng and the Bucktail veteran and hard-money man, Benjamin F. Butler. He never sought to turn banking reform into a cover for deregulating the state banks, as some state bankers desired. Quite the opposite: by empowering managers of the subtreasury system to accumulate state bank notes and demand specie payment, Van Buren's plan promised significant regulation of all state banks, above and beyond the former pet deposit banks. Although he couched his proposals in the familiar Jeffersonian doctrines of limited government—themes that later readers, critics and admirers alike, have sometimes confused for conservative laissez-faire—Van Buren, like Jackson, took them to mean that the government should not be enlarged to serve the interests of a privileged and ambitious few. ("It is not [government's] legitimate object," he bluntly asserted, "to make men rich.") Van Buren's conception of limited government did not preclude regulation for the public good, so long as government confined itself to the powers delegated by the Constitution.

Van Buren's message to a special session of Congress was lengthy but clear and direct, unburdened by the confusing verbosity that so often marred his public statements. Its stronger features included a sophisticated review of the panic's national and international origins, making points that economic historians would affirm more than a century later. The wording also displayed Van Buren's adeptness at making the dramatic sound routine, and the experimental sound like the most obvious affirmation of common sense. "[I]t is apparent that the events of the last few months," Van Buren said, calmly, "have greatly augmented the desire, long existing among the people of the United States, to separate the fiscal operations of the Government from those of individuals or corporations." Apart from a fleeting reference to "the laboring classes," the address shunned the class-inflected bombast of Jackson's bank veto message. Compared to the soaring eloquence of Jackson's nullification proclamation, Van Buren's subtreasury message had all the moral and political fire of a bill of exchange. But it was Jacksonian in substance and uncompromising about the main issue at hand, divorcing the government from the banks.

Whigs, Conservative Democrats, and the state bankers wailed, and the radical Democrats exulted. "He has identified himself wholly with the loco-focos—," the conservative *Boston Atlas* charged, "come forth a champion of the most destructive species of ultraism—and aimed at the vital interests of the country a blow, which if it [does] not recoil upon the aggressor, must be productive to the country of lasting mischief, perhaps of irretrievable anarchy." The new Conservative Democratic newspaper in Washington, the *Madisonian*, called Van Buren a convert to the wild-eyed radicalism of the original Working Men's parties. Hard-money Democratic officeholders sent letters of congratulations; Frances Wright hailed the plan as "the first practical, efficient, decisive realization of the Declaration of '76"; and the New York Loco Focos held a special meeting to congratulate the man they had distrusted for so long. Van Buren, having vindicated his self-image as a steadfast Jeffersonian, reveled in the praise and, without cutting his ties with moderates, reached out to the radicals. He sent a copy of the message to the New England Workie Theodore Sedgwick, asking for his opinion; Sedgwick replied warmly, calling it "unanswerable" and predicting that after "a great blow, a little thunder and lightning," the president would prevail. Van Buren soon befriended other radical writers and organizers, including a Free Enquirer-turned-Unitarian-turned-hard-money agitator in Boston, Orestes Brownson.

The special session of Congress made quick work of approving the White House's uncontroversial relief proposals, above all a suspension of surplus distribution to the states and the issuing of ten million dollars in new Treasury notes. But the independent treasury bill sharply divided the Conservatives as well as the Whigs from the pro-administration Democrats. The *Madisonian* called the contest over the plan nothing less than "a battle between civilization and barbarism." Senator Tallmadge denounced Van Buren's effort as "a war upon the whole banking system." Although support for the administration in the Senate seemed just large enough to win approval, the House, hopelessly divided into a multitude of factions, looked like a booby-trapped battlefield.

Suddenly, the wildcard of congressional politics, John C. Calhoun, commanded attention. After refusing to support either the Whigs or the Democrats in the 1836 elections, Calhoun had been thinking hard about how to strengthen his southern sectionalist political base. No longer, for the moment, a viable presidential candidate, he had subordinated his personal ambitions to defenses of slavery and nullifier doctrines—and into political maneuvering that, he hoped, would dominate the national government and sweep him back into contention for the White House. How, though, might his interests best be served in the wake of the panic? Many important southerners, like Waddy Thompson of South Carolina, had been making their peace with the Whigs, persuaded that what the wavering George McDuffie called "the wealth and intelligence of the northern and middle

States" would best protect the South against the growing threat of "unbalanced Democracy" and the abolitionism that it spawned. Yet Calhoun's loathing of industrialism had led him to reject his earlier similar musings and to fear and detest northern Whiggery as a threat to the South. Sooner or later, he calculated, northern businessmen would demand high tariffs and internal improvements in exchange for any alliance with the planters.

In Calhoun's view, the Democrats, now led by Jackson's second-rate sycophant Van Buren, presented better opportunities for manipulation. Calhoun would build on the earlier strategy of the pro-slavery Old Republicans: ally with northern Democrats; beat down the Yankee financiers and manufacturers; and then capture the Democracy, and the national government, for the South. And so, in October 1837, he decided not only to rejoin the Democratic Party and support the independent treasury bill but to add a tougher hard-money amendment, requiring that the Treasury accept only specie payments from state banks after 1840 and issue paper currency that would supplant bank notes. With the BUS dead, Calhoun had concluded, even before Van Buren's sub-treasury message, that any formal connection between the federal government and the banks would now only augment sectional favoritism and federal consolidation. But he would take that principled conclusion an additional political step forward. Confident, he wrote, that Van Buren had been forced "to play directly into our hands," Calhoun aimed to deepen the schism between his old foe and the Conservatives, and seize the balance of power for himself and the nullifers. Van Buren, with his independent treasury, would deliver a fatal blow to his own supporters, the New York bankers, while giving the South "a fair opportunity to break the last of our commercial shackles"—and open a path to political supremacy for Calhoun and his supporters.

As Tallmadge and the Conservatives would never back the subtreasury bill, pro-administration senators, commanded by the former Bucktail Silas Wright, immediately approved Calhoun's amendment, saying it was fully in line with administration policy. The amendment squeaked through; then the Senate narrowly approved the independent treasury. But the pro-treasury forces badly mismanaged things in the House, first by allowing Calhoun's foot soldier, Francis Pickens, to open debate on the bill's behalf (and deliver a harangue that, along the way, attacked Andrew Jackson and defended slavery), and then by permitting Churchill Cambreleng to mount a tactless tirade against the opposition that further alienated state bankers. The combined opposition—rallied by the Virginian Jacksonian-turned-Whig Henry A. Wise's slashing speech against the "Fanny Wright" campaign to destroy all banks—tabled the bill until the next congressional session in January.

Over the next two years, the fight over the subtreasury plan polarized national politics by emboldening the Whigs, sending the Conservative Democrats into irreversible rebellion, and pushing mainstream Democrats as never before into an embrace of the party's eastern, pro-labor, hard-money wing. The subtreasury bill again passed the Senate in 1838 and early in 1839, but it failed in the House. During the second of these rematches, the Whigs and Conservatives eliminated Calhoun's specie amendment by winning over a number of regular Democrats, chiefly from the western states (where, apart from Benton and a radical minority, there was little enthusiasm for hard-money policies). Calhoun duly turned against the bill, as did Pickens and other congressional nullifiers, and the House did not even bring the measure to a vote. All the while, the Conservative *Madisonian*, no longer pretending any Democratic allegiance, carried on with its vitriolic propaganda campaign, publicizing the speeches of Wise and Clay as well as Tallmadge, and depicting Van Buren as Nero to Jackson's Caesar. Outwardly cheerful, the president began looking, to some supporters, like a used-up man, "too easy & passive & willing to let things take their own course," according to John Milton Niles of Connecticut.

Thoroughly frustrated, many mainstream Democrats moved leftward, both in key eastern states like New York and Massachusetts and inside the administration. With patronage from Benjamin Butler, a new monthly, the *United States Magazine and*

Democratic Review, appeared in Washington under the editor-
ship of an energetic young radical, John L. O'Sullivan. (Dedicated to presenting the finest in American literary writing as well
as political reporting, the *Review* also lashed out, in December
1838, at the "dishonest factiousness" of the subtreasury's opponents.) One hard-money radical after another was rewarded with
either a federal job or a leadership post within the party—including (just before his premature death in 1839) William Leggett,
his antislavery attacks forgiven, as well as Charles Douglas and
the New York Loco Foco Moses Jaques. In July 1839, President
Van Buren visited Manhattan (where a large portion of Tammany
Hall had now embraced the radical program) and made a point of
being seen mingling with the Loco Focos in their own haunts,
including an evening at the Bowery Theater with Thomas Skidmore's former printer, Alexander Ming Jr., and Ming's wife. Not
only the New York radicals but the entire Democratic Party now
gained the nickname "Loco Foco"—a label that one meeting at
Tammany Hall accepted, much as in "the brightest days of the
illustrious Jefferson," the assembled declared, when the party
had not objected to being called Democrats.

The political costs of the Democrats' Loco Focoism—and of
the effectiveness of Whig and Conservative attacks blaming the
Van Buren administration for the hard times—began to become
apparent in the 1837 elections. In New York, where Tallmadge
and his Conservatives bolted and where Democratic Governor
William Marcy, a reluctant backer of the subtreasury, remained
cool to the radicals, the Whigs made stunning gains in local and
statewide contests. Elsewhere, from Connecticut to Mississippi,
the Whigs took command of state legislatures, committed to
defending democracy and enterprise, and repealed Democratic
hard-money and antibanking laws enacted over the previous two
years. Hard-money loyalists were inclined to blame their losses
on insufficient boldness by state leaders. ("What in hell is the difference between democratic principles this year and last year?"
the New Yorker Preston King asked another hard-money Democrat, furious at Governor Marcy's vacillation.) Plainly, however, as

long as the economy was depressed and the Conservative schism lasted, the Democrats' political position would continue to deteriorate—and the subtreasury plan would get nowhere.

A reprieve from the economic difficulties came in part from some of the more enlightened leaders of American business—and with Nicholas Biddle once again making trouble. In midsummer 1837, bankers in New York, restive over the suspension of specie payments, proposed a general meeting to agree on practical steps toward resumption. When the gathering finally assembled in November, the delegates were divided between those like Albert Gallatin and the other New Yorkers for whom resumption was a straightforward economic necessity, and the Philadelphia and Boston delegations, led by Biddle, who wanted to continue the suspension, exploit the crisis, and demand restoration of a national bank. Biddle and his backers prevailed. The debacle of 1834 seemed to be repeating itself, with Biddle once again trying to blackmail his way to a political victory by playing havoc with the economy. New York's leading private financier Samuel Ward complained that too many bankers had become so intimidated by Biddle and scared by their apprehensions about the subtreasury that "like a frightened school boy they have become frightened of a shadow."

Stymied at the national level, the New York bankers arranged for resumption of specie payments in their own state, to set an example to the rest of the nation. Biddle, as audacious as ever, issued a statement defending suspension on purely political grounds, and haughtily demanded that no general resumption begin until his Pennsylvania Bank of the United States was rechartered as a national institution. Late in June, he pressed the attack and boasted that the defeat of the independent treasury bill in the House had been "exclusively" the result of his bank's holding firm on suspension. But Biddle's latest game was nearly up. Exploiting his arrogance, the White House made overtures to other bankers, including an assurance that the Treasury would accept the notes of those institutions that resumed specie payments. Because the federal and state governments were using specie as much as possible in their own transactions, gold and silver had begun reappearing in American markets. Aided by the Bank of England's shipping of one million pounds in gold to New York in the spring of 1838, arranged by Samuel Ward, it was enough to turn bankers and public alike against Biddle's proposals and resume specie payments in July.

With the resumption came strong signs that the hard times were lifting, and for the ensuing fifteen months, the economic picture brightened. The Democracy's political situation duly improved. Although unable to prevent major statewide defeats in New York—including the election of William Henry Seward as governor—and significant losses in Connecticut and Mississippi, the Democrats carried six states in 1838 that they had lost the previous year and held two others. In Massachusetts, the radical Democratic historian George Bancroft finally replaced David Henshaw as party boss, which paved the way for the election as governor, in 1839, of the perennial Democratic candidate Marcus Morton, a hard-money convert. (After a prolonged counting of the ballots, Morton was awarded exactly the number of votes required to win.) The Whigs, as expected, ran well in the congressional races nationwide in 1838, but fell short of winning their first House majority; Conservative Democrats lost ground in the House and the Democrats held the Senate.

Thanks in part to some questionable dealings by Biddle's bank, enough leeway remained for Van Buren to hope that the independent treasury proposal might succeed in time for his reelection campaign in 1840. Gaining its new charter from the Pennsylvania legislature in 1836 had cost Biddle's institution nearly six million dollars, a steep price, but worth paying to survive. After the resumption of specie payments, several western state legislatures went on a borrowing binge, issuing bonds to pay for transportation improvements they expected would be serviced by future enhanced tax revenues. Biddle's bank led the way in aggressively marketing the state securities but badly overextended itself, and in 1839, when Biddle's and other institutions failed to meet their obligations to the borrowing states, the boom collapsed, forcing banks to close and nine states to default on their debts. Behind that disruption were additional dubious moves. Prior to the suspension of specie payments in 1837, Biddle borrowed heavily in Europe to try to corner the cotton market—just before cotton prices collapsed. Forced to draw on Pennsylvania Bank's credit until it completely evaporated, Biddle was suspected, in the spring of 1838, of attempting to raid the New York money market, which prompted Samuel Ward to negotiate the massive loan of bullion from the Bank of England. In ill health, Biddle resigned the bank's presidency in March 1839, but his successors continued his perilous policies. In early autumn, renewed financial difficulties prompted British banks to call in specie payments from the United States once again. The BUS was the first to resuspend specie payments on October 9, which sparked the rapid collapse of banks and the government defaults throughout the South and West. The latest panic plunged the nation into another, far deeper economic depression.

The second collapse would in time further damage Van Buren's public standing. In the short term, however, the BUS's perceived role as the trigger for the latest crisis had a very different effect, reminding the public of Biddle's counterattacks of 1834 and his obstructionism after the bank crisis in 1837. "In every respect," the wizened ex-Biddle supporter Albert Gallatin, now in his late seventies, would say of Biddle's operation, "it has been a public nuisance . . . the principal, if not the sole, cause of the delay in resuming and of subsequent suspensions." Biddle's disgrace linked Van Buren once again in the public imagination with the hero of the Bank War, Andrew Jackson. More generally the collapse of 1839, which could not be blamed on the Specie Circular or any other government action, bolstered the Jacksonians' contentions that the paper-fueled banking system was fundamentally unsound.

Despite the political turmoil and divisions that had hampered Van Buren during his first two years as president, the shift in public opinion gave renewed hope to the hard-money supporters of the subtreasury. But the fate of Van Buren's brand of Loco

Focoism also depended on more tangled political realities in Washington. Above all, the White House was anxious over how Calhoun, his firebrand followers, and the other southerners in Congress would react. And events outside Congress, connected with slavery, would ensure that those reactions, along with Van Buren's political strategy, depended on much more than specie flows and the ups and downs of wholesale commodity prices.

Since the mid-1830s, continued agitation by the American Anti-Slavery Society and other northern abolitionists had hardened pro-slavery sentiments in the South. The tabling of abolitionist petitions to Congress under the gag rule did not calm the situation as Van Buren and other Democratic leaders had hoped it would. Once Calhoun had decided, in 1837, to return to the Democratic Party, pressure intensified on Van Buren to mollify him, along with the milder southern Democrats, over slavery. And in trying as hard as he did to calm the South, Van Buren handed fresh ammunition to antislavery northern Whigs, abolitionist radicals, and even some hard-money radical Democrats who were already offended by his friendliness to the slaveholders and by his willingness to restrict Americans' rights to speak freely about slavery. The effect, ironically, was to reinvigorate an antislavery movement that was facing its own crisis.

ABOLITIONISM'S RECKONING

On April 28, 1836, in St. Louis, Francis McIntosh, a free black riverboat worker, was arrested and jailed on charges that he had killed a deputy sheriff and injured a second. A mob gathered, removed McIntosh from his cell, chained him to a large tree at the outskirts of town, and burned him to death. A grand jury was quickly impaneled, but on instructions of the presiding judge, one Luke E. Lawless, the jurors indicted no one. Near the end of his prepared remarks, Judge Lawless insinuated that the dead black McIntosh had been influenced by abolitionist doctrines, as "indicated by his peculiar language and demeanor," and he held up and read from a local antislavery newspaper, the *St. Louis Observer*, to prove his point. Lawless's words incited violence. On July 21, a large crowd smashed into the *Observer*'s office, destroyed hundreds of dollars' worth of printing materials, and threw the pieces into the Mississippi River. The paper's editor, a thirty-two-year-old former seminarian named Elijah Lovejoy, immediately quit St. Louis but reestablished his operation in the town of Alton, across the river in the free state of Illinois.

Lovejoy, a native of rural Maine, had come to the antislavery cause through his deep religious convictions. Raised in a devout household with his younger brother Owen (who would also become an abolitionist leader), he graduated first in his class from the Baptists' Waterville College, then traveled to St. Louis, where he established a school and became the copublisher of an anti-Jackson newspaper and a Sabbatarian reform activist. After having an intense religious experience in 1832, he returned East to complete ministerial training at the Theological Seminary of Princeton (later the Princeton Theological Seminary), the leading Presbyterian institution in the country. Then, in 1835, he doubled back to St. Louis to accept positions as Presbyterian pastor and editor of the *Observer*. Only peripherally perturbed by slavery, Lovejoy made his mark with slashing attacks on Roman Catholicism, and earned a deserved local reputation for religious bigotry. But living amid slavery in Missouri also stirred his conscience, and over the winter of 1835–36, he devoted increasing space in the *Observer* to antislavery articles and editorials. Lovejoy was not a Garrisonian immediatist, but the white citizens of St. Louis did not bother with fine distinctions and began hounding him as a promoter, in one vigilante committee's words, of "insurrection and anarchy, and ultimately, a disseverment of our prosperous Union."

After moving to Alton, Lovejoy vowed that his new *Alton Observer* would chiefly discuss religious matters. Although they lived without slavery, Alton's white citizenry, typical of central and southern Illinois, despised abolitionist agitation. Yet gradually Lovejoy expanded both his antislavery editorializing and his antislavery activism, aided by his typesetter, a self-taught black, John Anderson, who had moved from St. Louis to Alton when he learned Lovejoy had relocated there. In mid-August 1837, Lovejoy signed a petition calling for a meeting in October in one of Alton's Presbyterian churches to organize a state antislavery society. Local anti-abolitionists, believing Lovejoy had betrayed them, mobbed and destroyed his press; Lovejoy obtained a new one, but another mob destroyed it before it could be removed from its crates. When the antislavery delegates finally met in Alton in October, they arranged for the delivery of yet another press, courtesy of the Ohio Anti-Slavery Society. In an impassioned speech before a hastily organized public meeting, Edward Beecher, son of the renowned Lyman Beecher, denied Lovejoy had any intention to harm the community and insisted only on his American rights to "free discussion." But taking no chances, and lacking protection from town authorities, Lovejoy joined an ad hoc militia to protect himself and his new press once it arrived.

As expected, a mob turned out and threw rocks and brickbats at the warehouse where the new press was sent. One rioter attempted to torch the warehouse's roof; a group of Lovejoy's defenders ran out of the building and fired shots into the crowd; one of the mob fell, mortally wounded. Berserk, the crowd advanced, and the incendiary climbed back up his ladder to the roof. Lovejoy stepped outside and aimed his pistol at the arsonist, but five shots instantly hit the editor in the chest. He managed to stagger back to the warehouse, where he quickly crumpled and died. The mob then completed what it had come to do, routing Lovejoy's small band and destroying the accursed antislavery machine.

Elijah Lovejoy's martyrdom, the first murder of a white antislavery leader, shocked and emboldened the growing abolitionist movement, but its implications were much broader. For years, abolitionist meetings and speakers had been subject to physical attack. The abolitionist mails controversy and the congressional gag rule had raised charges that the South was trying to muzzle its critics. Yet never before had the issue of free speech arisen so dramatically. Lovejoy was, after all, an ordained minister. His major offense, prior to his appearance in Alton, had been to criticize a lawless lynching—and a lawless judge named Lawless who insisted on letting the lynchers go free. If Reverend Lovejoy's rights could be extinguished with impunity, and on pain of death, whose rights were then safe? Theodore Dwight Weld hammered the point home in an angry eulogy to Lovejoy:

> The empty name [of freedom] is everywhere,—*free* government, *free* men, *free* speech, *free* people, *free* schools, and *free* churches. Hollow counterfeits, all! FREE! It is the climax of irony, and its million echoes are hisses and jeers, even from the earth's ends. FREE! *Blot it out*. Words are the signs of *things*. The substance has gone! Let fools and madmen clutch at shadows.

What had begun in efforts to silence incendiary black agitators like David Walker and their white admirers like William Lloyd Garrison now looked like a lethal campaign to curtail free speech.

The renewed repression had contradictory effects on the abolitionist movement. Anti-abolitionist violence evoked public sympathy in the North, as did the growing impression that southern officials, supported by pliable northern Democrats, were violating constitutionally protected freedoms. Those perceptions fed antisouthern feelings, which in turn helped spike the membership of abolitionist societies in 1837 and 1838. Yet the unremitting anti-abolitionist reaction and Congress's obduracy were also discouraging. By the time Elijah Lovejoy was given a hero's funeral in Alton, the American Anti-Slavery Society had been hard at work for nearly four years but had failed to free a single slave. No practical reform of the nation's laws seemed imminent. The only major constitutional change in the North coincided with the abolitionist efforts in Pennsylvania in 1837–38, when a Democratic-dominated state constitutional convention eliminated voting rights for black men. The presidential election of

1836 offered no grounds for optimism. In the mainline northern Protestant churches, anti-abolitionists still prevailed, and even among evangelicals, abolitionists were in the minority. Among veteran field representatives and traveling speakers, the surge of rededication that followed the Lovejoy murder could not stem mounting frustration coupled with fatigue. The economic hardships after the Panic of 1837 drained the movement of vital funds as well as self-confidence.

Philosophical divisions also plagued the AA-SS. Especially troublesome was the growing breach between, on one side, Garrison and his loyalists and, on the other, the society's evangelical funders and managers, led by Lewis and Arthur Tappan. The evangelicals had never felt entirely comfortable with abolitionism's symbolic leader. Although he had been raised a Baptist and spoke of sin and Christian ethics, Garrison had never joined a church or experienced a religious conversion. In the fall of 1836, Lewis Tappan arranged for Garrison and his family to travel to New York, all expenses paid, to attend a three-week training session for AA-SS agents, where they could talk over the state of the movement. Garrison hoped to persuade Tappan that he was not some "great stumbling-block" to the cause, and Tappan was reminded how much he liked and admired Garrison. Tappan was distressed to hear, however, that his guest now abjured family prayer and church attendance, and that he believed the regular clergy was spiritually useless.

In the spring of 1837, Garrison took an even larger step away from the Tappans and toward the unorthodox netherworld of religious perfectionism when he became, briefly, a disciple of John Humphrey Noyes. A former student of Yale's Nathaniel Taylor, Noyes was one of thousands of northerners gripped by the Second Great Awakening whose spiritual journeys took them outside all orthodoxies and into a world of complete free will and total deliverance from sin. The perfectionists were particularly ubiquitous in New York's Burned-Over District. (Noyes eventually made Oneida his headquarters.) For Noyes, spiritual deliverance involved, among other practices, the downing of gin drinks in search of what he called "Gospel liberty," as well as a polygamous sexual arrangement that he called "complex marriage." Garrison accepted none of that, but he was captivated by Noyes's belief that sinful America would be destroyed by the Bible, once Americans renounced all of their corrupted institutions, including the federal government. This so-called come-outer impulse (based on the book of Revelation's command to sinners to "come out" of Babylon) brooked no compromise with sin, nor any connection with ungodly institutions. Garrison, impressed by Noyes's pacifism as well as his perfectionism, was soon reprinting one of Noyes's slogans in the *Liberator*: "*My hope of the millennium begins where Dr. Beecher's expires—viz*, AT THE OVERTHROW OF THIS NATION."

Garrison's newfound apocalyptic anti-institutionalism fused well with his already highly developed sense of moral absolutism and caused increased consternation in antislavery's ranks, as when he criticized the murdered Elijah Lovejoy for raising a small armed militia. (Although Lovejoy, Garrison allowed, "was certainly a martyr—strictly speaking—he was not . . . a Christian martyr.") But the truly important shift concerned what came to be known as "the woman question." Beginning with Lucretia Mott's insistent interventions at the founding convention of the AA-SS, women had always played a large role in the everyday life of the movement, especially as organizers of petition campaigns. Garrison took particular care to include the voices of women, black and white, in the *Liberator*, including the formidable black orator and organizer Maria Stewart. But the idea that women should have a role as speakers on behalf of the AA-SS, let alone help govern the movement outside of their own separate organizations, was disturbing to some in the mainline and evangelical antislavery leadership and anathema to others.

Ignoring complaints that he was promoting "Fanny Wright" heresies, Garrison strongly encouraged the women's work, above all the writings and speeches of Angelina and Sarah Grimké, South Carolina sisters who had moved north, converted to Quakerism, and joined the immediatist cause with Garrison as their mentor. By 1837, Garrison had added women's rights and pacifist nonresistance to the *Liberator* group's agenda for radical reform—a step the movement's conventional evangelicals denounced as at once a distraction from the movement's overriding cause and an endorsement of what one minister called "unnatural" presumptions about the sexes. Convinced that Garrison was injecting an impious "speculative antinomianism" into antislavery, Lewis Tappan and his allies braced themselves for a showdown over control of the AA-SS.

The Garrisonian fracture was not the only source of disunity. Although black abolitionists remained loyal to the AA-SS, blacks' failure in general to rise higher than the ranks of the group's secondary leadership, and their feelings that the whites (except for Garrison) were patronizing them, caused constant tension. Among the AA-SS leaders, meanwhile, a battle was brewing between what might be called the moralist and the political factions—those who wanted the movement to adhere strictly to moral suasion and those who believed it was time to participate actively in mainstream electoral politics. Garrison and the come-outers would, of course, steer clear of immoral institutionalized politics; so would the Tappanite evangelicals, with their high-minded attachment to converting souls through moral argument. Yet by 1839, a growing minority of immediatist leaders was pushing for new experiments in political abolition. They included a major funder of the cause, Gerrit Smith, as well as the movement veterans Henry B. Stanton, James G. Birney, Alvan Stewart, Elizur Wright, and Joshua Leavitt. To ignore the electoral franchise, Birney charged, was "inconsistent with the duty of abolitionists under the constitution."

While the abolitionists sorted out their differences, the focus of antislavery attention shifted to Washington—and to the persistent parliamentary attack on the gag rule undertaken by a small group of northern congressman led by the aging but feisty John Quincy Adams. Deeply depressed after his defeat by Jackson in 1828, Adams had recovered by indulging his appetite for political maneuvering, and in 1830, at the urging of his fellow

National Republicans and with the support of the burgeoning Anti-Mason movement, he won a seat in Congress in a landslide. ("My election as President of the United States," he wrote in his diary, "was not half so gratifying to my inmost soul.") Thereafter, propelled in part by political calculation, in part by his liberal piety, and in part by his dislike of Henry Clay—whom he now regarded as imperious and untrustworthy—Adams became, in his own words, a "zealous Antimason."

Anti-Masonry permitted Adams to find a political home free of the three groups whom he blamed for his own political woes and the nation's: old-line New England Federalists, especially in Boston (many Masons among them), who had regarded him as a traitor ever since he supported Thomas Jefferson's embargo; pro-Jackson slaveholders and their northern sympathizers (many Masons among them), who had turned him out of the presidency; and his longtime rivals for the leadership of the National Republicans, chief among them the Mason Henry Clay. Anti-Masonry fed Adams's distaste for political parties as corrupt vehicles for personal ambition. It also put him in contact with a kind of popular politics he had never before experienced—a democratic movement that, though commanded by political operatives such as Thurlow Weed, had been initiated by poor and middling farmers against the rich and privileged and retained its demotic character. Adams described his involvement in the movement in some unintentionally amusing passages in his diary, including one relating his arrival in Boston by chaise from Quincy to attend an Anti-Mason convention in 1831—where he found that "of the aristocracy, not one" was present. It was not the sort of meeting the Massachusetts mandarin was used to attending, and it gave him a taste for the way, with tempered ardor, that ordinary men could influence politics for the better.

By 1835, however, political Anti-Masonry was on its last legs, a victim of its own success once New England legislatures restricted the giving and taking of Masonic oaths and lodge membership plummeted. In Massachusetts, Daniel Webster reigned supreme over the new Whig Party, and when Webster crushed an

Anti-Mason effort to elevate Adams to the Senate, some of Adams's supporters, including his son Charles Francis Adams, urged him to back Van Buren instead of Webster for the presidency. Unable to support Jackson's loyal successor, Adams remained neutral in 1836. Thereafter, realizing that Anti-Masonry had no political future, he, like most of his fellow Anti-Masons, joined the Whigs. Yet if he was a Whig in name, Adams had no intention of becoming a party man, or abandoning his reputation, enhanced with age, as a splendidly independent figure, now known (sometimes admiringly, sometimes ironically) as "Old Man Eloquent." He would take, as his special mission, overturning the gag rule.

Prior to the 1830s, Adams had publicly displayed no desire to defend, let alone promote, the antislavery cause. His parents, and especially his mother, Abigail, had passed along to him their antislavery views. In 1820, during the debates over the Missouri crisis, Adams had some fascinating conversations with John C. Calhoun, after which he remarked in his diary on the perversity and hypocrisy of the slaveholders and noted that "[i]f the Union must be dissolved, slavery is precisely the question upon which it ought to break." Yet Adams, the nationalist, quietly endorsed the Missouri Compromise, adding to a long public record of seeming indifference on slavery and its spread. Nor did Adams think highly of the radical abolitionists, least of all Garrison and the Tappans, whom he regarded as fanatics. In 1831, Adams did obligingly present to the House fifteen petitions asking for the abolition of slavery and the slave trade in Washington. He also refrained from joining the anti-abolitionist chorus of Democrats and Whigs, and privately declared himself pleased that developments were "tending to universal emancipation." But as late as October 1835, Adams assured his constituents that he had no intention of getting mixed up in what he called the "Slave and Abolition whirligig." When new parcels of abolitionist petitions arrived in Washington in 1836, Adams berated the immediatists for engaging in tactics that would never win over a majority in the North and would only enrage the South.

The gag rule, coming so soon after the abolitionist mails controversy, changed everything. Both J. H. Hammond's proposal and Henry Pinckney's milder one to disregard abolitionist petitions struck Adams as fundamental violations of Americans' rights and an effort by southern congressmen to turn the House into their own private debating society. During the closing arguments over the Pinckney resolution, Adams rose to explain his opposition, but before he could proceed, southerners including Henry Wise blocked him with demands to call the question. "Am I gagged or not?" Adams asked, thereby giving the resolution its name.

Adams had only begun to fight. With the help of a handful of former Anti-Mason Whigs, he launched a hit-and-run campaign against the gag rule, trying to tie up the House in order to reopen debate over the matter. Careful never to say whether he thought slavery ought to be abolished, Adams rose on the floor virtually every day, always with a fresh abolitionist petition in hand, asking whether it fell under the gag rule's ban. He outdid himself on February 6, 1837, when he presented a petition signed by twenty-two persons "declaring themselves to be slaves." Waddy Thompson (earlier Ely Moore's antagonist) jumped to his feet, ripped into the Massachusetts madman, and proposed censuring Adams severely for his "gross disrespect to the House." It was bad enough for any Yankee to treat a petition from slaves as if slaves were citizens; even worse, from Thompson's perspective, the miscreant was a member of his own party, whose stunt reinforced southern Democratic claims that the Whigs were unreliable on slavery. "The sanctuary of age is not lightly to be violated," Thompson exclaimed, "but when that sanctuary is used to throw poisoned arrows, it ceases to be sacred."

Other infuriated southerners lined up to pummel Adams verbally, charging him with inciting a slave insurrection and demanding that he at long last be censured. Then Adams sprung his trap—for the slaves' petition, he now told his colleagues, was actually a request by the petitioners that they continue to be held as slaves. Did an effort to help slaves stay bondsmen deserve censure? Adams asked sardonically. Chuckles rippled through the

House. Thompson, embarrassed, denounced Adams anew for trying to turn his baiting of the South into a light amusement. Two more days of speeches followed. In his final address, Adams went in for the kill. Alluding to a threat by Thompson to have him indicted as an incendiary by a grand jury in Washington, he bid Thompson to educate himself about civil liberty and asked him whether a congressman should be indicted, let alone censured, merely for presenting a petition. "If that, sir, is the law of South Carolina," he cuttingly observed, "I thank God I am not a citizen of South Carolina."

Adams might as well have set off a bomb. (The transcript in the *Register of Debates* notes that "general agitation" followed his remark.) Not only had he made a laughingstock of the proud militant Thompson; not only had he made a mockery of the gag rule—Adams had focused the attention of the entire House on the slaveholders' willingness to limit free speech whenever, and wherever, they chose. A resolution condemning all House members who would present any petition from slaves then failed by a margin of 105 to 92, after which Thompson's effort to censure Adams went down to a greater defeat, with even Henry F. Pinckney voting against the motion. The pro–gag rule coalition reasserted itself very quickly, to be sure. In December 1837 and at the same time next year, the House endorsed gag orders similar to Pinckney's original, with northern Democrats once again lining up to support their southern counterparts, and northern Whigs standing in opposition. But for a moment, John Quincy Adams had blasted apart the gentlemen's agreement to keep the slavery issue out of national debates.

Two years later, the legal and political fallout from a shipboard rebellion by captive blacks brought Adams back to the center of antislavery politics, this time at the Supreme Court instead of the House, and in much closer connection with the abolitionists. On July 1, 1839, members of a cargo of fifty-three Africans (most of them from the Mende tribe) who were being held aboard the schooner *Amistad*, sailing from Havana, suddenly took over the ship, killing the captain and the cook. Most of the rebels had originally been part of a coffle of six hundred, shipped illegally from Lomboko on the west coast of Africa to Cuba. Bought by two speculators named Ruiz and Montes in Havana, they had been bound for the sugar plantations of Guanaja, on the other side of the island, when, under the leadership of a powerfully built man in his midtwenties named Sengbe Pieh (translated by one of the Spaniards as José Cinque), they slipped their chains.

Using as navigators Ruiz and Montes, whose lives they had spared, the rebels tried to change course for Africa. Sailing eastward by day but steered by the Spaniards at night in the opposite direction, the *Amistad* zigzagged around the Bahamas and farther northward. In late August, their supplies exhausted, the rebels caught sight of land and anchored the schooner at what turned out to be Culloden Point, just north of the settlement of Montauk on the eastern tip of Long Island. An American coast guard survey cutter spotted the ship, arrested the Africans, and towed the *Amistad* to New London, where U.S. District Judge Andrew Judson, a Democrat, ordered that the captives be tried in circuit court on charges of murder, mutiny, and piracy. Of the fifty-three Africans who had set out from Cuba, only forty-two had survived the mutiny and the haphazard trip north.

As soon as he learned of the arrests, Lewis Tappan enlisted Joshua Leavitt and Simeon Jocelyn in a Friends of the *Amistad* Africans Committee, to extend what aid they could to the captives. Here was a cause, Tappan recognized, that could bolster the flagging immediatist movement by patching up the widening differences between moralists like himself and politicals like Leavitt, while also offering to the public a stirring example of the oppression of Africans. On September 6, Tappan visited the prisoners in their jail cells—"[t]heir demeanor is altogether quiet, kind, and orderly," he wrote—and, true to form, gave them a quick sermon on Providence that they had no way to comprehend. Undaunted, Tappan hired a group of Yale students to attend to the Africans' spiritual needs, and located, on the New York City docks, a cabin boy from a British African patrol ship who understood Mende dialect and could act as translator. Tappan also hired a team of three talented antislavery attorneys to work on freeing the Africans—the chief lawyer, Connecticut Whig Roger Sherman Baldwin, scion of two distinguished old Federalist families; Seth Staples from New York, an abolitionist who had founded the legal academy that would become the basis for Yale Law School; and, also from New York, the lawyer and editor Theodore Sedgwick III, an outspoken hard-money Democrat, son of the Massachusetts class traitor and pro-Jackson radical Theodore Sedgwick Jr., and longtime colleague and friend of William Leggett.

Together with Tappan and his committee, the legal team covered the political spectrum from evangelical radicalism to Whig respectability to hard-money Loco Focoism. To solidify that coalition, Tappan kept the *Amistad* committee's operations completely separate from those of the AA-SS, with its taint of antislavery extremism. Knowing that the facts of the case would speak for themselves, Tappan was able to gain broad public sympathy with a minimum of abolitionist rhetoric. Wealthy notables who normally shook their heads in dismay at the abolitionists could feel a surge of liberal nobility in opening their hearts (and their purses) to help the wretched Africans. Ordinary northerners could feel sincere sympathy for the captives—and fury for the complacent federal officials who had jailed them. "Such base fraudulence—such *blood-hound* persecutions of poor defenceless strangers cast upon our shores," one Ohioan wrote to Tappan.

International politics also loomed large at the Africans' trial. The Spanish government insisted that, under existing treaty provisions, the United States had no right to try a case involving Spanish subjects only, arising from events that occurred on a Spanish ship on the open seas. Spain demanded the captives be summarily released to Spanish authorities in Cuba. President Van Buren and his cabinet basically agreed with the Spanish position, and but for the abolitionists' intervention might well have handed over the captives. But with his reelection campaign nearing, and the abolitionists making trouble, the president was eager not to appear to be giving in to a foreign power and abrogating due process, lest the affair inflame northern opinion. His secretary of state, John Forsyth, instructed the U.S. district attorney in Connecticut, a loyal Jacksonian named William Holabird, to take care that the Africans remain formally under the control of the federal executive—but the abolitionists also got the hearing they wanted. Although Van Buren was fully prepared to return the captives to Cuba on his own, he hoped and expected that the courts would order him to do so, relieving him of political pressure.

The legal arguments advanced by Baldwin, Staples, and Sedgwick sufficiently impressed Van Buren that in time he would order the State Department to release all its relevant documents on the case to the defense. But Secretary of State Forsyth, a Georgia slaveholder and state-rights extremist, was deeply involved in the case against the Africans, and he pressed hard for their conviction. After the circuit court, meeting in Hartford, ruled it lacked jurisdiction in the case, U.S. District Judge Judson ordered a new hearing, in his own court, to settle the Spaniards' outstanding property claims. Judson had overseen a high-profile conviction of the Connecticut abolitionist and schoolteacher Prudence Crandall six years earlier, and there was every reason to expect that he would be just as hostile to the abolitionists now. Forsyth assured the Spanish ambassador that the administration would immediately return the rebels once the federal district court had ruled.

The trial to decide the captives' status commenced in New Haven, after a postponement, in January 1840, and turned on the testimony of Dr. Richard R. Madden, the British Commissioner of the Anglo-Spanish board in Havana in charge of suppressing the slave trade. Madden had volunteered his services to help the Africans, and in a sworn statement completed in November, he asserted that, according to Spanish treaty agreements with Great Britain, the captured Africans were not slaves but illegal immigrants who now had to be returned to their homelands. Ruiz and Montes had produced transportation passports with the captives' names in Spanish, seeming to show that they were actually Spanish subjects and slaves, but Madden proved that the documents were forgeries. U.S. Attorney Holabird tried to discredit Madden's testimony, both at the original deposition and at the rescheduled proceedings in January, but succeeded only in bearing out Madden's claims.

While the trial was still in progress, President Van Buren, still confident of the outcome, assented to a secret executive order commanding the federal marshal, as soon as the proceedings ended, to deliver the prisoners to the schooner USS *Grampus*, which Secretary of the Navy James K. Paulding had directed to stand by in New Haven. As the abolitionists firmly and correctly suspected, the *Grampus* would whisk the Africans to Havana, and almost certain death, before their attorneys could file any appeal. But Judge Judson defied expectations by accepting the closing arguments of Baldwin and Sedgwick and ordering that the Africans be delivered back to Africa. "Bloody as may be their hands," he concluded, "they shall yet embrace their kindred."

Van Buren was embarrassed by Judson's ruling—and would be all the more embarrassed over the coming weeks as word leaked out about his secret order, which allowed unfriendly northern newspapers to denounce him as a court-tampering tyrant, guilty of a "heartless violation of the inalienable rights of man." By declining to submit summarily to Spain's demands over the *Amistad* and placing the matter in the courts, Van Buren may have thought he had successfully checked the controversy. But Tappan and the abolitionists, by turning the case into a national cause, placed him in an awkward position: if he failed to do his utmost to secure the blacks' conviction, and if they were left unpunished, he would appear to be condoning slave insurrection—which would have ruined what chances he still had for reelection. The center would not hold: Van Buren, by intervening in the case as he did, looked as if he had gone out of his way to win over the southern slaveholders, which alienated northern opinion; and the pro-abolitionist *Amistad* decision strengthened the political hand of pro-slavery southerners led by Van Buren's nemesis, John C. Calhoun.

Calhoun, unsatisfied by what he considered Pinckney's weak-kneed gag resolution, had worked tirelessly since rejoining the Democrats to push the party into toughening its stance against antislavery agitation. At the end of December 1837, he tendered to the Senate six resolutions aimed at protecting southern slavery. The first four restated Calhoun's version of the compact theory of the Constitution (contending that the individual states retained absolute sovereignty) and declared that all "open and systematic attacks" on slavery violated the spirit of that compact. All four passed by large margins. The fifth resolution, declaring the undesirability of any congressional effort to legislate on slavery in the District of Columbia or the territories, passed in amended form. Only the sixth resolution, declaring that any effort to prevent the annexation of new states or territories over the slavery issue would violate the rights of the slaveholding states, was tabled, mainly because the point was already pending in a resolution before the Senate calling for the annexation of Texas. Pro-administration Democrats were happy to approve what the Conservative Senator Rives mocked as "the abstractions invoked in Mr. Calhoun's resolutions" if it meant preserving party unity. But it came at the cost of appearing to follow Calhoun wherever he led them in order to protect President Van Buren—a man southern Democrats had begun to laud (and antislavery northerners begun to ridicule) as "a northern man with southern feelings."

And still Calhoun would not stop. After withdrawing his support for the independent treasury bill early in 1839, he consolidated his political command in South Carolina while wasting no opportunity to show off his growing mastery of the national scene. In December 1839, the Calhounites in the House brusquely broke with the Democrats and helped elect as Speaker the Virginian R. M. T. Hunter—a nominal Whig who supported the subtreasury idea but was also a strong supporter of Calhoun's. Soon thereafter, intermediaries arranged for Calhoun to pay a formal visit to Van Buren at the White House—the two had not spoken to each other in eight years—and an icy truce was arranged. But there was never much faith that the truce would last, at least from Calhoun's end. The outcome of the *Amistad* trial seemed custom-made as a pretext for Calhoun to inflame sectional antagonisms anew, especially after he denounced how the British had meddled in the affair and proposed Senate resolutions designed to deny rebel slaves on foreign ships any future protection from American courts.

Calhoun and his allies were not the only Democrats about whom Van Buren had reason to worry in connection with the slavery issue and the *Amistad* affair. In the aftermath of the gag rule controversy, Van Buren's efforts at compromise had also alienated antislavery opinion within the eastern radical Democracy. Some northern labor leaders and hard-money advocates, notably Ely Moore, stood by the administration and denounced the abolitionist petition drives. A tiny number, most conspicuously Theophilus Fisk, went even further to praise racial slavery as a much kinder system for degraded blacks than wage labor was for whites. Many of the antislavery radicals—including Frances Wright, Robert Dale Owen, and others—temporarily subdued their attachments to the antislavery Paineite tradition in order to preserve unity against what they considered the greatest immediate danger, pro-bank Whiggery. Yet the presence of Theodore Sedgwick III on the *Amistad* defense team was one sign of the growing antislavery commitments in some radical Democratic circles. The acidulous editorials of William Leggett—whose attack on what he called Van Buren's truckling to the slaveholders in his inauguration address and whose declaration that he was an abolitionist had temporarily made him a pariah with party leaders—represented another. The Massachusetts self-described radical Democrat Marcus Morton, shortly after his election as governor, pronounced slavery "the greatest curse and most portentous evil which a righteous God ever inflicted upon a nation." In Washington, the leading hard-money Jacksonian Senator Thomas Morris of Ohio was the only senator, of either party, openly to denounce the gag rule and defend the abolitionists—a courageous stance that would cost him renomination and his good standing inside the Ohio Democracy. On the Senate floor, Morris popularized a phrase that would later resound in antislavery politics—"the slave power," by which he meant the tightening alliance between southern planters and northern pro-bank Whigs, "both looking to the same object—to live upon the unrequited labor of others."

The Van Buren White House, preoccupied with the *Amistad* controversy, reasonably regarded the slaveholders as the greater immediate threat to its own self-preservation. Accordingly, the president, through Forsyth, directed U.S. Attorney Holabird to appeal Judge Judson's opinion, with the idea of sending it almost directly to the U.S. Supreme Court. Tappan, his committee, and the Africans were deeply disappointed. But as the court hearing date neared, yet another stroke of inspiration hit—that of adding Old Man Eloquent, John Quincy Adams, to the legal staff.

Adams had already been aroused by the *Amistad* story. Shortly after Judge Judson's first ruling, he wrote a public letter defending the Africans' uprising to secure their "natural right to liberty" and lamenting the lack of compassion and justice displayed by most federal officials. Adams had also helped the Friends of the *Amistad* committee obtain State Department correspondence relevant to the case. Although he would add little to the legal expertise of Baldwin and his associates, Tappan wrote, "his station, age, character, &c &c will give an importance to his services in this cause not to be overlooked." Adams hesitated at first, still wary of the abolitionists, but his outrage at the government's decision to appeal to the Supreme Court overcame his misgivings, and he threw himself into studying up on the case. Opening arguments were scheduled for February 22, Washington's birthday—only ten days before either Martin Van Buren or his opponent in the autumn election would be sworn in as president.

Successful as he was in galvanizing opinion over the *Amistad* matter, Lewis Tappan was having much greater difficulty holding together the AA-SS and the larger radical abolitionist movement. At the society's annual convention in 1839, the Garrisonians defeated efforts to condemn nonresistance and won the right of women to vote. All through late 1839 and early 1840, Tappan, discouraged but adamant, began laying the groundwork for a new antislavery organization. The final showdown came at the AA-SS convention in New York in May 1840, when the Garrisonians tried to elect the impressive come-outer woman Abby Kelley to the group's business committee. Although the woman question was the trigger, Tappan told Theodore Dwight Weld, the real battle was over what he called Garrison's wish to "make an experiment upon the public" by adding numerous new radical reforms to the abolitionists' agenda. Amid jeering, cheering, and considerable plotting, the Garrison faction managed to elect Kelley, whereupon Tappan and his men walked out and formed their own American & Foreign Anti-Slavery Society. The breach had become a schism.

Simultaneously, the tiny band of political abolitionists mistrusted by both Tappan and Garrison had begun getting somewhere. The AA-SS had endorsed certain kinds of political as well as moral action against slavery, as early as Garrison's original Declaration of Principles in 1833. Occasionally, immediatists had backed a particular candidate whom they viewed as sufficiently stalwart, most notably in 1834 when Garrison backed and voted for the Massachusetts abolitionist Democrat Amasa Walker in his unsuccessful race for Congress. But before 1840, antislavery political activists largely confined themselves to circulating questionnaires among candidates, challenging them to take sides on the slavery issue, and vowing to vote for no one deemed unsuitable. Not surprisingly, the tactic was ineffective. Abolitionist sympathizers held the balance of power in very few places, and most party nominees, with no interest in being linked in any way to the antislavery extremists, simply disregarded the circulars. Pushed by Garrison's deepening perfectionism, and by the disappointing results of 1836, the hardcore immediatists became even less enamored of electoral politics with the approach of the 1840 presidential elections—a contest in which no national candidate would be even remotely acceptable to them. Yet to a minority within the movement, the dire situation made it seem all the more urgent that they nominate candidates of their own.

In January 1839, James G. Birney and Henry B. Stanton tried unsuccessfully to persuade the Massachusetts Anti-Slavery Society to reject Garrisonian nonresistance and take up direct political action. But the wrangling continued at abolitionist meetings and conventions across the North. In a series of small gatherings in 1839, Myron Holley of Rochester, the former head of the New York Anti-Mason Party, tried to coax AA-SS members into making independent nominations for 1840. In November, Holley and his allies held a convention in Warsaw, New York, and nominated Birney for president on a ticket with Francis Julius LeMoyne, the president of a small college in Pennsylvania. The effort flopped: both Birney and LeMoyne declined their nominations, and antislavery societies passed resolutions rejecting the entire enterprise. The following April, however, Holley, now with the backing of Gerrit Smith, assembled more than one hundred delegates in Albany, New York. The group renominated Birney (who, this time, accepted) but with a different running mate, a well-known Loco Foco Jacksonian abolitionist editor from Pennsylvania, Thomas Earle. With only four months left in the campaign, the political abolitionists began stumping under a variety of names, including one apparently invented by Gerrit Smith, the Liberty Party. While the Garrisonians fumed and the Tappans prepared for the denouement of the *Amistad* affair, the first political party expressly dedicated to eliminating slavery began testing the limits of American democracy.

ANXIETY AMONG THE DEMOCRATS

One month after the political abolitionists named their national candidates, troubled delegates gathered at the Democratic presidential convention in Baltimore. The unanimous renomination of Martin Van Buren was a foregone conclusion, but there were bitter divisions in the ranks over whether to keep the clumsy, ungenteel Vice President Richard Johnson on the ticket. The eastern radicals still claimed the anti-Sabbatarian, hard-money man Johnson as their hero, and Van Buren wanted to keep him as well. But southern distaste over Johnson's combined sexual and racial improprieties had worsened since 1836, amid talk that he had entered into yet another illicit liaison with a mulatto woman, aged eighteen or nineteen, who was the sister of one of his previous consorts. (After a trip to Kentucky, Amos Kendall informed friends that Johnson was devoting "too much of his time to a young Delilah of about the complexion of Shakespears swarthy Othello.") Secretary of State John Forsyth, still embroiled in the *Amistad* affair, badly wanted the nomination but withdrew angrily when Van Buren, while taking a public stance of neutrality, would not give way on dumping Johnson and decided to leave the decision up to state party leaders. Andrew Jackson's favorite, James K. Polk, never formally backed down but issued a letter saying he did not wish to be an obstacle to the party, which was taken as a withdrawal. Johnson remained on the ticket.

Van Buren, having dodged a nasty brawl over the vice presidency, then received a party platform—the first such document in American history—that was completely to his liking, designed to unite all but the most recalcitrant Conservatives behind him. The platform promised "the most rigid economy" in federal expenditures in order to preserve the Republic; it denounced "all efforts by abolitionists or others, made to induce congress to interfere with questions of slavery"; and, above all, it called for "the separation of the moneys of the government from banking institutions." But a coherent platform did not mean a unified party, and Van Buren was in deep political trouble.

The obvious source of the worries was the enduring political impact of the Panic of 1837, but the Democracy's difficulties ran deeper than that. All of the divisions and contradictions that began emerging during Jackson's second term, in the Bank War and in the controversies over the abolitionists, had worsened under Martin Van Buren. By sticking to Jackson's banking and currency policies and allying with the Loco Foco radicals, Van Buren had kept the faith with the core concepts of Jacksonian politics, but at the expense of further fracturing the party. If the administration, building on renewed resentment at the banks, at last pushed the independent treasury plan through Congress, the president's supporters could claim that he had courageously stayed the course against the Money Power. If the economy showed any signs of revival, as it had in 1838, Van Buren could also proclaim his economic stewardship. But there were no guarantees that any of this would happen.

The slavery issue was getting to be just as difficult. Like Jackson and the rest of the party's mainstream, Van Buren believed strongly in keeping slavery out of national politics, for the good of the Union as well as the party. But more than Jackson, the northern broker Van Buren had always been on his guard against losing southern slaveholders' support. Now just as the radical abolitionist movement seemed to have peaked, the *Amistad* affair widened northern antislavery sympathies and aggravated sectional enmities. Although he tried to walk a delicate line while placating the South, Van Buren wound up reinforcing his reputation as the ultimate southern sympathizer, even as his administration failed to win its case against the black rebels. With a small but vociferous number of northern Democrats expressing sharp antislavery views, and with Calhoun back in the party, implacable as ever and making new trouble, the Democrats were in a tightening sectional bind—one that might cost them valuable votes in a close election.

Van Buren's and the Democrats' political difficulties exposed, once again, the deepening contradictions and dilemmas of Jacksonian egalitarianism. The Democracy's chances in 1840 would turn on whether the party could keep sectional enmity to a minimum, appeal in different ways to different parts of the country, and withstand any prolongation of economic hard times. They would also depend on whether the Whigs could at last nominate a credible candidate with a credible program and mount a credible national campaign. And as the Democrats would learn to their dismay, standards of credibility and campaigning were changing swiftly in national politics—as were the definitions of democratic idealism.

11

WHIGS, DEMOCRATS, AND DEMOCRACY

In the spring of 1835, William Henry Seward, having quit the collapsing Anti-Masons for the Whigs, accurately predicted the outcome of the presidential elections a year later: "It is utterly impossible, I am convinced, to defeat Van Buren," he wrote to his collaborator Thurlow Weed. "The people are for him. Not so much for him as for the principle they suppose he represents. That principle is Democracy. . . . It is with them, the poor against the rich; and it is not to be disguised, that, since the last election, the array of parties has very strongly taken that character."

Seward exaggerated Van Buren's invincibility—the 1836 election turned out to be surprisingly close—but he hit the crucial point: as long as the Whigs appeared to be the party of the rich and privileged, they would never win a national election. The difficulty was in part institutional—"Our party as at present organized," Weed had written in 1834, "is doomed to fight merely to be beaten"—but it was also intellectual, ideological, and sectional. To win power, the Whigs would have to square themselves, finally, with democracy—and bridge the divisions among state-rights southerners, border-state moderates, northern conservatives, and antislavery Yankees. In 1840, they figured out how to do so, and completed a revolution of American conservatism that stunned the Van Buren Democrats.

THE REVOLUTION OF AMERICAN CONSERVATISM: THE NEW-SCHOOL WHIGS

The absorption by the Whigs in the mid-1830s of some key northern Anti-Mason politicians, including Seward and Weed, was a crucial factor in the party's consolidation. Weed—who thought universal suffrage a curse but an inescapable political fact—brought with him a hardheaded mastery of popular flattery and insider manipulation, hammered out in the canal-town politics of the Burned-Over District. Weed's alter ego, Seward, was more of a crusader who envisaged government as a lever for commercial improvement and as a weapon to combat social ills, from crime in the cities to inadequate schooling in the countryside. Other former Anti-Masons—Thaddeus Stevens and Joseph Ritner in Pennsylvania, William Slade in Vermont—combined idealism and realism in varying degrees, at odds with patrician conservatives as well as what they perceived as the false democracy of the Jacksonians. Contrary to the high-toned Whigs, they would appeal to the voters to oust the Democrats in order to put government, as one sympathizer declared, "IN THE HANDS OF THE PEOPLE."

Weed was also responsible for recruiting the liveliest voice among a new crop of Whig newspaper editors, Horace Greeley. The son of a Vermont farmer and day laborer, Greeley had tramped across New York and Pennsylvania as a journeyman printer before settling in Manhattan in 1831. Three years later, he began his own literary review, the *New Yorker*, whose occasional pieces in praise of Henry Clay and Whig economics alerted Weed to his talents. Nearsighted, tall, and haphazardly vague in appearance, but a warm reform enthusiast, Greeley thought of Whiggery as the people's cause that would confound Democratic hypocrisy and uplift the masses. (When Weed arranged for him to edit a new Whig weekly, Greeley called it the *Jeffersonian*.) Greeley's Boston counterpart, Richard Haughton, editor of the *Boston Atlas*, was as much a political strategist as a journalist. With Richard Hildreth, a brilliant young polymath and humanitarian reformer, as its chief editorial writer, the brash, accessible *Atlas* pitched the Whig cause while proclaiming itself in basic harmony with "the abstract ideas of government advanced by the *Globe*, the *Advocate* and the *Bay State Democrat*."

By the late 1830s, other up-and-comers throughout the country were bringing energy and freshness to the party. In the Old Northwest and the newer western states, enterprising small towns produced a host of ambitious young Whigs from obscure backgrounds, attracted by the charisma of Henry Clay and the expansive promise of the American System—among them, in New Salem, Illinois, the young state legislator Abraham Lincoln. Some—including a pair of rural Ohio law partners, Joshua R. Giddings and Benjamin Franklin Wade, both sons of impoverished Connecticut families—burned with evangelical antislavery conviction. In the South, state-rights insurgencies by former Jacksonians swept capable young men from outside the planter elite into Whiggery, among them a Georgia country schoolmaster's son and follower of George Troup named Alexander Stephens. Scores of new anti-Jackson southern newspapers appeared, from the weekly *Washington Whig* and *Republican Gazette* in eastern Beaufort County, North Carolina, to the Vicksburg *Whig* in patrician black-belt Mississippi.

A democratization of Whig politics and ideology ensued, turning the party's earlier attacks on Jacksonian corruption and tyranny into a populist cause. The process did not unfold evenly in all parts of the country. In Massachusetts, where Jacksonianism only began to make inroads in state politics very late in the 1830s, established networks of family and business ties dominated the Whig leadership and ran the state party's affairs more like a private gentlemen's club than a modern party organization. Southern Whigs, who by the mid-1830s included most of the section's great planters, always evoked a more traditional, localist, patriarchal air than most of their northern counterparts, befitting the planters' increasingly unquestioned predominance over southern life. State-rights southern Whigs promised, above all, that they would be less compromising on slavery and the abolitionists than the Democrats. More nationalistic southern Whigs, especially in the great plantation districts, promised that their policies would restore economic stability and secure better markets for slaveholders and petty merchants alike. Yet even southern Whiggery learned to widen its appeal, proclaiming itself to white southerners of all classes as the true people's choice—devoted, one North Carolina paper declared, to "popular liberty"—while saving its worst condescension for outsiders, including unwashed Yankee Democrats like Ely Moore and, as ever, the abolitionists.

North and South, Whigs worked hard to create a truly national party organization. Having not even held a national convention in 1836, they would elect delegates to nominate a single candidate for the 1840 race. At the local and state levels, especially in the North, Whig managers and organizers paid close attention to raising funds and building a party infrastructure, from ward and township meetings on up. Whig committees and conventions picked candidates, passed resolutions, sustained members' loyalties, and, on election days, got out the vote, just as the Democrats did. Never again would the Whigs complain, as one New York loyalist had in 1835, that the party lacked "plan, purpose or principle," and that its "imbecility" and organizational maladroitness deterred "the young and ambitious."

A crucial shift in Whig ideology concerned the party's guiding assumptions about property and politics. The old Federalist prescription that property needed protection from the power of numbers had eroded badly, but it had not collapsed completely. The disdain for what John Randolph had called King Numbers still permeated the southern Tidewater elite. In the North, old-line conservatives like New York's Chancellor James Kent and business leaders like Nicholas Biddle believed that democracy menaced property, and they held in contempt the efforts by the expanded ignorant electorate to make economic policy through their equally ignorant elected representatives. "I think," William Sullivan of Massachusetts lamented in the year of the bank veto and Jackson's reelection, "that our experiment of self-government approaches to a total failure."

By the mid-1830s, American social realities and the force of democratic politics had rendered those assumptions obsolete—and, in national politics, self-defeating. In almost all of the states, poor white men had secured the vote, but private property had not been despoiled. Quite the opposite: the dynamic economy of the early republic had sufficiently widened opportunities so that ordinary freemen could at least hope to gain a measure of propertied security for themselves and their families through their own efforts. There were, of course, Americans, especially in the eastern cities, who found prosperity chimerical. The economic inequalities among the white male citizenry, North and South, were deep and growing. But these inequalities did not portend an uprising against property by the great masses of white Americans. Even at their most incendiary, neither the slaveholder Andrew Jackson nor the political professional Martin Van Buren was Thomas Skidmore. The illusion that they were—an illusion that recurred during the Bank War and the struggle over the subtreasury—had become such an encumbrance to those who sought the Democrats' overthrow that it made the Democrats appear unbeatable. Instead of resisting democracy in the name of protecting property, the new-school anti-Jacksonians now declared, better to embrace it and turn it against the Democracy.

This change in thinking, most visible in the rhetoric of the younger new-school Whigs, could also be seen in the adaptations of older national figures, none more dramatically than Daniel Webster. Early in his career, the young Federalist Webster, although less old-fashioned than some, had held to conventional conservative ideas about property and power. "We have no experience that teaches us, that any other rights are safe, where property is not safe," he declared at the 1820 Massachusetts constitutional convention, and on that basis, he joined a successful counterattack on a liberalized suffrage. "There is not a more dangerous experiment," Webster insisted, "than to place property in the hands of one class, and political power in those of another." Yet even then, Webster recognized that, at least in Massachusetts, the great majority of citizens actually did hold property and had an interest in its preservation. By the 1830s, he came to understand that by appealing for an even broader diffusion of property—to be achieved by sound conservative business policies and not by destructive Jacksonian foolishness—the experiment of democracy might be rendered safe. The masses, instead of posing a threat to property, could, if approached correctly, be turned into great defenders of property.

From this rejection of archaic Federalist politics followed a number of important consequences. The Whigs contended that in the United States all freemen shared a basic harmony of interests that had effectively banished the existence of classes. The older, tough-minded conservatism of John Adams, shared, in part, by James Madison and other Republicans, assumed that the clash between rich and poor would forever shape politics and government, even in the American republic. In the new conservative view, America was a great exception among nations, fundamentally different from Europe, where, as Webster remarked, there was "a clear and well defined line, between capital and labor." Thanks to America's abundance of land and wealth, its shortage of free labor, and its lack of hereditary aristocracy, the idea of the few and the many had been banished—and, contrary to the Democrats, rendered permanently antithetical to the genius of American politics. In America, rich and poor alike were workingmen, and all workingmen were capitalists, or at least incipient capitalists, ready to strike out on the road to wealth that was open to everyone. The Jacksonians and their labor radical friends understood nothing about this blessed nation, where expanding commerce and manufacturing, according to the *Amer-*

ican Quarterly Review, placed "within the reach of even the very poorest, a thousand comforts which were unknown to the rich in less civilized ages." What was good for the wealthy of the country was inevitably good for those of aspiring wealth, and what was bad was bad—worse for the aspirants than for the already affluent. "It is moneyed capital which makes business grow and thrive, gives employment to labor, and opens to it avenues to success in life . . . ," one Whig publicist observed. "The blow aimed at the moneyed capitalist, strikes over the head of the laborer, and is sure to hurt the latter more than the former."

A second corollary was political: Jacksonian politicians, and not privileged businessmen, were the true oppressors of the people. In place of the monied aristocrats whom the Democrats disparaged, the Whigs substituted what they described as a new class of selfish elected officials and appointees, led by King Andrew I—connivers who had turned government into their private trough, robbing the people of their money as well as their power. Attacks on Jackson as a despot expanded into charges that the Democrats' economic policies were subterfuges to create an empire of influence and self-enrichment with the people's money, most notoriously in the pet banks. Since Jacksonian power was greatest in the executive branch, those subterfuges (the Whigs observed) proceeded as expansions of presidential power, designed, as Justice Joseph Story wrote to Harriet Martineau, "to concentrate in the executive department the whole power over the currency of the country." That power would then be used for the exclusive benefit of Jacksonian insiders and their political clients.

The Jacksonians' alleged despotism led directly to another Whig theme: Jacksonian corruption. With the implementation of Jackson's spoils system, so the argument went, the Democrats had replaced occasional malfeasance by corrupt individuals with a vast apparatus of systematic plunder of the people's money. The discovery of the Swartwout affair in 1838, in which the long-time Democratic collector of the New York port had absconded to Europe with more than one million dollars in public funds, reinforced these charges. The ironies of that scandal for Van Buren—who had sharply opposed Jackson's original appointment of Swartwout in 1829, and who later moved to replace him because of his opposition to the subtreasury plan and other White House policies—only intensified the president's and his party's embarrassment. The old democratic political categories got turned inside out, allowing Whigs like Greeley to claim the Jeffersonian legacy and charge that Van Buren headed a political racket that regarded government "as an agency mainly of corruption, oppression, and robbery."

Democratic corruption was spiritual as well as material, the Whigs asserted. Playing off the stigma attached to freethinking radicals, Frances Wright above all, and the nativist fears of dissipated pro-Democratic immigrants, chiefly the Irish, Whig propagandists proclaimed their opponents dangerous to the very foundations of pious respectability and secure democratic government. If every Democrat was not an infidel, a libertine, or a drunk, the Whigs assured the upright, surely every infidel, libertine, and drunk was a Democrat. "Wherever you find a bitter, blasphemous Atheist and an enemy of Marriage, Morality, and Social Order," Greeley charged, "there you may be certain of one vote for Van Buren."

For the Whigs to purport to represent the people, they had to talk more like the people, or how they thought the people talked. Some of the party's Federalist and National Republican predecessors had already experimented with popular campaigning, notably in the Federalists' short-lived Washington Benevolent Societies. Some Jeffersonians-turned-National Republicans, most famously the gregarious Henry Clay, were excellent treaters and braggers on the campaign stump—forms of public performance that long predated the democratic breakthroughs of the Jefferson era. Suddenly, in the mid-1830s, Whig "cracker-barrel" philosophers and down-home wits began appearing in print. The most successful of them was the transformed fictional Major Jack Downing. As invented by Seba Smith, the sage of Downingville was a humorous figure who poked fun at Jackson and his coterie. In the mid-1830s, however, numerous "new" Major Downings appeared—the most brilliant of them being the creation of Charles Davis, a close friend of Nicholas Biddle's and a director of the New York branch of the Second Bank of the United States. Davis's Downing was a Whig ideologue through and through, praising bankers as benevolent people who "in the nature of things" would "never do any thing agin the gineral prosperity of this country," and who were locked in a struggle against the true "*monied aristocracy*" of "politicians [who] manage to git hold of the mony of the people, and keep turnin it to their own account—. . . buy up a party with it." Better a government of enlightened businessmen than of politicians out "jest to git into office; and then, to keep themselves in office." The first modern conservative folk hero was born in a branch office of the Second BUS.

There were other Whig populist heroes, some real, some imaginary, and some a combination of the two. David Crockett's emergence as a buck-skinned Whig celebrity was widely imitated. Whig favorites suddenly showed a fondness for manly, plebeian nicknames, including Tom "The Wagon Boy" Corwin, Henry "The Natick Cobbler" Wilson, and Elihu "The Learned Blacksmith" Burritt. Henry Clay, known widely as "Harry of the West," "The Great Compromiser," and even "Prince Hal," began to favor a name supposedly pinned on him in his youth, "Mill Boy of the Slashes"—a bit wordy but definitely down-home. On a more elevated level, the Whigs tried to match the Democrats' hard-money pamphlets with popular defenses of the credit system, the BUS, and high tariffs, the best of them written by Matthew Carey's son, Henry C. Carey.

Binding together these new-school Whig themes—American classlessness and underlying social harmony, the oppression and corruption of Democratic government, Whig populism—was the doctrine of self-improvement and reform. Attacks on the Jacksonians' dishonesty and class-war demagogy could only carry the Whigs so far in reimagining America for the electorate. Even in the Whigs' classless pastorale, some citizens were better off than others, and despite rapid economic development, the curses of crime, pauperism, and drunkenness appeared to be growing worse, not better. How could these disparities and pathologies be explained? Not, the Whigs insisted, with sinister talk of systemic social inequalities, class warfare, or corrupt institutions (apart from those the Jacksonian politicians had inflicted). Rather, the problems were individual and moral and their solution lay in individual self-reform, or what Boston's eminent Whig Unitarian minister William Ellery Channing called "Elevation of the Soul"—an elevation that benign Whig government would help to encourage.

Whig self-reform adapted ethical precepts from across the spectrum of post-Calvinist American Protestant belief, evoking the emotional revivalism of the Presbygationals and more proper of the southern evangelicals as well as Channing's rationalist Unitarianism. Their common theme, sacred and secular, was the all-surpassing importance of moral choice. The wealthy did not make the poor lazy and thriftless; the sober did not make drunkards drink; law-abiding, decent men and women did not make murderers murder, or thieves rob, or wife-beaters beat their wives. Rather, the lazy, the drunk, and the criminal chose wrongly, succumbed to sensuous temptation, and failed to exercise human faculties of self-control that could elevate their souls. What was at stake in the United States, the Whigs proclaimed, was nothing less than a battle over these self-evident facts—a momentous conflict between those who understood the basic moral conditions of human existence and those who rejected them. "We have, in truth, in the last eight or ten years, been in a continual state of moral war," the Tennessean John Bell said when he announced, in 1835, that he was joining the Whig Party. That war, as the Whigs depicted it, was essentially a democratic conflict, not between the privileged and the people or the wealthy and the poor, but between the righteous and the unrighteous.

Self-reform in turn became the basis for an uplifting idealism that defined Whiggery as a spiritual cause as well as a political party. Later writers have mistaken this aspect of Whig ideology as a belief in the corrective, liberal, "positive" state, in stark contrast to a Democratic laissez-faire, backward-looking liberal "negative" state. In fact, like virtually all American political parties and movements, the Whigs and the Democrats blended aspects of both "positive" and "negative" government. In some spheres, notably with regard to the currency and the national bank, Whigs greatly preferred private to public power and tried to limit government regulation. They wanted to halt what they called the Democrats' "war on the currency of the country . . . on the merchants and mercantile interests"—a war they said was designed "to support the power of the federal government." But the Whigs did promote the uses of government to help direct and even coerce individuals toward what they considered personal improvement—the basis, as they saw it, for social and political progress. Materially, this program had already reached its apotheosis in Clay's American System, a coordinated plan of federal-supported commercial expansion anchored by a privately managed BUS. Morally, it led new-school Whigs in the late 1830s, most auspiciously the more liberal Whigs in New York, to call for increased state support of institutions that would help keep the young on the path of righteousness and help lead the fallen toward the elevation of their souls: public schools, benevolent societies, rehabilitative prisons, reformatories, and, for the truly unfortunate, insane asylums.

"Of all the parties that have existed in the United States," John Quincy Adams's dyspeptic grandson Henry would later remark, "the famous Whig party was the most feeble in ideas." Given the subsequent intellectual history of other political parties, that judgment now seems severe. Whiggery did draw on some serious philosophical concepts, most of them derived from the Scottish so-called commonsense moral philosophers of the late eighteenth century, whose works were widely taught in American universities by the 1830s. In the area of economic thought, Henry Carey's pamphlets displayed a reasonably informed engagement with the writings of the political economists David Ricardo and

Thomas Malthus—although, finally, Carey's vaunting of the harmony of interests and the protective tariff relied as much on moral as on economic logic.

There was something of a Whig political and literary intelligentsia—mainly ministers and academics, under the leadership of cultural clerics and literary deacons. They included a few younger writers like the brash journalists Greeley and Hildreth, as well as others like Harvard's John Gorham Palfrey—at forty, the up-and-coming editor of the *North American Review* and later a courageous antislavery Whig congressman. In William Hickling Prescott, the Whigs could claim a lawyer-turned-historian whose scholarly reputation would eventually rank, for a time, near George Bancroft's. Southern Whigs produced the acclaimed novelist and congressman John Pendleton Kennedy, author of the picturesque *Swallow Barn* and, in 1844, of the pamphlet *A Defense of the Whigs*. Still, the Whig intelligentsia, even among the younger new-school Whigs, was meager in comparison to the Federalists and Jeffersonians before them—as well to the robust Jacksonians and those whom the Jacksonians attracted, including Orestes Brownson, Nathaniel Hawthorne, and a young New Yorker named Walter Whitman, among those whose work appeared in the *Democratic Review* during the *Review*'s early years. Harriet Martineau (whose work the *Review* also published) contended that although the Whigs embraced the men of learning and manners, the Democratic Party included "an accession small in number, but inestimable in power,—the men of genius."

Yet if Whig ideology lacked intellectual sparkle and strenuousness, it drew on and abetted powerful impulses in the popular American mind. Intellectually ordinary, the evolving Whigs were culturally and ethically rich. The classical learning that pervaded Whig literature, art, and oratory—leading some to compare Daniel Webster to Demosthenes and Edward Everett to Cicero—was not simply intimidating; it had genuine prestige and allure, in an America where spoken rhetorical grandeur still carried weight in legislative debates and on occasions of state. Spiritually, the liberalization of Calvinist doctrine among mainline believers became a fulcrum for the Whiggish moralism expressed most famously by Channing. And the fires of the Second Great Awakening, in its Finneyite version, blazed fallow fields for northern Whig politics, with its emphasis on the exertion of individual will and self-control in the search for redemption, and its imperatives of Christian stewardship. Charles Finney steered clear of party politics in deference to saving souls, but by 1840, Lyman Beecher was prepared to campaign publicly for the Whig national ticket. Many leading new-school Whigs, such as Joshua R. Giddings, were devout New School evangelicals. Areas where the Finneyite revivals of the 1830s hit the hardest, notably in western New York and in Ohio's Western Reserve, were Whig electoral strongholds.

Among more orthodox religious liberals and evangelicals alike arose the most compelling feature of new-school Whiggery, a broad Christian humanitarianism of the sort that had nourished the movements against Indian removal and, in the North, for the abolition of slavery. Just as post-Calvinist churchmen denounced human coercion and unbridled passion as unchristian, so they rejected everyday cruelties—the beating of children, wife abuse, the harsh treatment of convicts, and (according to some) the physical and mental torments of slavery—which other Americans took for granted as natural and even necessary forms of correction and social order. "The move toward a religion of the heart was a critical step away from the hard 'system' of Calvinism," the modern historian Elizabeth Clark put it succinctly, "and the revival meeting with its public prayer and testimony created a community of intense feeling."

Whig humanitarianism was distinct from that of the Democratic labor radicals and hard-money men, with their abstract political and economic theories of inequality and their Enlightenment rationalist affinities. The Democrats saw farmers and workingmen as society's chief victims, oppressed by greedy and (often) perfectly pious monopolists. Whig humanitarians turned to a very different set of victims. With faith, sentiment, and empathy, they set about relieving the misery of battered wives, abused blacks, and others who suffered deliberately inflicted hardship and pain—all with the higher aim of building a good society of benevolent men and women united by an affectionate regard for the lowliest of God's creatures. Self-reform was the more didactic side of Whig moralism; Christian benevolence and stewardship reinforced that moralism with effusions of Christ's gospel, and tightened the connections between Whiggery and various compassionate causes. In the South, the impulse would inspire, alongside movements for temperance and other moral reforms, slaveholders' efforts to persuade other planters to be truly Christian masters, treat their slaves with holy forbearance, and bring the gospel to the slave quarters—all as a means to strengthen the slaveholders' regime. In the North, a similar benevolent impulse pushed a small but disproportionate number of Whigs into antislavery work. Most northern Whigs had no particular antislavery commitments (while conservative Whigs were among the most prominent anti-abolitionists), and not all antislavery advocates were Whigs. Nevertheless, new-school Whigs, especially the middling farmers and artisans in their ranks, were far more ubiquitous in the antislavery circles of the 1830s than were Jacksonian Democrats.

Whig economics, as publicized by Henry Carey, also struck a nerve, especially after the Panic of 1837, among ordinary Americans enamored of a broad entrepreneurial ethos, sometimes labeled "middle class." The response was stronger in the free-labor North than in the slave South, but it arose in all sections. Over the decades since the American Revolution, with the collapse of old systems of deference, this ethos had practically become a version of the national creed, observed as a matter of principle if not always in practice—dignifying labor over affluent idleness, ennobling individual striving to make one's own way, glorifying humble efforts to improve opportunities for one's family by dint of hard work and delayed gratification. Early in the 1830s, the Jacksonians had turned that ethos to their advantage by mobilizing it, alongside labor-union discontent, against the politically privileged nonproducers. But after the Panic of 1837—

which the Whigs blamed on the Democrats' class warfare and on the man they now mocked as Martin Van Ruin—the political advantage shifted, especially in appealing to younger small farmers, shopkeepers, and workingmen laid low by hard times. Having shed the old guard's stigma of social exclusivity, the Whigs were able to position themselves and their credit-driven economic policies as the true allies of labor and honest ambition, and to proclaim proudly, as one leading publicist would, that "[t]his is a country of *self-made men*, than which nothing better could be said of any state of society."

This congeries of new-school Whig moral encomia and political polemics was completely in line with the well-being of business interests—northern and southern, insiders and outsiders alike—that had fallen on the political defensive during Jackson's presidency. Nicholas Biddle and his BUS may have been driven (and driven themselves) into disrepute, but the original friends of the bank, as well as the aggressive deregulating state bankers and the rest of the soft-money businessmen who despised the subtreasury plan and abandoned the Democracy, still formed one of Whiggery's chief political pillars. In the urban North as well as the plantation South, the overwhelming majority of the richest men were Whigs, and they contributed heavily to the party's coffers, sometimes ran for office, and exerted a pervasive influence on Whig policy at every level of government. No less than their National Republican forerunners, the new-school Whigs generally favored programs long championed by organized business, from government aid to internal improvements to the restoration of a national bank.

There were ideological fault lines within Whiggery that, if left unattended, could ruin everything. Old-line party conservatives remained suspicious of the new-school Whigs, like William Henry Seward, whom they believed carried the idea of humanitarian reform too far. The evangelical antislavery of northern Whigs such as Joshua Giddings repelled Whig slaveholders as well as northern conservatives who wanted to lay all controversy over slavery to rest. As they themselves would soon discover, men like Seward and Giddings were unrepresentative of the Whig Party as a whole, and especially of its national leadership. (The same was true for the sworn enemy of the gag rule, John Quincy Adams, who, after Anti-Masonry's collapse, became a Whig by default.) But with the entry into the party of capable political managers such as Seward's cynical sideman, Thurlow Weed, there was good reason to believe that at the national level, the Whigs could stifle their differences and unite against the common Democratic foe without sacrificing their newfound democratic affinities.

If kept within their proper boundaries, the main lines of the democratized Whig ideology, far from threatening pro-business conservatism, greatly strengthened it, by releasing men of property and standing from persistent fears of democratic overthrow, by merging their interests with those of the great people, and by transforming their search for profit and power into a moral and patriotic impulse—and a politically effective democratic impulse. ("[W]e maintain that the Whigs are THE Democrats, if there must be a party by that name . . . ," Henry Clay's publicist Calvin Colton would write. "Certainly they are the *true* Democrats, if there be any such in the land.") As for the rest of the country, democratized Whiggery gave another kind of hope—hope that the country might be delivered from hard times, hope that prosperity might yet be regained and enlarged, hope based on just enough of the realities of expansive American life that it could seem plausible.

LOG CABIN DEMOCRACY

The ascendancy of the new-school Whigs first became evident at the state level, most powerfully in New York. Upon his election as governor in 1838, William Seward transformed both the vocabulary and the programs that his constituents and his Democratic opponents had come to expect from Whiggery. His first message to the state legislature was a lengthy document filled with activist calls for reform and progress (in addition to vastly expanded internal improvements), couched in epithets the Democrats normally hurled at the Whigs. "What is the secret of aristocracy?" Seward asked. "It is that knowledge is power." Accordingly, Seward proposed a large new public school program, including a new state board of education, improved curricula for schools and colleges, and, for the rising tide of foreign immigrants to New York, equal education "with free toleration of their peculiar creeds and instructions." He also called for improved government-funded education for the state's black population, to help curb the unusually high crime rate in black areas. It was a manifesto of new-school Whig politics at their most liberal, promoting state aid to personal improvement without in any way disturbing—indeed, directly aiding—the state's vested economic interests.

A few months earlier, liberal Whigs in the New York legislature had affirmed not only their allegiances to state bankers but also their cleverness in co-opting the Democratic mantle of reform. Late in 1837, the long campaign for a free banking law, led by William Leggett, the Loco Focos, and the hard-money wing of the Albany Regency, seemed on the verge of victory. As proposed, the law would repeal the existing restraining law on the establishment of private banks of discount and deposit while imposing strict state regulations on the issue of paper money. Too radical for Governor William Marcy and even for Van Buren, the proposal had been the major source of division between Van Buren and the Loco Focos in 1836—but the suspension of specie payments a year later greatly stimulated interest in the proposal, and early in 1838, Marcy endorsed it. Old-line Whigs and Conservative Democrats rejected the plan out of hand. The pro-Seward legislative Whigs, however, seized on it, struck out the offensive passages about regulating paper money, and passed their rewritten version over Democratic objections. The new-schoolers had killed off hard-money reform, but had done so while looking as if they were the reformers.

These new-school victories were too much for old-guard Whigs in New York and around the country. "My principles are too lib-eral, too philanthropic, if it not be vain to say so, for my party," Seward would later write privately, dismayed at how conservative Whigs refused to cede control of the new party without a fight. Seward, Weed, and the rest had wrongly abandoned Biddle and the BUS, the conservatives charged; they were unseemly in their solicitations of immigrants, especially the Irish Papists; they were positively dangerous with their friendliness to abolitionists and their proposals to educate degraded blacks. These new Whigs lacked gentility and high-mindedness; they were too crassly inter-ested in the pursuit of power, too demagogic. They were, in fact, altogether too much like the Jacksonians. In 1839, Philip Hone, who had served as New York's mayor, expressed interest in run-ning for office again but was turned away on the ground that no gentleman could possibly succeed any longer in Whig politics. "If they are right in what they say," Hone complained in his diary, "the party is not worth sustaining; better it would be that everything should go back to the dunghill of Democracy."

Knowing that the Whig conservatives might well sink their own efforts to remold the party—and destroy a golden opportu-nity to capture the White House at last in 1840—the liberals and pragmatic new-schoolers set about eliminating from presidential contention the leading men of the party's National Republican establishment, especially those with conspicuous attachments to the unpopular Nicholas Biddle. First on the list was Daniel Web-ster. Hoping to unite New England and the North behind him, Webster in early 1837 announced his staunch opposition to a pending bill approving the annexation of Texas, declaring to one mass meeting that he would resist "anything that shall extend the slavery of the African race on this continent." After the panic, he advanced along a different line, blaming the Democrats' hard-money policies for the disaster and calling for the restoration of sound fiscal conservatism and the revival of the Bank of the United States. But Webster was more respected than he was loved by all but the crustiest of the Whig old guard, both in Con-gress and in the New England legislatures outside Massachusetts. When, in 1838, the new-school *Boston Atlas*, long one of Webster's chief supporters in the press, bitterly denounced him (along with Clay) as a favorite of the *"aristocratic Whigs"* and strongly endorsed the aging general and surprising vote getter from 1836, William Henry Harrison, Webster's candidacy took a nosedive from which it never recovered. Although he would not withdraw his name until the spring of 1839, Webster persisted chiefly out of jealousy, to see that his rival Clay would not succeed where he had failed.

Clay still had strong hopes that he would not fail, despite his ties to Biddle. Aware of how Texas annexation, abolitionism, and other matters connected to slavery were roiling just beneath the surface, and that his unfriendliness to Calhoun's pro-slavery resolutions of the previous congressional session was costing him southern support, Clay gave a major anti-abolitionist speech in the Senate in February 1839. The antislavery fanatics, he declared, were enemies to the Constitution, civil peace, and the antislavery cause they claimed to espouse—a cause which, Clay charged, they had set back by fifty years with their abstract incitements about good and evil. Although he proclaimed himself no friend to slavery—"[t]he searcher of all hearts knows that every pulsation of mine beats high and strong in the cause of civil liberty"—Clay charged that immediate emancipation would lead either to a war between the races, causing the extermination of one or the other, or to mongrelization and the ruination of both races. As a law-abiding American and as a white man, he had no choice but to defend the slaveholders' rights to hold their human property as they saw fit, and to sustain slavery as an inescapable exception to American liberty. The speech brought him closer than ever to the side of the pro-slavery state-rights men who formed the backbone of the Whig Party in the Deep South. Even John C. Calhoun, who understood perfectly Clay's underlying political motivations, flattered the Kentuckian on the Senate floor, claiming he had dealt abolitionism its death blow and commenced "a great epoch in our political history."

The next summer, in order to shore up his northern support,

Clay undertook a grand tour from Buffalo, across New York and into New England, then down to the elegant spa at Saratoga and after that Manhattan. "We never expect again," he told the faithful old-guard Virginian Benjamin Watkins Leigh, "to have such a great advantage in the contest." Huge, approving crowds and loud tributes greeted Clay at every stop along the way. At Saratoga—where the social season was in full swing, and where both President Van Buren and Thurlow Weed's new favorite, General Winfield Scott, were also plumping for votes—Clay gave a speech before a crowd of six thousand, the largest audience he had ever addressed, and whiled away the rest of his stay hobnobbing with Whig politicians. Among them was Weed, who broke the news that the triumphal tour was not all that it seemed, that although the Whig rank and file revered Clay's name and would always come out to see him and cheer, his political support was fading, and he had better save face by withdrawing from the presidential contest. Preferring to believe his own eyes and ears instead of Weed's intelligence, Clay carried on to Albany and New York City, and then farther down the coast, and finally to the spa at White Sulphur Springs in western Virginia. He returned to his Kentucky estate, Ashland, hopeful that he would command a plurality of the delegates when the Whigs held their nominating convention in Harrisburg, Pennsylvania, the following December.

All the while, Weed was personally supervising one of the most effective poison-pen campaigns in American political history, attacking Clay as unelectable because his political record was too unambiguous. In New York, a chain-letter scheme among local Whig leaders blew subtle and not so subtle anti-Clay propaganda all around the state and then as far west as Illinois, some of it suggesting that Clay was about to withdraw from the race. One Whig circular listed a formidable coalition of voters who would never vote for Clay—including the old Jackson men, most abolitionists, Anti-Masons, southern state-rights advocates, western squatters, and Irish immigrants—which precluded his winning more than a state or two. A string of Whig defeats in state and local elections over the summer and autumn of 1839 further persuaded party managers that almost any candidate would be preferable to Prince Hal.

In seeking a candidate with a wispier political background—or, better still, no political background at all—the new-school Whig managers believed they were reenacting what the Democrats had done so brilliantly in 1828. "The Whig party were broken down by the popularity and non-committal character of old Jackson," one western New Yorker wrote, "and it is but fair to turn upon, and prostrate our opponents, with the . . . weapons, with which they beat us." In Ohio, Indiana, and Pennsylvania, new-schoolers led by Thomas Corwin and the former Anti-Mason Thaddeus Stevens pushed for Harrison. Weed and the New Yorkers, unconvinced that the former general, at age sixty-six, could win, turned to General Scott, the colossal six-foot five-inch, three-hundred-pound commander who proudly wore his full-dress uniform bedecked with medals everywhere he went. The most capable officer in the American military, Scott had lately burnished his reputation by bringing to a successful close a nasty if bloodless boundary-dispute war between the state of Maine and the government of New Brunswick. Like Jackson twelve years earlier, a supporter declared, "Scott's name will bring out the hurra boys," who would then carry his massive frame into the White House.

At the Harrisburg convention—the first national convention in the Whigs' history—Clay's forces initially enjoyed a plurality, with solid support in a few of the northern delegations as well as in the border states and the South, but his position was precarious. Four slaveholding states, including South Carolina, failed to send delegations, which undercut Clay's earlier efforts to court pro-slavery opinion. That courtship, meanwhile, had alienated Weed and many northerners, giving Clay little room in which to maneuver. Still twenty-five votes shy of a majority, he only hoped that the pro-Scott and pro-Harrison supporters in the middle states and New England might deadlock and finally turn to him. Weed, chomping on his cigar and extroverted as ever, headed off that ploy by peeling individual northern delegates away from Clay in backroom negotiations. After several ballots, with Clay's support fading, Weed began coaxing some wobbly southern delegates to switch from Clay to Scott.

Thaddeus Stevens, however, had in his possession a devastating secret weapon for undoing both Clay and Weed: a private letter from Scott to Francis Granger, the New York Whig who had run for vice president alongside both Harrison and Webster in 1836. In the letter, Scott had attempted to win over antislavery Whigs with hints that he was favorably disposed to the abolitionists. Stevens took the letter to the headquarters of the Virginia delegation, mingled with the delegates, and calmly dropped his time bomb on the floor, where it was sure to be found. Frightened that Clay's chances were doomed and even more frightened, now, that the evidently antislavery Scott would win, the Virginians bolted en masse for Harrison. Weed then packed away the Scott bandwagon and switched to Harrison, whom the convention nominated on the next ballot.

To complete the ticket, the convention eventually gave way to the southern delegations and settled on the anti-BUS, former Democratic state-rights stalwart, John Tyler, who had run with Hugh Lawson White in 1836. Although basically at odds with Clay's nationalist political principles, Tyler had reportedly wept over Clay's defeat. He brought to the ticket both the blessings of the party's old guard and sectional balance that the delegates expected would help Harrison greatly in the depression-wracked South. Harrison, himself a native Virginian and scion of a great Tidewater family, was, on that account alone, acceptable to the southern delegates. But the addition of Tyler made the ticket more than acceptable to southern Whigs, including those in two of the four states, Georgia and Tennessee, that had not bothered to send delegations to Harrisburg.

In Washington, at the hour of Harrison's victory, Clay anxiously awaited word at Brown's Hotel, drinking heavily, expecting to hear of Scott's success but hardly reconciled to it. As the alcohol supply dwindled, Clay launched into a stormy, vulgarity-rich monologue about his perfidious friends and devious enemies.

Snapping to, he noticed two strangers in the room, dressed in black, who had come to meet him. "Gentlemen," Clay said, "for aught I know, from your cloth, you may be *parsons*, and shocked at my words. Let us take a glass of wine." He filled some glasses, then abruptly left the room, his visitors staring in shocked disbelief. ("That man can never be my political idol again," one of them said.) Clay walked across Pennsylvania Avenue to his boardinghouse, where he finally received word that Harrison, and not Scott, had bested him, prompting a fresh outburst of fist-shaking fury and self-pity. "My friends are not worth the powder and shot it would take to kill them! . . . If there were two Henry Clays, one of them would make the other President of the United States!" It would take several days for Clay to regain his grip and do the right thing, warmly endorsing the Harrison-Tyler ticket at a Whig campaign dinner in Tyler's honor back at Brown's Hotel.

The Democrats, scornful of the opposition's mediocre nominee, tried to exploit Clay and his supporters' bitter disappointment—with disastrous results. Shortly after the convention, the pro–Van Buren *Baltimore Republican* baited the Whigs with an insult reportedly delivered by a Clay man against Harrison: "Give him a barrel of hard cider, and settle a pension of two thousand a year on him, and my word for it, he will sit the remainder of his days in his log cabin." The superannuated general—"Old Granny" Harrison, some Democrats called him—was simply too old, too befuddled, too undistinguished to be a credible president. But the insult played directly into the hands of Weed as well as the old-guard Whigs. Richard S. Elliott, a Harrisburg Whig editor, was one of the first to grasp fully the implications, in a postconvention conversation over some rare Madeira with the banker Thomas Elder at Elder's mansion on the Susquehanna. The Van Burenites' mockery could, the two figured out, become the Whigs' pride, projecting Harrison and his party as paragons of plain rustic virtue while condemning the Democrats (the possibilities grew richer with each sip of the Madeira) as scornful, out-of-touch nabob politicos. And so the Whigs' famous Log Cabin and Hard Cider campaign began, with an enormous Harrison transparency mounted in Harrisburg depicting a log cabin with a cider barrel by the door. New-school party managers were fully aware of political genius behind the ballyhoo. "The Log Cabin is the symbol of nothing that Van Burenism knows, feels, or can appreciate," Weed later explained to the readers of the *Albany Evening Journal*. "It tells of the hopes of the humble—of the privations of the poor—. . . it is the emblem of rights that the vain and insolent aristocracy of federal office-holders have . . . trampled upon."

The Democrats, not taking this new Whig campaign symbolism at all seriously, entered the lists in their time-tested ways. Van Buren, outwardly unflustered as ever, did not reply to the volleys of personal attacks on him, preferring to have his supporters calmly restate his positions on the issues and leave it to the state and local Democratic campaign committees to stir up the faithful. His greatest boost came at the end of June 1840, when, after three years of dogged maneuvering and bargaining—and pushed hard by Van Buren following the bank collapse of the previous autumn—Congress finally passed an independent treasury bill. Hard-money Democratic radicals and their administration allies were ecstatic, all the more so because they thought their victory cleared the way for Van Buren's reelection. (The Massachusetts Democrat Robert Rantoul told the president that the new law would "purif[y] the political atmosphere" by finally destroying the "corrupt alliance between Bank & State.") Van Buren held off signing the bill until the Fourth of July, amid great celebrations of both American freedom and the independent treasury. Out on the campaign stump, Democrats hailed Van Buren as the new Thomas Jefferson and the subtreasury law as the second Declaration of Independence.

Would it ring true? Months before July 4, it had become clear that economic depression had returned with a vengeance, that there would be no quick recovery, and that, though the fallout might win the subtreasury bill, Van Buren would bear an enormous political burden with the voters. Some radicals, notably John L. O'Sullivan, urged the administration to undertake even more direct efforts on behalf of the nation's hard-pressed wage earners. Van Buren complied by issuing, on March 31, an executive order establishing a ten-hour day for laborers on all public works with no reduction in pay. Although presented in the mildest possible way as a step toward ending "the inconvenience and dissatisfaction" that arose from having different work rules at different work places, Van Buren's order was a clear indication that his government would act on behalf of the nation's workers. New-school Whigs, caught off guard, complained that the order would have little positive effect and charged that it was, in any case, an unwarranted interference with the free market. The length of the workday, said the self-proclaimed champion of labor Horace Greeley, ought to be left to "mutual agreement" between workers and employers: "What have Governments and Presidents to do with it?" Shipyard workers thought differently. Looking back, a free black Washington Navy Yard hand named Michael Shiner wrote in his diary that "the Working Class of people of the United States Machanic and laboures ought to never forget the Hon ex president Van Buren for the ten hour sistom, . . . his name ought to be Recorded in evry Working Man heart."

Otherwise, the Democrats hoisted their old banners emblazoned with slogans about defending the rights of labor against the paper-system aristocracy, and once again they celebrated their man as the anointed successor of Old Hickory. ("The *Paper Plague* affects us all," ran one broadside, "Its pains are past enduring;/Still we have hope in Jackson's robe,/Whilst it wraps around Van Buren"—the forced rhyme, loaded with a tired message, misfiring like a rusty musket.) Southern Democrats added their own twist, charging that the Bank Whigs wanted to violate state rights. Early in the campaign, Democrats remained confident that their old campaign weapons would suffice, and that the Whigs' demagogy about "Old Tippecanoe" Harrison, the heroic Indian fighter, would flop. "The Logg cabin hard cider and Coon humbugery is doing us a great service every where," Andrew Jackson wrote to Van Buren from his retirement at the Hermitage, "and none more so than in Tennessee." When the Whig chorus swelled ever louder, puzzled Van Buren men responded unavailingly with sweet reason. "The question is not whether Harrison drinks hard cider," William Cullen Bryant remonstrated. ". . . The question is what he and his party will do if they obtain the power." Bryant may have been right, but he missed the point by a mile.

The Democratic side contributed the only intellectually forceful product of the 1840 campaign, an astonishing, rebellious essay by George Bancroft's discovery, Orestes Brownson, entitled "The Laboring Classes." A former associate of Frances Wright and the New York Working Men, Brownson had lurched between radical politics and religious exhortation in what his biographer has called "a pilgrim's progress," before winding up in Boston in the mid-1830s as the head of something he called the Society for Christian Union and Progress and as the editor of a little periodical, the *Boston Reformer*. After the Panic of 1837, the *Reformer* endorsed hard-money Loco Focoism in what Brownson described as the great contest between capital and labor. Bancroft, alerted to Brownson's polemical gifts, handed him a federal patronage job to cover the costs of establishing a larger journal, the *Boston Quarterly Review*. To the horror of Boston conservatives, Brownson's magazine, a local equivalent of O'Sullivan's *Democratic Review*, became a successful outlet for the radical Democracy and helped turn Brownson—a tall, striking man, not yet forty, who orated as forcefully as he wrote—into a political celebrity.

"The Laboring Classes," formally a review of a brief book on Chartism by the famed British writer Thomas Carlyle, appeared in the *Boston Quarterly* just as the presidential campaign heated up. In part it was a biting restatement of the radical economic ideas that had become mainstream Democratic principles, directed against "the chiefs of the business community"— "nabobs, reveling in luxury," while "building miniature log cabins, shouting Harrison and 'hand cider.'" Some of the essay's fiercest diatribes pierced through the moral reformism typical of the new-school Whigs—"priests and pedagogues," Brownson called them, who "seek to reform without disturbing the social arrangements which render reform necessary." Brownson strongly endorsed the divorce of bank and state through the independent treasury system (enacted just after his article went to press). But Brownson also moved well beyond the radicalism of the hard-money Democracy, picking up themes developed earlier by the Free Enquirers, Thomas Skidmore, and the class-conscious trade unionists and reshaping them into a new manifesto of working-class revolution. Brownson demanded an abolition of the wage system, "to emancipate the proletaires, as the past had emancipated the slaves." (Perversely, Brownson also claimed that the wage system was a more efficient means of exploitation than the one oppressing southern slaves—whom, he failed to note, the past had hardly emancipated, and whose masters' defense of slavery were toughening.) He demanded the abolition of the corrupt existing churches and the rebirth of Christ's true gospel. Above all, he demanded the abolition of inheritance. Brownson had little faith that these changes could be won by elections or political parties. Only a cataclysmic final conflict—"a war," he wrote, "the like of which the world as yet has never witnessed," horrific yet unavoidable—would usher in the new just society, where labor and capital would be combined in the same individual and exploitation would cease.

Based on his own volatile mixture of Workeyism, Loco Focoism, and Christianity, Orestes Brownson, in Boston, pushed the hard-money logic far beyond Jacksonian Democracy into a proletarian revolutionism every bit as startling as the one that Friedrich Engels and Karl Marx would proclaim in *The Communist Manifesto* eight years later. Seeing an opportunity, even liberal Whig publicists and politicians grabbed hold of the essay and denounced it as the pluperfect statement of what Martin Van Buren and his friends intended to inflict on the ordinary citizens of the United States. Here was definitive proof, if any was really still needed, that Loco Focoism was "utterly subversive of all Rights of Property whatever," Horace Greeley said, determined to seize what honest men had worked so hard to earn. The clamor grew so loud that Secretary of the Treasury Woodbury desperately asked Bancroft in October why he had not yet removed Brownson from his government job.

But the truly remarkable thing was that Bancroft, a contributor to Brownson's *Quarterly*, steadfastly refused to listen to Woodbury. Several Democratic papers, including Bryant's *Evening Post*, criticized what they called the campaign to censor Brownson far more than they did Brownson's outlandish ideas. Even as the election campaign drew to a close, Brownson remained a mainstay of the Massachusetts Democracy, stumping across the state for Van Buren and local Democratic candidates. Nothing approaching Brownson's revolution would be in the offing if the Democrats won the election, but the reaction by Bancroft, Bryant, and others to the attacks on him exposed the depth of the anti-Whig animus among considerable portions of the party—and how far to the left they had moved by 1840 on issues of labor and banking.

In 1840, however, the new-school Whig campaigners carried much more weight with the public than defenses of the free-speech rights of a revolutionary intellectual. One facet of the Whigs' assault was to update the personal attacks on Van Buren, portraying him as a callous, aristocratic pervert. The smears of the president became increasingly baroque. One best-selling Whig campaign pamphlet—the reprint of a speech by Charles Ogle, an obscure Whig congressman from Pennsylvania, entitled "The Regal Splendor of the Presidential Palace"—accused Van Buren of living in said splendor and dining on fancy expensive delicacies prepared by a French chef, while hard-hit Americans went hungry. The electorate learned from Whig partisans that the degenerate widower Van Buren had instructed groundskeepers to build for him, in back of the Executive Mansion, a large mound in the shape of a female breast, topped by a carefully landscaped nipple. Van Buren, the Whigs cried, was a depraved executive autocrat who oppressed the people by day and who, by night, violated the sanctity of the people's house with extravagant debaucheries—joined, some whispered, by the disgusting Vice President Johnson and his Negro harem.

The attacks on Van Buren's alleged dissipation reinforced the old Whig charges about presidential power run amok, but they also added spice to the new charges that he and the Democrats had ruined the economy with their bank and currency policies— charges that conveyed genuine principles about authentic issues. "Harrison and Prosperity or Van Buren and Ruin," ran the title of one Whig pamphlet, which pretty much summed up the party's line of attack on the economic front: in times of contraction and low prices, currency inflation and eased credit seemed imperative. Some stump orators (notably, in Illinois, young Abraham Lincoln) called for the restoration of the BUS in order to supply needed credit for the common man. Others lashed out at the Democrats' restriction of paper money and at the subtreasury act, which Harrison vowed to repeal. Still others, especially in traditionally protectionist Pennsylvania, vaunted the protectionist tariff as the cure for hard times. In the South, however, the politics of slavery overshadowed the more orthodox economic issues. Whereas the antislavery elements among the northern Whigs pilloried Van Buren for supporting the gag rule, southern Whigs dismissed his anti-abolitionism, claiming that his despotic proclivities menaced their rights to hold slaves as well as the prosperity of the cotton economy. Harrison, by contrast, they deemed far safer on the slavery question as well as on economic policy, a son of Virginia who, according to the *Richmond Whig*, "breathes the most ardent and devoted attachment to the rights and institutions of the South."

The Whigs, as ever, embedded their arguments about both economics and slavery in their arguments about politics and the Constitution, arguments that further confute later blanket descriptions of the Whigs as the party of active government and the Democrats the party of laissez-faire. Even the candidate, Harrison, normally limited to mouthing platitudes about liberty and log cabins, made it clear that the Whigs, and not the Democrats, were the party of restrained government, the true heirs of Jefferson and Madison. Instead of meddling with the economy and usurping power, the Whigs would undo the Jacksonians' mischief and then leave well enough alone. "The administration . . . now say to the people, 'You must not watch us, but you must watch the Whigs! Only do that, and all is safe!'" Harrison told a mass meeting in Indiana. "But that, my friends, is not the way. The old-fashioned Republican rule is to watch the Government. See that the Government does not acquire too much power. Keep a check on your rulers. Do this, and liberty is safe."

The Whigs also applied more practical lessons from the Democrats' national campaigns. To Weed and the other party managers, establishing an effective national campaign organization was of equal importance as taking positions on issues. After the Harrisburg convention, an executive Whig committee set up shop in two rooms at the Washington city hall, which quickly became the national party's nerve center. Whig congressmen, making generous use of their franking privileges and the unpaid labor of loyal government workers, turned the place into a fountain of propaganda, largely financed at the public's expense. Down the chain of command, state committees, county committees, town committees, and the all-important local Tippecanoe Clubs geared up to oversee stump speaking, campaign festivities, patronage matters, and the crucial details about getting Whig voters to the polls. At Harrison's home in North Bend, Ohio, the national campaign supplied the general with his own personal committee—to shield him from troublesome correspondence, prepare whatever public remarks he might have to make, and otherwise ensure that he said or did nothing that might offend anyone. Campaign workers also hastily restored Harrison's commodious residence to look more like the log cabin it had originally been, in which Harrison had lived only briefly.

The Whig campaigners showed great ingenuity in exploiting the broadened avenues of commerce and commercial culture and pitching their message into every cranny of American life. Log cabins turned up everywhere, in every imaginable form, as cheap trinkets, parade floats—and, in innumerable towns and cities, as actual edifices, surrounded by barrels of hard cider to treat all who cared to enter, often with a raccoon skin on the wall or even a live raccoon prowling the premises as a rustic finishing touch. Engravers and lithographers churned out endless streams of decorative vignettes and cartoons featuring Harrison as patriot-general, as farmer-citizen, as champion boxer. Medallions of brass and copper turned up like newly minted coins, with the log cabin on one side, Harrison on the other, and the motto, "He leaves the plow to save the country." Porcelain makers supplied campaign mugs and pitchers and platters of every grade to help voters eat, drink, and be merry in the unending presence of the Log Cabin campaign. One of the campaign's consumer items wound up permanently enriching the American vocabulary: the popularity of "Old Cabin Whiskey" (distributed for free along the Erie Canal) brought fame to its makers, the E.C. Booz Distillery of Philadelphia—thus, the birth of booze.

The partisan Whig press also played a crucial role, most successfully a new paper edited by Horace Greeley and named, naturally, the *Log Cabin*. Greeley, always at least two cuts above the average party hack or penny-paper sensationalist, filled his columns with some of the more earnest efforts at explaining new-school Whig political thought and programs, including William Ellery Channing's sermon on self-reform, "Essay on the Laboring Classes." But Greeley also made sure to include song lyrics and other gems of ready-made Whig literary and musical entertainment. (One Whig song stole the tune of an old Thomas Jefferson theme and ended with the words, "For HARRISON and LIBERTY!") Elsewhere these entertainments became as hard to miss as the Whigs' gewgaws. At the very moment that mass-produced pianos and sheet music were entering American parlors as markers of respectable middle-class taste, the Whigs came rushing after with their "Tippecanoe Song Sheets" and "Log Cabin Cotillions." Black-faced minstrel shows—a city-born entertainment, originally popular with young workingmen, that had swept the country in the 1830s—now featured players performing pro-Whig skits and caricatured Negro dialect ditties, to the accompaniment of banjoes and rat-a-tat bones sets. Glee clubs, urban and rural, and popular itinerant singers sang the Whigs' praises. Greeley's *Log Cabin* and the *Boston Atlas* tried to whip up a stir by announcing that Chang and Eng Bunker—the famed Siamese twins who had recently quit touring and retired to Wilkesboro, North Carolina—had most definitely decided to vote the Whig ticket.

The Whigs also took to the political stump as never before. National figures joined in with gusto. Henry Clay, an excellent campaigner, regained his public dignity once he had recovered from his bitter loss and managed to tell voters with a straight face that they had to choose between "the log cabin and the palace, between hard cider and champagne." The austere, godlike Daniel Webster got fully into the swing of things, dropping his classical cadences in favor of a more conversational and at times rip-snorting delivery. Not to be outdone, the erudite, elegant South Carolina editor and ex-congressman Hugh Swinton Legaré conducted a "slangwhanging" expedition through five states, declaring it unthinkable for southerners not to vote for "a man born and educated in the South."

Even the candidate made a historic breakthrough on the hustings. Perturbed by Democratic criticism of their efforts to keep Harrison under wraps—rendering him "General Mum," Van Burenite papers snickered—the Whigs broke with campaign tradition and gave their candidate some formal public exposure. It began on July 6, with an unscheduled speech by Harrison on the steps of the National Hotel in Perrysburg, Ohio—the first approximation of a formal campaign speech ever delivered by an American presidential candidate. The old general turned out to be quite good at it, delivering some twenty-three speeches, each one more melodramatic and carefully crafted than the last. ("I am in favor of paper money," he declared in one public statement, which was an orthodox Whig sentiment; then he added straightaway, "I am not a Bank man," which was not.) Harrison milked his old soldiers' glory, timing his speeches to coincide with anniversaries of his military victories and always making sure to have some local old veteran from the War of 1812 totter up on stage beside him. In mid-speech, he would suddenly stop and ostentatiously take a few swigs from a barrel plainly marked "Hard Cider," throwing the audience into an uproar. As to substance, his addresses mainly took unterrified stances against monarchy in government and all unnecessary uses of the executive veto, and pledged he would serve only one term. Harrison showed his gray head to the people, said nothing too dangerous, and played wonderfully to the crowd.

It was not merely theater: it was political theater, with several messages at once. With a combination of calculation and improvisation, the Whig campaign reformulated their broader economic, cultural, and moral precepts and packaged them for the voters. Appeals to labor, hard hit by the depression, were ubiquitous, not only in speeches and pamphlets but in banners and illuminations that freely borrowed trade union insignias—especially the familiar emblem of a brawny arm lifting a hammer—while praising Old Tip and the overarching harmony of economic interests. Evangelical Protestants could not only hear and read their local ministers extol Whig morality; they could read of how Lyman Beecher himself heartily endorsed Harrison's candidacy. The hard-cider motif, and all of the alcohol served up at the village-green log cabins, did pose a potential obstacle in winning over the pro-temperance evangelicals. But Whig strategists took care of that by releasing testimonials claiming that the party's efforts coaxed men away from taverns and distilled spirits toward loftier pastimes and less dangerous beverages, thereby rendering hard cider a temperance drink and the Whig log cabins halfway houses to sobriety. In a major campaign innovation, the Whig planners made sure to include women supporters by the tens of thousands, and feature them in their festivities—parading not as Fanny Wright feminists but as exemplars of the blossoming evangelical cult of domesticity who looked to General Harrison as their worthy protector. Here and there, women actually gave speeches; more typically, Whig advance men gathered the ladies together, supplied them with Harrison handkerchiefs for waving at the appropriate moments, and placed them conspicuously before the crowds. Obviously, there was no women's vote to be won, but wives and daughters could certainly exercise domestic moral suasion to help direct their men to attend the rallies and vote correctly on election day. The surviving evidence about their thoughts and perceptions suggests that Whig women were fully caught up in the politics as well as the theatrics of the campaign.

The Whigs' ability to infuse these beliefs, values, and loyalties into giant rallies and processions, demotic and sometimes light-hearted spectacles, made the Log Cabin campaign so successful. Enormous contingents of pro-Harrison marchers gathered with torchlights behind their banners—"The Eleventh Ward Young Man's Whig Club," "Boot and Shoemakers for Old Tip"—and then set off, one after the other, along the designated route. In Cleveland, an industrious band of Whigs banged together an immense tin ball—a symbolic gibe at the Democrats—which they then pushed through towns and hamlets to a Whig convention and the state capital, Columbus, over a hundred miles away, cheered and sung to by the faithful:*

> As rolls the ball,
> Van's reign does fall,
> And he may look
> To Kinderhook.

After arriving in Columbus, the Clevelanders met up with another, even larger ball, covered in cowhide, which had been sent on a wagon by the Whigs of Muskingum County. Similar rollings occurred around the country. Even by the Democrats' systematic undercounts, the reported turnouts for these events and others were enormous, numbering upwards of a hundred thousand by the end of the campaign.

As if these crushing events were not bad enough for the

---

* The ball-rollings were a joking reference to Thomas Hart Benton's speech when he began a campaign to expunge the Senate's censure of Jackson: "Solitary and alone, I set this ball in motion." Now the anything-but-solitary Whigs would get their own ball rolling—and roll it right over the Democrats.

Democrats, the last-minute efforts of the political abolitionists were also irritating the Van Burenites in pockets of the North. Van Buren's support of the gag rule and involvement in the *Amistad* affair, and the abolitionists' charges that his complicity with the slaveholders ran even deeper, left him vulnerable. Although the Liberty Party men might have been counted on to draw support chiefly from Yankee Whigs, they seemed at times to be directing themselves chiefly toward dissident Democrats. Whig abolitionists—who scolded the Liberty men as sectarians and as the spoiler promoters of a "Van Buren trick"—stayed loyal to their party, joined the Tippecanoe Clubs, and left the Liberty men to appeal elsewhere. "They had nothing to fear for themselves," one Ohio Liberty man said of the Whigs, "and stumped it for Harrison, for weeks throwing out insinuations against the third party as an affair got up to help Van Buren."

Both of the Liberty candidates, James Birney and Thomas Earle, had Democratic backgrounds, Earle with the hard-money Loco Focos. The Van Burenite editor of the *Albany Argus* became so fearful of the Liberty Party insurgents that he refused to follow instructions from higher-ups to deliver the usual Democratic attacks on abolitionism. Benjamin Butler had to calm Van Buren's fears that a local Democratic Party meeting in New York would favorably consider the abolitionist cause. In Massachusetts, western New York, and Ohio, Liberty Party committees included a healthy proportion of artisans, workers, and nominal Democrats who worked hard to bring Democratic voters into the fold. Their numbers, to be sure, were miniscule overall, and their political campaign was too quickly knocked together to make much of a difference. (In the final tally, the Liberty men would win, in the nonslaveholding states, barely seven thousand votes out of more than 1.7 million cast.) But as the electioneering wore on, the anxieties that pro-slavery forces had long caused Van Buren were complicated by antislavery anxieties that might only grow in the future, even if the Democrats squeaked out a victory. In some marginal northern districts, anger at the administration's placating of the slaveholders, endlessly stoked by the Liberty men, threatened to cost Van Buren valuable votes.

By early autumn, it was obvious that a Democratic victory was impossible. The Maine elections, held in September, brought a narrow Whig win—and with it the latest version of the most famous chorus of the 1840 campaign:

> And have you heard the news from Maine
> And what old Maine can do?
> She went hell-bent for Governor Kent,
> And Tippecanoe and Tyler too,
> And Tippecanoe and Tyler too.

So went the nation. When the final results arrived, Harrison had won a respectable 53 percent of the popular vote and had humiliated Van Buren in the Electoral College by a margin of 234 to 60. The Whigs had won states in every section of the country; they had won all of the large states except Virginia; and they had captured both houses of Congress, gaining majorities that appeared impregnable. The results from the South were staggering: Louisiana, Mississippi, Georgia, North Carolina, and Tennessee, once the heartland of Jacksonian electoral success, had broken for Harrison, swayed by southern Whig arguments that their sound economic principles and zeal for state rights would protect slavery far better than the Yankee Loco Foco Van Buren and his corrupt coterie. And the northern states? All except New Hampshire and Illinois also voted for Harrison.

Thurlow Weed and the new-schoolers, with energy, imagination, and all the luck they could ask for, had completed their masterpiece. Once the Whigs had rallied behind a single national candidate and mounted a spectacular campaign, they captured the electorate's imagination. More than 2.4 million voters, nearly a million more than in 1836, had surged to the polls, representing roughly 80 percent of those eligible to cast their ballots—by far the highest turnout ever in a presidential election, and a quantum leap from the figure of about 55 percent four years earlier. Democracy had spoken as never before—and democracy turned out to be Whig. Some alert Democrats saw what was happening as early as the summer. "[T]hey have at last learned from defeat the very act of victory!" the *Democratic Review* exclaimed. "We have taught them how to conquer us!"

ANDREW JACKSON, JACKSONIAN DEMOCRACY, AND DEMOCRACY

"Corruption, bribery and fraud has been extended over the whole Union," Andrew Jackson howled after Harrison's victory. Jackson was burdened with financial difficulties once more, and dying, he said, as fast as he could get on with it. Like other Democrats, he had expected that the virtuous working masses would thwart the Whigs' campaign of gaiety and bunkum, in Tennessee as in the rest of the country. Rousing himself from his physical agonies, he had even ventured out of the Hermitage to give a speech in praise of Van Buren late in the canvass. But Harrison trounced Van Buren in Tennessee as he did nationwide (and pulverized him by a 5 to 1 margin in Jackson's own district), and now it looked as if the Whigs were in a position to destroy the independent treasury, restore the BUS, and then undo everything Jackson had achieved as president. Jackson could still muster his old faith in Providence as well as the people and look to the future. "The democracy of the U[n]ited States have been shamefully beaten," he consoled the defeated president, "*but I trust, not conquered.*" Yet the words rang hollow, with the insistent confidence of a fog-bound old campaigner.

Jackson would live long enough to have a last laugh. Neither American democracy nor his own party—the Democracy—had been conquered in 1840. The Whig triumph raised questions, though, about how democratic the Democracy had been, still was, and would remain. More precisely: how had the Jacksonian ascendancy shaped, for better and for worse, the democratic impulses that had arisen out of the American Revolution and had evolved so furiously after 1815?

In its embryonic form, the Jackson Democracy was a political coalition produced chiefly by three crucial developments. The Panic of 1819 and subsequent depression shattered the overextended Republican Party that had led the nation to war against Britain and, at war's end, had promised new national development and prosperity. The coincident crisis over Missouri statehood produced arguments over the future of American slavery that threatened to rearrange the shattered political allegiances along sectional lines. The presidential election of 1824, instead of resolving these upheavals, ended in deadlock and an alleged corrupt bargain that, as far as Jackson and his supporters were concerned, was a virtual coup d'etat against the will of the electorate. In 1828, Jackson, running chiefly as the warrior-avenger against the plotters of 1824–25, John Quincy Adams and Henry Clay, took moderate and, to some, ambiguous stands on major issues like the tariff and internal improvements. But the promises that he did make to cleanse the Augean stables in Washington stirred planters, small farmers, and workingmen hit hard by the depression and wary of Adams and Clay's American System. They also attracted voters who feared that fights over slavery would tear the nation apart. With an electoral base that was strongest in the South and West, Jackson benefited greatly from the sophisticated political operations of his supporters in the middle states, above all the New Yorker Martin Van Buren, and swept to victory. "They believed him honest and patriotic," the veteran Washington politico Nathan Sargent later recalled of Jackson's supporters, "that he was a friend of the *people*, battling for them against corruption and extravagance, and opposed only by dishonest politicians."

Jackson's winning coalition was not yet, however, the Jackson Democracy, which only emerged from the convulsive labors of Jackson's first term. The new president's comprehensive Indian removal policy reinforced, for a time, the allegiances of southern planters and small farmers, especially in states that contained the bulk of newly cleared land. But Jackson's bank veto and subsequent war with Nicholas Biddle alienated northern business interests (including the so-called Bank Democrats) as well as southern planters who saw the BUS as an anchor of financial stability. The nullification crisis, in turn, completed the schism that had begun with debates over the tariff and John C. Calhoun's fall from Jackson's political good graces, and that in time drove state-rights planters into the opposition. Although South Carolina wound up isolated from the other slaveholding states in 1833, sympathy for nullification and resentment of Jackson gripped a substantial portion of the southern planter elite—including "original" Jacksonians who, once the Indian removal issue was virtually settled, were repelled by both Jackson's democratic nationalism and his attack on the BUS. But Jackson threw down the gauntlet: "the tariff was only the pretext and disunion and a southern confederacy the real object," he observed immediately after the nullification crisis ended. Nullification's defeat, along with Biddle's one year later, nearly completed the first important stage of the Democracy's formation, which would culminate under President Van Buren with the Conservative defections over the independent treasury.

What, then, was the Jackson Democracy in its mature form? One powerful interpretation, refuting earlier descriptions of Jacksonianism as a western movement, claims that the party actually owed more to eastern labor, and that the political conflict of the 1830s can be better understood in terms of classes than of sections. Other writers, asserting an entrepreneurial consensus over economic issues, have posited either that these conflicts were insubstantial clashes between rival "ins" and "outs," or that religion, ethnicity, and other cultural issues actually drove Jacksonian politics. Still others have charged that Jacksonian Democracy was an alliance of slaveholders and racist "northern men with southern feelings" dedicated to clearing out the Indians, expanding U.S. territory, and keeping the imperial republic safe for slavery. More recently, historians have revived the economic and class interpretation but without its eastern focus, depicting Jacksonianism as a movement of subsistence farmers and urban workers resisting the encroachments of capitalist development. Each view has something to recommend it, but all of them slight the dynamic and unstable character of the Democracy's rise and development, and the primacy of politics and political thinking in the conflicts of the era.

Jacksonianism hardly began as an eastern movement concerned with labor, money, and banking, and some westerners remained vital loyalists. Support for Jackson in 1828 was far sturdier in the South and West than it was in the East. Through the 1830s and beyond, Jacksonian rhetoric always reserved a prized place for the noble independent farmer and the landed interest—what the neo-Jeffersonian Martin Van Buren called the great irreplaceable bulwark "against the political demoralizing and anti-republican tendency of the Hamiltonian policy." Yeoman portions of the South and West generally stayed loyal to the Democrats in local and national elections through the 1830s and after. But the Democracy did evolve in ever closer association with eastern hard-money radicalism during the Bank War and its aftermath, merging Jackson's own antibanking views with those that arose out of the Workie and Loco Foco movements. Some western anti-BUS men—Thomas Hart Benton, Amos Kendall, Francis Blair—were also steadfast and influential hard-money Jacksonians for the duration of the 1830s. There is a case to be made that, apart from Jackson, these westerners, especially Kendall and Blair, exerted the most important pressure inside the administration to keep it on the hard-money path. Yet large numbers of anti-BUS westerners also deserted the party when the war on eastern privilege became a war on the paper system and speculation, including land speculation. And although many anti-BUS easterners did the same, eastern radicals supplied the intellectual and political firepower to support the removal of the deposits, the Specie Circular, and the subtreasury plan. If anyone was the intellectual architect of Jacksonian economic policy after 1832, it was the Philadelphia radical William Gouge.

When, during Van Buren's presidency, the Whigs began labeling the Jacksonians as "Loco Focos," the attempted slur had merit. The meter as well as the rhymes of the Democrats' appeals may have slipped off-kilter by 1840, but their sentiments rang out clearly enough, as in one pro–Van Buren broadside:

> Then let the working class,
> As a congregated man,
> Behold an insidious enemy:
> For each Banker is a foe,
> And his aim is for our woe—
> He's the canker-worm of liberty!

The guarded Van Buren, long an ally of upstate New York bankers, would never go as far as the Loco Focos desired. But in his own careful way—praised by no less a radical than Frances Wright—Van Buren vindicated the core of hard-money radicalism. The rest of the Democracy, shorn of its Conservative wing, was increasingly a party dominated by the same ideas, advanced most coherently by eastern radicals with their roots in the old city democracy.

The claim that these appeals betrayed an underlying entrepreneurial consensus with the Whigs stretches the idea of consensus beyond recognition. The Democrats favored private property, commercial growth, individual labor, and the personal accumulation of money, at which many of them excelled. None (apart from Brownson and whatever small coterie shared his ideas) were social revolutionaries of the sort that, in the last century, became widely considered the sine qua non of genuine radicalism. But the Democracy's economic radicalism, based on creating a hard-money currency regulated by the federal government, was predicated on a form of commerce and a way of life that were fundamentally at odds with the Whigs' credit-and-paper, boom-and-bust system—a system, Roger B. Taney complained, driven by "speculation and the desire of growing rich suddenly without labor" that had "made fearful inroads upon the patriotism and public spirit of what one called the higher classes of society." Whereas the Whigs savored the romance of risk and capitalist investment (where the greatest spoils belonged to the greatest victor), Democrats favored a more secure and egalitarian commercialism—not what the *Globe* called "a succession of throws of the die"—which they believed would distribute wealth more evenly while keeping political power in the hands of the majority of the citizenry. At stake in the politics of the 1830s, or so the participants believed, was which form of commerce would prevail.

The depth of that conflict did not mean that Democrats and Whigs fought it out solely on class or on economic grounds, especially in the North. Like all successful parties, the Democrats and Whigs contained coalitions that included elements of all social classes. Economic interests—or voters' responses to the effects of rapid commercial growth, what some historians have called the "market revolution" of the era—were not the only interests in play. Part of the genius of new-school Whiggery was its ability to turn the Panic of 1837 against the Democrats while also describing political and economic issues culturally, reorienting debates along ethical and cultural lines that cut across differences of wealth and class. It was not merely a calculated sideshow: the "continual state of moral war" that the Whig John Bell described in 1835 tapped into a clash of ideologies far greater than any mere partisan subterfuge could invent. The Whigs' morality, in turn, attracted disproportionate numbers of Presbygational evangelicals, just as it consigned Irish Catholics (despite Seward's efforts in New York) and most of those masses who remained indifferent to religion to the Democrats. Class and economics were always central to Jacksonian politics, but the Whig revolution of conservatism encouraged voters to understand economic success and failure in cultural ways that reinforced the legitimacy of Whig economics. In the 1840s, that understanding, in polyglot northern polities like New York, would yield partisan voting returns that divided sharply along ethnic and (especially) religious lines.

Race, slavery, and antislavery also shaped Jacksonianism. Jackson's anti-abolitionism (restated pointedly by Van Buren in his inauguration address) was a salient feature of the larger Democracy. The efforts by congressional Democrats and the White House to placate the party's southern wing without succumbing to the Calhounites became a running theme after 1833. Although this expediency, and toleration of "the Slave Power," alienated some northern Democrats, a minority of middling new-school Whigs appear to have greatly outnumbered the Jacksonians who gravitated to the abolitionists before 1840. Democrats, North and South, were friendlier than the Whigs to expansionist efforts that would widen opportunities for the spread of slavery. The propensity of Democratic leaders to see antislavery agitation in partisan terms led them to equate, falsely, political ambition and opportunism with genuine humanitarianism, much as they did in the fight over Indian removal—or as the antirestrictionist compromisers did during the Missouri crisis in 1819–21. To halt the abolitionist agitation and quiet southern counteragitation, both Jackson and Van Buren attacked the abolitionists' civil rights, in the mails and gag-rule controversies—and, in the latter, were resolutely opposed by a small group of House Whigs led by John Quincy Adams. Although Whigs and Democrats shared in the Negrophobia dominant among all whites in the 1830s, northern Democrats did take the lead in disenfranchising blacks (as in Pennsylvania in 1837–38), even as they celebrated the growing political participation of lower-class white men.

None of this, however, made the Jacksonians a pro-slavery party—or even, as one milder critic has argued, "*functionally* pro-slavery"—fighting a proto-abolitionist Whig Party in order to protect a status quo that left the slaveholders the dominant class in American politics. The Jacksonians did not oppose interference with slavery where it existed or obstruct the abolitionist efforts to arouse the South, because they wished to sustain the slaveholders as a national ruling class. They wanted, as the Whigs did, to keep slavery out of federal politics to protect constitutional order, national harmony, and party unity. Sustaining the slaveholders' power was the goal of Calhoun and others, who saw the planter class not as dominant but as beleaguered, and to whom the Jacksonians would never, after 1830, come close to measuring up.

(The Jacksonians, by contrast, generally spoke of slavery as a misfortune that would eventually disappear.) As time passed, the most vociferous pro-slavery elements in the original Jacksonian coalition actually left the party—first the Calhounites, then the state-rights Whigs such as John Tyler, then the anti–Van Buren planters, and finally the southern bank Conservatives. When Calhoun temporarily rejoined the Democrats in 1838, he aimed chiefly to destroy it as it existed and remake it into a genuine slaveholders' party.

Even the profound and sometimes vicious racism commonly found among northern Democrats was less uniform, less singular, and more complicated than it might appear. There were at least some important antislavery Democratic partisans, including William Leggett, whose radicalism also extended to race. And as the anti-abolitionist violence of the mid-1830s showed, conservative Whig gentlemen and nominal Democratic conservatives were just as drawn to hair-raising, inflammatory racist attacks on blacks as mainstream Democrats were. Even Democrats who led fights for black disenfranchisement were trying to sustain their egalitarian ideals against racist conservative hierarchy, in ways that now seem cruelly paradoxical and are difficult to comprehend. According to the Democracy's conception of citizenship, political equality was indistinguishable from social equality. And yet, prodisenfranchisement Democrats argued, their Whig opponents were proposing political equality for black men without granting them social equality—to the Democrats, an absurdity that made a mockery of equal rights. "[Y]ou could not admit the blacks to a participation in the government of the country," one New York Democrat argued, "unless you put them on terms of social equality," something that neither the Whigs nor the Democrats intended to do. At the state constitutional convention of the new state of Michigan, another Democrat swore that he would oppose giving the vote to any blacks "until we consent to treat them as equal with us in all respects." Only with the rise, very late in the decade, of the more liberal of the new-school Whigs such as Seward and Giddings did the opposition make any clear moves in the direction

toward greater social tolerance of blacks—much to the consternation of more moderate and conservative northern Whigs and the
horror of southern Whigs. Even then, mainstream northern Democratic racism was not the same thing as pro-slavery.

At bottom, the Jackson Democracy was chiefly what its proponents said it was—a political movement for, and largely supported by, those who considered themselves producers pitted
against a nonproducer elite. Moral clashes, and the simmering
disputes over abolitionism and slavery, helped further define the
movement. Yet even these connections can mislead, for on all of
these fronts, Democrats assumed that politics and government
institutions remained the primary locus of power. Here was the
key to Jacksonian politics: a belief that relatively small groups of
self-interested men were out to destroy majority rule and, with it,
the Constitution. The nonproducing few were able to oppress the
productive many, the Democracy proclaimed, because of deliberate political corruptions that thwarted the great principle under-
girding American government, popular sovereignty. The corrupt
bargain of 1824–25 had negated the people's will and launched
an administration awash in peculation and extravagance. The
Second BUS had been granted enormous powers with no
accountability to the people. The entire paper-and-credit system,
unless properly reformed and regulated, created illegitimate
authority at war with popular sovereignty and equal rights. The
twisted doctrine of nullification proposed to allow a few designing men, under the pretext of opposing the tariff, to usurp powers
delegated to the people's representatives by the Constitution—
and then to permit those men, if challenged, to dissolve the
Union. Abolitionists were deluded philanthropists, dupes of
northern BUS aristocrats and southern nullifiers who wanted to
create political havoc and destroy the Democracy. In all these
cases and others, political abuses formed the matrix of oppression. Accordingly, the cure was political as well—above all, prom-
ulgating the central Jacksonian principle that the majority is to
govern.

The Jacksonians hardly invented that democratic principle,

nor did they initiate the expansion of democratic rights and power for ordinary white men that posterity too often associates purely with Andrew Jackson. But they greatly encouraged as well as benefited from that expansion, giving the politics forged earlier by the city and country democracies and then the Jefferson Republicans an unprecedented presence and power in national affairs. The Jacksonians' chief institutional innovation within the operations of government, apart from Jackson's rotation-in-office reform, was to vaunt the power of the executive—selected, as never before, by the ballots of ordinary voters and not (with the glaring exception of South Carolina) by state legislators—as the only branch of the national government chosen by the people at large. Jackson used that authority to the fullest extent granted him by the Constitution, turning a democratized version of Hamiltonian doctrines about an energetic executive toward goals that would have shocked Alexander Hamilton.

The destruction of the Second Bank of the United States and the creation of the independent treasury became the foremost of those goals—and, in attaining them, the Jacksonians made fundamental and lasting changes in the nation's political economy. At the time, and well over a century later, many observers misunderstood Jackson's and Van Buren's banking policies and the evolving hard-money Democracy. "Those who regard it in no higher aspect than a mere financial arrangement," John Niles declared in the Senate, "a question of temporary expediency, cannot appreciate the motive of those who consider it the first important stop in the reform of our wretched paper money system, on the one hand, and of our political institutions on the other." By ending Nicholas Biddle's privately controlled national bank, Whigs and Conservative Democrats predicted, Jackson and Van Buren threatened the nation with a revolution against property and a descent into barbarism. Instead came what Niles called "the entire separation and exclusion of the organized moneyed power from our political institutions," a final rejection of the Hamiltonian idea that the private banking and business community should have special powers in deciding economic policy.

The Jacksonians' solutions would be tested over the decades to come, by pro-business forces and private corruption schemes, as well as by the ups and downs of a rapidly industrializing economy—ups and downs that no reform could completely quell. The decentralized arrangements that the Jacksonians inaugurated would eventually prove so unwieldy and ineffective that a later southern Democratic president, Woodrow Wilson, would help replace it with the Federal Reserve System. But never again would formal institutional control over banking and currency policy fall so far from the purview of the president and Congress—and, thus, the voters—as it had under Biddle's BUS. In the final analysis, it would be the government and its direct appointees, and not the business community, that would make the nation's decisions. Coupled with the Jacksonians' announced friendliness to labor, the reversal announced a momentous shift in concerns, with an increased wariness of the corrupting power of wealthy businessman and speculators, and a great receptivity for the view, expressed by William Gouge, that "[i]f any classes of the community deserve the favor of the government, in any country, they are the farmers, mechanics, and other hard-working men." If they did not invent democracy, the Jacksonians did make this way of thinking the basic credo of American liberal democracy.

Jackson's emphatic presidential style affected American politics as well as government. By the end of his second term, Jackson had twice smashed and remade his cabinet, ostracized one vice president and handpicked his successor, hired and fired large batches of other civil servants at will, vetoed more legislation than all of his predecessors combined, destroyed nullification and the Second BUS—and seen a Senate resolution condemning him for constitutional misconduct officially expunged from the record. Thomas Jefferson had been an effective president, but Jackson transformed the office and its potential and made it the focus of national leadership based on boldly democratic premises unavailable to Jefferson. And although Jackson's performance as president would loom above his successors' for decades to come, his elevation of the presidency, coupled with the rise of a credible national opposition in the late 1830s, helped complete the process that turned presidential elections into quadrennial democratic frenzies. During the flush period of voting by eligible citizens between the 1790s and 1816, rates of participation in presidential contests generally lagged behind those for state and local offices. The "one-party" politics of the inaptly named Era of Good Feelings brought a general falling-off of participation, but when the pattern began to change in 1828, the nationwide turnout for the presidential election more than doubled, to 56.3 percent. There the figure stabilized until the battle over the reelection of Jackson's successor in 1840, when it jumped again to about 80 percent, a level that would be roughly sustained for the rest of the nineteenth century. The irony is that Jackson and the Jacksonians had made contests over the presidency, as well as the presidency itself, matter as never before, but the great surge of 1840 came on behalf of an anti-Jacksonian candidate and party pledged to curtailing presidential power.

The Jacksonians also created the first mass democratic national political party in modern history—the institutional basis for mobilizing and then consolidating political loyalties and participation. Earlier approximations of mass parties had arisen over sharp ideological differences and devised effective means to spread their messages, get their supporters to the polls, and struggle over government policy at the local and national levels. More than the conventional historical wisdom on the "deferential-participant" politics of the era allows, there was a great deal of democracy in Jeffersonian Democracy. But to the founding generation, the idea of parties still remained tainted with associations to vicious factions that would corrupt and divide the republican commonwealth, and a great deal of power in national and state politics remained formally concentrated in the hands of small and constricted elites, concretized in the congressional nominating caucus.

The Jacksonian party that emerged out of the collapse of the "one-party" period and the death of the caucus system dispensed with those fears and greatly enlarged on earlier forms of party organization. Elections were the crucial events for this new democracy, toward which all organizing efforts led. But elections were only the culmination of a continual effort to draw together the faithful. In place of the discarded nominating caucuses, the Jacksonians substituted a national network of committees, reaching up from the ward and township level to the quadrennial national convention, each a place where, at least in principle, the popular will would be determined and ratified. The political ferment continued almost year-round, with local committees calling regular meetings to approve local nominations, pass public resolutions, and mount elaborate processions. Sometimes, as in the Tammany Hall meeting that brought the Loco Foco schism in 1835, these party gatherings could get out of hand, further reinforcing conservative prejudices like Philip Hone's about "the dunghill of Democracy." But even at their most tumultuous, the Jacksonians could claim that more than any previous party or faction, they honored what New York's *Evening Post* called "[t]he democratic theory . . . that the people's voice is the supreme law."

The Jacksonians did not, however, fully reconcile themselves to the idea of what later historians and social scientists would call a party system. Seeing themselves as the authentic legatees of the Jeffersonian Republicans, they assumed that if they did their work correctly, they would forever hold the opposing aristocratic party at bay. Far from regarding themselves as simply an electoral machine, they believed they were the constitutional party of the sovereign people. They were an organization, as Jacksonians ceaselessly reiterated, "of principles, not of men," in which active devotion to the party would sustain the classless Constitution. Lacking the private resources of the aristocrats of "associated wealth," the people had no choice but to organize as a party—virtually along military lines with ballot boxes as their weapons—to sustain their sovereignty. The few, in response, would be free to organize their own opposition party—a focus of competition that would make the Jacksonians' own political efforts more disciplined. But the Jacksonians never envisaged an operational contest between rival political organizations, or what the *Evening Post* called "the mere struggle of ambitious leaders for power." Instead, they expected a two-party system in which they, the party of popular sovereignty, would hold power more or less in perpetuity, unless, as Van Buren said, diminished zeal led to "the gradual abandonment of the principles it sustained."

The politics of the 1830s proved how elusive Van Buren's party vision actually was—and how unstable the Democracy remained. Thanks, chiefly, to the new-school Whigs, the opposition not only improved on the Democracy's electioneering tools; it devised a contrasting democratic message that struck a deep nerve in the electorate that the Democrats did not even realize was there. And quite apart from Van Buren's defeat in 1840, the Democracy confronted internal difficulties and external challenges that majoritarian politics could not fully handle. The return of John C. Calhoun threatened to turn the party into a handmaiden for Calhoun's pro-slavery nullifier views. The appearance of the political abolitionists, although only a minor force in 1840, promised to prolong and intensify agitation over slavery. The stigma of the depression forced Democrats to think anew about the hard-money principles that had become a cornerstone of their democratic politics. So did the loss of both the White House and the Congress.

Larger ideological questions arose as well. How long could Democrats, in the name of preserving sectional harmony, back the gag rule and other attacks on free speech without fatally compromising their own ideals of equal rights? How long could the Democracy present itself as the party of the producing classes and still defend the interests of slaveholders—men whom some Democrats had begun regarding as nonproducers who lived, as Thomas Morris declared in the Senate, "upon the unrequited labor of others"? The very raising of those questions, meanwhile, caused consternation among southern Master Race Democrats, for whom the bondage of blacks had become a basic precondition for securing political equality among whites. How, in their eyes, could equality be preserved if the very foundation of equality came under question? How could democracy endure without slavery, or with slavery under assault?

The ironies of the Jacksonians' predicament were enormous—and, as far as the future of the Jackson Democracy was concerned, tragic. Their success in the 1830s had been so great that even when the opposition finally beat them, it was on their own democratic political terms that old-guard conservatives had abhorred. By decade's end, Whigs and Democrats alike could agree in principle with Jacksonian paeans to the people and majority rule. Two different intersectional, partisan versions of democracy had emerged, both propounded by diverse political coalitions. Yet by opening up popular politics and by enshrining the popular will, the Jacksonians also exposed the political system to new forms of agitation over precisely the issues they and the Whig Party leadership tried so hard to suppress. The first flickering of that new political agitation was the electoral debut of the Liberty Party in 1840. Over the years to come, the rising flame would consume both the Democracy and the Whigs—and ignite a democratic revolution more profound than anything discernible amid the torchlit furies of the Log Cabin campaign.

SELECTED FURTHER READING

This list of suggested readings is far from exhaustive. Readers interested in exploring particular topics in greater depth, especially concerning local and state politics, may wish to consult the relevant endnotes in the full one-volume Norton edition of *The Rise of American Democracy*, available in paperback.

John Ashworth, *Slavery, Capitalism, and Politics in the Antebellum Republic, Volume I: Commerce and Compromise, 1820–1850* (New York, 1995).

Samuel Flagg Bemis, *John Quincy Adams and the Foundations of American Foreign Policy* (New York, 1949).

———, *John Quincy Adams and the Union* (New York, 1956).

Donald B. Cole, *Martin Van Buren and the American Political System* (Princeton, 1984).

———, *The Presidency of Andrew Jackson* (Lawrence, 1993).

George Dangerfield, *The Era of Good Feelings* (New York, 1952).

Richard E. Ellis, *The Union at Risk: Jacksonian Democracy, States' Rights, and the Nullification Crisis* (New York, 1987).

Daniel P. Feller, *The Jacksonian Promise: America, 1815–1840* (Baltimore, 1995).

Ronald P. Formisano, *The Transformation of Political Culture: Massachusetts, 1790s–1840s* (New York, 1983).

William W. Freehling, *Prelude to Civil War: The Nullification Controversy in South Carolina, 1816–1836* (New York, 1966).

———, *Road to Disunion: Secessionists at Bay, 1776–1854* (New York, 1990).

Eugene D. Genovese, *Roll, Jordan, Roll: The World the Slaves*

Made (New York, 1974).

———— and Elizabeth Fox-Genovese, *The Mind of the Master Class: History and Faith in the Southern Slaveholders' Worldview* (New York, 2005).

Paul Goodman, *Towards a Christian Republic: Antimasonry and the Great Transition in New England, 1826–1836* (New York, 1988).

————, *Of One Blood: Abolitionism and the Origins of Racial Equality* (Berkeley, 1998).

Bray Hammond, *Banks and Politics in America from the Revolution to the Civil* War (Princeton, 1957).

Richard Hofstadter, *The Idea of a Party System: The Rise of Legitimate Opposition in the United States, 1780–1840* (Berkeley, 1969).

Michael F. Holt, *The Rise and Fall of the American Whig Party: Jacksonian Politics and the Onset of the Civil War* (New York, 1999).

Daniel Walker Howe, *The Political Culture of the American Whigs* (Chicago, 1979).

Alexander Keyssar, *The Right to Vote: The Contested History of Democracy in the United States* (New York, 2001).

Richard B. Latner, *The Presidency of Andrew Jackson: White House Politics, 1829–1837* (Athens, 1979).

Bruce Laurie, *Artisans into Workers: Labor in Nineteenth-Century America* (New York, 1989).

Henry Mayer, *All on Fire: William Lloyd Garrison and the Abolition of Slavery* (New York, 1998).

Richard P. McCormick, *The Second American Party System: Party Formation in the Jacksonian Era* (Chapel Hill, 1966).

John McFaul, *The Politics of Jacksonian Finance* (Ithaca, 1972).

William G. McLoughlin, *Revivals, Awakenings, and Reform: An Essay on Religion and Social Change in America, 1607–1977* (Chicago, 1978).

Glover Moore, *The Missouri Controversy, 1819–1821* (Lexington, 1953).

Mark A. Noll, *America's God: From Jonathan Edwards to Abraham Lincoln* (New York, 2002).

James Oakes, *The Ruling Race: A History of American Slaveholders* (New York, 1982).

Merrill D. Peterson, *The Great Triumvirate: Webster, Clay, and Calhoun* (New York, 1987).

Benjamin Quarles, *Black Abolitionists* (New York, 1969).

Robert V. Remini, *Andrew Jackson* (New York, 1977–83).

———, *Henry Clay: Statesman for the Union* (New York, 1992).

———, *Daniel Webster: The Man and His Time* (New York, 1997).

Leonard L. Richards, *"Gentlemen of Property and Standing": Anti-Abolition Mobs in Jacksonian America* (New York, 1970).

———, *The Life and Times of Congressman John Quincy Adams* (New York, 1986).

Michael P. Rogin, *Fathers and Children: Andrew Jackson and the Subjugation of the American Indian* (New York, 1975).

Arthur M. Schlesinger Jr., *The Age of Jackson* (Boston, 1945).

Charles G. Sellers, *James K. Polk, Jacksonian, 1795–1842* (Princeton, 1957).

———, *The Market Revolution: Jacksonian America, 1815–1846* (New York, 1991).

James Roger Sharp, *The Jacksonians Versus the Banks: Jacksonian Politics in the States after the Panic of 1837* (New York, 1970).

John Stauffer, *The Black Hearts of Men: Radical Abolitionists and the Transformation of Race* (Cambridge, 2002).

Anthony F. C. Wallace, *The Long, Bitter Trail: Andrew Jackson and the Indians* (New York, 1993).

Harry Watson, *Liberty and Power: The Politics of Jacksonian America* (1990; New York, 2006).

Sean Wilentz, *Chants Democratic: New York City & the Rise of the American Working Class, 1788–1850* (New York, 1984).

Charles M. Wiltse, *John C. Calhoun* (Indianapolis, 1944–51).

ACKNOWLEDGMENTS

I am deeply grateful to the John Simon Guggenheim Memorial Foundation and the American Council of Learned Societies for their financial support. An intellectually challenging fellowship year at the Woodrow Wilson International Center for Scholars in 1998–99 transformed my understanding of American democracy, for which I am indebted to the Center and its excellent staff. I am equally indebted to the Princeton University Research Board, the Shelby Cullom Davis Center for Historical Studies, and the Princeton University History Department for their generosity over many years.

Gerald Howard, then of W. W. Norton & Company, showed faith in this book and its author when he signed me up long ago, and he remains a steadfast ally. At Norton, I have been blessed to work with Drake McFeely, a friend for more than two decades and a wise editor, who also possesses the patience and fortitude of a saint. His assistant, Brendan Curry, offered me his energy, encouragement, and shrewd expertise. Mary Babcock's superb copyediting improved my prose and pushed me to omit large amounts of extraneous material. Thanks go as well to Starling Lawrence and Jeannie Luciano for their support. During the final stages, Nancy Palmquist, Anna Oler, Gina Webster, Don Rifkin, Bill Rusin, Louise Brockett, Elizabeth Riley, Sally Anne McCartin, and their staffs performed splendidly in turning out the finished book.

Tom Wallace of T. C. Wallace, Ltd., and Andrew Wylie of the Wylie Agency handled business matters with sagacity and efficiency.

Judith Ferszt, the manager of the Program in American Studies at Princeton, has helped me in matters large and small nearly every day for the past dozen years and given me the gifts of her singular intelligence and good cheer.

Amanda Ameer and Samantha Williamson put in many hard hours checking footnotes and quotations.

Numerous friends, loved ones, colleagues, students, teachers, librarians, research assistants, technical wizards, counselors, and confessors have helped me beyond measure, in everything from suggesting sources, locating documents, and reading drafts to making allowances for my exasperating distraction. To praise them here as they deserve would add many more pages to an already long book. I have thanked them, and will continue to thank them, personally. Above all, thanks go to my beloved and forbearing family, who make me wish I could have been a poet instead of a historian and said it all much better and quicker.

The dedication is a toast to essential companions and decades of companionship—and to decades more, through thick and thin.

CREDITS

1. Library of Congress
2. Library of Congress
3. National Portrait Gallery, Smithsonian Institution / Art Resource, NY
4. Library of Congress
5. Picture History
6. The Granger Collection, New York
7. Virginia Historical Society, Richmond, Virginia
8. Library of Congress
9. Library of Congress
10. *John C. Calhoun* (1782–1850), 1838, by Rembrandt Peale (1778–1860), oil on canvas, Gibbes Museum of Art / Carolina Art Association, 1959.23.01
11. National Portrait Gallery, Smithsonian Institution / Art Resource, NY
12. The Historical Society of Pennsylvania (HSP) James Forten, Leon Gardiner Collection
13. Library of Congress
14. National Archives and Records Administration
15. Oberlin College Archives, Oberlin, Ohio
16. State Preservation Board, Austin, Texas
17. Library of Congress
18. Library of Congress
19. Library of Congress
20. Courtesy of the author
21. Ross County Historical Society, Chillicothe, Ohio
22. The Granger Collection, New York
23. Library of Congress

INDEX